THE WORD OF GOD MINISTRIES

Whole Bible Prophecy

Horror and Hope

Bruce S. Bertram

Presenting a view of biblical prophetic writings, interpreted using the whole Bible.

© Bruce S. Bertram 2022

Whole Bible Prophecy

Published by The Word of God Ministries

This book may not be reproduced in whole or part without the express written consent of the author or his agent, except for small sections for personal use or quotes that are properly attributed.

www.wholebible.com
YouTube channel: The Whole Bible Christian

ISBN 978-0-9975014-4-5

All art © 2022 Bruce S. Bertram except for the basic outline map drawing of the Fertile Crescent © 2022 Isaiah Wilhelm and front cover art background © 2022 Lynette Wilhelm

ESV Scripture quotations are from the English Standard Version, The Classic Reference Edition, © 2016 by Crossway Bibles, a publishing ministry of Good News Publishers. All rights reserved.
KJV Scripture quotations are from the King James or Authorized Version.
NASB95 Scripture quotations are from the New American Standard Bible 1995 update copyright 1981, 1998 by the Lockman Foundation.

Table of Contents

1 Horror and Hope 1
- Repent 3
- The Church 10
- Peeking 16
- Peace and Safety 18
- Three Keys to Understanding 21
- The Basics 24
- Hate, Love, Curse and Blessing 26
- Defining Faith 28
- The Person and Work of the Prophet 31
- False Prophets 36
- Spirit Sight 38
- The Deceiver 40
- Prophecy Reveals a Spiritual Battle 44
- Learn the Past, Know the Future 45
- Tribulation 49
- An Overview 50
- The Reason for the Season 53
- Judgment Begins in His House 55

2 Interpretation 57
- Prophetic Timing 60
- The Time of John 63
- Cycles of Fulfillment 65
- Prophetic Language 69
- Words, Association, and Wordplay 72
- Dreams and Visions 76
- Movie Trailers 79
- Newspaper Exegesis 80
- Stand-Ins or Types 85
- Goddess of Reason 87
- Evolution 92
- Notions We Already Have 94
- Name Changes 96
- Sacred Names 98
- Numerology 101

Expositional Constancy	102
How Do We Know?	104
What Good is Prophecy?	106

3 God's Promise and Prophecy ... 109

The Promise	109
The Body of Sin	112
The Body of Christ	116
Idolatry	121
Chronology	124
Event Orientation	127
The Ripe Time	128
The Old World Order	129
The United States in the Bible	133
The Church in the Bible	135
Families of Man	138
What is the World?	141
Nations and Nature	143

4 The Apple of God's Eye ... 149

Hate for Israel	151
The Adulteress Redeemed	152
Prophecy in God's Holidays	157
Times and Seasons	160
Faith-Filling	164
Much More	166
Appointments with Yeshua	171
Jerusalem	173
The Temple	174
The Ark	184
Gathering the Outcasts of Israel	187

5 Tribulation Like No Other ... 190

The Four Beast Kingdoms	192
Babylon	194
Dress for Action	200
The Earthquake	202
Stars	205
Numbering the Days	206

    Kings of the North & South 210
    The Hot Spot 212
        Image of The Fertile Crescent 213
    The Endurance of the Saints 216
    God's Wrath and Man's Wrath 221
    Anointing 222
    The 70 Weeks of Daniel 224
    The Agreement for One Seven 227
    The Temple Rebuilt 229
    A Tale of Three Women 230
    Image: Scroll of Authority 234

6 Scroll of Authority 235
    Judgment Belongs to Yeshua 239
    Seven Seals 240
    Seal 1: The White Horse Rider 243
    Seal 2: The Red Horse Rider 246
    Seal 3: The Black Horse Rider.. 246
    Seal 4: The Pale Horse Rider 249
    Seal 5: Martyrs Under the Altar 251
    Seal 6: Earthquake, Blood Moon, Black Sun 255
    Elders 257
    144,000 Sealed from 12 Tribes 257
    A Great Multitude 262
    Seal 7: Eye of the Storm 265

7 Day of the Awakening Blast 267
    Trumpet 1: Mix of Fire, Blood & Hail 275
    Trumpet 2: Burning Mountain 277
    Trumpet 3: Wormwood 278
    Trumpet 4: Third of Sun, Moon, Stars 280
    Trumpet 5/First Woe: Poisonous Locusts 281
    Trumpet 6/Second Woe: Army, Witnesses 285
        Mouths 289
        Mighty Big Angel, Little Sweet Scroll 292
        The Two Witnesses 294
    Trumpet 7: Mystery of God Fulfilled 297
        Third Woe: Dragon, Beasts, Messages 299

Signs in the Heavens 301
　　　The Dragon Thrown Down 303
　　　An Unholy Trinity 306
　The Blasphemous "Little Horn" or Worthless Shepherd 307
　The Abomination(s) Causing Desolation................................. 314
　The Second Beast: Antichrist.. 317
　　　The Image 320
　　　The Mark... 321
　　　Buying and Selling... 330
　The 144,000 Victorious 335
　Listen Up! Last Chance! 336
　　　First Angel: Choose God 337
　　　Second Angel: Your Kingdom Babylon is Toast 339
　　　Third Angel: Go With the Beast, Go All the Way............ 341
　The Hour to Reap Has Come 343
　A Note on Conquering 345

8 Yom YHVH 347
　Bowl 1: Painful Sores on the Mark... 349
　Bowl 2: Sea of Blood.. 349
　Bowl 3: Springs of Blood 351
　Bowl 4: Scorching Sun 352
　Bowl 5: Darkness They Will Feel... 353
　Bowl 6: Euphrates Dry, Frog Spirits Gather Armies 354
　Bowl 7: Great Earthquake, 100 Pound Hailstones................. 356
　Prostitute Riding a Scarlet Beast.. 358
　The Fall of Babylon the Great 363
　Rider on a White Horse... 366
　Armageddon: Treading the Winepress 368
　Refusal to Repent... 374

9 Resurrection & Rapture... 375
　The Last Trump.. 377
　The Timing of the Rapture 378
　Wrath and the Rapture 381
　The Resurrection.. 382
　Three Phases of Resurrection... 384
　What Does 'Coming' Mean? 385

In the Air or On the Ground	387
Taken	389
The Church in Revelation 4-19	390
Meta Tauta, "After These Things"	395
Hidden From Wrath	397
Falling Away	401
End Like a Flood	402
10 Your God Reigns	**405**
Marriage Supper of the Lamb	406
Yeshua Touches Down	408
Cleaning Up	410
Survivor Population	411
The Spirit is Poured Out	413
A New Name	414
A New Temple for Everyone	414
Return to Eden	415
Yeshua on the Throne	417
Israel Completed	418
God's Rest	418
The Earth Subdued	421
Life Expectancy	423
Living Under the Rule of Iron	424
The Deceiver's Final Defeat	426
The Last Enemy is Destroyed	428
The Books Are Opened	428
New Everything	432
Yeshua Gives It Up	433
11 The New Jerusalem	**434**
Almost 1,400 Miles Square	434
Living Accommodations	436
Life in the Big City	436
No Temple	438
Gates and Jewels	438
Who's In, Who's Out	439
12 Happily Ever After	**441**
What is Certain	441

A Different Sort of Timeline 444
Timeline in Outline Form 452
    Daniel Lays Out the Full Scope of God's Plan 452
    Image: Daniel Lays Out the Full Scope of God's Plan 454
John Fills in Some Details 455
    Image: Agreement for One Week; Middle to End 457
    Image: Agreement for One Week; Before Start to Middle . 458
    Image: Yeshua Takes the Throne of David 462
Kingdoms and Spiritual Forces 463
What Do We Do? 464
Choose God 468
Topical/Scripture Index 473

A note on the cover art: It's sideways in order to emphasize that this book is a different way of looking at Bible prophecy.

1 Horror and Hope

Malachi 4:1–6 ESV. "For behold, the day is coming, burning like an oven, when all the arrogant and all evildoers will be stubble. The day that is coming shall set them ablaze, says the LORD of hosts, so that it will leave them neither root nor branch. But for you who fear my name, the sun of righteousness shall rise with healing in its wings. You shall go out leaping like calves from the stall. And you shall tread down the wicked, for they will be ashes under the soles of your feet, on the day when I act, says the LORD of hosts. "Remember the law of my servant Moses, the statutes and rules that I commanded him at Horeb for all Israel. "Behold, I will send you Elijah the prophet before the great and awesome day of the LORD comes. And he will turn the hearts of fathers to their children and the hearts of children to their fathers, lest I come and strike the land with a decree of utter destruction."

These words from God through Malachi summarize the horror and the hope of prophecy. The arrogant and evildoers will be destroyed, but those who fear His name will be made whole and will tread down the wicked. There's a lot more to it, which is explored in this book (and His), but that's the basics.

Because of the prophetic horror described in this and so many other Scripture texts, many philosophies have been developed by Church leaders that have churchgoers avoiding the horrible prophetic events. One such is that The Church will convert everyone before Jesus comes back, making the horror unnecessary. Another is that everyone who believes in Jesus will be whisked away; disappearing before the final horrors start in something called the rapture. A third is that most or all of prophecy has already happened and we don't have to worry at all.

Comparing these philosophies of men and others like them with the Bible, many inconsistencies become apparent. When questioned about them, the teachers of these philosophies are unable to adequately "give an answer for the hope that is in you." It is painfully obvious that none of the philosophies matches the whole of Scripture. There are big holes in all of them because verses that contradict are ignored or given a "spiritual" meaning that is entirely manufactured. After years of study and questioning, the conclusion is that these philosophies are "vain hopes" and "visions of their own minds, not from the mouth of the Lord."

Jeremiah 23:16–17 ESV. Thus says the LORD of hosts: "Do not listen to the words of the prophets who prophesy to you, filling you with vain hopes. They speak visions of their own minds, not from the mouth of the LORD. They say continually to those who despise the word of the LORD, 'It shall be well with you'; and to everyone who stubbornly follows his own heart, they say, 'No disaster shall come upon you.' "

The inconsistencies are resolved, not in more of the philosophies of men, but in going back to reading the whole Bible and doing all of what God tells His children to do. Embracing the whole of the Word causes understanding to flower, and bore the fruit recorded in these pages. We cannot "despise the word of the Lord" by ignoring all or part of His Laws and hope that it will be well with us. Real hope lies in the whole of God's living and active Word, applied in every way to everyday living.

Ezekiel 7:26 ESV. Disaster comes upon disaster; rumor follows rumor. They seek a vision from the prophet, while the law perishes from the priest and counsel from the elders.

Perhaps this is a self-evident truth, and one might ask why make a big deal out of it in this book (and our other books). The reason is that the whole of the Word is most assuredly not being taught by The Church, much less lived. Therefore, the Bible is misunderstood and misapplied, including prophecy. Spiritual maturity is weak, and churchgoers are not prepared for horror either in daily living or what is coming.

God tells us what will happen (prophecy) for several reasons. One is to show that dumb idols can't do what He can do. Another is to tell His servants what is going to happen, and give us hope that He is always ahead of the game and will protect us. A main reason for prophecy is to reveal iniquity.

Lamentations 2:14, ESV. Your prophets have seen for you false and deceptive visions; they have not exposed your iniquity to restore your fortunes, but have seen for you oracles that are false and misleading.

Revealing iniquity (literally lawlessness) is full of hope, because the soft hearted person has a chance to correct behavior not in line with God's Word before it's too late. Since judgment begins in His house (1 Peter 4:17) we need to heed God's warnings and sweep the iniquity out of every room in our own houses.

This book was written to give real hope to those who hunger and thirst for God's Word, and address the vain hopes and deceptive visions with clarity from the mouth of the Lord. Together we will unravel the fictions, reveal iniquity so it can be remedied, strengthen faith, advance spiritual maturity, build up hope, and prepare for whatever God has in store for us, both in daily living and the future.

Repent

There was about 400 years of silence from God after Malachi. But His Words from that time easily connect us to the words of John the Baptizer arriving on the scene after that silence: "Repent, for the kingdom of Heaven is at hand" (Matthew 3:1). John ministered in the spirit of Elijah, commanding people to repent or "remember the Law" as Malachi said. After John was arrested, Jesus kept the message of the ages going by repeating the same command.

Matthew 4:17, ESV. From that time Jesus began to preach, saying, "Repent, for the kingdom of heaven is at hand."

Momentous prophetic events were occurring right before the eyes and ears of the people present at the time. The kingdom of God was at hand. The hope of man, given in the promise from our Father, arrived in the body and teachings of His Son.

The announcement of His Kingdom, certified by miracles of healing and signs of power, was prefaced by a command of repentance for entry (remember the Law). Repent means to change direction. The change God has always had in mind is for people to stop stubbornly following their own heart (or doing what seems right in their own eyes) and follow God's heart. Those who obey the command enter into the kingdom, and the kingdom is established further in the hearts of those who respond. This part of the kingdom has been growing steadily since the Garden.

Yet the physical part of the kingdom at the time of the Incarnation was not established on earth as it is in heaven. The throne of David still awaits its rightful occupant. Repentance is a continuing command, but now it is more urgent than ever because the time is short and the horrible part of the prophecies is imminent. King Yeshua is coming with His armies and an iron rod.

The son of Zechariah was the voice of one crying in the wilderness in the spirit of Elijah, warning people to make straight paths for the King. Many paths were straightened in repentance at that time, but "The Day" announced by Malachi and many other prophets got postponed. Alas, the King was rejected by His subjects (or the leaders of His subjects) and His reign wasn't completely realized on earth as it should have been.

Our King wasn't honored and crowned with gold the first time as was His right. Instead, He was mocked, despised, crowned with thorns, tortured and killed in the worst way imaginable. His ascension to the throne of His kingdom on earth was delayed, but now we are in the time of the end of worldly kingdoms when that will be rectified. The King is coming a second time, and on this trip, He will not be denied. In preparation, the cry from the wilderness is going out again, and repentance is still commanded.

Luke 3:4–6 ESV. As it is written in the book of the words of Isaiah the prophet, "The voice of one crying in the wilderness: 'Prepare the way of the Lord, make his paths straight. Every valley shall be filled, and every mountain and hill shall be made low, and the crooked shall become straight, and the rough places shall become level ways, and all flesh shall see the salvation of God.' "

The promised kingdom of heaven has always been "at hand." It is as near as a soft, faithful and obedient heart. "Make his paths straight" is another way of saying "Repent." John and Jesus are still crying out by the Spirit and from the pages of Scripture, telling people to stop going the way that seems right in their own eyes and walk in God's ways instead. The wise will heed the command and make His house ready.

Matthew 24:45–46 ESV. "Who then is the faithful and wise servant, whom his master has set over his household, to give them their food at the proper time? Blessed is that servant whom his master will find so doing when he comes.

The son of Zechariah and Elizabeth and the son of God adopted and fostered by David's son Joseph had to deliver their message outside the recognized religious system of the day. That system had become very corrupt. The religious leaders mishandled the Word of Life in such a way as to block people from gaining spiritual maturity and getting close to the Father.

Matthew 23:1–4 ESV. Then Jesus said to the crowds and to his disciples, "The scribes and the Pharisees sit on Moses' seat, so do and observe whatever they tell you, but not the works they do. For they preach, but do not practice. They tie up heavy burdens, hard to bear, and lay them on people's shoulders, but they themselves are not willing to move them with their finger.

Jesus is still standing at the door knocking with the same message of repentance, and it is still directed at a people who claim to know His name. Religious leaders are still corrupting the plain teachings of God's Word of Life, and the solution again has to be repeated from outside that corrupt system. God continues to command The Church along with people everywhere to return to straight paths, fill in valleys of sin with righteousness, and make low the hills and mountains of pride.

The message to repent was directed at a people who claimed to know, and should have known, their God, and "the time of your visitation" (Luke 19:44). It has echoed down through the centuries and settled in the hearts of believers everywhere. We wait for another time of visitation soon, and prepare by filling our hearts with His Word in every way we can. We don't want to miss the next time of our visitation (although it will be much harder to miss than before). Whole Bible Prophecy is another echo of that repentance message, needed today perhaps more sorely than ever.

Whole Bible prophecy proceeds from Whole Bible Christianity. Whole Bible Christianity is taking in the whole Bible and establishing it in a soft heart, living all of God's instructions every day. This is explained more thoroughly in our book <u>Whole Bible Christianity</u>. Without living all of His Word, prophecy won't make a lot of sense.

The process of whole Bible living can be compared to the "good ground" in the Parable of the Seed in Matthew 13:8, Mark 4:8 and Luke 8:8. Good ground is a soft heart responsive to every word spoken by God. Another example is in John chapter 6:52-58, where Jesus tells His disciples to eat His body and drink His blood.

By this, He means our souls are to consume all of God's Words and live them in the same way we consume food for our bodies and live. His Words are Spirit and Life.

John 6:63 ESV. It is the Spirit who gives life; the flesh is no help at all. The words that I have spoken to you are spirit and life.

Every word God speaks is always moral, living and active. Believers "in humility receive the Word implanted" (James 1:21) in the good ground of a soft heart of flesh. This Word was from the misnamed Old Testament, because the likewise misnamed New Testament had not been written at the time of the gospels. The New Testament is Scripture, but none of the words or events recorded in those books overrides or replaces any of the so-called Old Testament. There is no "old" word, no "new" word, no divisions of "civil" "ceremonial" or "moral." The only thing "old" about the covenant is our hearts of stone before conversion.

If the heart is hard, fully or partially, the seed of the living Word either cannot find purchase or just bounces off the hard ground. A hard heart sits in judgment on the Word, handing down false and deceptive visions. We are told by the hard hearted that some of the Word is old and no longer part of daily living, or that it is "fulfilled" which somehow means eliminated.

A person with a hard heart is like a spectator at a sporting event who does not understand the game. All the plays except the most basic are just a puzzle. In the spiritual game, a spectator has only a limited understanding of the most basic concepts such as repent because the Word is a puzzle. Hard hearts aren't conducive to following much about the Word or prophecy (Hebrews 5:12-13).

Ezekiel 33:31–33 ESV. And they come to you as people come, and they sit before you as my people, and they hear what you say but they will not do it; for with lustful talk in their mouths they act; their heart is set on their gain. And behold, you are to them like one who sings lustful songs with a beautiful voice and plays well on an instrument, for they hear what you say, but they will not do it. When this comes—and come it will!—then they will know that a prophet has been among them."

To understand prophecy the Bible has to become a part of us by living all of its Words all of the time. That is the starting point. This doesn't mean living the Law only externally or as doctrines of men learned by rote. It means a planting of the Word in a soft heart that yearns to be guided by His Spirit in every way.

Without actually doing what God says, prophecy will be nearly incomprehensible and subject to all sorts of false visions. If we don't follow what He plainly says He wants His people to do, then how will we be able to believe something like prophecy, which takes more insight and wisdom?

Deuteronomy 8:1–2 ESV. "The whole commandment that I command you today you shall be careful to do, that you may live and multiply, and go in and possess the land that the LORD swore to give to your fathers. And you shall remember the whole way that the LORD your God has led you these forty years in the wilderness, that he might humble you, testing you to know what was in your heart, whether you would keep his commandments or not.

Prophecy cannot be studied as an isolated subject apart from the rest of the Word and expect to fully understand it. His people are to be careful to embrace the "whole commandment" and "remember the whole way" of God. Rejecting any part of the Word (it's old, eliminated, or for someone else) creates gaps in understanding all of it. The Bible is an integrated whole, and in order to achieve a balanced understanding of any one part of it, the entire book must be read and God's instructions followed. Like our brother Israel, Gentile believers must also be careful to do the whole commandment.

The foretelling of events is an extension of all the plans and purposes of God, of living as He wants us to live.

Nehemiah 9:13–14 ESV. You came down on Mount Sinai and spoke with them from heaven and gave them right rules and true laws, good statutes and commandments, and you made known to them your holy Sabbath and commanded them commandments and statutes and a law by Moses your servant.

When we apply all of His Law or Instructions filled with love and the Spirit as much as we are able, it changes us from spectators to active participants. It's the difference between sitting in the stands and getting a personal experience of the game right in the thick of things. If, instead of living it, we stand around judging the Word, cutting it in pieces and parceling it out to different people groups (Jews, the Church) and refusing to follow the most basic instructions, then how could we possibly understand prophecy?

God is really the only prophet, since all knowledge of the future comes from Him. He made the first (Genesis 3:14-19) and last (Revelation 22:12) prophecies in the Bible, which makes Him the Alpha and Omega (beginning and end) of prophecy as in everything else. He has declared to whoever would listen what was going to happen (the end) from the beginning, to accomplish His purpose and pleasure. Happily, He is a loving God.

Hope is in living as He instructs, and is what He asks of us on many occasions. This is what it means to be faithful. Our Father uses words like "watch," "stay awake," "conquer," and "persevere" quite a bit in His preaching and prophecy. He doesn't ask us to hunt down the beast and kill him. He doesn't say we should be salvation police and judge someone else's walk with Him. There is no assignment from our Father to find out exactly what constitutes the mark of the beast. We are to grow in His love and grace, practice the fruit of the Spirit, encourage one another to love and good works, and stay alert for His return. Believers can study the

Bible and prepare for bad stuff happening as we need to, but our focus is on glorifying God in our behavior and our teaching.

The Church

Before we really get into the prophecy stuff, we have to address the elephant in the room. And it's not the symbol of the Republican Party in the United States, either. The elephant in the room is The Church.

We have to talk about it because it claims for itself the authority to declare what is biblical and what is not. Often this is while ignoring the very Bible they supposedly endorse in favor of philosophies of men. Leaders constantly preach about acceptable and unacceptable Christian behavior, presuming to dictate lifestyles and discipleship methods apart from the Word. They sit in judgment on the Word and pass their judgments on to unsuspecting sheep, and in turn cast out and shun those who actually follow the whole of the Word. Leaders keep their sheep in malnourished ignorance as they focus on sentiment and dole out tiny pieces of the Word, reserving for themselves the sole authority to interpret.

Of course, 'The Church' in this book is a general way of referring to the visible Church, and all the secret organizations connected with it, in all its fractured, denominational (or non-denominational), bureaucratic, backbiting, Word-denying glory. The Church is all the churches, organizations, para-church groups, denominations and related entities claiming to follow the Bible and Jesus, and/or the God of Abraham, Isaac and Jacob, and presume to speak for Him. This includes Catholics, Protestants (or non-Catholics), Muslims, Messianics, and Jews. It is organized in groups around schools of theology, traditions or personalities using by-laws, statements of faith, extra-biblical books, creeds or confessions, and has only a smattering of the Word of God. This is a fair generalization as we'll see when we get to the Prostitute.

The Greek word *ekklesia* (a-clay-see-ah), is translated in the New Testament by the English word "church." But The Church as we see it today was unknown until about the third century and after. An *ekklesia* is simply a gathering or group of people, also known as an assembly. The Church is an ekklesia, and the Body of Christ is an ekklesia, but the Church is not the Body of Christ.

In the Old Testament, the Hebrew words *edah* (a-daw) or *qahal* (ka-hall) are the similar words for congregation or assembly. The Septuagint (sept-to-a-jint or sept-to-jent), is the Greek translation of the Old Testament made by Hebrew scholars about 300 years before the Incarnation. Since it is a translation of the OT Hebrew into Greek, the Hebrew words for congregation or assembly (*edah* or *qahal*) are usually translated by the Greek word *ekklesia*, even when talking about Israel. But Church translators do not use the word Church in the translations of the Old Testament.

In general, the Bible only mentions believers and non-believers (sometimes in an assembly or congregation). Believers are called the Body of Christ, the Bride, branches of a vine, an olive tree, the remnant, saints, and other such names. As Jesus said, where two or more are gathered in His Name He is there in the midst. But He also says of others that "I never knew you."

A "churchgoer" is one who simply attends a church (or other congregation) and is not necessarily a believer. They tend to "draw near with their words and honor me with their lip service, but they remove their hearts far from me, and their reverence of me consists of tradition learned by rote" (Isaiah 29:13 NASB95). In this book, "believer" means a born-again person, grafted into the Body of Christ, whose heart is dedicated to following all of what God says to the best of their understanding and ability.

The Church grew out of a well-intentioned effort by believers to extricate themselves from first century Jewish and Roman wars and persecutions. But it has ended up as something that is completely unrecognizable compared with Paul's ideal of the Body of Christ. People in The Church have done many good works, but the good has been outweighed by many serious bad things from leadership. Most of the good has been done in spite of The Church, not because of it. A big chunk of The Church regards itself as a replacement for Israel, which the Bible never verifies. It has manufactured philosophies to shore up its position, authority and power, but most of them only touch on the Word at best.

There are many genuine believers in God and His only begotten Son *within* The Church (perhaps misled), and those believers are part of the Body of Christ. But the word "church" is not in the original languages. It is only in translations of the Bible. There is also not a single reference to Lutherans, Baptists, Methodists, Calvary Chapels, Vineyards, Catholics, Protestants or any others anywhere in the Bible. These have developed into what could be thought of as clubs. There are different flavors of clubs (churches, synagogues, mosques) but they all pursue whatever is right in their own eyes rather than wholly and specifically what God says in the Bible. The clubs have appropriated Bible culture and names and strained very hard to be included with the Body, without really doing what the Head of the Body commands.

Though the word *ekklesia* is used of assemblies in Israel throughout the Septuagint (and even one in Acts 7:38), no one in the Church translates *ekklesia* as "church" in the OT. Church translators only use "church" in English translations of the (erroneously named) New Testament. They want to see the Church as unique and separate from Israel, starting at the time of the apostles. "The assembly of believers" or *ekklesia* is much different from "the Church." His assembly includes all believers everywhere and every-when. The Body of Christ has always been around since the foundation of the world. It did not just pop into existence at the time of Acts chapter 2, it was just energized. It has multitudes of members from all nations and tongues. Believer's names have been written in the book of life from the foundation of the world.

Revelation 17:8 ESV (underline added). The beast that you saw was, and is not, and is about to rise from the bottomless pit and go to destruction. And the dwellers on earth whose names have <u>not been written in the book of life from the foundation of the world</u> will marvel to see the beast, because it was and is not and is to come.

The identity of a believer is in Jesus our God and Messiah, and in the eating and drinking of His Words (meaning to hear and obey). Believers can be recognized by the combination of their behavior and their testimony. Those who do what He says and testify that Jesus the Christ is God in the flesh and the Messiah are different from other ekklesias.

Some clubs talk about Jesus all the time but don't do what He says ("Lord, lord" Matthew 7:21, 25:11, Luke 6:46). Other clubs fancy themselves as obedient but deny that Jesus is God in the flesh (1 John 4:2,3; Revelation 2:9) such as Jehovah's Witnesses and Mormons. The "congregation in the wilderness," as Stephen called Israel at the giving of the Law (Acts 7:38-39), heard the gospel but didn't unite it with faith. In other words, they didn't do what God said (Hebrews 4:2). Churchgoers are in the same boat. True believers on the other hand hear "God with us" in the Law, follow it, and recognize Jesus for who He is. Law, of course, is all the instructions for living coming from God and Jesus (both instruct the same things) given to God's people at any time.

The Church as a whole resembles physical Israel at a low point instead of the Body of Christ at its best. It is teaching some of the milk of God's Word, but not the complete nutrition of the whole Bible. A little truth is mixed with a lot of lies. As a result, most inside The Church are malnourished and spiritually weak, with impaired hearing and needing salve for their eyes (Revelation 3:18). Being ignorant of large portions of the Bible causes them to be unable to hear God speaking, and won't respond as He directs to the horrors of prophetic fulfillment coming soon.

Nicolaitan is a general name for the false teachers who infest The Church and lead astray from the Bible. They are mentioned only twice by name in the Bible, but they are still with us. "Wolves from among your own selves" is another name in warnings to us by Jesus and Paul.

Matthew 7:15–16 ESV. "Beware of false prophets, who come to you in sheep's clothing but inwardly are ravenous wolves. You will recognize them by their fruits. Are grapes gathered from thornbushes, or figs from thistles?

Acts 20:29–30 ESV. I know that after my departure fierce wolves will come in among you, not sparing the flock; and from among your own selves will arise men speaking twisted things, to draw away the disciples after them.

We are seeing the fruit of wolves all throughout the Church. Biblical correction is rejected in favor of dictates commanded by personalities. There are no grapes on the thorn bushes or figs on the thistles. It's easy for The Church to point the Nicolaitan finger at cults, but it's much harder to admit that The Church as a whole is now overrun by ravenous wolves in sheep's clothing. Your own pastor, rabbi, imam or priest is likely in that category. Anyone who teaches that parts of the Word are "old," "for Jews only," or are "fulfilled and eliminated," and so on is a suspect. Especially as they refuse to repent.

Clubs denying that Jesus is God in the flesh, and those who deny that the Law is a valid lifestyle and discipleship method, are in the same sinking boat with wolves such as Jezebel, Balaam, the Nicolaitans and the synagogue of Satan (Revelation 2-3). The choice is the same as that presented by John the Baptizer and Jesus. Stay in the sinking boat and keep uselessly bailing, or repent and row to the shore of the complete Word of God.

We can clearly see that the biblical Body of Christ is not the same as the Church. The Body concerns itself with trust in God and obedience to all of His Words. Modern-day Nicolaitans in The Church promote loyalty to man-made theology, Confessions, Creeds and By-Laws however good. If you don't regurgitate what they teach then you are a "divisive person" and shunned or encouraged to search for fellowship elsewhere. After all, they do not want their deceptive visions destroyed by the Truth, which would take away their power and blow away their house of cards.

The Church is a man-made construct not unlike the Tower of Babel. It does not follow God very well at all, which is likewise illustrated for us by Israel and Judaism through the centuries. The squishiness of philosophies of men cannot be relied upon as a foundation for spiritual maturity. It turns out the Bible is enough, when you just read it and do it. You might need some help here and there, if only to navigate through the twisted teachings of the Nicolaitans. But believers have to want to do all of His Words. His Word works best when we hunger and thirst after righteousness.

Bad shepherds lord their power, education and/or position over lay people. They teach falsely, telling us things like the unchanging Word of God (John 10:35) was changed or eliminated by Jesus. These wolves are everywhere present in the entire Church, and have mostly obscured the plain message of the Word. One gains wisdom and understanding enough to see through all the childish, outside the Bible stuff by diligent study and application of all of what God says to the Body.

Hosea 14:9 ESV. Whoever is wise, let him understand these things; whoever is discerning, let him know them; for the ways of the LORD are right, and the upright walk in them, but transgressors stumble in them.

It's hard for Nicolaitans to see past ideas they are convinced are truthful, even if they aren't. But this is not a book about all the different opinions. Scripture interprets Scripture, and here prophecy is analyzed by the whole Bible. Some of the revelations herein will scare the daylights right out of you, but overall they will give hope. These revelations will be explained more thoroughly and biblically here than you may have heard.

Peeking

Nope, this is not a city in Asia. We love to peek at the future. If we can get a handle on what's going to happen we can adjust our plans to take advantage of good things, or make tracks to get away from the bad. This is why astrology and other forms of fortune-telling are so popular. Even though it's wrong, comfort is seemingly offered and a little confidence given in the midst of uncertainty. It doesn't matter that the confidence is mostly false; even false confidence goes a long way toward easing the anxiety (or guilt) that so often plagues us.

Isaiah 46:9-10 NASB95. ⁹"Remember the former things long past, For I am God, and there is no other; *I am* God, and there is no one like Me, ¹⁰Declaring the end from the beginning, And from ancient times things which have not been done, Saying, 'My purpose will be established, And I will accomplish all My good pleasure';

As Isaiah declares, our God of hope showcases His unique knowledge, power and control in prophecy. He will accomplish all His good pleasure (emphasis on the word "good"). Biblical prophecy comes from God and gives us a solid peek into the real future. Its main purpose is to glorify Him. It encourages believers and warns unbelievers. It gives people a chance to repent. It shows that no other god or spirit can even come close to being in His class. He "declares the end from the beginning," meaning both that He knows what is going to happen before it happens, and also that He guarantees His purposes or goals will reach fruition.

People don't like God's prophecies, in part, because they are completely accurate and true. This is in stark contrast to man's astrology, crystals, omens, witchcraft, deceptive visions, philosophies of men, and much of Church teaching. God tells us things we don't want to hear; astrology and other philosophies tickle our ears. Humans prefer our own methods using our own understanding (divination, communication with spirits, witchcraft, pastors or rabbis cheerleading messages, and so on) because we want the power to know what will happen and change it to suit ourselves. It's another way of unseating God from His throne.

The other part of our dislike of God's prophecies is that they point out our disobedience and require a change. He doesn't make syrupy, non-specific prophecies designed only to build our self-esteem. God is painfully honest and direct about humanity's shortcomings. He also demands changes, and has provided a Way for us to get clean and get back to Him. Usually, He attaches a message of repentance from lawlessness to His prophecies. In other words, stop doing our own thing and do His. But we're too busy worshipping images of ourselves, making our own decisions and following our own inclinations (known as narcissism). We just don't want to be bothered with reminders that the end of those efforts is death. We close our eyes and think that if we can't see death then it isn't really coming for us. One of the reasons the end comes like a flood is from ignoring what He says.

Nahum 1:8 ESV. But with an overflowing flood he will make a complete end of the adversaries, and will pursue his enemies into darkness.

Peace and Safety

Whole Bible prophecy is melding, blending or weaving all of the words God has given us into a complete picture of what He wants from us, what happens when we don't give it to Him, and what will happen if we continue to reject Him. Each prophecy or verse is like a color in a paint-by-number kit. When all are applied, the picture becomes clearer.

Too often, interpreters grab parts of Bible books or verses and patch them together while attempting to plug in current events. They ignore passages that don't bear on the message they want to convey, and over-emphasize those passages that seem to confirm their thinking. Some well-meaning scholars spend a great deal of time on such things as textual accuracy, word definitions, and cultural changes, all of which are important. But meaning and application frequently escapes them because they don't actually do what God requires. The question is, can the average non-scholar type person (such as this writer) take the scholar's efforts in delivering a text in his or her own language and reach the truth without having it explained by a scholar? This book answers yes!

None of the Bible stands alone. God has breathed out a complete picture of His will and plans in His Word, and anyone who wants to understand that picture not only has to look at all of it, we need to live all of it. All of the colors He provides must be used. It's not easy to do this because so many calling themselves teachers (pastors, rabbis whatever) are teaching so many wrong things. It can be confusing. These teachers want secure jobs, so they make it seem as if a scholarly education is necessary to properly understand the Bible. But an education is no guarantee of understanding. In fact, a scholarly education tends to get in the way more often than not because pride rears its ugly head.

James 3:1 ESV. Not many of you should become teachers, my brothers, for you know that we who teach will be judged with greater strictness.

Imagine if a scholar worked years to get to be a tenured professor, pastor, priest, rabbi or famous author, only to find out they were almost completely wrong. Do you think that person would simply admit it and change their approach? Would they confess to leading people astray for many years? Could they admit that they doled out such tiny parts of the Word to their followers, mixed with huge doses of philosophies of men, that the followers stayed malnourished and unable to handle even the smallest of life's problems? Generally, that's a big no to all those questions. It's more likely that a long-time leader in that position would rather defend his position to the death than repent. We see an example of that when the bulk of the Pharisees and Sadducees are confronted by the King standing right in front of them and they refused Him.

Many church leaders lose a faith they never really had in the first place and turn to the self-worship of atheism. Other deluded leaders suddenly decide there is no hell or some other such false teaching. These are obvious and their positions are self-destructive. On the other hand, the pastor or rabbi convinced their group is right and who is, perhaps, a real believer, but then have their eyes opened to the whole of the Word, is in a tougher position. Like Paul. A leader like that would have extremely difficult decisions to make, and you don't see the choices being made in the right direction very often at all.

If it does happen, and they start living and teaching the whole Bible, it means the end of their reputation, income and position in whatever church (or related organization) of which they were part. Paul and a few others did it throughout history, but it is a very difficult path to follow. No wonder there is such a heated defense made by churchgoers when trying to present the truths in this book and others like them to The Church.

Scholars have done great work for the most part in delivering a text in a language non-scholars can understand. After that, however, many tend to spend too much time on scholarly viewpoints and not enough on just how the texts apply when compared together and brought into daily living. We can benefit from the scholarship and at the same time take into consideration one of the biggest impediments to understanding the Word: the unwillingness to do everything God says. The scholars have their place in the Body of Christ, but what is more important is a loving heart intent on following every Word with diligence, reading and doing the whole Book.

All the world's troubles can be traced back to rebellion against anything to do with God. Imagine a place and time with no war, disease or pestilence. Paradise. Perfection. Eternal life with a loving Father and Messiah. We had peace and safety, and didn't want it. We chose and still choose to pursue our own ways and goals. But apart from God and His life, we just create death and destruction.

It is apparent that our world has already gone to the dogs and is ready for judgment. You can see it in the way churches cater to people with money, and the way people with money use it to further the destruction of godly culture. It is in the distancing of ourselves from the morality and life in God's Law, with the Church leading the way. It is illustrated for us in so many of the ways we treat each other, from the ho-hum reactions concerning the slow disappearance of our God-given rights, on around to the spinelessness of political leaders who take them. People think everything is fine and getting better, but while we are thinking "peace and safety," the storm bearing sudden destruction is on the horizon and coming fast.

Three Keys to Understanding

The place to start for understanding prophecy is, well, The Beginning. Genesis 3:15 is a promise of a Messiah, and the rest of the Book traces this promise through to the end of world kingdoms. The book of Genesis is the back drop for every succeeding event or prophecy. In loving grace, God made a perfect world and created perfect beings to live in and take care of it. Dad and mom (Adam and Eve) decided to ignore His Word and go their own way, and every child since has done the same thing. Some of us have repented and strive to order our lives after His wisdom and ways. But the majority of people insist on continuing the sin of Adam, doing what seems right in their own eyes.

Writing a book on prophecy isn't easy. There are a lot of philosophies of men through which we have to wade to get to the biblical truth. Lots of books have been written, lots of sermons preached, and there's lots of interpretations. It's taken a long time of wide-ranging, intense study to get to this point, and a lot of the effort has been spent struggling through the extra-biblical jungle of Church theology.

This book was written to help shorten your learning curve, and so you won't have to do as much struggling. The insights and connections presented here are intended to give you a head start in your own education. Continued study, mostly by just reading and doing the Word, will firm up your ability to see the Truth. As you read it and do it, you'll see that false teachers use the Bible only as a touch point for the imagination and philosophies of men.

Jeremiah 8:9 ESV. The wise men shall be put to shame; they shall be dismayed and taken; behold, they have rejected the word of the LORD, so what wisdom is in them?

The first key to understanding God's Word, whether it's for the future or not, is a spirit of humility and obedience.

1 Peter 5:5-7 NASB95. ⁵You younger men, likewise, be subject to *your* elders; and all of you, clothe yourselves with humility toward one another, for GOD IS OPPOSED TO THE PROUD, BUT GIVES GRACE TO THE HUMBLE. ⁶Therefore humble yourselves under the mighty hand of God, that He may exalt you at the proper time, ⁷casting all your anxiety on Him, because He cares for you. (Caps quote is from Proverbs 3:34)

Humble people get God's grace; proud people get opposition. This means opposition to understanding His Word, too. Without submission to God, the Bible is just a 31,102 piece puzzle with no picture on the box. For the same reason this book will not be understandable either. Many of the perspectives here will make a prideful person angry, which should be a clue perhaps that for them the Father is not quite the Lord they say they worship. God wants us to depend on Him and His Word alone, to love Him and trust Him and do what He says when He says it.

The second key to understanding prophecy, and this will be emphasized repeatedly, is to keep in mind that the Word is one complete, unified package. As Paul says, it is one faith given to one Body. God hasn't stopped and started different programs as a reaction to what people or fallen angels did to mess things up. Every part of His inexorable plan is intact and moving forward just as He wills. He doesn't second guess Himself or scramble to come up with a new plan because the other one didn't work. He is still on the plan He started, and no one is able to sidetrack it or cause it to fail. Every prophecy, from start to finish, is directly related to every other prophecy, and to every other word of God.

Most Church interpretation looks at the Bible from outside in. Many would-be interpreters don't make all of the Word a part of their walk with God. They pick and choose what they will and won't do by classifying parts of His Word as old and outdated. Or they'll dismiss parts as merely 'civil,' and 'ceremonial.' A third philosophy rejects much that is inferior because it is 'physical' and not 'spiritual,' ignoring the fact that they are connected. This chopped up teaching, thinking and doing leads to chopped up understanding when it comes to prophecy, too. There are many who have found their way to God anyway, and parts of the sliced and diced teaching are effective sometimes, but nothing satisfies or helps with living as does living the whole of the Word.

Examining parts of something through a microscope might allow you to identify some parts, but it doesn't give you the firsthand understanding that comes from actually being involved. Instead of chopping, the best way to understand God is to become part of His household, through complete and absolute humble obedience to every one of His living oracles.

Studying prophecy from the outside doesn't work very well to gain understanding and change lives. We need to have it on the inside; eat His body and drink His blood as He said in John chapter six, again meaning to hear and obey. Doing this imparts wisdom, and then we can understand prophecy from the inside out.

Proverbs 1:22–23, ESV. "How long, O simple ones, will you love being simple? How long will scoffers delight in their scoffing and fools hate knowledge? If you turn at my reproof, behold, I will pour out my spirit to you; I will make my words known to you.

Speaking of every word from God being related, **the third key** to understanding prophecy is to use the Bible to interpret the Bible. Much of prophecy is explained several times in several different ways and several different contexts. Many of the prophecies in Revelation are in various forms in previous books.

A great earthquake like no other, for instance, is mentioned a number of times (Isaiah 29:6; Ezekiel 38:19; Zechariah 14:5; Revelation 16:18) in connection with God appearing "on that day" or on "his day" (of wrath and judgment). There have been, and will be, lots of quakes, but one in particular is like none of the others. We can identify similar events by their descriptions given to us in other parts of the Word. We have to be careful of this, because even if two things look the same that doesn't mean they necessarily are the same. On the other hand, if they look the same they might very well be closely related to each other.

Some understanding is obscured from us and will only come as we experience the events at the time. Believers will recognize what is happening then because we have the Word in our hearts and are living it out. It is like salve for the eyes and unplugs our ears. God's Word will be living and active in us, so our humility and practiced obedience will allow us to respond to events according to His will. We will be able to put two and two together in those few instances where God has delayed giving the specifics.

The Basics

This book is organized with short sections and titles so that you can jump to places that have a particular interest for you. There is some repetition to make jumping around easier, but you will probably understand better if you go all the way through it. You know, like we should do with the Bible. Feel free also to check the context of the Bible references used. Read a chapter or two before and after to get the whole flavor of what God is telling us. Don't take our word for it; take His.

God tells us a lot, but some information He is holding in reserve for His own reasons. Of the revealed portion, more and more will become plain as humility and obedience increase. Much of His revelation that may seem obscure to you is due to philosophies of men that pick and choose from Scripture instead of using the Bible to interpret the Bible. Obscurity is the calling card of people who do not follow all of God's Word, including the Law.

God's message is to be understood (or why give it?), but some parts are yet to be revealed. Many of the parts are assembled here into an understandable coherent whole. Use this as a start point to help prepare God's people for what is coming, because the Bible indicates that it's going to be rougher for everyone than conventional Church teaching claims. There is no special direction or spiritual knowledge from Him in here, such as a special anointing or visions, other than what can be gleaned from what He has already delivered. All believers are anointed (1 John 2:20), but we have to exercise that anointing by working to rightly handle the Word of Truth (2 Timothy 2:15).

Psalm 111:2 ESV. Great are the works of the LORD, studied by all who delight in them.

On the one hand, information presented here might not have a school's stamp of approval. On the other, it means there are no blinders on. There is freedom to read the Word and ask as many questions as needed. There is no worry about getting fired, thrown out of a denomination, or have any degree repossessed by the school that granted it. You can be free too. All you have to do is read the Word and do what He says. You don't have to agree with this book, but you do have to listen to Him. One way or the other.

Hate, Love, Curse and Blessing

You wouldn't think we'd have to talk about this in a prophecy book. One of the reasons we *do* have to talk about it is the flip that is happening in the world right now. By "flip," it is meant that right is becoming wrong and wrong is becoming right.

Isaiah 5:20–21 ESV. Woe to those who call evil good and good evil, who put darkness for light and light for darkness, who put bitter for sweet and sweet for bitter! Woe to those who are wise in their own eyes, and shrewd in their own sight!

The flip is happening all over the world, because we have turned away from His commands. We cut ourselves loose from the standard, so we can do what is right in our own eyes. Wrong is defined by God as turning from His commands. Turning away from even one of them is wrong, evil, wicked and rebellious.

Daniel 9:3–5 ESV. Then I turned my face to the Lord God, seeking him by prayer and pleas for mercy with fasting and sackcloth and ashes. I prayed to the LORD my God and made confession, saying, "O Lord, the great and awesome God, who keeps covenant and steadfast love with those who love him and keep his commandments, we have sinned and done wrong and acted wickedly and rebelled, turning aside from your commandments and rules.

Included in this flip of light to darkness and evil to good are the definitions of hate and love.

Malachi 1:2–3 ESV. "I have loved you," says the LORD. But you say, "How have you loved us?" "Is not Esau Jacob's brother?" declares the LORD. "Yet I have loved Jacob but Esau I have hated. I have laid waste his hill country and left his heritage to jackals of the desert."

Biblically, neither hate nor love are emotions. There are emotions perhaps frequently attached, but the basic definitions do not include emotion. Love means to do things, actions, for the benefit of others, even if one doesn't "feel" like it. Hate means to withhold an action that would benefit others. So when God says He "hates Esau," it means that He isn't going to help Esau. In other words, Esau is on his own, which is the usual preference demanded by people in general anyway. When He "loves Jacob," it means He is going to actively work to benefit Jacob.

We can also use the word "blessing" for love. This word at its root means to have the presence of God. The presence of God makes blessing possible. Blessings and God go hand in hand. A curse, on the other hand, is literally the absence of God. If God, the source of all blessing, withdraws His presence even a little bit, by that much there is a curse. After Adam and Eve decided to act on their own apart from God, He "cursed" the ground by withdrawing some of His help or blessing. This caused the ground to produce thorns and thistles in spite of our best farming efforts. God "blesses" everyone with sunshine and rain in season, because while farming or gardening is hard work He hasn't completely withdrawn His presence, and the ground is still fruitful.

Many non-believers want to hit believers with "Isn't your God a god of love?" What they are implying is their opinion that He should work on the behalf of others no matter how sinful they are and even if they don't follow Him, which is false. This is where love and hate definitions come into play in prophecy. Even though God will be dropping judgment on the kingdoms of the deceiver, it is still love because He will not allow them to continue harming others with their anti-God ways.

People have a hard time admitting, because the definitions are upside down, that God would hammer the earth with judgments as are described in Revelation and other places. Since He is a "god of love" (falsely defined), then to these people (in or out of the Church), it doesn't make sense God would judge even a little bit.

One of the ways that the beast will be "loved" by the population is that he'll use the sentimental version of love, and paint God as hateful because He is pouring out judgment on the world. "Destroying the earth" is already set up as a bad thing. It's assigned to people in modern culture, for instance, who don't march in lockstep with the globalist hoax idea of man-caused global warming. Globalism is another name for the deceiver's one-world government. "Destroying the earth" is also the label for those who don't think that renewable energy is going to be the salvation of mankind. Labels like "destroyer of the earth" illustrate how God-haters have flipped the meanings of hate and love, blessing and curse, upside down.

Technically, the globalists are correct, but not in the way they think. God is going to warm up the globe and it will actually be "man caused." However, there will be no remedy by man except to repent, which will not be offered to God.

God wants to save the earth. He'll save anyone in it that wants to be saved. But it is infested with corruption, evil and haters who do everything in their power to usurp anything God says and take His place. You wouldn't want to move into a new home if filth was everywhere, would you? Neither would our Father. God is going to save the earth by first cleansing the existing planet. Then He'll show how it could have been had we just trusted Him and did what He said. The kingdom of heaven with Jesus on the throne of David will demonstrate a truly green new deal. Later He's going to make a new heavens and new earth, in which all of the filth will be relegated to a place of warming chosen by hater's rejection of Him.

Defining Faith

Romans 12:3 NASB95. For through the grace given to me I say to everyone among you not to think more highly of himself than he ought to think; but to think so as to have sound judgment, as God has allotted to each a measure of faith.

Looking at faith in the Bible, we get two definitions. There is "faith" which is connected to "faithfulness," and the other faith that is a set of instructions, prophecies, warnings and admonitions from God. In other words, there is "your faith" and "The faith."

Jude 3 ESV. Beloved, although I was very eager to write to you about our common salvation, I found it necessary to write appealing to you to contend for the faith that was once for all delivered to the saints.

Galatians 1:23 ESV. They only were hearing it said, "He who used to persecute us is now preaching the faith he once tried to destroy."

"The faith" is the Bible. "Your faith" is trust in, and obedience to, "the faith." Technically, and practically, we can have faith in the faith. Faith is sticking with God; faithlessness (or sin) is departing from Him and following our own desire or knowledge.

Many people equate faith with belief, but then turn around and define belief as merely recognizing or apprehending an idea. In truth, faith or belief must have a corresponding action. Recognizing an idea or a truth, by itself, is worthless as James tells us. For belief or faith to be worthwhile, we need to do something from or because of our belief. The Bible defines faith, and believers are defined by their faith, with actions. Loving God and faithfulness go hand in hand.

What can be known about God is plain, because God has shown it in creation. He has given everyone a conscience that testifies of God's existence, and His invisible attributes are clearly perceived by all humans. In other words, He has given everyone a measure of faith. But many put it in the wrong ideas or person.

Romans 1:18–23 ESV. For the wrath of God is revealed from heaven against all ungodliness and unrighteousness of men, who by their unrighteousness suppress the truth. For what can be known about God is plain to them, because God has shown it to them. For his invisible attributes, namely, his eternal power and divine nature, have been clearly perceived, ever since the creation of the world, in the things that have been made. So they are without excuse. For although they knew God, they did not honor him as God or give thanks to him, but they became futile in their thinking, and their foolish hearts were darkened. Claiming to be wise, they became fools, and exchanged the glory of the immortal God for images resembling mortal man and birds and animals and creeping things.

Knowing about God, and putting faith in God, are two vastly different things. His instructions and prophecies are directed at all men, and He requires a response: "He commands all people everywhere to repent" (Acts 17:30). No one will have any excuse for not acting on the prophecies in the Word.

Faith is a set of statements and prophecies given by God in the Bible, and when we act on those statements, we gain faith or put our faith into action. Faith is shown by actions. Faith is trusting God and doing what He says.

Luke 17:6 ESV. And the Lord said, "If you had faith like a grain of mustard seed, you could say to this mulberry tree, 'Be uprooted and planted in the sea,' and it would obey you.

If we have faith as small as a mustard seed, which is to say trust in God and obedience to His will even a tiny amount, then as Jesus said we can do amazing things. Not the least of these is when we share the Word of God with someone and it changes his or her heart of stone to one of flesh. If we trust Him, and do what He says, our faith can move mountains. Or mulberry trees. But we need to be aligned with God's will, which comes from taking in all of His Words and acting on them.

"Obedience to the faith" or "obedience of the faith" in some Scripture verses shows us that obedience is a big part of faith. It proceeds from trusting that God's Word is a rock on which we can rest. The Word doesn't change. When we hear a prophecy to repent and then believe it, we repent or change direction. We stop doing what is right in our own eyes and do what is right in God's eyes. God is not messing around, and commands men everywhere to obey the faith.

Acts 6:7 ESV. And the word of God continued to increase, and the number of the disciples multiplied greatly in Jerusalem, and a great many of the priests became obedient to the faith.

Romans 16:25–27 ESV. Now to him who is able to strengthen you according to my gospel and the preaching of Jesus Christ, according to the revelation of the mystery that was kept secret for long ages but has now been disclosed and through the prophetic writings has been made known to all nations, according to the command of the eternal God, to bring about the obedience of faith— to the only wise God be glory forevermore through Jesus Christ! Amen.

Faith is decreased if we back away from doing any part of His Words to us, including the Law. Many Church philosophies nibble away at our ability to obey and thus destroy faith by casting doubt on the whole of the Word and encouraging disobedience.

The Person and Work of the Prophet

God uses people to help deliver His Word, and some of those who do it on a regular basis we call prophets. Almost anyone can prophesy (Numbers 11:25-26 elders; 1 Samuel 10 Saul; John 11:51 Caiaphas). But a true prophet has to be consistent with other revelations from God, including whatever books of the Bible are in existence at the time (in particular the Torah or first five books). If there are events foretold they have to happen accurately, and the message cannot compromise worship of God alone.

Worship includes taking in and doing all of His Words as if they were bread for our souls (John 6:53-58). It means to obey God; to do what He says. Idolatry is obeying someone or something else. If any prophet, teacher, or leader tells us not to follow any part of God's Word, for any reason such as "it's for the Jews" or "it's old" or "it was fulfilled and eliminated by Jesus," that person is a false prophet or teacher. Modern Nicolaitans all over are telling us even now that believers shouldn't follow all or part of what some call the Law of Moses.

A prophet's main job is not just to tell the future, but to deliver the Word of God. He or she '**forth tells**' (preaches, teaches) as well as '**fore tells**' (the future). An example of forth-telling is in 1 Chronicles 25:1-3, where musicians are said to prophesy with music and song. The Psalms in many ways are prophetic songs.

With forth telling, the delivery of a 'future-gram' is usually prefaced by "Thus sayeth the Lord." Prophecy frequently includes admonitions to turn from wicked behavior back to God's Living Oracles, and so avoid His upcoming judgments.

All prophecy from God conforms to His Word recorded for us in the 66 books of the Bible, and especially the first five. Another issue is authority, which is clarified for us by Jesus.

John 7:17–18, ESV. If anyone's will is to do God's will, he will know whether the teaching is from God or whether I am speaking on my own authority. The one who speaks on his own authority seeks his own glory; but the one who seeks the glory of him who sent him is true, and in him there is no falsehood.

Prophecy glorifies God. If it does not glorify God, it is not from God. True prophecy points people to God, comforts people that God is in control, and shows His power in knowing what will happen. Our faith (remember, trust and obedience) should be in Him, not in somebody's theology or a philosophy of man. Though man might have some power, God has ultimate power and will always do what He says He will do.

One word used to characterize a prophet's message is **"remember."** The word remember includes the idea of speaking or acting on behalf of someone or something, which also fits right in with the idea of "don't forget." Remember the things God has done, remember His Word or covenant, remember that He isn't finished with you yet, and the nations should remember that they too will be judged for disobedience.

As discussed before, another word that characterizes the message of a prophet is **"repent."** Prophecy generally comes under the heading of "Things that will happen if you follow (or do not follow) God." The overall idea is to stop doing your own thing and do His instead. That's why most of the time real prophets are killed - people don't want to submit to God. False prophets seem to keep popping up because they tell people only what they want to hear.

Amos 5:10 ESV. They hate him who reproves in the gate, and they abhor him who speaks the truth.

No one likes the message of 'repent or die,' so unbelievers tend to silence God's messengers permanently if they can. In a way Jesus was just one in a long line of prophets that people wanted to silence. To the consternation of unbelievers, there are always people that God can call on to continue delivering His Word.

A prime purpose for the prophet was to **reveal iniquity or sin**, so that believers would confess and repent. Iniquity is literally "lawlessness" or no law. Lawlessness can be complete law-breaking or just one law broken. Once revealed and changed, God restores people back to what they had in Him before they sinned.

Ezekiel 13:4–5, ESV. Your prophets have been like jackals among ruins, O Israel. You have not gone up into the breaches, or built up a wall for the house of Israel, that it might stand in battle in the day of the LORD.

On top of sending pesky prophets and prophetesses, God made sure to write most of it down and preserve the Book so no one could ever say, "Nobody told me." God has spoken through prophets, the written Word, and through His Son.

Hebrews 1:1-2 NASB95. ¹God, after He spoke long ago to the fathers in the prophets in many portions and in many ways, ²in these last days has spoken to us in His Son, whom He appointed heir of all things, through whom also He made the world.

The prophets and Jesus spoke most of what is recorded for us, at least the stuff we need to know. The Bible is the Word of God, absolute truth, complete and inerrant in what it teaches, and written in plain language so that anyone can read and do what God says. It wouldn't make any sense to communicate things people need to know in a way that they couldn't understand. God is very clear and His Words literally mean what He says.

Of course, just because it is in plain language doesn't mean that people rush out to do what God says. Our own flesh gets in the way. That's one reason we need to encourage one another to love and good works. Doing what God says isn't easy. There are also wolves which hinder our progress with false teachings.

Foretelling is one way that God informs His people of His plans and purposes in advance. He told Abraham what was going to happen with his family (blessing to the nations) and what was going to happen in Sodom and Gomorrah.

Genesis 18:17-19 NASB95. ¹⁷The LORD said, "Shall I hide from Abraham what I am about to do, ¹⁸since Abraham will surely become a great and mighty nation, and in him all the nations of the earth will be blessed? ¹⁹"For I have chosen him, so that he may command his children and his household after him to keep the way of the LORD by doing righteousness and justice, so that the LORD may bring upon Abraham what He has spoken about him."

God tells His prophets, and then the prophets inform the people. Amos says that a prophet can't help but relay the Word of God, likening it to a reaction from a lion's roar.

Amos 3:6-8 NASB95. ⁶If a trumpet is blown in a city will not the people tremble? If a calamity occurs in a city has not the LORD done it? ⁷Surely the Lord GOD does nothing Unless He reveals His secret counsel To His servants the prophets. ⁸A lion has roared! Who will not fear? The Lord GOD has spoken! Who can but prophesy?

Believers respond to what God says through the prophet, unbelievers do not. Nineveh responded to God's Word from Jonah, once he did what he was supposed to, and they averted disaster. At least for a while (later they fell back into sin and were destroyed). Abimelech responded correctly to a dream from God (Genesis 20) concerning Sarah, received healing and avoided death.

Notice that God speaks to everyone, not just those who supposedly wear His name. His Word is for all people. Whoever follows His Word is saved. We can be saved from immediate consequences, as in the case of Nineveh (warned by Jonah), or we can be saved from hell if we persevere. When God speaks, He expects a response; humble hearts hear what He says and obeys. Eternal life is for those who persevere in following His Word.

The first prophet mentioned in the Word is God (Genesis 3:15). He is the pattern and the motivator of all other true prophets. The first use of the actual word "prophet" was in describing Abraham to Abimelech after that king grabbed Abraham's wife Sarah (Genesis 20:7). Abraham in his office as prophet was supposed to intercede (or intervene) for Abimelech with God so that God didn't kill Abimelech for taking Sarah. We don't really see much direct foretelling from Abraham, but we do see quite a bit of him standing between God in His wrath and people who didn't deserve it. So besides forth-telling and foretelling the Word, a prophet also intercedes for people as needed. Interceding is the root of prophecy, because people are warned about what will happen if they continue on a path away from God.

False Prophets

The Bible tells us there will be false prophets and false Christs (or anointed). Sure enough, we see them frequently. But not all are right out there in front of people saying so. False prophets are all around. We have to check everyone, and the standard is the Bible.

Matthew 24:24 ESV. For false christs and false prophets will arise and perform great signs and wonders, so as to lead astray, if possible, even the elect.

The first check is that if the prophet foretells the future, and the event does not come about the way they said, they are false. The second check is that the event comes to pass, but the prophet says to follow other gods. Then he or she is false. A third would be, as mentioned before, that if it doesn't glorify God it doesn't come from God. To glorify God is to give Him the credit, praise, obedience, and worship that is rightfully His in the first place.

There are prophetic utterances that come from God to a false prophet but are a test. Sometimes a person will foretell something that comes to pass. However, then he or she will tell people to worship another god. God tests His people on occasion with false prophets. The idea is to make sure we stay true to Him.

Deuteronomy 13:1–4 ESV. "If a prophet or a dreamer of dreams arises among you and gives you a sign or a wonder, and the sign or wonder that he tells you comes to pass, and if he says, 'Let us go after other gods,' which you have not known, 'and let us serve them,' you shall not listen to the words of that prophet or that dreamer of dreams. For the LORD your God is testing you, to know whether you love the LORD your God with all your heart and with all your soul. You shall walk after the

LORD your God and fear him and keep his commandments and obey his voice, and you shall serve him and hold fast to him.

Worship is not necessarily just making or bowing down to a statue. Worship is primarily obedience, so worship of other gods means to ignore God and His commands and do what the other god (or person) suggests or commands. Idolatry is ultimately a worship of self, because we do what we think or feel instead of what God commands. Adam and Eve were guilty of idolatry because they did what they thought was right in their own eyes instead of following the command of God not to eat one particular fruit.

Following other gods includes worship of, or obedience to, anyone (or anything) other than God. This means those who teach something different from the Word are false prophets also. All those wolves in sheep's clothing, who tell us, for instance, that Jesus terminated the Law at the cross, are in effect telling us to worship other gods. They may sound good, but the ideas are false.

False prophets don't always come right out and say worship another god. They just cast doubt on God's Word (especially His Law). Chipping away at the Rock, they hope to recast God's message into something more comfortable and permissive. Again, it's worth repeating the quote of this passage from a true prophet.

Jeremiah 23:16–17 ESV. Thus says the LORD of hosts: "Do not listen to the words of the prophets who prophesy to you, filling you with vain hopes. They speak visions of their own minds, not from the mouth of the LORD. They say continually to those who despise the word of the LORD, 'It shall be well with you'; and to everyone who stubbornly follows his own heart, they say, 'No disaster shall come upon you.' "

This is the message of most of the modern Church. It says, "We can ignore most of God's Laws and it will be well with us because Jesus fulfilled and eliminated them" and other such nonsense. The Church is full of "vain hopes" and "speak(s) visions of their own minds, not from the mouth of the Lord." But our God says, "Do not listen!"

Our Father tells us to stay away from false prophets (Deuteronomy 18:9-14). This includes necromancers (calling up the dead) mediums (a bridge for spirits) witchcraft (essentially substance abuse whether ingested or as potions) spell casters, omen readers (astrology), and those who use divination (the use of objects mostly to tell the future). God doesn't tell us to avoid the false stuff because it doesn't work to some extent (most of it will at least partially work); it's because the methods go around Him and frequently include lies. Instead of God, the wrong methods depend on the power of the deceiver and his demons.

The category of false prophet also includes those who claim to follow Him, but introduce just enough error in their teaching of the Bible that people get lost a little at a time. False prophets might look good in wool suits but promote philosophies of men such as that the Law (or part of it) has been eliminated. These prophets don't mislead people all at once with in-your-face false teachings. It's more effective to just nudge us sheep away from the whole Word by a little bit here or there.

Spirit Sight

Taking in all of God's Words and doing them is a very spiritual process. We might start out seeing only a little bit of God's promises and plans and choose to follow Him. As we feed on His Words, trust Him more, and consequently do more of what He says, the eyes of our soul or spirit open wider. The more we do, the more our faith grows, the more we see. As our hearts open to Him, the salve of His Word opens our eyes and our ears.

Isaiah 29:18 ESV. In that day the deaf shall hear the words of a book, and out of their gloom and darkness the eyes of the blind shall see.

Trust in God grows as we feed and water our little mustard seed of faith with the body and blood of the Christ. Jesus tells the congregation of Laodicea to buy salve to anoint their eyes that they may see. This salve is the Word of God, not just in the reading but also in the doing. We are told in a number of places to circumcise our hearts and our ears (Deuteronomy 10:16, Jeremiah 4:4). We do this by trusting God and doing His Word.

Jeremiah 6:10 ESV. To whom shall I speak and give warning, that they may hear? Behold, their ears are uncircumcised, they cannot listen; behold, the word of the LORD is to them an object of scorn; they take no pleasure in it.

As our spirit sight gets stronger from reading and doing His Word, we can see more of the spiritual realities behind or overlaying our physical world. Our understanding grows as our trust and obedience grows, which is the nature of faith. For instance, with open eyes we can see how worldly tyrants and dictators are moved by the hate of the deceiver for God. The causes of wars are more obvious, including the causes for wars connected with God's judgments. Love and the Spirit flow from obedience to His Words, which in turn salves our eyesight and makes it clearer.

We need spirit sight in order to understand what's really going on with prophecy. The principalities and powers that Paul mentions in several of his letters are the big players in prophecy.

Ephesians 6:12 ESV. For we do not wrestle against flesh and blood, but against the rulers, against the authorities, against the cosmic powers over this present darkness, against the spiritual forces of evil in the heavenly places.

The book of Revelation shows us the character and the goals of the dragon and his followers. It also shows us the real power of God and agents acting on His instructions. It takes "spirit sight" to understand the message God is communicating.

1 Corinthians 2:14 ESV. The natural person does not accept the things of the Spirit of God, for they are folly to him, and he is not able to understand them because they are spiritually discerned.

Sadly, mankind is way too wrapped up in a selfish, self-centered, disobedient viewpoint to make sense of things that are spiritually discerned. In general, even in the Church, people are immature and unwilling to properly handle the message from God. The most obvious and easy-to-see proof of this is refusal to acknowledge or follow God's Law.

1 John 2:3–6 ESV. And by this we know that we have come to know him, if we keep his commandments. Whoever says "I know him" but does not keep his commandments is a liar, and the truth is not in him, but whoever keeps his word, in him truly the love of God is perfected. By this we may know that we are in him: whoever says he abides in him ought to walk in the same way in which he walked.

If a person can't see the life and love in God's commands, live them and promote them, he or she is spiritually blind and won't see the other parts of the Word properly. The main message of the Word, repeated many times in many ways, is to choose God and live as He wants us to live. Follow His Words, stay in Him, make His commands as close to you as a heartbeat. This is what clarifies spiritual eyesight.

The Deceiver

Ephesians 2:1–3 ESV. And you were dead in the trespasses and sins in which you once walked, following the course of this world, following the prince of the power of the air, the spirit that is now at work in the sons of disobedience— among whom we all once lived in the passions of our flesh, carrying out the desires of the body and the mind, and were by nature children of wrath, like the rest of mankind.

One of the biggest con jobs in world history is the effort by the deceiver to make people think he doesn't exist. He has done excellent work there, aided by willing agents or people willing to blind themselves. But he really does exist, and he really, really hates God and everything connected with God. He hates Israel, he hates believers, he hates Jerusalem and he really hated the Temple when it was around. He couldn't wait to tear it down with his agents the Babylonians and then the Romans.

It is important to know the prince of the power of the air because he is the agent of suffering throughout world history. He is the driving force behind all disobedience of God and sin. But he isn't the direct cause of all of it because people do evil well enough on their own. We can't really say "the devil made me do it".

Some people might think he is all powerful, all knowing and all present but he isn't. His power is monitored and controlled by God (see Job, for instance). God allows the deceiver to do certain things when it suits His purposes, but he cannot just do whatever he wants. He is limited. He's not all present, although through his agents the fallen angels and many humans it might look like it. While powerful, he is not all powerful. Only God has the "all" qualities.

You might be asking, "Why does God allow evil and suffering?" which is a good question, but lacking in depth. What we really need to ask is, "Where would He stop it?" At which point in history should He stop the evil? Or at which point in the individual sinning process, thought or action, should He stop it? Because when He stops it, there is a definite end. He doesn't kid around. To stop it He would have to stop people. Stop them from being born, stop them from exercising the ability to choose, stop them from sinning the moment they sin by ending their existence.

If He struck people with a lightning bolt at the moment of sinning, there wouldn't be any people around! Adam and Eve would've been burnt to a crisp, instead of merely receiving banishment from intimacy with God along with chances to repent and (eventually) return to Eden. The deceiver may be the instigator of much of the evil in history, but people all by themselves do an excellent job of inventing evil on their own. God, in His gracious love, waits for people to change direction and choose His way.

The deceiver is also known as the dragon, the serpent, a son of the morning or dawn, and Day Star or Lucifer meaning "shining one" (Isaiah 14:12). Originally, he was an angel of the type called cherub, a guardian of the righteousness or holiness of God. He decided that he wanted what God had, without having God (Ezekiel 28:11-19). Apparently, he was beautiful and can still appear that way. He is the power behind world kingdoms such as Assyria and Babylon (Isaiah 14) and kings such as the king of Tyre (Ezekiel 28). The deceiver will also be the power behind his protégé the beast or little horn in the Tribulation. He will give his power to the beast for a short time to help establish the world kingdom, but will not succeed.

Part of the great con job the deceiver has managed to pull on the world is to get people to see him as a cartoonish figure in red pajamas with a pointy tail and carrying a pitchfork. That is opposite of what he really is. He doesn't even own a pair of pajamas, let alone red ones, although I'm sure he owns a closet full of wool suits. He is one of those people who look good on the outside but inside is all putrid, rotten, 100% against God and completely evil. His hair is combed in the latest style, he is a compelling speaker, and very intelligent. He isn't a clown; he's a deadly enemy of everything life-giving. He is death walking, because of his opposition to God.

It's not so much that he wants to destroy good things. He just doesn't want God in the picture. This doesn't work out for his ultimate success, because God is the source of all good. Jesus is the one who upholds everything by the word of His power. If God were to somehow leave completely everything would fall apart.

The little horn will be a weak echo of the deceiver. On the surface, he will in many ways look like the ultimate villain in a James Bond movie: smooth talking, attractive, and convincing, with the appearance of wisdom masking the character of a raptor in a dinosaur movie. While God is described for us as "holy, holy, holy" and His Son our Messiah as a lamb that was slain for our sin, the beast (and his father and mentor the deceiver) won't even come close to holiness and goodness.

Everything the deceiver does turns out bad. He tries to shore up his works by appropriating some of God's goodness, like some of His rules, but cannot quite do it completely. He incorporates some of God's Word in what he does, but the effort falls short because of a lack of love. He doesn't want to obey God unless he has to, and without the Giver and Creator of light, life and love, he's got pieces missing from a sure foundation. Anything he builds is bound to fall apart from corruption.

Matthew 12:25 ESV. Knowing their thoughts, he said to them, "Every kingdom divided against itself is laid waste, and no city or house divided against itself will stand.

Another reason the deceiver's kingdom cannot stand is because it is divided against itself. He builds on hate, and all of his plans and his people hate. As mentioned in a previous section, hate is defined as anything that is against God or outside of His Word or will, or refusing to do anything for the benefit of others. The deceiver wants to be the big cheese, but everyone who sides with him also wants to be the big cheese. As he did with Jesus, the deceiver offers the kingdoms of the world to people if they would just do what he says. So they fight and scheme and backstab each other, and ultimately destroy themselves trying to obtain those kingdoms. The problem is, as with all con jobs, the deceiver over-promises and under-delivers.

We cannot underrate the deceiver, which is what we do when we picture him as a guy with red makeup, horns, a pointy tail and red pajamas. He is sophisticated and sneaky, powerful and persuasive. It isn't always with a direct confrontation that he fools people; it's with a little bit of error introduced over a long time. He knows the Bible backwards and forwards (he just doesn't obey it), and uses a little of it here and there to bolster and disguise his temptations. Our defense is to know the entire Bible and follow it without hesitation. When he gives us a little bit of the Bible with a lot of error, we respond as Jesus did with, "It is also written."

Prophecy Reveals a Spiritual Battle

We have to remember too that there is a spiritual battle going on, and all we see in the physical world is not all there is (see Ephesians 6:12 for instance). Many of the events God tells us will happen are puzzling on the surface but seem to be in the Bible because of the spiritual powers behind them. For instance, Daniel (10:13, 20) is told of a battle between the angel and a prince of Persia, and that prince is definitely not a human. The prince of Persia is mostly likely a fallen angel, or the deceiver himself.

In another instance the king of Babylon in Isaiah 14 is described as 'star of the morning' (or 'Day Star, son of Dawn' in the ESV) which is actually the title of the deceiver. Not so far-fetched when we remember that Babylon, (or the people of

Babylon called Chaldeans), is related to one of the deceiver's first projects on earth; the tower of Babel.

It also makes sense because the power behind kings and presidents are principalities in high places. The king of Tyre is said by God to have been in Eden (Ezekiel 28:13) which was only true about the power *behind* the throne (the deceiver again). The character of the human king and the spiritual king are the same, and will share the same fate. The real king (behind the flesh and blood king) of Babylon and Tyre are the same deceiver, though he acted through different human agents.

Prophecies directed at city-states or countries are better understood if we remember the spiritual agents that energize and control those countries. We can tell who their rulers are by the actions of the people in the kingdom. This is why we know that dictators like Stalin or Mao are atheists, though they may not openly declare themselves as such. To identify the driving force behind a government or tyrant just look at their works or actions.

By looking at actions, we can tell that Islam and Islamic governments are a creation of the deceiver. Most governments in the world today belong to, or are animated and powered by, the deceiver. Israel might not act like it sometimes, but is protected by Michael the archangel who is backed by God. The power struggles go back and forth, in direct relation to the condition of the people and whom they worship. Which brings up the question: Who is the spiritual power behind the United States government?

Learn the Past, Know the Future.

1 Corinthians 13:8 ESV. Love never ends. As for prophecies, they will pass away; as for tongues, they will cease; as for knowledge, it will pass away.

As we read through the whole of the Word, we are confronted with a series of statements from God that, from the perspective of the people to whom He delivered them, were yet to occur. Many of them have not been seen even now. Others seem to repeat again and again. At the time it is revealed, prophecy is history that hasn't happened yet. What was future becomes the past, depending on where you are on the timeline.

To God, there is no past and future except as it relates to humans. He is in a 'present' that includes past and future. He sees it all from start to finish, and always has every part of it under His control, while granting to man the freedom to make choices. Prophecy and history are closely related because all prophecy becomes history. Studying how prophecy changes from future to past helps decipher what is yet to happen. If we study prophecy that became history, we can use the patterns to perhaps interpret prophecy that hasn't happened.

For instance, there are over 300 prophecies speaking of the Incarnation, crucifixion and resurrection of the Christ such as those in Psalm 22. Each one was specific and happened just as foretold. In that Psalm evildoers are described as "bulls of Bashan" and "dogs" who gloat and cast lots for His clothing. We can perhaps interpret that the dogs were Roman soldiers, while the bulls (making loud sounds like bulls roaring) were unbelieving Israelites cheering the death of Jesus. Bashan was part of the land of Israel at the Exodus, taken from Og as described in Numbers 21, and located somewhere in Samaria (north Israel) according to Amos 4.

Large chunks of the Word that were prophecy at one time are now history, but the past is just as important as the future. The history of God's dealings with people gives us a complete education on how to interpret the things that haven't happened yet from our perspective.

Prophecy comes directly from God in the form of the spoken word, visions, and dreams. It is a statement of God's will, and we know it will happen because God said it would.

Daniel 8:26 ESV. The vision of the evenings and the mornings that has been told is true, but seal up the vision, for it refers to many days from now."

The foretelling function of prophecy is, of course, about the future. This is part of the nature of prophecy. A large part of what was future at one time may now be history, but some of the prophesied events have not transpired. The Bible itself sometimes says events are unique[1] (never occurred before and never will again) and sometimes says it's for the "distant future."

2 Samuel 7:19 NASB95. "And yet this was insignificant in Your eyes, O Lord GOD, for You have spoken also of the house of Your servant concerning the distant future. And this is the custom of man, O Lord GOD.

Daniel 12:1 NASB95. "Now at that time Michael, the great prince who stands guard over the sons of your people, will arise. And there will be a time of distress such as never occurred since there was a nation until that time; and at that time your people, everyone who is found written in the book, will be rescued.

So there are events that we know haven't happened yet because they are so unique or pertain to a distant future. No one who is a preterist (thinks prophecy has already happened) is paying attention to the Word, nor do they truly believe it. You have to decide: Does God really mean what He says, or not?

We also have to understand that God's perspective is different from ours. He made a perfect universe and earth, and then

---

[1] Exodus 11:6 where the outcry from the death of Egypt's firstborn is "such as will never be again." Compare with other instances of "never again" (Isaiah 2:4, 24:20; Jeremiah 31:12, 50:39; Joel 2:2; Micah 4:3).

there was rebellion. This rebellion began with Lucifer, extended to Adam and Eve, and then to most of the rest of the people of the world throughout history. When God talks about sin, He is including not only an individual action but also the tendency in men to go their own way. The Day of God's Wrath is the judgment and wrap-up of the rebellion to that point.

The love of money is a main driving force in this rebellion. The kingdoms of the world are motivated primarily by the love of money (unjust gain), which generally relates also to power over, and control of, other people. This is one of the reasons that "the prostitute sitting on many waters" known too as "Babylon the great, mother of prostitutes and of earth's abominations" (Revelation 17) is decked out in gold, jewels and pearls. This prostitute is also marked by trading in cargos of valuable products and even men's souls (Revelation 18:11-13). Money, for the people in Babylon, has replaced God as an object of worship.

A huge point to make about history is that many historians have at the very least been misled and at worst have outright lied about the past. The twisting of history affects how we look at prophecy, because our understanding shades our viewpoint when trying to understand how God sees things.

What God says in prophecy is accurate but is obscured sometimes because of what we've been told about history. Let's face it: none of us were there. What we know about history we've learned from fallible people, who not only have to make many guesses about events but also frequently pursue their own agendas. The Catholic Church in particular had and has an agenda to reinforce their position and authority.

We can trust the Bible, but unbelieving humans not so much. If the Bible, and history as we have heard it, disagree, choose the Bible account every time. Remember that the basic idea of prophecy is that God will judge the earth, purify it, and bring believers into a kingdom under His rule again.

Tribulation

It will be helpful if we talk a little bit about tribulation here, even though we don't really get into "the Tribulation" or Day of the Lord until chapter 5. There has always been some kind of trouble or tribulation in the world. It started when mom and dad got booted out of the Garden, because God withdrew somewhat from direct involvement with them and their kids (a curse). We don't get to walk with Him in the cool of the evening as did Adam and Eve.

Tribulation in general is any suffering, from stubbing a toe to something like losing a crop for a farmer, all the way up (or down) to disease and death. John says there is "tribulation in Jesus" (Revelation 1:9) which is suffering or martyrdom that comes with believing in Him.

However, there is a special tribulation like no other. Jesus speaks of it in Matthew 24:21-22. Other names for this Tribulation are "the Day of the Lord," the "time of trouble," "a day of smoke and burning," and "the Time of Jacob's (Israel's) Trouble. It is going to be a time of God's judgment on the anti-God forces of the deceiver's kingdom with events including the sun darkening, the moon turning to blood, earthquakes (including one really massive earthquake), famines, brimstone, pain and death on a huge scale.

Some think believers will escape this time by something called the Rapture, and others think that most of the Scripture that applies to this time is simply poetic imagery and isn't literal. If we take God at His Word though, it is apparent that the Tribulation really happens and it is a very harrowing and horrible time. It is also apparent, if you believe Paul's writings, that believers will be going through it or most of it. We are protected from God's wrath, but not necessarily from the wrath of man. More of the arguments for the inclusion of believers are in the following pages.

Secular prophets are predicting a huge upheaval coming, even if you aren't a believer in Jesus. For instance, look up the book The Fourth Turning by William Strauss and Neil Howe. Most everyone can sense it; it's just a matter of time.

An Overview

This section is a quick outline or overview of the timeline for God's wrath. All of the Word is combined to arrive at this understanding, but there may be some events out of order or more information is needed. God has given us all we need in the Word to figure out most of His message. Keep in mind that the key to understanding is reading and doing all He says that applies to believers. We are admonished to watch and be ready, not try to figure it all out beforehand.

Matthew gives us the outline from Jesus for future events which he recorded for us in chapters 24 and 25 of his gospel. Jesus tells the apostles that the Temple will be destroyed at 24:2. They come to Him privately later and ask for more information.

Matthew 24:3 ESV. As he sat on the Mount of Olives, the disciples came to him privately, saying, "Tell us, when will these things be, and what will be the sign of your coming and of the end of the age?"

They ask a seemingly simple question, but it has a compound answer. They are thinking the destruction of the Temple will be at the end of the age, perhaps. But there is more to the answer, and Jesus lays it out for them. Verses 4 through 14 are a brief overview from that point to the end. Then Jesus gives another outline, starting with the abomination of desolation (24:15) and ending with the coming of the Son of Man in a much more obvious fashion than when He arrived as a baby.

Four times in both outlines (two each), Jesus tells us of false prophets and false or anti-Christs (Christ is a word that simply means "anointed") and are sometimes called an "abomination of desolation" (AoD). One of these anti-Christs or AoD's arrived when the Roman army destroyed the Temple. Another AoD arrived at the destruction of Jerusalem in 135 A. D. But there is still a future AoD or anti-Christ.

Jesus tells us that immediately after the tribulation the sun will be darkened, the moon won't give light (which happens when the sun doesn't provide light) and He will come back, gathering His elect from the four winds (meaning all over the world). A partial gathering has occurred, but more gathering is coming.

There was great tribulation when the Romans destroyed the Temple, and after they destroyed Jerusalem. But Jesus says there will be another time of trouble unlike any other.

Matthew 24:21–22 ESV. For then there will be great tribulation, such as has not been from the beginning of the world until now, no, and never will be. And if those days had not been cut short, no human being would be saved. But for the sake of the elect those days will be cut short.

Roughly speaking, fairly normal events are going to proceed until a period of time known as the Tribulation. Before that time, there will be wars and earthquakes and famines increasing in frequency and intensity (Matthew 24) but these are not the final events. They are only what Jesus calls "birth pangs."

The tribulation is from the Word given to Daniel concerning 70 weeks of years for Israel (Daniel 9:27-24). 69 of these weeks were counted up to the time of the "cutting off" (crucifixion) of Jesus. The seventieth week has events that are unique and have not yet transpired, so it is still to come.

This week of years is apparently kicked off by the rise of the beast (little horn or AoD) with his fellow anti-christ the false prophet. He signs an agreement for seven years (one week) "with many" (Israel, probably through a democratic vote). This agreement will likely include a provision to build a new temple.

God's two witnesses (the "second woe" of Revelation 11:1-14), probably Elijah and Enoch, create havoc for the beast's efforts to create one world kingdom united against God. The work of the two witnesses contains penalties similar to the seven trumpets. Somewhere around the middle of the week of years, the dragon or deceiver is kicked out of heaven permanently and gives his power to the little horn. The beast figures out how to kill the witnesses, although they don't stay dead.

About this time the false prophet or anti-christ creates a talking image of the little horn on or around the Temple site or in an actual rebuilt temple. The beast then declares he is God, which causes all heaven and hell to break loose. Everyone worshipping the beast or little horn receives the mark of the beast (666) on the forehead or back of the hand.

The Tribulation is broken into two sections by the declaration of Godhood from the little horn, the second half of which is called the Great Tribulation or more specifically the Day of the Lord. It seems many of the most terrible events recorded in the book of Revelation take place during this time (hence the term Great Tribulation) including the bowl judgments of Revelation 16.

About the end of the seven year period the unholy trinity of the little horn, false prophet and the dragon send out three evil frog spirits to gather the armies of the world. These armies attempt the destruction of Israel by fighting against God at the valley of Megiddo, the battle otherwise known as Armageddon. Yeshua is sent back to earth by the Father. On the way, Jesus resurrects His Body and raptures living believers, and together they crush the armies of the deceiver. The beast and false prophet are finally thrown into the lake of fire.

Jesus sets up shop as the real King of the world for a thousand years, during which the dragon or deceiver is chained in the abyss. At the end of this millennium, the deceiver is let loose, and he immediately incites another rebellion against God. This rebellion is also summarily squashed and the perpetrators sent to the lake of fire. The dead who died unrepentant to that point are resurrected, judged, and thrown in there too. God remakes the heavens and earth, and the heavenly city of New Jerusalem is brought down for the Body of Christ to live in forever.

The Reason for the Season

The centerpiece of the tribulation is, as John has put it, "The revelation of Jesus Christ." Our Messiah is going to take control of His kingdom and go to town on evil. Daniel says this:

Daniel 9:24 ESV. "Seventy weeks are decreed about your people and your holy city, to finish the transgression, to put an end to sin, and to atone for iniquity, to bring in everlasting righteousness, to seal both vision and prophet, and to anoint a most holy place.

These are the goals God has in His dealings with people throughout history. He wants to put an end to sin and bring in everlasting righteousness. The penalty for iniquity (lawlessness) was paid at the cross. All people have to do is accept that sacrifice for their own sin. Those who won't do it need a thrashing and consignment to a place that doesn't have the presence of the God they hate. The transgression is not finished yet, and the Tribulation will go a long way towards putting an end to sin leading into everlasting righteousness. These goals are the reason for the Tribulation season.

Isaiah 57:4–6 ESV. Whom are you mocking? Against whom do you open your mouth wide and stick out your tongue? Are you not children of transgression, the offspring of deceit, you who burn with lust among the oaks, under every green tree, who slaughter your children in the valleys, under the clefts of the rocks? Among the smooth stones of the valley is your portion; they, they, are your lot; to them you have poured out a drink offering, you have brought a grain offering. Shall I relent for these things?

Isaiah 24:5–6 ESV. The earth lies defiled under its inhabitants; for they have transgressed the laws, violated the statutes, broken the everlasting covenant. Therefore a curse devours the earth, and its inhabitants suffer for their guilt; therefore the inhabitants of the earth are scorched, and few men are left.

Not only are sins part of the reason for the season of the Tribulation, so is lack of repentance. Compounding the issue of lack of repentance, people use the tongue and breath the Creator gave them to mock Him, refusing to give credit to God, or give thanks to Him, for His many blessings. This includes the supreme blessing of the blood poured out by Jesus in a torturous death that paid the penalty for their many evils. The rejecters and mockers of our holy and loving Father spurn even the freely given blood of His forgiveness, purchased at the cost of His only begotten Son.

It's easy to use words like sin, or even lack of repentance, but it doesn't really do the subject justice. Words fail in describing the depth of the filth, degradation, hate, defilement, duplicity, and hypocrisy that marks much of the earth's population now and throughout history. It is amazing that God is holding off so long in judgment. But He is a longsuffering, patient, loving God who is unwilling to drop the hammer, hoping that people will see the misery and destruction resulting from rejecting Him and repent.

Revelation 11:18 ESV. The nations raged, but your wrath came, and the time for the dead to be judged, and for rewarding your servants, the prophets and saints, and those who fear your name, both small and great, and for destroying the destroyers of the earth."

Judgment Begins in His House

The judgment of the world culminating in the Tribulation has already started in the house of God. Israel has been severely chastised for not following God in centuries past. The Jews spent several thousand years wandering in exile because of failure to obey the Word of God. If the Father did this to His covenant children for failing to follow His Laws, how much more will He judge everyone else for rejecting the sacrifice of the Messiah?

Ezekiel 5:5–8 ESV. "Thus says the Lord GOD: This is Jerusalem. I have set her in the center of the nations, with countries all around her. And she has rebelled against my rules by doing wickedness more than the nations, and against my statutes more than the countries all around her; for they have rejected my rules and have not walked in my statutes. Therefore thus says the Lord GOD: Because you are more turbulent than the nations that are all around you, and have not walked in my statutes or obeyed my rules, and have not even acted according to the rules of the nations that are all around you, therefore thus says the Lord GOD: Behold, I, even I, am against you. And I will execute judgments in your midst in the sight of the nations.

Much of The Church thinks it is immune. It misuses the claim of "the blood of Jesus," like some sort of cosmic eraser which can even erase the Word of God. Nicolaitan theology has The Church either escaping judgment with a rapture or eventually conquering the world. In reality, it is as far removed from God, as a group, as Israel ever was at its low points. The Church has twisted the Word of God so far out of shape to get permission to sin that the teachings are unrecognizable compared to the Bible. At heart, people do not want to follow His Laws, not even a simple one like "don't eat the fruit." Most of The Church is no different from the nations who do not claim to believe in Him, and will suffer the same fate.

Jeremiah 25:15, 28-29 ESV. ¹⁵Thus the LORD, the God of Israel, said to me: "Take from my hand this cup of the wine of wrath, and make all the nations to whom I send you drink it... ²⁸"And if they refuse to accept the cup from your hand to drink, then you shall say to them, 'Thus says the LORD of hosts: You must drink! ²⁹For behold, I begin to work disaster at the city that is called by my name, and shall you go unpunished? You shall not go unpunished, for I am summoning a sword against all the inhabitants of the earth, declares the LORD of hosts.'

The Tribulation is not for believing Israel. It is for all unbelievers. You don't really think that God judges His own as severely as He has Israel, the apple of His eye, and won't judge the nations also, do you? If Israel was punished and exiled for not following God's Laws, other countries surely won't escape punishment for ignoring them either.

1 Peter 4:17–18 ESV. For it is time for judgment to begin at the household of God; and if it begins with us, what will be the outcome for those who do not obey the gospel of God? And "If the righteous is scarcely saved, what will become of the ungodly and the sinner?"

The Church needs to repent. We all need to repent. We need to judge ourselves by His Word, stop following our own stone hearts and allow the Spirit to write His Law on a new heart of flesh. We better do it now, or He will do it for us later.

1 Corinthians 11:31–32 ESV. But if we judged ourselves truly, we would not be judged. But when we are judged by the Lord, we are disciplined so that we may not be condemned along with the world.

2 Interpretation

Isaiah 42:9 ESV. Behold, the former things have come to pass, and new things I now declare; before they spring forth I tell you of them."

Not everyone who wears His name believes there are events prophesied in the Bible that haven't happened yet. As mentioned before, a *preterist* insists that all or almost all of what is considered prophecy is already history. These people clearly belong in Peter's category of "scoffers" in the last day.

2 Peter 3:3–4 ESV. knowing this first of all, that scoffers will come in the last days with scoffing, following their own sinful desires. They will say, "Where is the promise of his coming? For ever since the fathers fell asleep, all things are continuing as they were from the beginning of creation."

In order to see all prophecy as having happened already, one must spiritualize many passages. Spiritualizing ignores the plain meaning of the words in favor of a "more spiritual" or "fuller" meaning. What the text says is not what it means in this teaching. This destroys the meaning intended by the author and transfers authority from the Word to the spiritualizer. The spiritualizer supersedes God and grabs the final authority on meaning, because there is no objective way to verify the "fuller" meaning. There are no rules in spiritualizing as there are in normal language.

You may notice that the word eschatology, meaning the study of "end times" events, is not used in this book. That's because the word has been frequently misused, and there really is no "end time." There is a transition, marked by many horrible events, from the kingdoms of the world to a Kingdom ruled by Jesus, but His kingdom has no end.

There is a large difference between spiritualizing and the use by prophets of symbolic language. Though perhaps a little more obscure sometimes, symbols still have a plain meaning. In reading and doing the whole of the Word, they become easier to understand. Many symbols are repeated in different ways or are used with explanatory text, such as in Proverbs with the woman called Wisdom.

In marked contrast to spiritualizing, the literal interpretation method, which is defined as the meaning the author intended, is used in this book. Another way to say this is that the plain meaning of the words is to be preferred. God said what He meant and means what He says, even when using symbols or types.

Most in the Church claim to use and teach a literal method of interpretation. But then they add in other fanciful philosophies such as dispensationalism. This extra-biblical philosophy of men means that God deals differently with different people in different ages. In this philosophy, each age has little to do with the others. Another such fanciful philosophy is covenantalism. This can be summarized as God making mythical covenants with Himself such as the covenant of redemption (allegedly between God and Jesus about dying on the cross). Then He is supposed to deal with man on the basis of other mostly imaginary covenants such as a covenant of works (the Law) and a covenant of grace (Jesus). If you don't know these types of philosophies, you can safely ignore them and just concentrate on the Bible text.

Gradualism is another one of these philosophies, and it proposes that things should and do change over time, including God's Word. The Church has been quietly, and gradually, using this to sneak away from The Law for a long time because it is in the way of their self-serving philosophies of men. This is another of many Church interpretation methods and philosophies developed over time giving the appearance of adhering to His Word, but in reality just give it lip service.

In the United States, there are those who want to apply gradualism to our Constitution. They want to change it because it interferes with the deceiver's (or deep state's or globalist's) desire to develop a worldwide tyrannical government. The Church is doing the same thing with God's Law. His Law, like the U.S. Constitution, interferes with the tyrants who desire to participate with the deceiver in a worldwide tyrannical government.

Gradualism has always been around in the Church, because men (and women) don't like God's Laws and want permission to go their own way. So they "gradually" change things to suit their whims (and flesh).The Church and the deep state, or as some call it "the Cabal" or globalists, are united in their desire to further the kingdom of the deceiver. This cooperation will be more obvious as time goes on, and the fruit of their efforts shows up in the person of the beast and his tyrannical kingdom.

One reason The Church rejects parts of the Bible is because they don't fit with the philosophy of The Church as an independent and separate entity from Israel. Sadly, its' lack of acceptance or refusal to see relevance for today in the Bible (or parts of the Bible) creates holes in understanding. More Church philosophies try to fill in the holes, but they just create confusion and make God look like He doesn't know what He's doing.

You may not know the methods or philosophies, but we don't really need to know them to understand the Bible. You might want to learn them to figure out where your church stands and refute their false teachings, though. Or just get away.

Every one of the previously mentioned philosophies and others like them developed while trying to justify the existence of the Church, which is not The Body of Christ. The visible Church has people in it who are part of the Body, but is not itself the Body. Israel is not the Body either, though there are also many members from Israel in the Body. The Church and Israel are in fact separate, but the Body is one. The extra-biblical notion that the Church has replaced Israel is just plain wrong. Like the split between the north and south kingdoms of Israel, two bodies were never in the plan of God. Thinking that there are two bodies presents difficulties when trying to interpret or apply prophecy, because these assumptions color the understanding of the prophecies and make them virtually impossible to decipher.

There is only one Body or Bride. This Body (also called the remnant, the olive tree, the saints, elect lady and so on) has been in existence since the beginning. Entry is by spiritual birth following physical birth (blood and water). Spiritual birth ('born again') is and always has been by God's grace through faith or trusting obedience. All believers are in this Body. Unbelievers are the only other group. It is given to a man once to die (Hebrews 9:27) and there is only one resurrection with a new body for each believer. Not only is the man-created Church unbiblical, but the idea of separation or replacement also causes interpretation difficulties, especially when it comes to prophecy.

Prophetic Timing

As stated previously, the study of prophecy is not intended by God to be by itself. Prophecy is part of the whole of His Word, which is so unified and interconnected it is impossible to interpret or understand one part without referring to others. Although about half the Bible is (or was) prophetic, prophecy is just one of the subjects God wants us to learn. We must study prophecy in context with all the rest of Scripture.

If we want to understand prophecy we must submit to God's will as much as we know and understand. Submission requires humility, also known as a soft heart, and humility improves our sensitivity to God's voice as expressed in the Bible. Pride hardens the heart and dulls the hearing. If you don't want to hear and do the easy stuff that God says, you will not be able to understand more than a few basics of prophecy, such as that of "repent or die." The skills used in matching prophecy with current events come from learning obedience to all of God's Word. Disobedient people can expect nothing from God except admonishment to repent, and eventual consignment to a place that doesn't have the presence of the God they hate.

A lot of prophecy had an immediate audience and fulfillment, meaning that it was short term. It was given to people who understood what it meant and the application for them came about quickly compared to the whole of history. An example of an immediate fulfillment is in 2 Kings 7. There Elisha tells a captain of the army that the siege-caused famine will end the next day, and the captain expresses his disbelief quite emphatically. Elisha responds that it will indeed happen but the captain won't see it. The next day the captain is trampled by the starving mob going out to pick up the food left by the God-encouraged, panic stricken retreating Syrian army. This also illustrates a principle that we might not know *how* God is going to do something, but rest assured He will do it.

Some prophecies had a little longer term such as the 70 years of Judah's captivity in Babylon (Jeremiah 25:11-12, 29:10). Other portions of prophecy have much longer chunks of time in mind, such as the span of empires Daniel mentions in Daniel 7, or those for "the time of the end" (of earthly kingdoms) later in the book (Daniel 8:17, 19, 11:35, 40, 12:4, 9 for instance). However, much of even the immediate prophecy still contains the pattern of what will happen later, because of the aforementioned tendency of man and the deceiver to keep trying the same tactics over and over.

What a prophet can see can be likened to a person who is just below the crest of the hill in front of him and can see the crest of the next hill or series of hills. But he might not see the valley of time in between. Well, either he can't see or perhaps he just reports the pertinent information. Or we can compare it to a series of transparencies for an overhead projector laid on top of one another, each having only part of the whole picture.

The prophet doesn't always have the complete picture. He or she has just enough for the purpose of the message. There is an instance of this in 2 Kings 4:27. The Lord had hidden the cause of a woman's distress from Elisha. She had to tell him the problem before he could take care of it. However, all prophets are aware of the Promise and the plan of God.

There are times a prophet is given just enough information to make a point, or to encourage His people, or perhaps to inform His servants of future events. The messages are consistent with God's revealed word and seemingly repetitious, especially given that they are delivered over a very wide block of time. But the main point of prophecy is to glorify God.

Sometimes the Bible describes events as for the "distant future," sometimes "the time of the end" and other times as happening "soon" or "at hand." Interpreters tend to think all of these relate to a calendar, or only to the people living when the prophecy was given. In other words, if something were to happen "soon" then many interpreters think it had to occur during those people's lifetimes.

The "distant future" or "time of the end" types of statements are self-explanatory. The prophet is speaking (or being told) of an event related to the day of the Lord or day of burning. A problem becomes apparent when speaking of an event happening soon. The "soon" or what seems to be immediate timing statements (Revelation 1:3 "the time is near" or Revelation 2:16 "I will come to you soon") are also related to time, but sometimes this is more in line with people's life spans than a calendar.

Since humans have short life spans, a distant event might still be "soon." Believers go to sleep, and when we are resurrected (1 Thessalonians 4:14) a lot of time might have passed, but to the person who just woke up it would seem to be no time at all.

Another meaning of "soon" connects to behaving with the awareness that it could happen at any moment. Jesus tells us to watch and be ready at all times, for instance, because we don't know when the bridegroom will arrive (Matthew 25). So when a prophet says something like "the things that must soon take place" (Revelation 1:1) we are to be ready all our lives, which may be short, or it may be after we wake up.

The Time of John

Since we will be focusing quite a bit on the book of Revelation, it will be helpful to review a little background about the writer. John was a "son of thunder" with his brother James (not the James who was the physical half-brother of Jesus and wrote the book of James). The brothers James and John were two of the three disciples that stood on the mount of transfiguration with Peter. John wrote his gospel, the three letters that bear his name (1, 2, and 3 John) and the book of Revelation. He very likely wrote all these close to the end of his life.

If we accept a date of 95 A.D. for the writing of Revelation (and this writer does), John was probably getting close to 90 or more years of age. He had seen a lot of success in the spread of the good news, and a lot of tribulation. Not too many years before, he had probably seen Christians thrown to the lions and otherwise tortured and killed. John himself is said to have been tortured and dunked into a pot of boiling oil, which didn't work to kill him apparently. Afterwards he was exiled to the island of Patmos. Historically, we know that one of the Roman emperors named Nero during this time dipped Christians in oil and lit them on fire to illuminate his parties, so it seems the legend of John's tribulations has at least a grain of truth.

Some people claim that the book of Revelation must have been written before the rebellion of the Jews against Rome and the resulting destruction of the Temple in 70 A.D., because John doesn't mention its destruction. However, the destruction would have been no surprise to him, because he knew and firmly believed the prophecy from Jesus that no stone would be left on another (Matthew 24:2; Mark 13:2; Luke 19:44, 21:6). He was probably with the believers who evacuated Jerusalem just before the Romans went to work on the city the first time (70 A.D.).

John was well aware of the animosity of the Jewish leaders towards believers, and the persecution of both Jews and Christians by the Romans. He knew that the important thing was the love of God in believer's hearts moving them to follow all of the commands in the Law. Revelation has many encouragements to persevere or endure, and two of them specifically mention the commandments (Revelation 12:17 and 14:12).

One school of thought about the book of Revelation is that John wrote it in code to get it off of the island of Patmos, past the Roman guards, and in to the hands of the seven congregations. This supposition sounds plausible, except that the Romans had no reason to think that an old man, possibly crippled from the reported attempt to kill him, and exiled to a tiny island away from people, could be any threat to the iron empire that had already put down a Jewish rebellion and destroyed their main place of worship. Christianity was spreading, but posed no threat. Christians were mainly just for entertainment in the gladiator arenas. Perhaps John had some anger at his tormentors which caused him to put some of the book into what might be considered obscure language. Even if true, it doesn't take away from the accuracy or certainty of his God-given visions. The "code" John used was simply the Word of God, and all his writings had to match or agree with the writings that came before. The whole Bible is a "code" to the natural man who refuses to follow it in the first place.

John was hyper-aware of governments that persecuted the people of God. As he was writing down the visions given to him, he also wrote encouragement to believing people everywhere subject to the same mistreatment. Jesus gives promises of benefits through and beyond tribulation to all seven congregations in Revelation 2 and 3 if they "conquer." John calls for the endurance and faith of the saints in Revelation 13:10 and 14:12.

Cycles of Fulfillment

Ecclesiastes 1:9–10 ESV. What has been is what will be, and what has been done is what will be done, and there is nothing new under the sun. Is there a thing of which it is said, "See, this is new"? It has been already in the ages before us.

Complicating our interpretation of prophecy is the fact that some of the events contained in prophecies have happened, while other parts or events have not. Or as mentioned before, events keep happening repeatedly. For instance, the prophecies concerning the Messiah have "partial" fulfillment, meaning that some parts of prophecies He did while He was walking around as an itinerant rabbi, but some parts He hasn't done yet. Many of the prophecies were literally born out or fulfilled at His physical birth, ministry, death and resurrection. But others of them still haven't been realized. Malachi 3:1-5 records a prophecy where "the Lord whom you seek will suddenly come to his temple."

Malachi 3:1–5 ESV. "Behold, I send my messenger, and he will prepare the way before me. And the Lord whom you seek will suddenly come to his temple; and the messenger of the covenant in whom you delight, behold, he is coming, says the LORD of hosts. But who can endure the day of his coming, and who can stand when he appears? For he is like a refiner's fire and like fullers' soap. He will sit as a refiner and purifier of silver, and he will purify the sons of Levi and refine them like gold and silver, and they will bring offerings in righteousness to the LORD. Then the offering of Judah and Jerusalem will be pleasing to the LORD as in the days of old and as in former years. "Then I will draw near to you for judgment. I will be a swift witness against the sorcerers, against the adulterers, against those who swear falsely, against those who oppress the hired worker in his wages, the widow and the fatherless, against those who thrust aside the sojourner, and do not fear me, says the LORD of hosts.

Jesus suddenly came to His temple, in a way, when He chased out the money changers (Matthew 21:12). However, Malachi goes on to say, "who can endure the day of his coming...For he is like a refiner's fire and like fullers' soap." This is much more dramatic and final than merely chasing moneychangers or criticizing hypocrites. It's obvious that on the one hand Jesus has a purifying function like refiner's fire for believers even now through His death and resurrection. It's equally obvious on the other hand that there's more to be done worldwide.

An example of repeated events is in the book of Nahum. The prophet records for us the end of the mighty Assyrian city called Nineveh (and the rest of the kingdom). God destroyed them because of their cruelty, immorality, greed and arrogance. All of the events foretold happened just as Nahum said. However, it looks like not only is his book a prophecy for Nineveh, it is a prophecy against any kingdom (including the deceiver's) that has the same behavior (and they all do) and is backed by the same spiritual powers.

God says in verse 1:8 He "will pursue his enemies into darkness," pointing to all enemies everywhere. In 1:15 God says "for never again shall the worthless pass through you, he is utterly cut off." On the one hand, this is certainly true for the city of Nineveh, but it is directed at Judah, which still to this day has worthless people in it. We can see that there is a fulfillment at the time, but also a fulfillment that is still future.

There is also a hint of the coming "worthless counselor" of the little horn and anti-Christ (false prophet) in Nahum 1:11.

Nahum 1:11 ESV. From you came one who plotted evil against the LORD, a worthless counselor.

There was a worthless counselor at the time, but it also applies to worthless counselors throughout history and the final worthless counselor on the day of the Lord at the Tribulation. The little horn or beast is also the "worthless shepherd" of Zechariah 11:17.

Zechariah 11:17 ESV. "Woe to my worthless shepherd, who deserts the flock! May the sword strike his arm and his right eye! Let his arm be wholly withered, his right eye utterly blinded!"

Assyria is called a prostitute (3:4) and a whore, and so is Tyre (Isaiah 23), Jerusalem (Jeremiah 13:27; Ezekiel 16 and others), Samaria (Micah 1), and Babylon (Revelation 17). All of these and others had immediate prophecies fulfilled against them, but any other empires who have the same behaviors will meet the same fate.

Prophecy has a cyclical nature because people keep repeating the same mistakes, and the deceiver keeps trying the same plans, again and again (and so do individual unbelievers). Some people also call this "history repeats itself." People forget history and forget God and, like a broken carnival ride, just keep going in circles. The deceiver continues to jump the gun in building his own world empire, so God smacks him down and makes him get back behind His line until it is the right time in His plans. This is one explanation for the apparent partial fulfillment of some prophecy.

Empires rise and conquer other empires, then dominate for a while only to fall back into the dustbin of history. Dictators come into power and behave exactly like their predecessors; so much so that we can't tell one from another without name tags. Hitler was not the first to try and wipe out the Jewish people. He was only one of the latest in a long string of murderers, used by the deceiver, who have tried to sidetrack God's plans.

When Nebuchadnezzar got his dream interpreted by Daniel (chapter 2) he found out that his kingdom was only the head and was not going to last as long as he was thinking. In response, he had an image made entirely of gold (Daniel 3) as if to say, "I repudiate the dream and my kingdom will last forever." What a bummer for him that it only lasted a few years after his death. God was right and ol' Nebby was wrong.

The deceiver has to start fresh all the time because he just can't get his human puppets to live long enough. He also bases his kingdoms on the unsteady foundations of selfishness and greed, and his followers keep trying to knock each other off. Truly the deceiver's kingdom is divided against itself and cannot stand (Matthew 12:25-26).

Another "cycle" that keeps repeating is the cycle of repentance. People do what is right in their own eyes; life descends into hopeless death and suffering, then God steps in with judgment and His Word. Those who respond He returns to a semblance of rightness and rescues us from ourselves. The United States started out as one such return to rightness, but it too has rejected God and descended into depravity. Sometimes His judgment is exile from the Land of Israel for instance, and other times it is the destruction of worldly kingdoms. Let us hope that repentance comes soon.

God keeps short-circuiting the deceiver's plans because He has His own, much better, plan. A few paltry efforts at world domination by also-rans aren't going to get in God's way. The only reason the little horn or beast has any kind of success at the end is because God allows the deceiver to do what he wants. Finally. For a while, anyway.

Prophetic Language

Job 32:17–18 ESV. I also will answer with my share; I also will declare my opinion. For I am full of words; the spirit within me constrains me.

The language of prophecy is no different from language in general. The difficulty in understanding is not in the language but a frame of reference and the willingness to see. God sees things differently than we do. He sees further and deeper, past the surface appearance and without time or calendar limitations, straight into the true nature of created things and beings. He really knows us, and our kingdoms, inside and out.

A statue represents the world empires in the first vision of Daniel 2, with various metals representing their declining value but increasing strength (at least until the ten toes of iron mixed with clay). Later, Daniel describes the same world kingdoms as animals in chapter seven of his book. God shows that their true natures are like animals, rending and tearing and ruling by strength rather than the love, truth, wisdom and goodness of God.

There is a tendency when trying to interpret prophecy (or other Bible parts) to wrangle over words. We think that if we can just get an exact definition then we would understand. This idea is not born out considering the many scholarly arguments over word definitions. Not to mention ignoring the words spoken by God in much of His Law. Word definitions are important. So are translation accuracy, sentence structure, history, geography, and other tools. But these tools aren't the be all and end all of interpretation, especially prophetic interpretation.

The main interpretive method is reading and doing the whole of the Word. This involves faith, which is trusting obedience. We fear and trust God; do what He says, and then understanding flowers. If we don't trust God or know Him very well, how could we possibly understand any prophecy? You'll find that people who doubt prophecy or can't figure out much of it will generally have a problem with God and a living faith in the first place.

John 8:43 ESV. Why do you not understand what I say? It is because you cannot bear to hear my word.

We do not understand His word because we won't let it in and do what He says. Good ground is needed for receiving the seed of the Word and showing growth. The Word is not the problem; the problem is hearts of stone.

The Bible interprets itself very well. Much of the message is repetitive, because people are kind of dense and need a lot of repetition. We also keep repeatedly doing things wrong. God obliges our stupidity by telling us the same thing in many different ways and at many different times. As mentioned a number of times already, the big keys to understanding God are taking in all of His words and doing them in humble love. That'll clear things up better than the most in-depth parsing of words or sentences, no matter how detailed and accurate we think of our parsing.

The philosophies of men frequently interfere with understanding the Bible rather than helping. For instance, there is that pesky fact that there is no Church in the Bible, only in the translations. Paul tells us clearly that there is only one body, one faith, one God and one Messiah, yet the Church defines itself as something new, separate and unique.

For another example mentioned previously, dispensationalism, which claims that God dealt differently with different people in different ages, is mostly false. While there are different ages, God has always dealt with people on the basis of His gracious, loving character. Many philosophies such as these have fogged up our picture of God, Jesus and the Bible, and prevented spiritual growth or understanding.

In spite of the (to us) odd way of giving us some information, the interpretation and meaning of God's Word is literal and certain. Even though we might not understand right away, prophecy is interpreted literally or as the author intended. For instance, Daniel in chapter 9 of his book realizes that Jeremiah was given a time limit of 70 years for Israel to serve Babylon (Jeremiah 25:12). Since Babylon was taken over by the Medes, and 70 years had passed, Daniel understood that it was literally time for Israel to go back to their land.

Many times, because we can't understand a prophecy, we resort to spiritualizing. Remember that this is defined as looking for hidden "spiritual" meanings under the plain meaning. On the one hand, there is a spiritual component to His Word.

1 Corinthians 2:14 ESV. The natural person does not accept the things of the Spirit of God, for they are folly to him, and he is not able to understand them because they are spiritually discerned.

But on the other hand most of the time the practice of spiritualizing just confuses rather than clarifies. Plus, it takes understanding out of the hands of the average person and gives it to the spiritualizer, so we have to depend on the spiritualizer to tell us the meaning or significance.

Spiritualizing gives permission to the interpreter for all sorts of imaginative flights of confusing fancy. The preference should be to take God at His Word and stick with the plain meaning. This is why accurate Bible teaching is needed: because wolves in sheep's clothing continue to interfere with plain Bible teaching in order to draw away followers after them (Acts 20:29-30). The big part of spirituality is in doing what God says. We might not understand it all, but that doesn't mean God doesn't mean what He says. It also doesn't mean that we can't see spiritual meanings when the text calls for it.

Words, Association, and Wordplay

God builds meaning for us by using events and language to reinforce concepts that are difficult to understand or that we tend to forget. He uses association, wordplay (like puns), hyperbole (exaggeration for the sake of emphasis), poetry, synonyms (words that sound different but have similar meaning) antonyms (words that are opposite in meaning) and other useful language techniques to get His message across. Fun with words plays a big part in God's prophecies.

Association with something concrete defines some words in prophecy. A well known instance is in one of the titles for Jesus. He is the "lamb of God" even though obviously He isn't a four-footed fuzzy offspring of a sheep. His title comes from His sacrifice on the cross and because He was gentle and didn't do anything wrong during the Incarnation. When John writes about a beast rising out of the earth having two horns like a lamb and speaking like a dragon (Revelation 13:11) we get the meaning because of the association of the word "lamb." It means that the "anti-christ" or "instead-of-anointed" looks like Jesus but speaks like the dragon or deceiver.

Jesus gives us a comparison with a definite meaning when speaking of His resurrection.

Luke 11:29–30 ESV. When the crowds were increasing, he began to say, "This generation is an evil generation. It seeks for a sign, but no sign will be given to it except the sign of Jonah. For as Jonah became a sign to the people of Nineveh, so will the Son of Man be to this generation.

Jonah spent three days in the belly of a big fish (a whale maybe?) and was "resurrected" when the fish spit him out on land. Jesus spent three days in the belly of the earth but death could not hold Him and He was "spit out" back to life. We can see the "sign" of Jonah is the same as the sign of the resurrection of Jesus. Both were signs of the power of God over death, and a path to life for those who repent.

In another example, an abomination is something detestable, disgusting, unclean and outside of God's wonderful Word or will. Sometimes it can be an action, such as sexual immorality (Leviticus 18:22, 20:13). Sometimes it can be eating unclean items like pork or shellfish (Deuteronomy 14:3). When applied to a human, as in the case of the "abomination that makes desolate" in Daniel 12:11 (ESV), it is the nature of the person that is highlighted for us. The person so indicated is outside of God's holy and perfect will and is acting in a manner that is against His will, up to and including actually claiming to be God. By association with the word "abomination," we know that this person is an agent of the deceiver doing the deceiver's work.

An example of wordplay is in Isaiah 21:11 where he gives us an "oracle concerning Dumah." The literal meaning of Dumah is silence, stillness or the underworld. It is also the name of one of Ishmael's descendants (Genesis 25:14) and Ishmael is likely the founder of the Arab nations or just Arabia. The specific nation of which Isaiah is speaking is Edom because of the reference to Seir, a major city in Edom. The implication is that Edom will be silent as death, or almost destroyed. God uses loads of wordplays in His announcements to fill out specific meaning or application.

Israel is associated in her rebellious, idolatrous state with Sodom and Gomorrah (Isaiah 1:10, Revelation 11:8). God uses the association to convey the depth of depravity into which Israel has descended at times. The imagery is instantly recognizable and communicates to us how bad it really is without very many words. As the saying goes, a simile is worth a thousand words.

An animal's horn is its power, so God uses "horn" to indicate the power or strength of a kingdom, a king, nation or empire. The word "mountain" describes a kingdom such as God's kingdom we read about in Daniel.

Daniel 2:35 ESV. Then the iron, the clay, the bronze, the silver, and the gold, all together were broken in pieces, and became like the chaff of the summer threshing floors; and the wind carried them away, so that not a trace of them could be found. But the stone that struck the image became a great mountain and filled the whole earth.

On the one hand, we don't want to get carried away with associations. People or ideas or events might look the same but it doesn't mean they are the same. On the other hand, we miss out on a lot of meaning by not recognizing those people, ideas or events that really are the same, but just have a little bit different phrases of speech to describe them. For instance, the little horn is also a beast and a worthless shepherd, as well as a smooth liar and military genius.

Remember, though God is the same throughout the centuries, the people that He tasks with relaying His messages have different frames of reference, different cultures, and different environments. So while it might be a challenge to match all those factors and come up with a right understanding in the present day, we shouldn't be afraid to draw conclusions when commonality is apparent. God is the "unifying theory" of creation, and He has given us one Messiah, one Spirit and one faith to bind us together in one Body to help make one understanding possible.

We are aided in our reach for understanding by matching actions with actions and natures with natures. For instance, a godless nation has certain characteristics such as a lack of justice, sacrifice of children, and no compassion or love of God and His ways. You know, similar to many nations of the world today. Especially the United States, which fancies itself a Christian nation while denying justice in her courts and killing millions of babies.

In another instance, we see in Revelation 1 through 3 examples of congregations already in decline 65 years after the resurrection, and given many admonitions to repent. So later in Revelation 17, when there is a vision of "mystery religion Babylon" characterized by many of the issues pointed out by Jesus in the first three chapters, we can see the relationship to the "Church." Looking at the history of the Church over the last 1,800 years, it's obvious that the "Church" (all of it, not just the Catholics) is in pursuit of wealth and sexual immorality, is full of blasphemous names, tells the world they speak for Jesus while denying most of His Words, and is drunk with the blood of the saints or martyrs of Jesus.

Put it all together and it is easy to make the association of the Church with Babylon in Revelation 17. The connection between the biblical description of mystery religion Babylon and current practices of religious people is plain, as long as we aren't afraid to look in the mirror.

Dreams and Visions

Job 33:15–18 ESV. In a dream, in a vision of the night, when deep sleep falls on men, while they slumber on their beds, then he opens the ears of men and terrifies them with warnings, that he may turn man aside from his deed and conceal pride from a man; he keeps back his soul from the pit, his life from perishing by the sword.

Much of prophecy is delivered in dreams and visions, but the ethereal nature of the delivery does not take away from the reality of the experience, or the guarantee from God that He will execute His plans as He has says He will. We may not be able to identify with certainty every detail of every prophecy now. Regardless, all of it is real and certain. The events will take place, and they will happen just as described, if we have eyes to see.

Hosea 12:10 ESV. I spoke to the prophets; it was I who multiplied visions, and through the prophets gave parables.

Jewish leaders misinterpreted the prophecies about the arrival of the seed of the woman, whom we know to be Jesus. They couldn't reconcile the suffering of the servant in places like Psalm 22 with the victorious King of Kings in places like Zechariah 9:10. Some of them thought there were two Messiahs. Some thought Israel was the servant or Branch. Whatever the popular thinking was, Jesus arrived right on time and did exactly according to all the prophecies about Him. The opinions of men that didn't match the Word didn't amount to a hill of beans. God did what He said He would do in the case of our Messiah, and He will continue to do exactly what He says even now.

All prophecy centers on Jesus. Revelation is actually "The Revelation of Jesus Christ" (Revelation 1:1). The Lamb of God is front and center in all of the visions given to John. He is the Alpha and Omega, beginning and end, of all of God's Words. He used a lot of parables when He was walking around Israel as an itinerant rabbi, which is another way to make prophecies, along with directly informing His people about future events. He spoke about the kingdom, for instance, through parables, which is realized in the heart now and will be worldwide eventually.

One of our helpful tools for interpreting prophecy is Joseph's dreams and interpretations of them. All the dreams he interpreted were not specifically his, but he was given a facility for interpreting that is rivaled in the Bible only by Daniel's gift. Genesis 37:1-11 is the first couple of dreams from Joseph, and from these Joseph gets a message that his brothers and parents will bow down to him. The brothers get upset; Joseph is sold into slavery, and ends up in Egypt. When he is falsely accused of a crime, he goes to jail and interprets dreams for a baker and a cupbearer (Genesis 40) which turn out to be accurate. Later, Pharaoh has a dream in two parts that he needs interpreted, and Joseph is called out of jail to do it. He ends up as a ruler second to Pharaoh, and the family bows down to him just as he dreamed.

Two things among many in these accounts are important for us here. One is that prophetic dreams and interpretations come from God. Two is that dreams from God depict events that are certain to happen. In Genesis 41:32 Joseph adds a principle for us that the doubling of the dreams means the events foretold "are fixed by God," meaning no appeal and no changing. Since the baker only had one dream, perhaps he could have appealed to God and possibly cancelled his fate.

The events of the first dreams of Joseph, the ones where his family bows down to him, are realized when Joseph rescues his family from the famine. In spite of their best efforts to get rid of him and thus make his dreams nothing but fantasies, his brothers have to accept Joseph as a ruler, showing that God's plans will not be sidetracked. Joseph's dreams may also be related to the description of the woman in Revelation 12.

Daniel is another person who receives visions or dreams and interprets them for other people such as the king of Babylon. Many parts of the visions and interpretations given to Daniel are to represent concepts rather than specific realities. For instance, the kingdoms represented by beasts aren't really led by a lion or leopard or goats and rams. The beasts represent the nature of the kingdoms and their actions. The leopard with four wings just means that king or kingdom conquered very rapidly. The bear represents a kingdom a little slower but way stronger and more vicious. When we look at other visions, we have to remember things are not always what they seem on the surface.

The visions in the Revelation more probably convey concepts or ideas also. The woman in chapter 12 for instance is a symbol of Israel, but since she gives birth to the Messiah, it is more likely that she is the part of Israel that has faith in God. Reading and doing the whole of the Word, and taking pains to study carefully and compare, helps us to discern the nature of the visions instead of getting caught up in the symbols.

Narratives in the Bible sometimes give the "big picture" in one chapter and then fill in details in the next chapter or two. An example of this is in Genesis chapters one and two. Chapter one covers the whole of creation, and chapter two gives details on the creation of Adam and Eve. John employs this technique when he records the rise of the beast starting in Revelation 13, then fills in details of Babylon in chapters 17 and 18.

Movie Trailers

Speaking of the "big picture," another comparison to help with interpreting prophetic visions is to think of them like movie trailers. The scenes in trailers aren't sequential as they appear in the movie itself. They show scenes out of order, only parts of scenes, and so on just to get you interested in shelling out a lot of money to see it in the theater.

God's movie trailers are the same type of thing (except they are free). He doesn't need to give away every detail of the plot. He also has a purpose in showing a dream or a vision, and usually it's to warn or reassure. He warns people and nations of the penalties for continuing to ignore His Law or attack His people. He reassures His people that, while there may be some tough times now, ultimately we are going to make it through to the eternal peace of His kingdom.

An excellent example of a trailer is in Revelation 4 through 7. There are four groups of believers mentioned: elders, martyrs, 144,000 and a multitude. At the time of the "trailer" the elders are presumably deceased (except for John). The number of martyrs has yet to be completed. The 144,000 are gearing up for future tasks, and the multitude is from a later time ("the great tribulation). These groups seem to be out of sequence, like a movie trailer.

Movies are different from a book. With movies, you can show feelings or intent with a look from one character to another. An approaching storm can seem ominous, or merely rain for crops, by the selection of music. The bad guy sneaks around with a gun to strident music and we know he's up to no good. A good guy with a gun might have soaring or triumphant music. The leading man exchanges a smoldering look with the leading lady and we know what happens next. By the way, stop showing this last one to us in graphic detail. We get the message without the pictures for crying out loud.

God's short movies are visual, but He puts the scripts in a Book. Even then, the meaning comes across loud and clear if we pay attention to everything He says. He describes concepts or what is to happen with powerful symbols and words, and builds on meaning with repetition over the centuries. He's not hiding anything we need to know. So when we are looking at the various pieces of prophecy and trying to fit them together, remember that it is all one storyline or plot, with one purpose for His people.

Jeremiah 23:20 ESV. The anger of the LORD will not turn back until he has executed and accomplished the intents of his heart. In the latter days you will understand it clearly.

Newspaper Exegesis

Next to wrangling over words, another popular way to interpret prophecy is to try and interpret prophecies using current events. Mostly this misses the boat because the wannabe dream interpreters don't proceed from a Scripture-centered base. *Exegesis*, meaning to interpret or get meaning *out* of words (expose meaning), is different from *eisegesis* (eye-sa-gee-sis), which is to put meaning *into* words (impose meaning). Newspaper exegesis, a term I coined a few decades ago, is a combination of these because we attempt to interpret prophecy by reading popular thought (including headline news) back into the Word. Maybe it should have been "newspaper eisegeses."

Many teachers use newspaper exegesis for interpretation or application of prophecy. They sell a lot of books trying to match current events to the Bible. The problem is they are frequently wrong because they don't start with an understanding and practice of the whole Bible in the first place. The point of this book is to show how much the Bible defines prophecy itself. Our exegesis should be focused on the Bible first and then maybe on current events. If we aren't rightly dividing the Word of God in the first place, then going to the newspaper isn't going to do a lot of good. Especially since most news people are liars anyway.

Ezekiel 39:3 NASB95. "I will strike your bow from your left hand and dash down your arrows from your right hand.

From the verse above, Hal Lindsey in his book <u>The Late Great Planet Earth</u> interprets bow and arrows as possible "missiles and launchers," equating these with modern weapons. He gets points for trying to make Scripture relevant, but a couple points are deducted for not looking at the whole Bible picture. The Hebrew words for bow and arrows might actually apply to launchers and missiles, but probably not of the fighter jet or ICBM varieties.

It might mean that this army will literally use bows and arrows, but it probably means whatever weapons are used will be rendered useless. Is God confining His judgment here only to missile launchers or only to people with hand-carried weapons? No, He would include any weapon used against Israel, including rocks and dirt. Or even economic weapons like stocks and bonds. Jeremiah records another way of saying bows and arrows when he quotes God about weapons of war.

Jeremiah 21:4 ESV. 'Thus says the LORD, the God of Israel: Behold, I will turn back the weapons of war that are in your hands and with which you are fighting against the king of Babylon and against the Chaldeans who are besieging you outside the walls. And I will bring them together into the midst of this city.

It is better to understand the phrase simply as 'weapons of war' as said by Jeremiah and leave it at that. It is interesting to note, however, that Israel and the U.S. have developed a missile that will intercept other missiles, and they call it the Arrow (at this writing Arrow-2 and Arrow-3). So maybe the passage does literally refer to "arrows." That should bring a smile to the face of people who think the Bible is literal.

In the late '70's and early '80's the boogey man of the moment was the Russians and communism. Back then, books were written on the communist threat and how it related to the beast and prophecy. Not now. Today the perceived threat is Islam, although Russia and China are still in the mix and working through agents such as the misnamed Black Lives Matter and Antifa organizations to bring governments down.

There are still communists and Democrats trying to take down the United States, but the big threat of the USSR is more or less neutralized. In the '80's what is now called the European Union was identified with the ten toes of Daniel's image and the ten horns of the beast in Daniel 7:7 because there were ten member nations. That is, until member nations grew to more than ten. At present, there are 28 nations, so even if we count all fingers and toes they are still way over. This doesn't mean the ten toes are not European nations; just that it will probably be a different combination of nations and tribes. In any case, panic over ten nations getting together isn't necessary.

At that time also (the early '80's) there was a great deal of excitement, especially in the Calvary Chapel branch of The Church, about a computer in Belgium that could number the entire world's population and was nicknamed 'The Beast.' There were those such as this writer who tried to tell whoever would listen in Calvary Chapel that it wasn't a big deal because computers aren't that smart. Giving every person on the planet a number did not mean the computer (or the person controlling it) was the little horn. Nor did it mean that the computer was capable of enforcing a restriction on buying and selling, because it wasn't tied into the banking or point of sale systems. Today your average home computer is capable of numbering everyone on the planet, but that doesn't make your desktop computer "the beast" either.

Something similar happened in the Y2K hysteria. You might remember, some people were preaching that computers were going to crash because of a date glitch in computer software changing between the 1900's and 2000's. Computer-controlled missiles were going to launch by themselves because the software controlling them would get confused. We would not be able to buy food, because cash registers weren't coded with the right date format. So it was said that when the calendar turned over at the end of 1999 everything was going to go nuts.

Again, there were those such as this writer who told whoever would listen (this time maybe three or four people listened) that none of it would happen. The worst that could happen, knowing computers and programming, was that a computer would just stop working or lock up. Maybe it would give out false data because a math equation based on the date would not return correct answers. Anyone who has seen the "blue screen of death" or had a computer lock up knows the drill. Turned out there wasn't a single missile launch because the computer date went screwy, and we were able to buy groceries just like any other day.

Just before 2012, people were nearly hysterical about the Mayan calendar, because it indicated that some huge cosmic event would end the world in the year 2012. We're still here. There were some efforts to "spiritualize" the meaning in order to make their interpretations work, but obviously the "prophecy" was just flat out wrong. There have been lots of other false prophets too, from comet-worshipping idiots to people sitting on roofs waiting for a rapture on a specific date. But these have all just been leading people astray.

Newspaper exegesis is also not a very good way to interpret prophetic Scriptures because the newspapers (and TV news) lie. Their main goal is money and power, and it doesn't matter to them how they get it (Babylon in a nutshell). They need high ratings (or views or clicks) so they can charge more for advertising. They convey some facts, but with a heavy slant towards their own understanding and their mostly liberal/globalist agendas.

There is a tendency towards hysteria (a problem in the Church too), blowing certain events all out of proportion compared to their real effect. Especially their effects on prophecy. We've got to remember that we're dealing with a 6,000 year timeline, and a God who has a whole different perspective on what's important and what isn't. Believers need to keep in mind the warning of John about adding to the prophecies.

Revelation 22:18–19 ESV. I warn everyone who hears the words of the prophecy of this book: if anyone adds to them, God will add to him the plagues described in this book, and if anyone takes away from the words of the book of this prophecy, God will take away his share in the tree of life and in the holy city, which are described in this book.

Whether it is well-intentioned or not, we add to the prophecies or take away from them when we come up with interpretations that are not biblically sound or accurate and keep teaching them in spite of being corrected by the Word. Believers are told to "attend carefully all that I have commanded you," "watch and be ready," and "wash our robes," meaning to believe Jesus and do what He says. A false teacher or prophet will ignore parts of the Word that are uncomfortable such as parts of the Law.

Yeshua wants us to diligently obey His commands, stay faithful to the end, and teach others the same. We are not to run around like the proverbial headless chickens.

Matthew 25:13 ESV. Watch therefore, for you know neither the day nor the hour.

Matthew 28:19–20 ESV. Go therefore and make disciples of all nations, baptizing them in the name of the Father and of the Son and of the Holy Spirit, teaching them to observe all that I have commanded you. And behold, I am with you always, to the end of the age."

Revelation 22:14 ESV. Blessed are those who wash their robes, so that they may have the right to the tree of life and that they may enter the city by the gates.

Stand-Ins or Types

One of the interesting features of prophecy, indeed most of the Bible, is the use of stand-ins or types. A type is a symbolic picture for God's truth. For instance, Jesus is called the Lamb of God, but He's not really a four-footed fuzzy offspring of a ewe. He is like a lamb in that He's gentle and doesn't do anything wrong. He's also like a lamb in that He was slaughtered without a fight. So Jesus is a symbol or "type" of a sacrificial lamb (or the lamb is a type of the Christ). Other lambs have been slaughtered for sacrifice or meat, and other people have been slaughtered. But there is only One Lamb of God who was sacrificed for the sins of the world.

Any of His truths can be represented by different types but the truths stay the same. As an example, God Himself is personified at various points as a woman (wisdom - Proverbs 1), a rock (Deuteronomy 32:4), a shield (Proverbs 2:7), a burning bush not consumed (Exodus 3:2), and so on. All of these, and others, are God or parts of His character.

The nation of Edom (descended from Esau) can be an example of a type or a stand-in for all nations sometimes, because they picked on, or attacked, or rejoiced when others attacked, Israel. Isaiah 34 starts out with God speaking to the nations.

Isaiah 34:1–2 ESV. Draw near, O nations, to hear, and give attention, O peoples! Let the earth hear, and all that fills it; the world, and all that comes from it. For the LORD is enraged against all the nations, and furious against all their host; he has devoted them to destruction, has given them over for slaughter.

In just a few verses, God through Isaiah seems to switch to a focus on Edom.

Isaiah 34:5–7 ESV. For my sword has drunk its fill in the heavens; behold, it descends for judgment upon Edom, upon the people I have devoted to destruction. The LORD has a sword; it is sated with blood; it is gorged with fat, with the blood of lambs and goats, with the fat of the kidneys of rams. For the LORD has a sacrifice in Bozrah, a great slaughter in the land of Edom. Wild oxen shall fall with them, and young steers with the mighty bulls. Their land shall drink its fill of blood, and their soil shall be gorged with fat.

Bozrah was the capital city of Edom. We can see how oxen, young steers and mighty bulls are also stand-ins for the men of Edom. We can also see how Edom and Bozrah are stand-ins or types of kingdoms run by the deceiver. Isaiah continues:

Isaiah 34:8–9 ESV. For the LORD has a day of vengeance, a year of recompense for the cause of Zion. And the streams of Edom shall be turned into pitch, and her soil into sulfur; her land shall become burning pitch.

We know this hasn't happened yet, and we can guess that it will probably happen in a future battle. A huge army, numbering 200 million men, coordinated by four angels that are bound at the river Euphrates (which goes right through the middle of Iran) will kill a third of mankind at a time yet to come, for instance. Revelation 9:17-18 describes sulfur, fire and smoke coming out of the mouths of this army's lion-headed horses. Perhaps this is where the soil of Edom is turned into sulfur and streams turned to pitch.

The point is that types are another way of describing the natures of events, people or God's truth. Edom attacked Israel in a representative way, as many others nations or kingdoms have done. Anyone who participates in trying to destroy or even just pick on Israel will receive similar penalties as outlined for Edom.

There are many other types or symbols used by God in His Word. Ezekiel is shown a valley of dry bones in chapter 37 of his book, and they live again because of God's command. We understand that the task was impossible with man, but Israel is now living in a similar astounding fashion. Two sticks are used by Ezekiel in the same chapter to show how Israel will one day be united in one kingdom, which we can see has happened before our eyes today.

The parables of Jesus are also a way of communicating truth with figurative language. Types, similes, metaphors, symbols and the like all help us understand what God is meaning when He fills His Word up full by acting for His glory in human affairs. They show us the nature of people and events, use natural things to illustrate spiritual principles, and prepare us for further revelation.

Goddess of Reason

An important example of a type that can have different looks but still represent the same truth is the Prostitute of Revelation 17. A little history review is in order here, because it will help give perspective on the woman riding the scarlet beast and the effect of her identity on interpretation of the Bible.

Revelation 17:3–6 ESV. And he carried me away in the Spirit into a wilderness, and I saw a woman sitting on a scarlet beast that was full of blasphemous names, and it had seven heads and ten horns. The woman was arrayed in purple and scarlet, and adorned with gold and jewels and pearls, holding in her hand a golden cup full of abominations and the impurities of her sexual immorality. And on her forehead was written a name of mystery: "Babylon the great, mother of prostitutes and of earth's abominations." And I saw the woman, drunk with the blood of the saints, the blood of the martyrs of Jesus. When I saw her, I marveled greatly.

This typical woman has been around a long time and has known many names throughout history. Sometimes the woman is personified as a goddess such as Astarte, Ashtaroth or Ishtar. Other times she has names that are more general such as mother earth, Mother Nature or Gaia. The Bible has some names for her such as Folly, Mammon, the forbidden woman, and the adulteress. Going out on a limb here, the worship of Mary the mother of God by the Catholics is another version of the woman. Not for Mary herself, but for how she is elevated and changed into an idol.

One other name should be applied to the woman riding the scarlet beast. This name is perhaps closer to the true nature of all false gods (or goddesses), and is the Goddess of Reason. This was a name given to a so-called "goddess" during the misnamed Age of Enlightenment, which occurred from about the late 1600's through the 1800's. Enlightenment was the term for people who at that time reacted violently to the corruption and control of government by the Catholic Church. They elevated their version of science and "reason" to the status of a literal "goddess" instead. Some of these people murdered churchgoers by the thousands as sacrifices to their goddess.

But all they really did was exchange one tyrant for another. Both of these tyrant types (Religion and Reason), by the way, are really the same goddess. Man's reason (or religion), goddess or not, is built on knowledge that denies God and so is lacking in wisdom. The fear of God is the beginning of wisdom, and through the knowledge of God one gains understanding. But fear of God is not a part of the goddess of Reason, or the worship of that goddess.

Proverbs 9:10 ESV. The fear of the LORD is the beginning of wisdom, and the knowledge of the Holy One is insight.

Reason by itself is simply another name for self-worship, which is the root of all idolatry. It is "doing what is right in our own eyes" instead of in God's eyes. False gods and idols are made in man's image with human traits and weaknesses, including the tendency to be manipulated by their worshippers.

The goddess Reason is the true name of the woman on the scarlet beast because all God-rejecting and idol-worshipping people worship human reasoning in the end. She didn't just pop up newly created in the Age of Enlightenment. She's been around for a very long time. Adam and Eve worshipped her, Cain was her slave, Nimrod and Balaam and Jezebel and many others have worshipped at her shrines down through the ages.

A big part of the Age of Enlightenment was a violent reaction to the violence and corruption of the Catholic Church. In addition to many other abuses of power throughout the centuries, the Church used Inquisitions from the late 1100's well into the 1500's to torture and kill "heretics." These so-called heretics were often nothing more than people who disagreed with or spoke against the corruption in the Church. Galileo (1564 to 1642) was one of these heretics.

Another "heretic" was Martin Luther (died in 1546). He had his say against the excesses of the Catholic Church and was a pivotal figure in the Protestant Reformation. Although an extreme anti-Semite, his efforts, along with other reformers in the 1500's (and even before), helped kick off not only the Reformation, but also hurried along the Age of Enlightenment.

By the 1600's the Church had fallen so far away from the teachings of Jesus and the rest of the Bible it was almost unrecognizable in comparison to the Word. Power was hoarded like Gollum with his ring, and the primary purpose of the leadership was to hold onto that power using all the force at the Church's disposal.

People of the 1600's finally got fed up and tore down the idols of the Catholics, only to substitute their own goddess of Reason and science. This goddess was, and is, just as corrupt and bloody, seeing as how they are the same abomination. The goddess of Reason was pictured literally riding in a seat carried on the shoulders of men, which is eerily similar to the mother of prostitutes or religious Babylon in Revelation 17. She has been riding on, or carried by, people since the day Adam and Eve decided to follow her in opposition to the will and Word of God.

It is not hard to see the commonality between all of the goddesses (and gods) of history and the woman riding the scarlet beast. Babylon the great, mother of prostitutes or goddess of Reason is truly the parent of all anti-God religions. She is "full of blasphemous names," which are all the names she has had since the beginning.

Proverbs 5:3–6 ESV. For the lips of a forbidden woman drip honey, and her speech is smoother than oil, but in the end she is bitter as wormwood, sharp as a two-edged sword. Her feet go down to death; her steps follow the path to Sheol; she does not ponder the path of life; her ways wander, and she does not know it.

Don't be fooled for a second into thinking that much of the Church, Islam, and even Judaism are not included with her. Any philosophy of man or "religion" that does not follow God, (and in general these don't) and is "drunk with the blood of the saints the blood of the martyrs of Jesus," are part of the Prostitute.

The "Church" with its Inquisitions, Crusades, anti-Jewishness, idolatry, and other atrocities is a member. Islam is just a branch of Babylon with its wars, forced conversions, racism, history of selling people into slavery and persecution of anyone not a Muslim. Judaism gets a membership nod with its rejection of Jesus and Jesus believers, secularism, and hard-heartedness regarding the Covenant new or old. The Goddess of Reason is included in Babylon by the killing of many Christians after her modern public ascension to the throne, baby sacrifice through abortion, and the many deaths and racism driven by its evolutionary theory with its modern cultural degradation. Atheists and many others are part of Babylon, all have the blood of believers on their collective hands, and all have a part in the "mother of prostitutes."

In contrast to the goddess of Reason is the goddess of wisdom. Wisdom is a type of a woman in many places in the Bible, and wisdom is from God. His Word or Law is the essence of wisdom, and wisdom stands in direct contrast to man's reason. Especially since man's reason is not really reason at all, but simply a group of excuses to reject God and deny the science the "reason worshippers" say they worship.

Proverbs 1:20–31 ESV. Wisdom cries aloud in the street, in the markets she raises her voice; at the head of the noisy streets she cries out; at the entrance of the city gates she speaks: "How long, O simple ones, will you love being simple? How long will scoffers delight in their scoffing and fools hate knowledge? If you turn at my reproof, behold, I will pour out my spirit to you; I will make my words known to you. Because I have called and you refused to listen, have stretched out my hand and no one has heeded, because you have ignored all my counsel and would have none of my reproof, I also will laugh at your calamity; I will mock when terror strikes you, when terror strikes you like a storm and your calamity comes like a whirlwind, when distress and anguish come upon you. Then they will call upon me, but I will not answer; they will seek me diligently but will not find me. Because they hated knowledge and did not choose the fear of the LORD, would have none of my counsel and despised all my reproof, therefore they shall eat the fruit of their way, and have their fill of their own devices.

Evolution

Evolution also came out of that misnamed Age of Enlightenment. After replacing The Church and enthroning their goddess of Reason in the 1600's, the self-blinded people of the deceiver groped around in the 1700's and 1800's trying to find a replacement for the account of creation in the Bible. Charles Lyell (died in 1875) proposed the idea of Uniformitarianism where, to paraphrase Peter's prophecy (2 Peter 3-7), "all things are continuing as they were from the beginning of creation."

Lyell formalized the thinking that long periods of time coupled with natural events brought forth what we see in the earth today. His disciple was the racist Charles Darwin, who further refined many of the anti-God ideas floating around at the time and offered "natural selection" as part of the theory of evolution. Modern publishers won't print, and most progressives will not cite, the original full title of his book, because it is obviously supporting racism. For those who are curious, the title is "On the Origin of Species by Means of Natural Selection, or the Preservation of Favoured Races In the Struggle for Life." He was also looking for an excuse to justify slavery of anyone not white.

Evolution is in a book on prophecy because it has done a lot to destroy the interpretation of the Word for many people. This theory pushes the idea that people have gone from simpler, dumber man-type forms to smarter and more advanced forms in the current time. Therefore, all the older writings of the Bible are "myths" created by dummies who didn't know any better. In this philosophy, anyone who still worships a "god" other than the god of reason is just backwards and "unenlightened." Many in The Church have prostituted themselves to this philosophy of men.

One of the many glaring examples of Church Nicolaitan investment in evolution is with the interpretation of leviathan and behemoth in the book of Job. The descriptions are exact enough that it is obvious they were dinosaurs. Since the Nicolaitans have bought into evolutionary theory, they believe that dinosaurs did not coexist with man. So instead of dinosaurs, they say that leviathan was a crocodile and behemoth was a hippopotamus. It's apparent that man is getting dumber as time passes, not smarter.

It is much more biblical to realize that God created Adam as the epitome of human intelligence, and starting with the fall we have been getting dumber and dumber ever since. People several thousand years ago were undoubtedly much smarter than we are now, and would've had no trouble at all telling us about mechanical devices (they knew what wagons and chariots were for sure) or exploding warheads. They may very well have understood how to make an internal combustion engine, but had the sense not to develop it.

There are Mayan temples, for another instance debunking the philosophy of evolution, that are made with multi-ton blocks of stone, fitting together so well that a sheet of paper can't pass between them. Not only can we not make them that way anymore with the tools they had, but also our strongest machines cannot lift the ones that are already made. How did they do it? Not so surprising if you realize that evolutionary theory, the stupid idea that things start out simple and get more complicated as they develop, has flipped knowledge and understanding upside down. The Mayans and Egyptians were probably much more on the ball than we are today at least as far as building things.

There isn't a shred of evidence to support evolution. Even setting aside the fact that it is anti-God, it is still anti-science and anti-common sense. The only reason it is accepted by unbelievers so thoroughly is that they desperately need something to replace God. Scientists were able to make up a theory out of whole cloth in the 1700's and 1800's simply because the science of the time did not have the investigative tools that we now have. For instance, they knew nothing of electron microscopes which can see DNA. Or even DNA itself for that matter.

Evolutionary theory could only be temporary, because as real scientists have developed better tools and discovered more and more about the world God created, the flimsy proof offered for evolution is evaporating.

Anti-God scientists stubbornly hold to their corrupt theories, however, because the alternative (God) holds so much terror for them. In the meantime, the pseudo-science of evolutionary theory has corrupted many people's views of the Bible and God's plans. Truly, the people who frantically hold to the bankrupt teachings of evolution will be living life like normal, "eating and drinking, marrying and giving in marriage," as the flood of God's judgments in the Tribulation overtakes them.

Notions We Already Have

Much of prophecy interpretation is colored by notions we have before we start, notions that have been greatly shaped by philosophies of men laundered through the Church. The philosophies are slanted towards, among other things, the idea of the Church as the body of Christ, which cannot be substantiated by the Bible. Other notions include a lack of trust in the written Word, a belief that the average person can't just read the Bible and understand it, and Jesus was just a good teacher. The philosophies men have come up with over the centuries have taken us far afield from the Bible.

The notion of chapters and verses, applied by men, can help us navigate but they also frequently change our understanding. They make breaks that shouldn't be there, and keep ideas together that perhaps should be separated. Believers should work at reading without paying attention to the artificial breaks, because then the whole text will make more sense.

Even apostles had notions which caused them to misunderstand prophecy. John in his gospel account tells us of one wrong notion.

John 21:20–23 ESV. Peter turned and saw the disciple whom Jesus loved following them, the one who also had leaned back against him during the supper and had said, "Lord, who is it that is going to betray you?" When Peter saw him, he said to Jesus, "Lord, what about this man?" Jesus said to him, "If it is my will that he remain until I come, what is that to you? You follow me!" So the saying spread abroad among the brothers that this disciple was not to die; yet Jesus did not say to him that he was not to die, but, "If it is my will that he remain until I come, what is that to you?"

The point was the will of Jesus, not that John was going to keep living until Jesus came back. John makes sure to correct the misunderstanding, but people still spread around the wrong ideas.

Evolutionary notions, as was mentioned already, infect a lot of philosophies of men, frequently without people even noticing, because there is a built-in tendency to reject God. It is assumed by many that the prophets did not understand their own visions, and could not tell what a missile launcher was from a lion-headed horse having fire coming out of its mouth. But what the prophets usually saw were the *natures* of the things, not necessarily the things themselves. Either that or they saw the actual missiles and launchers but understood them differently, and more accurately, than we do, again because they were seeing more than the physical outline. They also weren't as enamored of technology as men are.

Daniel shows us some of this when he speaks of the (at the time) future empires that would take turns trying to rule the world for a while. He compared them to beasts such as winged leopards and bears (Daniel 7). It wasn't that he didn't know better, or couldn't identify what he was seeing. It was that he saw (or was shown) the natures of the kings/kingdoms as related to certain aspects of wild animals. It is the way God sees them. A glance at the way earthly kingdoms operate will confirm that.

Our first notion is to listen to the words of God rather than the words of men. Second is that of course God has delivered to us a text anyone can understand. Third is that if we are not willing to follow that text, it is like a clanging gong because we are not returning the love He has for us in the first place. So are you ready for events that may not match what you are currently thinking? If something happens differently than you imagined, will you be able to refer to the Word and allow it to change you? Can you even do it now? Is your hearing sharpened by constant practice of reading and doing, so that if God penetrates your understanding unexpectedly later on, you will hear and do?

Name Changes

It's difficult sometimes to identify a place or kingdom in the Bible on modern maps. We know where a lot of places are because of archeology or tradition, but there is still some uncertainty for some places. City names for instance got changed several times depending on who is doing the conquering. Rulers tended to change names to suit their worship of pagan gods or simply for vanity. Modern day Istanbul was called in the past Constantinople and before that Byzantium.

The location of the ancient Canaanite city of Megiddo is uncertain and has been associated with a couple of Arabic place names. We know where the plain of Megiddo is, but not the exact location of the city. The plain of Megiddo is probably the same as the Valley of Decision, the valley of Jehoshaphat (Jehoshaphat means "the Lord has judged") and the plain or Valley of Jezreel (a little north of Jerusalem), all of which seem also to be names for Armageddon. Some maps identify the valley of Jehoshaphat with the Kidron Valley (next to Jerusalem on the east), but they don't match. Armageddon is another way to refer to the "hill of Megiddo" (Armageddon is actually *har-meggido* or hill of Megiddo).

This naming or location ambiguity is deliberate on the part of our enemy. He has made an effort to obscure place names and locations in order to throw us off the scent when trying to cross-reference events of the Bible. It also creates doubt about the veracity of the Bible. Scholars debate back and forth about exact meanings and locations of various place names from the Bible, which is illustrative of the confusion the deceiver has generated.

By obscuring Bible names with new names given by conquering armies, the deceiver can disassociate Bible events from actual places, making the events prophesied seem removed from real life or even imaginary. Uncertainty produces doubt in the accuracy of the Bible, which leads to unbelief. If the place doesn't seem to exist now, then maybe the Bible accounts can be dismissed as myths or bedtime stories, not having any relevance to life today.

However, enough is known of ancient cities and kingdoms that we can couple this information with Bible information to get a good idea of where they are now. Geography plays an important part in the movement of armies, as we can see with the seventh bowl judgment and the drying up of the Euphrates River.

Sacred Names

Speaking of name changes, there are groups around that are insisting on using what they call "sacred names" for God and Jesus. The thought is that Jesus, for instance, wasn't actually called by the English word Jesus, which comes from the Greek word transliterated Iesou (e-yo-sue). They maintain that His name was actually Yeshua, from the Hebrew word transliterated Yehoshua which means "God saves." This is probably true, but controversies like this tend to obscure meaning and create detours away from doing what He says. This includes acting like His body.

Other groups insist that the New Testament was originally written in Hebrew, and that the Greek texts we have now have caused people to misunderstand the teachings of Jesus and others. This goes on and on with many other groups. Karaite Judaism has their problems with calendars. Jehovah's Witnesses deny Jesus is God and insist on a different pronunciation of the Tetragrammaton (YHVH). Many, many groups have many similar issues with the modern Bible (or even the original language texts).

Some who insist on a Hebrew New Testament will create an issue of doubt in His Word by using, for example, the parable of the rich man and the eye of a needle. They'll say that Jesus didn't mean a camel, He meant a thick rope. Again, the result of arguments like these, intended or not, is to ruin hearers of God's Word. Whether He meant a camel or thick rope or a Ford truck, the point by Jesus is that it is difficult for a rich man to enter the kingdom.

I respect the opinions of people who genuinely want to honor Jesus and God with what they think is the "correct" name or the "correct" language or word. We should watch, however, for the sin of pride in thinking we know how words should be used. These types of teachings are distractions that confuse people about God's messages and create doubt in the Word. We don't want to get lost in meaningless side issues. In this book, the names for Jesus and God switch around here and there. The reason is simple: the name is not the problem. Lack of obedience is the problem.

2 Timothy 2:14 ESV. Remind them of these things, and charge them before God not to quarrel about words, which does no good, but only ruins the hearers.

There may really be a specific name to use for the Father or our Messiah. If so, the Bible doesn't say. There isn't a place informing us that such-and-such a name is the correct one and the only one we are to use. The Father and our Messiah have many names and titles in many different languages, each one illustrating some aspect of their character or work. Jesus even has a name only He knows (Revelation 19:12). Jeremiah tells us of a future name for Yeshua:

Jeremiah 23:6 ESV. In his days Judah will be saved, and Israel will dwell securely. And this is the name by which he will be called: 'The LORD is our righteousness.'

It is good to learn and use names as best as we are able, but not to judge and destroy another's faith with doubt. This brings up another issue, which is pronunciation. We don't really know how to pronounce older words or phrases. Scholars have researched thoroughly, but at best, they can mostly just guess at many of the words. So to argue over a favorite word or even sacred names just contributes to ruining the hearers, intended or not. The meanings of names are important, and can help our understanding of prophecy, but to focus and divide over what are essentially non-issues is confusing people at best and discouraging at worst.

If a person wants to go be a missionary in, say, Germany, wouldn't you think that person would need to learn the German language? And wouldn't the main communication be in German?

So if we are going to communicate with Church people, shouldn't we try not to let language get in the way and speak in ways they understand? These are rhetorical questions by the way.

As far as calendars, again we don't really know for certain which is the only one to use (or even where we are at on the calendar). There's Roman or solar, Hebraic (12 months of 30 days with an adjustment every so often), Lunar and so on. It's best if we just try to follow God's ways as we understand, and change if we need changing. Again, there is no reference that commands a particular calendar and only that one.

When Israel was in the Land and functioning properly, they knew what calendar to use and still they didn't keep using it as they should. Believers should have a soft heart and want to do their best to follow God's ways, which is the important thing. We are not going to hell because we celebrated Passover on the wrong day or use the wrong Name. We can't, because Jesus paid the penalty for our sins, and God won't hold it against us anyway if we are truly in ignorance. He is pleased and will honor us if we are trying to follow Him from the heart.

Zephaniah 3:9 ESV. "For at that time I will change the speech of the peoples to a pure speech, that all of them may call upon the name of the LORD and serve him with one accord.

Obviously, if Zephaniah is speaking to us of a return to a "pure" speech, it means it's not so pure now. The scrambling of languages (and thought patterns) at the Tower of Babel served to derail an empty challenge to God's kingship. It also makes God's Word stand out like a spotlight attracting believers to its purity. Not just in the words used, because they are common words used by all, but in the concepts the words convey.

When we get to the difference between Hebrew and other languages, the bottom line is that one language is not more holy than another. God used the prophet's language of the time to record what He wanted us to hear. The message is clear even so, because the basic message is to FOLLOW ALL OF HIS WORDS. Let us stick with the plain meaning of the Word and the important things God is trying to explain. Don't get sidetracked or ruined by wrangling over words.

Numerology

Lots of numbers are used in prophecy, and usually have a very specific meaning. God's numbers are three and seven (one supposes He actually has all numbers). Three is because of the Father, Son and Holy Spirit (or even "thrice holy"), and seven is the number of completeness or perfection (7 days of creation). Three is also the number for certainty, meaning that if something is repeated three times (such as holy, holy, holy is God almighty) it is a certainty.

Joseph tells Pharaoh (Genesis 41:32) that the doubling of his dream means that "the thing is fixed by God, and God will shortly bring it about." The number of government is 12, so we have 12 tribes and 12 apostles. Multiples of numbers are also used, such as seven times seven or 49 years in between Jubilee years (the 50th year) and 12,000 from 12 tribes sealed during the tribulation totaling 144,000. Seventy years was the length of time of the first captivity or exile of Israel, and Jesus sent out 70 disciples.

A number used for Jesus is eight, the number of new beginnings. Four is a number describing the earth (four winds, four corners) or perhaps "everywhere." Six is one short of the number seven indicating completeness, and is used as the number for man because we are incomplete without God. That's why the little horn or beast is given the number 666, because it is the number of man and this man is certainly three times incomplete.

Numbers are used a lot in Revelation. We hear of seven seals, seven trumpets and seven bowl judgments, all referring to completeness or fulfilling. John confirms the idea of completeness, for instance, when he says that the wrath of God is finished with the seven bowls or plagues.

Revelation 15:1 ESV. Then I saw another sign in heaven, great and amazing, seven angels with seven plagues, which are the last, for with them the wrath of God is finished.

The point here is that numbers are meaningful, but exercise caution and don't go too far afield when interpreting a prophecy containing numbers.

Bible codes, where numbering letters and counting them is supposed to reveal hidden prophecies, are just so much fantasy. Maybe God really did arrange it so that counting letters and substituting numbers for some of them has some hidden meaning. It isn't beyond Him to do something like that. But it doesn't factor into interpretation of prophecy, because to judge from the calculations of Bible code believers the results lack certainty and don't really tell the future. Only as they work hard to shape the codes to past events do they make any sense at all, which is related to newspaper eisegeses.

The language of math itself shows us the glory of God, and probably the more we learn the more of His glory will show up. But getting all excited about Bible codes is just another one of those distractions that get us away from the Word rather than encouraging us to do what God says.

Expositional Constancy

Some teachers use the concept of "expositional constancy" when interpreting the Bible. This philosophy of men simply means that when a type was defined the first time in Scripture, then that type always means the same thing later on. For instance, since Israel is compared to figs (or a fig tree) as in Jeremiah 24, then if expositional constancy is true, figs and fig trees always represent Israel. So the philosophy states that when Jesus in Matthew 24:32 says we know that summer is near when the fig tree puts out leaves, we will know that the time of the Son of Man is near when Israel (the fig tree) is showing growth again. People relate this to when Israel became an official nation once again.

The problem with this is that constancy depends on context. Adam and Eve made loin cloths out of fig leaves (Genesis 3:7). Does this mean that somehow they covered themselves with Israel? No. It simply means that they covered themselves by their own hands or works. Although on further reflection, Israel (like man in general) had a habit of covering their sins with their own works, too. Expositional constancy doesn't really work as well as the teachers who use it maintain.

Leaven is another example. During Passover (or Unleavened Bread), leaven, as a symbol of sin, is removed from homes. However, at Shavuot (Pentecost) two loaves of leavened bread are part of the offerings. Does this mean the loaves are filled with sin? No.

Later, in the parables from Jesus, He uses leaven as a symbol for sin or hypocrisy (which is sin anyway) (Matthew 16:6, 11, 12). Not always, however. In the parable of the kingdom in Matthew 13:33, the kingdom of heaven is compared to leaven that a woman took and hid in three measures of flour, till it was all leavened. So either Jesus is saying the kingdom is like sin, or instead He is clearly saying that the kingdom will work its way through the world until it is all over the place.

Leaven, as a symbol or type, just means something that works its way throughout another type. Used as symbol for hypocrisy, we have a picture of it working its way through the world (and the Church). Used as a symbol for the kingdom of God, we see how the kingdom works its way through the world also. The kingdom, of course, is the rule of God in the hearts of men. As the Kingdom increases, the hypocrisy of people who want to look like believers but don't really do what God says also increases. They go hand in hand, sadly.

Egypt is a good third example. Sometimes it is just a kingdom or a country. Other times it is a stand-in or symbol for the godless world system. When Israel departed Egypt in the Exodus, we can use that as a comparison for coming out of the world and into God's kingdom.

Exodus 13:14 ESV. And when in time to come your son asks you, 'What does this mean?' you shall say to him, 'By a strong hand the LORD brought us out of Egypt, from the house of slavery.

When many in Israel wanted to go back to Egypt, we can then see that desire as wanting to abandon God and go back to the slavery of the death-bound sinful world.

Expositional constancy fails quite frequently. In fact, if fails so often that the only thing constant about it is the failure to help us understand much of anything. Context changes the meanings of a lot of phrases, symbols, types and words if we are paying attention. If we rely on philosophies of men, such as expositional constancy, to interpret the Word, we will invariably fall short of a balanced, complete understanding. Sometimes a fig is just a sweet tasting fruit, and sometimes leaven is just something that makes bread light and fluffy.

How Do We Know?

Job 33:5–7 ESV. Answer me, if you can; set your words in order before me; take your stand. Behold, I am toward God as you are; I too was pinched off from a piece of clay. Behold, no fear of me need terrify you; my pressure will not be heavy upon you.

The easy answer to the question of how do we know is...we'll know it when we see it. This writer hasn't been given any special knowledge, except perhaps the grace and discernment to read His Word and follow it in the first place. The resulting book is an attempt to figure out prophecy according to The Book. That's what we should all be doing, both for prophecy and for daily living. Everything written here is just commentary or opinion. We'll just have to keep watching events, do what He says for us to do, and cling to the hope of the return of our Messiah.

He tells everyone what will happen and it's not so hard to figure out a lot of it. He wrote it all down so there's no surprise. The way to interpret prophecy is by the Word, and we don't have to spiritualize in order to make the events fit some preconceived notion either. Compare the nature of events with other events to match them up, including descriptions and key words or phrases.

For instance, the term "Day of the Lord" or "that day" or "a day of smoke and burning" generally refer to the Great Tribulation. It depends on the context. Other imagery can be matched to the Feasts of the Lord, such as smoke and burning to the Day of Atonement, or the trumpet judgments of Revelation to the warnings in the appointed time or holiday of the Feast of Trumpets.

A mallard duck and a pintail duck may look different, but they both have bills, webbed feet, love water and quack, so they are both ducks. Of course, we have to be careful in our comparisons and do a lot of cross checking Scripture with Scripture. Things might look the same but may not be related at all. That's not to say there are many things that *are* the same even if they don't look the same on the surface.

Part of the ability to tell what is what comes from submitting to God in every detail of living. If we read large portions of His Word on a daily basis, and submission in humility to everything He instructs becomes part of daily living, that humility is rewarded by God with ever increasing understanding. Jesus calls this "eating His flesh and drinking His blood" (John chapter 6). This concept freaks people out, but is a true description for the believer who hungers and thirsts after righteousness.

What Good is Prophecy?

1 Corinthians 14:3 ESV. On the other hand, the one who prophesies speaks to people for their upbuilding and encouragement and consolation.

Some of the benefits of prophecy have already been discussed, such as the comfort that comes from knowing what God intends to do. God tells us that whatever happens we will be able to overcome it and persevere. He is always in control, always way ahead of our enemies, always trustworthy, always faithful, and never turns His back on His children. He is a God of His Word, never saying anything He doesn't mean and meaning what He says. There is no shadow of turning in Him, and because of His unchanging character we can trust what He says without question or doubt. We wait on the Father to reveal what we need when we need it. In the meantime we continue to sharpen our sight, our hearing and our understanding by taking in His Word and practicing it every minute of the day. So when He speaks, say for instance if He directs His people to a hiding place in the midst of the tribulation storms (see the section **Hidden from Wrath**), we will hear and follow Him.

More than these, however, are the benefits of demonstrating His power, wisdom, and knowledge. Prophecy glorifies God, and rightly so. Prophecy gives hope. We know that righteousness will prevail, that evil-doers will get their just desserts, and no matter what we go through in this life, it will not stay this way.

Jeremiah 23:18–20 ESV. For who among them has stood in the council of the LORD to see and to hear his word, or who has paid attention to his word and listened? Behold, the storm of the LORD! Wrath has gone forth, a whirling tempest; it will burst upon the head of the wicked. The anger of the LORD will not turn back until he has executed and accomplished the intents of his heart. In the latter days you will understand it clearly.

God teaches us through prophecy. He knows the end from the beginning, nothing is outside the range of His knowledge and plans, and He does not change. He is a rock on which we can rest. His Word doesn't change (despite what many in the Church say) so we know His promises are sure and solid.

He proves He is God all by Himself, with no other gods who can do anything close to what He can. God tells us stuff before it happens so we can't say we, or our idols, knew it.

Isaiah 48:6–8 ESV. "You have heard; now see all this; and will you not declare it? From this time forth I announce to you new things, hidden things that you have not known. They are created now, not long ago; before today you have never heard of them, lest you should say, 'Behold, I knew them.' You have never heard, you have never known, from of old your ear has not been opened. For I knew that you would surely deal treacherously, and that from before birth you were called a rebel.

One of the main points of prophecy is that God's Words are health and life and peace, and none of the bad things would have to happen if we just stayed within the boundaries of what He says.

Isaiah 48:17–19 ESV. Thus says the LORD, your Redeemer, the Holy One of Israel: "I am the LORD your God, who teaches you to profit, who leads you in the way you should go. Oh that you had paid attention to my commandments! Then your peace would have been like a river, and your righteousness like the waves of the sea; your offspring would have been like the sand, and your descendants like its grains; their name would never be cut off or destroyed from before me."

There are a lot of science fiction books that try to foretell the future. Every single one of them is written without God, and therefore without hope. There might be new gadgets for the kitchen, different ways to get around the planet, and even faster ways of traveling between planets or stars. But the one thing they all have in common is that people (or even aliens) remain the same. Their characters have the same faults, the same sins, the same wars, the same everything. Even when they stretch their story line thousands of years in the future, they can only show depressing cycles of war and destruction. Without God, we are locked into a repetitive lifestyle of death and hopelessness. God tells us He will not put up with that forever. He is going to stop it. Hope is what prophecy is all about for those who believe Him and do what He says.

3 God's Promise and Prophecy

Luke 4:42–43 ESV. And when it was day, he departed and went into a desolate place. And the people sought him and came to him, and would have kept him from leaving them, but he said to them, "I must preach the good news of the kingdom of God to the other towns as well; for I was sent for this purpose."

God's plan is a Kingdom that is clean and pure, ruled by love, justice, mercy and compassion, peopled by those who love and live by every word from His mouth. That is real paradise. Obviously, we don't have the full Kingdom now, except in the hearts of believers everywhere. Rebellious people of the world will eventually be winnowed out and sent to a place that they prefer over the Kingdom of God. In that place there is weeping, wailing and gnashing of teeth, because their choice was really stupid.

The foundation, chief cornerstone, the Promise, and king of the Kingdom of Heaven is Yeshua haMashiach. He isn't on the throne of David yet, but once the world is judged and world kingdoms destroyed, He will take up His rule on earth as it is in heaven. Jesus will show us how things would have been had we just done what He said in the first place. The promise of this King and kingdom is the backbone of the Bible and prophecy.

The Promise

God gave The Plan right away to Adam and Eve after their exile from the Garden of Eden. The outline and first announcement of The Plan is the Promise of the Messiah in Genesis 3:15.

Genesis 3:15, ESV I will put enmity between you and the woman, and between your offspring and her offspring; he shall bruise your head, and you shall bruise his heel."

Some have termed this the "Protoevangelium" meaning the first evangelistic or gospel message. God's Promise to believers is that the deceiver will not prevail and our Messiah (seed of the woman) will reunite us with God in every way. The separation from Him will not be permanent. This gives new meaning to the name Immanuel (God with us). It is the good news or gospel of God's Kingdom, which is also another way of saying God with us. It is the blessing to the nations coming through Abraham.

Noah gets more details of the Plan and Promise in Genesis 6:18, 9:9 and 9:25-27. It's a different form of promise, called a covenant. But it is a one-sided covenant, where God says He will do something. God cannot be forced to fulfill His side of the deal, so we can also call this a promise, and it is combined with the previous general Promise in Genesis 3:15. Later on Abraham gets more details when God includes him in the Promise in Genesis 12:1-3.

Genesis 12:1–3 ESV. Now the LORD said to Abram, "Go from your country and your kindred and your father's house to the land that I will show you. And I will make of you a great nation, and I will bless you and make your name great, so that you will be a blessing. I will bless those who bless you, and him who dishonors you I will curse, and in you all the families of the earth shall be blessed."

When God says "in you all the families of the earth will be blessed" it is yet another way of saying God with us, because God is the source of blessings. Isaac and Jacob receive the Promise (Genesis 13, 15, 17, 22, 24, 26 and 28) and it carries on to the delivery of The Law and gospel at Mt. Sinai. Why is the giving of the Law included with the gospel? Because the writer of Hebrews (4:2) tells us, "good news (literally the gospel) came to us just as to them," and the gospel is "God with us."

Hebrews 4:2 ESV. For good news came to us just as to them, but the message they heard did not benefit them, because they were not united by faith with those who listened.

The Law and the establishment of Israel as a nation in their own land was a part of the Promise. It was "added" according to Paul (Galatians 3:19). God was going to be "with" Israel, literally in their midst in the Tabernacle and later the Temple.

David was given additional details of the Promise in 2 Samuel 7:12-16. His Son (whom we know to be Jesus) he is told, will sit on the throne of God's kingdom forever.

2 Samuel 7:12–16 ESV. When your days are fulfilled and you lie down with your fathers, I will raise up your offspring after you, who shall come from your body, and I will establish his kingdom. He shall build a house for my name, and I will establish the throne of his kingdom forever. I will be to him a father, and he shall be to me a son. When he commits iniquity, I will discipline him with the rod of men, with the stripes of the sons of men, but my steadfast love will not depart from him, as I took it from Saul, whom I put away from before you. And your house and your kingdom shall be made sure forever before me. Your throne shall be established forever.

Similar words are in 1 Chronicles 17:1-15. House is a figure of speech for family, clan, tribe or Kingdom. The "house" that God is going to build for David we know as the people who make up the Body of the Messiah Jesus the Christ. We are "the house," and the head of our house is our King, the Son of David. God has been building this house for a long time, and it is the culmination of much prophecy.

All the prophets saw the coming of the seed of the woman such as Isaiah (Isaiah 7:14, 11:1 and others) Amos (Amos 7:7-8), Jeremiah (Jeremiah 33:14-17) and Zechariah (Zechariah 3:8-9). Even Balaam saw the promised Messiah (Numbers 24:17).

The apostles were aware of the promise also and its fulfillment in Yeshua haMashiach a.k.a. Jesus the Christ.

Romans 1:1–4 ESV. Paul, a servant of Christ Jesus, called to be an apostle, set apart for the gospel of God, which he promised beforehand through his prophets in the holy Scriptures, concerning his Son, who was descended from David according to the flesh and was declared to be the Son of God in power according to the Spirit of holiness by his resurrection from the dead, Jesus Christ our Lord,

If you look up the word "promise" in the New Testament, you will find it described dozens of times. This promise is a central feature of the Scriptures and the foundation for all of God's interactions with men. It is a central feature in prophecy too. For instance, the book of the Revelation is actually The Revelation of Jesus the Christ. All prophesied events lead up to the destruction of the deceiver's kingdom (bruise his head) and the revealing to the world in all His glory of Yeshua HaMashiach. He is victorious even after all the attempts to destroy God's Promise, including His crucifixion (heel was bruised).

The Body of Sin

The flesh, also called the sin nature, is that part of created beings that moves us to feel, think or act apart from our Creator. God describes this as sin. Sins are the specific actions of the sin nature. One of the main features of prophecy is to deal finally with sin and its penalty; death or separation from the God of life.

Desire and pride are big parts of the sin nature. In some ways, desire is not such a bad thing. We desire to have a stable, secure home out of the storms, to satisfy hunger, and to marry and have kids. God gave us these desires and had provided these things for us at the time of Adam. We didn't even have to work for them. He places desires in our hearts and delights also in providing for them (including giving of Him).

Psalm 37:3–4 ESV. Trust in the LORD, and do good; dwell in the land and befriend faithfulness. Delight yourself in the LORD, and he will give you the desires of your heart.

Out-of-order desire, on the other hand, is different in that it works for self-satisfaction as opposed to God satisfaction. After the first parents reached out in ungodly desire and took of the fruit that God told us was off-limits, we had to work for our basic needs or desires. Desiring material things such as wealth or physical stimulation outside of our basic needs and God's design is sin. Eve desired the fruit of the wrong tree and convinced herself that it would make her wise. Adam desired Eve and forsook the paradise God had provided (and turned his back on God) in order to stay with her. The deceiver desired to be like God, and left the position that God had given him to set up a kingdom without God. Men desire gold (money), extra wives, sex outside of marriage or the God-designed order of male and female, position, and power.

Ecclesiastes 5:10 ESV. He who loves money will not be satisfied with money, nor he who loves wealth with his income; this also is vanity.

Matthew 6:24 ESV. "No one can serve two masters, for either he will hate the one and love the other, or he will be devoted to the one and despise the other. You cannot serve God and money.

1 Timothy 6:10 ESV. For the love of money is a root of all kinds of evils. It is through this craving that some have wandered away from the faith and pierced themselves with many pangs.

Hebrews 13:5 ESV. Keep your life free from love of money, and be content with what you have, for he has said, "I will never leave you nor forsake you."

This desire for gain above or beyond our basic needs (or what God provides) is a driving force in the kingdoms of the world, and is one of the things destroyed in the Tribulation.

Revelation 18:15–18 ESV. The merchants of these wares, who gained wealth from her, will stand far off, in fear of her torment, weeping and mourning aloud, "Alas, alas, for the great city that was clothed in fine linen, in purple and scarlet, adorned with gold, with jewels, and with pearls! For in a single hour all this wealth has been laid waste." And all shipmasters and seafaring men, sailors and all whose trade is on the sea, stood far off and cried out as they saw the smoke of her burning, "What city was like the great city?"

Wealth or gain is power in worldly terms, and is connected to all evil including sexual immorality, idolatry, coveting, murder, and any other sin you can name. Desire for power over others will drive the beast and false prophet to try and knock God off of His throne and take it themselves. Desire for God's position drives the deceiver to create much of the misery, war, poverty, disease, pestilence and death in the world.

The "great prostitute" of Revelation 17 is said to have committed sexual immorality with the kings of the earth, and is wrapped in wealth (gold, jewels and pearls). The desire for gain or power is part and parcel of all the other sins, especially sexual immorality. To understand the identity of this prostitute is to understand the desire for immoral gain that marks all kingdoms of man, and especially the kingdom of the little horn or beast.

The beast's desire for illicit gain is not necessarily economic or sexual, but he uses these things to entice people into his kingdom and away from God's. He desires the power to challenge God for the position of Big Cheese, and uses the Prostitute to weld together a coalition of spiritual but not religious people in order to replace Him with the beast. The Prostitute is a symbol of evil desire clothed in wealthy array, and all the world's religions have some part in her.

Like many prostitutes, she might be beautiful on the outside but inside she is rotten to the core. We can tell she is the personification of corrupt religion because she is drunk with the blood of the saints. The Prostitute in Revelation is shown in her true nature. She can be hard to spot from a believer's point of view though, due to her use of sheep's clothing covering the gold and pearls. One way to spot her in The Church is that she cannot abide the saints, due to their testimony for the truth of God's word and Yeshua our Messiah. She claims to follow God's Laws, but reacts negatively if it is even lightly suggested that she doesn't and should. She must remove any threats to her wealth or control by any means available.

The war between believers and the Prostitute has been going on since the beginning. She is disguised at times by appearing to be the same as believers, holding to some of God's Word perhaps but not all of it. There are gaps in her wool suit if you know where to look (my grandma, what big teeth you have!).

2 Corinthians 11:12–15 ESV. And what I am doing I will continue to do, in order to undermine the claim of those who would like to claim that in their boasted mission they work on the same terms as we do. For such men are false apostles, deceitful workmen, disguising themselves as apostles of Christ. And no wonder, for even Satan disguises himself as an angel of light. So it is no surprise if his servants, also, disguise themselves as servants of righteousness. Their end will correspond to their deeds.

For instance, an obvious part of the war between the Prostitute and believers was when Jewish leadership (the Prostitute) handed Jesus over to the Romans (another member of the Prostitute) who crucified Him. The book of Acts shows more of this war when we see unbelieving Jewish leadership (the Prostitute) chasing and killing Jewish believers, or unbelieving Gentiles (the Prostitute) persecuting believing Gentiles in order to protect their idol businesses or for political reasons. The beast will use this Prostitute for a while, but he will ultimately destroy her.

The desire for wealth and satisfaction of the flesh is the reason that many people will gladly take the mark of the beast. They will lust for power and hope that the beast can give it to them. This is the reason the mark is associated with buying and selling, and the reason that merchants and sailors mourn the destruction of wealth-trading Babylon in Revelation 18 and 19.

A collective term for the desires of the flesh is the body of sin. Paul uses this term in Romans 6:6 when writing about crucifying it with Christ to obtain freedom from sin. Our desire should be for God and His Word, not for the flesh. The flesh can never be satisfied, and the self-seeking pursuit of wealth excludes God in every way.

If our desire is for Him and His words, we will desire those things that please Him, which are good things for us anyway. Seek first the kingdom of God, and God will provide the other things in His time and by His measure.

The Body of Christ

Paul in Romans nine through eleven speaks of an olive tree with natural branches and "grafted in" branches. He uses this analogy of an olive tree to illustrate the concept of the body of Christ. In another place, Paul tells us about being baptized by one Spirit into one body of Christ (1 Corinthians 12). The olive tree and the Body of Christ are the same thing. Believers were chosen in Him before the foundation of the world (Ephesians 1:3, Revelation 13:8) to be part of the tree or body.

Matthew 25:34 ESV. Then the King will say to those on his right, 'Come, you who are blessed by my Father, inherit the kingdom prepared for you from the foundation of the world.

At first we might think of the tree as physical Israel, and in a way we might be right, but only because Israel is part of the tree, not the tree itself. They were supposed to establish the Kingdom of Heaven on earth. The root of the olive tree is Yeshua, and the tree is His kingdom. Israel is part of the kingdom, and was intended to be the representative of God's kingdom on the earth, but they frequently fail to stay on the path.

Branches of the olive tree that do not show fruit, even natural branches, are broken off and burned in the fire. "Natural branches" means physical Israel, and wild branches are Gentiles. Wild branches (not physical Israel) are grafted into the kingdom, but if they don't bear fruit, they can be broken off too. New (more properly "renewed") covenant fruit is from a heart made soft by the Holy Spirit and written with God's commands.

Jeremiah 31:31–34 ESV. "Behold, the days are coming, declares the LORD, when I will make a new covenant with the house of Israel and the house of Judah, not like the covenant that I made with their fathers on the day when I took them by the hand to bring them out of the land of Egypt, my covenant that they broke, though I was their husband, declares the LORD. For this is the covenant that I will make with the house of Israel after those days, declares the LORD: I will put my law within them, and I will write it on their hearts. And I will be their God, and they shall be my people. And no longer shall each one teach his neighbor and each his brother, saying, 'Know the LORD,' for they shall all know me, from the least of them to the greatest, declares the LORD. For I will forgive their iniquity, and I will remember their sin no more."

Ezekiel 36:25–27 ESV. I will sprinkle clean water on you, and you shall be clean from all your uncleannesses, and from all your idols I will cleanse you. And I will give you a new heart, and a new spirit I will put within you. And I will remove the heart of stone from your flesh and give you a heart of flesh. And I will put my Spirit within you, and cause you to walk in my statutes and be careful to obey my rules.

People in the Body of Christ are marked by holding to the testimony of Jesus and obedience to God's Law (Revelation 12:17). They do what God says. Fruit grows from a soft heart inhabited by the Spirit and written with the law of God and His Son.

Galatians 5:22–23 ESV. But the fruit of the Spirit is love, joy, peace, patience, kindness, goodness, faithfulness, gentleness, self-control; against such things there is no law.

Ephesians 5:5–11 ESV. For you may be sure of this, that everyone who is sexually immoral or impure, or who is covetous (that is, an idolater), has no inheritance in the kingdom of Christ and God. Let no one deceive you with empty words, for because of these things the wrath of God comes upon the sons of disobedience. Therefore do not become partners with them; for at one time you were darkness, but now you are light in the Lord. Walk as children of light (for the fruit of light is found in all that is good and right and true), and try to discern what is pleasing to the Lord. Take no part in the unfruitful works of darkness, but instead expose them.

The olive tree has been in existence since the beginning. The Promise is the heart of the tree, our Messiah Jesus is the root of the tree and the head of the Body, and believers are nourished from the sap of the tree which is the blood of Yeshua or Word of God. He is the life of the tree and of the Body. Physical Israel is part of the tree because God "promised" Abraham, Isaac and Jacob to make from them a great nation (Genesis 46:3; Exodus 2:24; Leviticus 26:42; 2 Kings 13:23). Israel is supposed to be the visible part of the kingdom of heaven. They have first place in many ways, but only as they show fruit. Fruit comes out when we are nourished by the sap of the tree.

In another sense, Gentiles are part of Israel but not through genetics. We partake of the Promise the same as our brothers, but the tree of which we are all part is the Kingdom of God. We might be called "spiritual" Israel because we are born again and have inherited the promises to Abraham by grace through faith. Believers are children of Abraham, not be genetics but by trusting and obeying God (faith - Galatians 3:7). Obedience to His Word is what ties us together.

Romans 9:6–8 ESV. But it is not as though the word of God has failed. For not all who are descended from Israel belong to Israel, and not all are children of Abraham because they are his offspring, but "Through Isaac shall your offspring be named." This means that it is not the children of the flesh who are the children of God, but the children of the promise are counted as offspring.

In a similar fashion as Israel, people in the Church can be part of the Kingdom, olive tree or body, but the Church is not the Body. As a group it has become little different from a series of country clubs or fast food franchises, holding to a form of religion but denying the power of the Promise and the New Covenant. The "new" part of the New Covenant is the heart, not the Law or Word of God. Those who do what God says are the Body, and those who do not will be thrown into the fire. That is how it has always been.

There are different roles and responsibilities for people in the Body and the kingdom. For instance, the 144,000 from the 12 tribes of Israel have a different role than others. There are the 24 elders (Revelation 4:4), and the "great multitude" of Revelation 7:9-17 and Revelation 19:1-3 from every nation standing before the throne. There will be survivors of the Tribulation, if only a few and perhaps mostly physical Israel, who go into the millennial kingdom.

We can also add in here the different roles of apostles, prophets, teachers, miracles, healings, helping, administrating, tongues (1 Corinthians 12:28-29), along with evangelists and shepherds (Ephesians 4:11). Different gifts are distributed by the Spirit for these roles. All have obedience to God's Word in common. For another example of different roles, apparently the resurrected (and raptured) believers get new bodies, are like the angels, and don't marry.

Matthew 22:30 ESV. For in the resurrection they neither marry nor are given in marriage, but are like angels in heaven.

Yet in the kingdom there will be babies and old men, people building houses and planting crops (swords into plowshares (Isaiah 2:4 and Micah 4:3) and enjoying the work of their hands.

Isaiah 65:19–23 ESV. I will rejoice in Jerusalem and be glad in my people; no more shall be heard in it the sound of weeping and the cry of distress. No more shall there be in it an infant who lives but a few days, or an old man who does not fill out his days, for the young man shall die a hundred years old, and the sinner a hundred years old shall be accursed. They shall build houses and inhabit them; they shall plant vineyards and eat their fruit. They shall not build and another inhabit; they shall not plant and another eat; for like the days of a tree shall the days of my people be, and my chosen shall long enjoy the work of their hands. They shall not labor in vain or bear children for calamity, for they shall be the offspring of the blessed of the LORD, and their descendants with them.

So what happens to the Body of Christ in the Tribulation? Well, it is terrible to contemplate but we will be going through some pretty tough times. Some of us will be (and are being) killed. Some will be hidden, overlooked or protected by supernatural means. Others will go (and are going) into captivity, which might mean jail or relocation.

Whatever is going to happen, however, we have to put our trust in God and maintain our witness by doing what He says. The one Body of Christ is the Kingdom and the tree, and He will not allow us to be extinguished. Read the Word and do what it says now as if your life depended on it, because it does. Hearing and doing His Word will sharpen our hearing and eyesight so we can follow any instructions He has for us as the times get tougher.

Romans 5:1–5 ESV. Therefore, since we have been justified by faith, we have peace with God through our Lord Jesus Christ. Through him we have also obtained access by faith into this grace in which we stand, and we rejoice in hope of the glory of God. Not only that, but we rejoice in our sufferings, knowing that suffering produces endurance, and endurance produces character, and character produces hope, and hope does not put us to shame, because God's love has been poured into our hearts through the Holy Spirit who has been given to us.

Idolatry

Faith is sticking with God's will and Word. Idolatry is faithlessness or cheating on God. Idolatry is a reflection of man's selfish and self-centered desire in rejecting the rule of God and creating for themselves gods they can control. Pagan gods created by men conform to the image of man, but men are only healthy and whole as they conform to our loving Father. Through the sacrifice of Yeshua, believers strive to be more like the God of Abraham, Isaac and Jacob. Unbelievers have only empty husks incapable of rescuing them from a hopeless eternity of horror, flame and agony.

As mentioned before, one reason that God tells us what is going to happen is so that no one can say other gods cause the events to happen.

Isaiah 48:3–5 ESV. "The former things I declared of old; they went out from my mouth, and I announced them; then suddenly I did them, and they came to pass. Because I know that you are obstinate, and your neck is an iron sinew and your forehead brass, I declared them to you from of old, before they came to pass I announced them to you, lest you should say, 'My idol did them, my carved image and my metal image commanded them.'

God's perspective is that man in general (not just Israel) is obstinate, stiff necked and all-around resistant to God's plan and words. He declares what is going to happen to show that man's imaginary idols and other gods cannot. This goes for fallen angels or something like the goat demons mentioned in Leviticus.

Leviticus 17:7 ESV. So they shall no more sacrifice their sacrifices to goat demons, after whom they whore. This shall be a statute forever for them throughout their generations.

Most gods spring from the minds of corrupted people seeking some sort of deity they can control. All of them are directly related to the Goddess of Reason mentioned earlier. If they say the right things, give the right sacrifices (many times including children, as in abortion), then the "god" has to respond to the manipulation by granting the request. The control is with the worshipper of the imaginary god. Sometimes there might be a real spiritual power, such as a fallen angel or demon, that is operating outside of its God-assigned boundaries and allowing what appears to be manipulation for its own purposes. But the goal of all idolatry is to further the kingdom of the deceiver, or at the very least destroy the kingdom of God.

Idolatry does not always involve a statue or a specific god. Daniel, for instance, mentions a previously unknown god of forces or fortresses.

Daniel 11:38–39 ESV. He shall honor the god of fortresses instead of these. A god whom his fathers did not know he shall honor with gold and silver, with precious stones and costly gifts. He shall deal with the strongest fortresses with the help of a foreign god. Those who acknowledge him he shall load with honor. He shall make them rulers over many and shall divide the land for a price.

Paul tells us of people who have their belly for a god (Philippians 3:19) or serve their appetites (Romans 16:18). People who claim to contact the dead (necromancers), mediums, sorcerers and similar practices are included in idolatry. Anything that is not

God, yet is obeyed or worshipped or served contrary to God, is an idol, and all idols will be destroyed.

Isaiah 2:17–19 ESV. And the haughtiness of man shall be humbled, and the lofty pride of men shall be brought low, and the LORD alone will be exalted in that day. And the idols shall utterly pass away. And people shall enter the caves of the rocks and the holes of the ground, from before the terror of the LORD, and from the splendor of his majesty, when he rises to terrify the earth.

Idolatry, with or without statues, is on the rise in modern times. Interesting that Revelation mentions idol worship in prophecies that occur at the end of the world's kingdoms. Yet worship of false gods has always been around, as long as there have been people. Some of the gods have name changes, and some aspects of idolatrous practices have died out, but in one form or another people have always made gods they can manipulate. As Jeremiah says, "the work of your hands" (or even "doing what is right in our own eyes") is still idolatry.

Jeremiah 25:4–7 ESV. You have neither listened nor inclined your ears to hear, although the LORD persistently sent to you all his servants the prophets, saying, 'Turn now, every one of you, from his evil way and evil deeds, and dwell upon the land that the LORD has given to you and your fathers from of old and forever. Do not go after other gods to serve and worship them, or provoke me to anger with the work of your hands. Then I will do you no harm.' Yet you have not listened to me, declares the LORD, that you might provoke me to anger with the work of your hands to your own harm.

There are many idolatrous religions around even now such as Buddhism, Islam, Mormonism, Catholicism, Wicca or witchcraft, Satanism, and Taoism to name a few. But now idolatry seems to be coming out of the closet without shame more than in recent memory. There are the statues of "Mami Wata" in New Orleans or "Cybele" and "Oracle" in New York. College students are chanting worship of old Aztec gods of human sacrifice. Witches are demanding recognition as a legitimate "religion." Pagan practices thought to have had died out long ago are being revived. In the past we might have wondered how the beast or little horn of the Tribulation could make an image and have much of the world worship it or him. But now we can easily see worship of the beast will be thorough and worldwide, and receiving the mark of his name will be an honor to those who are perishing.

Chronology

This subject complements the section from Chapter 2 on Prophetic Timing. Prophecies, such as those in the book of Revelation, are not necessarily sequential or chronological just because they appear one after the other when written down. Some are sequential, such as the seals, trumpets and bowl judgments in Revelation (although there may be long periods of time between them). But some are not, such as Revelation 12. Even if they are sequential or chronological, we don't know how much time passes between events.

Sometimes in the text, there are intervals where we get some history in order to explain what is coming. The books of Isaiah and Ezekiel list visions that may look like the events described arrive one after the other, but they actually occur over years, decades or millennia. They may be connected, and in the overall scheme of God's plan the events are in fact connected, but not necessarily directly to each other in time.

Malachi 3:1–4 ESV. "Behold, I send my messenger, and he will prepare the way before me. And the Lord whom you seek will suddenly come to his temple; and the messenger of the covenant in whom you delight, behold, he is coming, says the LORD of hosts. But who can endure the day of his coming, and who can stand when he appears? For he is like a refiner's fire and like fullers' soap. He will sit as a refiner and purifier of silver, and he will purify the sons of Levi and refine them like gold and silver, and they will bring offerings in righteousness to the LORD. Then the offering of Judah and Jerusalem will be pleasing to the LORD as in the days of old and as in former years.

Malachi here is an example of timeline gaps. He says that "my (God's) messenger" is sent to prepare the way, and then the Lord will "suddenly come to his temple." We know that John the Baptizer was a messenger for Jesus, and that Jesus "suddenly" came to the temple and chased the money lenders out. This can be seen as one way of purifying the sons of Levi.

The tone shifts radically however with verse two when Malachi asks, "But who can endure the day of his coming, or who can stand when he appears?" This part didn't happen when Jesus was traveling around as a humble, itinerant rabbi, even if He was rough on the money changers in the temple. So it will happen when He returns.

Apparently, there is a very large time gap between the way Jesus did it the first time and when He does it the second time. Perhaps the first visit would have followed Malachi's prophecy more closely had Israel's leaders accepted Jesus. The first visit was a sort of rehearsal for the second, more spectacular visit, perhaps because of the rejection of Jesus. Anyway, the hope here is that you understand that prophecies might have large time gaps.

Even the trumpets and bowl judgments could have weeks or years between them. When we get to the bowl judgments, the pace seems to pick up quite a bit. The events of the bowls feel like they are happening very quickly, judging by the way John writes. Still, they may be stretched out over, oh, say three and a half years. Or they may be jammed together much more rapidly.

It appears that many visions are self-contained and give some history along with revealing future events. An example of this is Revelation 12. The chapter seems to include history such as the birth of the Messiah and His ascent into heaven, as well as the protection of the woman for time, times and half a time. But the vision could also describe an increased focus on, or renewal of, the war with the saints during that same three and a half year protection period.

In addition to schooling, we learn how to interpret by understanding the nature of people and their attempts to modify God's plans, and by humbly submitting to God and His Word. Nebuchadnezzar tried to repudiate his vision of the statue kingdoms by making an image of solid gold, implying that his kingdom would last longer than the time encompassed by the gold head in God's vision. He was wrong.

Some prophesied events could even be ongoing. For instance in Revelation 12:17 the dragon "went off to make war on the rest of her offspring, on those who keep the commandments of God and hold to the testimony of Jesus."

1 Peter 5:8 ESV. Be sober-minded; be watchful. Your adversary the devil prowls around like a roaring lion, seeking someone to devour.

John in Revelation 12 may be referring to this ongoing war. Remember, too, that prophecies were made of the Messiah for 4,000 years before He incarnated and many people missed some of the significance. Prophecies we are dealing with in this book mostly were made starting about 6,000 years ago. The book of Revelation was written almost 2,000 years ago. God has been silent for a long time about new revelation, but that doesn't mean the plans He made aren't in the process of working out just as He designed.

2 Peter 3:8–13 ESV. But do not overlook this one fact, beloved, that with the Lord one day is as a thousand years, and a thousand years as one day. The Lord is not slow to fulfill his promise as some count slowness,

but is patient toward you, not wishing that any should perish, but that all should reach repentance. But the day of the Lord will come like a thief, and then the heavens will pass away with a roar, and the heavenly bodies will be burned up and dissolved, and the earth and the works that are done on it will be exposed. Since all these things are thus to be dissolved, what sort of people ought you to be in lives of holiness and godliness, waiting for and hastening the coming of the day of God, because of which the heavens will be set on fire and dissolved, and the heavenly bodies will melt as they burn! But according to his promise we are waiting for new heavens and a new earth in which righteousness dwells.

Event Orientation

Most people are not calendar oriented as much as they are event oriented. In other words, when we think about an event in our lives, we usually think of the event first and then fit it into a calendar. We remember a special event such as a birthday party; we think of the party first and then try to remember which birthday it was and when it happened. We do this all the time in my family. We might say, "Do you remember when we had that cake that looked like the Death Star from Star Wars?" Then we'll try to remember which kid's birthday it was and which calendar year it happened. Or we'll remember a particularly heavy snowstorm we had where we got a foot of snow all at once (that much snow is kind of a rare thing where we live) and it stuck around for a month. Then we'll try to figure out what year it was. We might remember a particularly bad or good year, or the year we graduated or started a new job, but even then, we remember those dates because of the events occurring during that time.

It looks like God does the same thing when He is giving us prophecy. It is oriented around events rather than specific years on some calendar somewhere. Especially since, He's communicating across centuries, and calendars change frequently. So when we are trying to fit prophecies together, we have to line up the events first, and then we can maybe figure out the timing better.

A prophecy example is when we look at the 70 weeks of Daniel. They are divided into three sections. Each of the three sections is marked by the arrival of an anointed one or prince with certain other events, not by a date on a calendar. The book of Revelation seems to be divided in a similar fashion. So remember this as you study.

The Ripe Time

When it comes time to harvest, fruit is checked to see if it's ripe. At first, people just squeeze a little. If grapes are hard then it's not time to harvest. When they are a soft, one is picked and tasted. It might still be tart, so the rest are left on the vine for a little while longer. The same thing happens with apricots, peaches, cherries, plums and so on. Apples are a little different - just watch the color then taste to see when it's okay to pick. Once the okay is given, then people start harvesting.

Mark 4:26–29 ESV. And he said, "The kingdom of God is as if a man should scatter seed on the ground. He sleeps and rises night and day, and the seed sprouts and grows; he knows not how. The earth produces by itself, first the blade, then the ear, then the full grain in the ear. But when the grain is ripe, at once he puts in the sickle, because the harvest has come."

This is the reason Jesus did not know the day or the hour. It didn't mean He had no knowledge, it meant that He is timing the harvest differently than by a clock or a calendar. He waits for the "ripe time" when He and the Father agree that it's time to go.

Matthew 24:36-37 NASB95. [36]"But of that day and hour no one knows, not even the angels of heaven, nor the Son, but the Father alone. [37]"For the coming of the Son of Man will be just like the days of Noah.

Prophecies are not intended to be a detailed account of every tiny action (although sometimes they are). Mostly they are broad brush pictures and event oriented. The main thrust of most of God's prophetic messages is "repent," so enough of the message is given to encourage repentance or give hope. Specific times are rarely given down to the day or the hour. The trigger will be an event that develops apart from being tied to a day or hour.

In other words, knowing when something is going to happen might be a result of a culmination of *events* or behavior rather than on clocks or calendars. Humans are as predictable as ripening fruit, so He just adds more sun, drops rain occasionally, and even sometimes throws on some fertilizer to coordinate events with His timing. Sometimes He directs certain things, but most of the time all He has to do is let us go. This is what is meant by the phrase "when the harvest is fully ripe." Harvest happens by the weather, fertilizer, water and ground conditions.

Revelation 14:15 ESV. And another angel came out of the temple, calling with a loud voice to him who sat on the cloud, "Put in your sickle, and reap, for the hour to reap has come, for the harvest of the earth is fully ripe."

God is not willing that any perish, but wants all to come to repentance. One of these days the harvest will be ready, and He will gather the wheat while the grapes are thrown into the winepress of His wrath.

The Old World Order

An important thing to understand about our world is that all the unbelievers and anti-God spiritual powers are geared toward the deceiver getting his kingdom (or destroying God's). This is the mother of all conspiracies. The New World Order we've been hearing about for years is just another name for it. It's actually an old world order, started when the deceiver rebelled against God.

Luke 11:23 ESV. Whoever is not with me is against me, and whoever does not gather with me scatters.

Every invention, technological advancement, and major political move is for the express purpose of setting up the final try at a world government by the deceiver. The telephone, computer, TV, internet, airplanes, the automobile, and so on were developed so that the deceiver could run his own worldwide kingdom. The conspiracy behind all other conspiracies is that political systems also were developed by the deceiver, but we are not to fear.

Isaiah 8:11–13 ESV. For the LORD spoke thus to me with his strong hand upon me, and warned me not to walk in the way of this people, saying: "Do not call conspiracy all that this people calls conspiracy, and do not fear what they fear, nor be in dread. But the LORD of hosts, him you shall honor as holy. Let him be your fear, and let him be your dread.

Every story science fiction writers tell pushes the idea that more technology (or knowledge) means better and longer lives. This is a hollow hope, because knowledge without God will never produce the paradise desired. Nifty devices are only going to develop enough for the deceiver to make a try for a globe-spanning kingdom. Faster-than-light travel and colonizing other planets are dreams of the deceiver too, but his dreams will be dashed at Armageddon. Sure, technology is used for good purposes, and it's not inherently evil. But ultimately, the inventions have another purpose than the "good" uses.

Increasing communications, data processing, and travel will make it easier for the deceiver and his minions the beast and the antichrist to make a try for world domination. They can't be everywhere present like God can, so they need worldwide communications. Flesh and blood can't travel as fast as spirits can, so the deceiver's subjects will need jets and cars. The unholy trinity can't keep track of everyone on the planet without computers because they don't know everything like God does. These things are what makes this time in history so much different from any other, and have brought the dream of the deceiver closer to reality.

The deceiver has been running many of the world's kingdoms or countries since the beginning. He keeps trying to build a world kingdom. The second-to-last try at a world government will be different in that it will all be out in the open. Unbelievers are being groomed to make the transition easier.

Grooming can refer to the process of making oneself clean and presentable such as combing hair or putting on makeup. The word is also used to describe preparing someone for a position or task, such as a political office. There is a third use of the word for when a predator is preparing a target for a heinous act, such as when a homosexual grooms a young male for a sexual partner.

One of the main methods homosexuals use to make more homosexuals are to find a troubled youth, show sympathy for his or her problems, and give gifts of money or access to special activities. Slowly the target is brainwashed into anti-god thinking, and when the young man or woman develops trust in the predator, the predator lures him or her into sexual sin.

Synonyms for grooming are educate, coach, train, and tutor. The word is used here to describe how the population of the world is being groomed for the arrival of the little horn or beast and his attempt at a kingdom.

The methods used by sexual predators are remarkably similar to the grooming methods used on the world population today because they come from the same source. The deceiver is the originator of grooming methods as we can see from the exchange in the Garden of Eden. His goal with grooming is to get people to reject God and worship (or obey) the deceiver instead. We can see some of the deceiver's methods at work when he tried to groom Jesus by offering Him the kingdoms of the world; tempting Him to act on His own apart from the Father's will (Matthew 4).

Matthew 4:8–9 ESV. Again, the devil took him to a very high mountain and showed him all the kingdoms of the world and their glory. And he said to him, "All these I will give you, if you will fall down and worship me."

Movies, television and music play a large role in the grooming of the populace. Sexual immorality is portrayed as not having any penalties, and if there are a few downsides such as disease or abortion, they are passed off as "normal" or just bad luck. Love is redefined as emotion (or sex) only: whatever feelings are involved are paramount, and what God says about right and wrong is not even part of the picture.

Superheroes started out just having different abilities; now they are coming out of the closet as gods. I'm sure that part of the deceiver's deception will include the idea that the "next evolutionary step" for mankind is super powers, as long as people worship him. Maybe it will also include the temptation to transfer the consciousness into a machine and live forever, which is discussed later.

If you've ever wondered at the push for globalism, wonder no more. The deceiver needs to erase, or mostly erase, the effects of the Tower of Babel. To get his worldwide kingdom, he has to get rid of country borders, language differences, and any form of independent thought or government, such as that in the United States. He doesn't want anybody independent - he wants all of us dependant on him; otherwise known as obedient slaves.

The United States in the Bible

Jeremiah 17:13 ESV. O LORD, the hope of Israel, all who forsake you shall be put to shame; those who turn away from you shall be written in the earth, for they have forsaken the LORD, the fountain of living water.

Some people are puzzled that the United States doesn't show up in the Bible anywhere. Since we are arguably one of the most powerful nations ever, if not the most powerful, how come we're not mentioned in Scripture like most of the others? Actually, the U.S. is mentioned; very prominently too. You just have to know your history. It is part of the old Roman Empire, the west leg of Nebuchadnezzar's statue (Daniel 3).

The Roman Empire split into two parts (or was always sort of that way) around three to four hundred years after the birth of the Christ. It was roughly split between the west part (what is now Europe and North Africa) and the east (Russia, the Balkans, Turkey, Asia, Greece, Israel, Egypt). Rome ruled the west leg, and Constantinople (which was supposed to answer to Rome) the east leg. It went back and forth for a while, but that's basically how it played out.

A side note here that might be important is that both Rome and Constantinople were built on seven hills. Constantinople was the birthplace of the Church (Council of Nicea 325 A. D.) and both cities were Roman, although Byzantium or Constantinople had a heavy Greek influence. Modern Istanbul is the name of Constantinople now, because the Muslims conquered it (after a number of attempts) in 1453 A. D. Emperors in Byzantium, or Constantinople, with the Church, ruled a huge empire in the east for perhaps a thousand years after Rome declined. Whether seated in Rome or Constantinople, and regardless of how many hills they are on, the Church has a long history of killing those who disagree with them. This factors into the prophecies of Babylon the Great in Revelation 18 and 19.

So from Europe (the west part of the Roman Empire) and Africa most of the settlers of the United States have come. Take a good look at our culture and compare it to Roman culture. We have laws and customs handed down from the Romans (who also borrowed from Greeks and others). They built roads and aqueducts that stand to this day. We build roads (many built on trails and roads from our colonial era) and large water distribution systems, which have also lasted.

Romans liked to build huge stadiums where athletes entertained the crowds. Gee, that doesn't sound familiar, does it? Most of our major cities have huge taxpayer-funded coliseums, some actually called 'coliseums,' where athletes perform for the masses. Rome tolerated any religion and incorporated many of the pagan practices into their own. Our presidents have had Muslim Ramadan meals in the White House and Churches are full of pagan bits and pieces.

The Roman Empire rotted from the inside out; so too is the United States (and most of the world). Baby killing is legal and applauded. Homosexuals, non-binary and many other sexually immoral people are honored, and our no-justice system lets murderers go free while locking up alleged tax law violators.

Politicians spend millions on elections and end their time in office wealthier than when they started. Like their ancient Roman senator counterparts, most of today's politicians are corrupt influence peddlers more concerned with pandering for the next election than doing anything to reverse our slide into the pit. All they need are some togas and peeled grapes and the comparison would be complete.

It's easy to see that the United States is just an extension of the old Roman Empire. That empire might've declined and fallen, but their kids live on and keep the family customs alive and well, at least for a while. The United States had a chance to be better (and stay better), but we turned our backs on God, and now the proverbial chickens are coming home to roost. The United States may be the most powerful nation ever, but that doesn't mean a drop of water in a bucket-full to the Maker of the heavens and the earth.

Isaiah 59:1–4 ESV. Behold, the LORD's hand is not shortened, that it cannot save, or his ear dull, that it cannot hear; but your iniquities have made a separation between you and your God, and your sins have hidden his face from you so that he does not hear. For your hands are defiled with blood and your fingers with iniquity; your lips have spoken lies; your tongue mutters wickedness. No one enters suit justly; no one goes to law honestly; they rely on empty pleas, they speak lies, they conceive mischief and give birth to iniquity.

We can't just blame the baby killing, toga wearing people that we now call "elites" however. We have to blame ourselves and our complacent, apathetic attitudes. The elites have been allowed to get away with their crimes for too long because we are just too comfortable and "tolerant." The Church is an accessory to the crimes, because they commit the greatest crime of all: claiming to teach the Bible, then twisting and changing and deliberately misinterpreting His Words to give themselves permission to follow the flesh. The world just follows suit.

The Church in the Bible

It's curious that Jesus wonders whether He'll find faith on the earth or not when He returns.

Luke 18:7–8 ESV. And will not God give justice to his elect, who cry to him day and night? Will he delay long over them? I tell you, he will give justice to them speedily. Nevertheless, when the Son of Man comes, will he find faith on earth?"

The person expecting a rapture before the Tribulation might say that, well, Jesus won't find faith on the earth when He comes at the end of the Tribulation because all believers are taken away at the beginning. Other persons believing the Church will eventually conquer the earth have a real problem. Why would Jesus have doubts about finding faith on the earth if the Church has converted everybody? Neither idea makes sense according to a plain reading of the Word.

As mentioned before, translations of the Bible into English make you think that the Church, as we see it today, is in there. But it isn't. There is no Church in the Bible at all, except for Mystery Religion Babylon in Revelation 18 which will be explained later. None of the variations of Church we see in history or modern times are mentioned anywhere in the Bible text. The Church has grabbed hold of the "wool" of some of the Bible to cover their ultimate anti-God behavior.

Remember that the word translated "church" in English versions is the Greek word transliterated as *ekklesia*, meaning "gathering" or "assembly" or "congregation." It's just a group of people. In the Greek translation of the Old Testament (Septuagint), the same word is used for gatherings such as the assembly of Israel at Mount Sinai in Deuteronomy 9:10 (translating the Hebrew word for assembly which is *qahal*). The modern Church steals the word, translates it by the English word "church," and claims they follow the Christ. But they don't, as a group, do what He says. This is exactly the attitude exhibited by the Pharisees and Sadducees right before they crucified God's Anointed. All you have to do to confirm that is compare Church behavior with the Bible.

The Catholic Church (catholic means "universal"), founded by the Roman emperor Constantine around 325 A. D. and lasting until now, was the only Christian game in town for quite a while in the past. It has drifted so far from the Bible that it has become something other than what God intends (if it ever was what God intended). Reform attempts are squashed without mercy, and the Catholic Church government is responsible for the death of many real believers. However, they are not the only ones to blame for getting away from God's original intent.

The Protestants started with good intentions trying to reform the Church beginning around the 1200's to 1400's, but over the centuries, they too have drifted from God's Word until they are likewise unrecognizable compared to the Bible. They "protest" the Catholic Church, but other than a few cosmetic changes, they do the very same things the Catholics do that are not found in the Bible. More details of these concepts involving all sections of the visible Church and its Nicolaitan leaders is in the book <u>Nicolaitan: Lords of Hypocrisy</u> if you want to know more about them. They lord their position, power and education over the "lay" people and teach as doctrine the commandments of men.

Matthew 15:7–9 ESV. You hypocrites! Well did Isaiah prophesy of you, when he said: " 'This people honors me with their lips, but their heart is far from me; in vain do they worship me, teaching as doctrines the commandments of men.' "

Think of the Church as being similar to Israel. The nation of Israel in the Bible was supposed to belong to God, yet by and large was mostly idolatrous. There were (and are) some God-followers here and there, and sometimes they did what God said as a nation, but mostly they had the name and didn't follow through. The Church can be described in the same way. They claim the name but they're just playing a lip-service game.

The Church will be in the Tribulation, all parts nearly intact and following the beast along with many other pagan religions. As a whole, the Church does not follow the Word; it just puts on a show with wool-costumes. This is one reason Jesus warns us to beware of the leaven of the Pharisees, which is hypocrisy (Luke 12:1). Pharisaical leaven has worked its way throughout the Church in a way that makes the whole thing rotten, just as it was (and is) with Israel. Faith is a combination of trust in God and obedience to what He says, so it's no surprise Jesus questions finding faith on the earth at His return.

Families of Man

Deuteronomy 32:8 ESV. When the Most High gave to the nations their inheritance, when he divided mankind, he fixed the borders of the peoples according to the number of the sons of God.

God divided the people of the earth at the Tower of Babel into families or tribes or nations (Genesis 10 and others). This is important because the names of nations or countries as we call them today have changed here and there. But the people that compose the nations are still the same genetic family descended from those mentioned in Genesis 10, and share the same characteristics.

Canaanites, for instance, especially the seven tribes in the area promised to Jacob and sons, had very marked wicked and worthless practices. They were terribly bad and there was no hope of change. The only answer for their way of Godless living was to excise the corruption and send it to hell. Apparently, they not only practiced every kind of sexual immorality (Sodom and Gomorrah were two of their cities), murder and theft were a way of life, and they did things like sacrifice their children to worthless, made up gods in hideous ways. Kind of like much of the world today. So they were erased from the earth, like Sodom and Gomorrah and the people in the Flood.

This is important for studying prophecy because nations in prophecies are usually referred to by names that were given long ago and are not used much in modern times. Ezekiel for instance (Ezekiel 27:13, 32:26, 38, and 39), centuries after Genesis 10, receives information about some of the nations mentioned before. Specifically he's told about Magog, Tubal and Meshech who were all children of Japheth (Yaphet), one of the sons of Noah. Each of these went on to found large tribes or nations. But the future history doesn't end with Ezekiel. John in Revelation also mentions nations that are at the four corners of the earth, Gog and Magog, to gather them for battle at the end of the millennial phase of the kingdom of heaven (Revelation 20:8).

Ezekiel tells us about a major war between Gog and Israel that has not happened even now in chapters 38 and 39 of his book. God will put hooks into the jaws of Gog, chief prince of Meshech and Tubal, to draw him down to destruction. This is probably referring to a fallen angel who is actually the spiritual power behind Gog. Other nations such as Persia (modern day Turkey and surrounding area), Cush and Put (northern Africa) will join in and launch a major attack on the mountains of Israel. This appears to be the battle of Armageddon at the end of the Tribulation.

The point is that the nations mentioned are not called by the same names in the present day. Gog and Magog, Tubal and Meshech are "far north" of Israel which identifies them as the families or tribes we now call Turkey and Greece. God sees the nations as He has divided them, and prophecies are given using the ancient family names. John tells us also about tribes.

Revelation 1:7 ESV. Behold, he is coming with the clouds, and every eye will see him, even those who pierced him, and all tribes of the earth will wail on account of him. Even so. Amen.

The words "all" and "of the earth" plainly refers back to Genesis 10, as well as the Tower of Babel, and includes everyone. John knew that families of the earth still existed. Modern man might not know who belongs to which family, but the original tribes are still around. Jesus speaks of them at the writing of the Revelation the same way He did in Genesis. In prophecies of the future, He still refers to the families of man in the same ways.

The borders of nations have changed, and peoples are mixed together genetically somewhat (probably illustrated as the feet of clay and iron mixed in Daniel 2). In our time this makes it harder to determine who is who when we are trying to understand prophecy. But it is possible to determine families by the way people behave.

For instance, as already mentioned, Canaanites were known for their wickedness in sacrificing babies to false gods. In modern times, we don't find much of this. Or do we? The priests of false gods wore special robes or other forms of clothing. They used special instruments to kill, and had special religious rites to follow. Now the question is, "Are abortionists a modern version of Canaanite priests?" They wear special robes and other clothing, have special washings for preparation, and perform their wicked actions in special facilities as they sacrifice babies to appease their god of convenience or the Goddess of Reason. If this doesn't sound like Canaanites, then you are easily fooled. Forms may change, clothing might differ, family trees might be obscure, but actions are a dead giveaway.

Believers know Hitler, Stalin, Mao and others were in the atheist or anti-God family because of the way they behaved. Hitler was a churchgoer, and supported the German Lutheran church for a while (as long as it suited his purpose), but that doesn't mean he followed God (or that the Lutheran Church followed God). His actions against the Jews in the Holocaust revealed him as a tool of the deceiver, and atheists make excellent tools. Other dictators and despots reveal themselves as "no god" or anti-god people by similar actions, even if they don't claim the name atheist. Usually they target the Jews, but they also end up hammering all people of faith too, just like the little horn will.

The people of the beast will be known by behaving in the same way as he does. To prove it, they will gladly take his mark. This mark will be an outward sign of an inward condition, taken freely and openly because they are part of the family. It won't be a vaccination, a chip under the skin, or a replacement for a credit card. It will not be accepted by accident, but will be a mark of honor to the recipients who swear allegiance to the beast, the deceiver, and the kingdom for which they stand. The mark will stamp all of his people with a signature telling everyone the exact nature of the family tree to which they belong.

What is the World?

Genesis 41:57 ESV. Moreover, all the earth came to Egypt to Joseph to buy grain, because the famine was severe over all the earth.

Revelation 12:9 ESV. And the great dragon was thrown down, that ancient serpent, who is called the devil and Satan, the deceiver of the whole world—he was thrown down to the earth, and his angels were thrown down with him.

When we read in the Bible something about the whole earth or the whole world, it does not necessarily mean every individual. Sometimes it does, as in the case of Genesis 11:1 and the incident at the Tower of Babel.

Genesis 11:1 ESV. Now the whole earth had one language and the same words.

Sometimes it doesn't. In modern English, we might say instead something like "the world over" for an experience (such as a famine or disease) that is widespread but not affecting every single person. In the Genesis 41:57 reference, however, does the writer mean to say the famine was on every continent? It is possible that this was the writer's intended meaning, but that would also mean that people from every continent came to Egypt to buy grain. It could mean that people were not spread out as much.

Or it might be that at the time, the continents were connected and people could walk from one to the other. This is gleaned from a small, easy-to-miss reference from just after the flood. It seems that at the time of Shem's great-grandsons, Peleg in particular (born about 101 years after the flood with a name that means "division"), the earth was divided.

Genesis 10:25 ESV. To Eber were born two sons: the name of the one was Peleg, for in his days the earth was divided, and his brother's name was Joktan.

There are at least two possibilities for what is meant by "divided." One is that it could refer to the Tower of Babel, mentioned next in the text (Genesis 11). Or it could be that this is a hint that, for a time after the flood, the continents were connected. As the seas perhaps rebounded to higher levels, maybe due to ice caps melting, the land bridges were inundated and the continents separated by water.

If "all the earth" came to buy grain from Egypt, and that means "every person," then many of the trips were very long and made by very hungry people, which isn't likely. Even if "all the earth" or every person living at the time did in fact come to buy grain from Egypt, that *still* means there were a lot of long trips by very hungry people. The point is that "all the earth" does not always mean each and every person living on the planet.

For another instance, in our Revelation 12:9 verse, the "deceiver of the whole world" does not mean each and every person is deceived. It is more obviously a general term for "people everywhere" or "the world over" or something of the sort, because believers are not deceived.

Matthew 24:24 ESV. For false christs and false prophets will arise and perform great signs and wonders, so as to lead astray, if possible, even the elect.

To "lead astray" is the same as "deceive," and according to Jesus, it is not possible for the elect to be deceived. So when we get to some passages in Revelation concerning the "whole earth" and similar phrases, they don't mean every single person. The passages more likely are speaking of every corner of the earth, or perhaps even the known world at the time, in a general sense. If the phrase is limited to the known world, that would be around the Mediterranean and throughout the Fertile Crescent. See the section in chapter five titled **The Hot Spot** for additional information.

Nations and Nature

Speaking of families, most of the nations of the world are prominent in prophecy. Few of them have operated (or are operating) according to God's Word, many have attacked or threatened Israel over the centuries, and every one of them is included in the Tribulation festivities when they commence. Most of them are compared to beasts in various prophecies, and will receive the brunt of God's anger in the Day of the Lord.

Isaiah 34:1–2 ESV. Draw near, O nations, to hear, and give attention, O peoples! Let the earth hear, and all that fills it; the world, and all that comes from it. For the LORD is enraged against all the nations, and furious against all their host; he has devoted them to destruction, has given them over for slaughter.

Again, the happenings at the tower of Babel way back in Genesis (about 4,000 years ago) play a central role in history, prophecy and the events of Revelation. As mentioned before, at Babel God split the families or tribes of the world at the time into groups that have developed into what we now call nations. Each group not only had its own language but its own way of thinking and viewing the world. If the groups were just split by language, they would have worked out some method of communicating.

Even now, if two people meet that don't speak the same language, they will eventually work out some sort of limited communication method. That's why more than language separated the groups; it was also ways of thinking and probably feeling too. Add in natural suspicion, hatred, envy and the like and these would harden the divisions. Interestingly, John seven times (Revelation 5:9, 7:9, 10:11, 11:9, 13:7, 14:6 and 17:15) refers to languages (also see the word "tongues") as part of the dividing line between nations or tribes and peoples.

Revelation 10:10–11 ESV. And I took the little scroll from the hand of the angel and ate it. It was sweet as honey in my mouth, but when I had eaten it my stomach was made bitter. And I was told, "You must again prophesy about many peoples and nations and languages and kings."

This is important when looking at symbols such as the beast in Revelation 17. The great prostitute sits on many waters (the nations), but also on a scarlet beast with seven heads and ten horns. The heads are perhaps best understood as people groups, nations, kingdoms or governments divided by language. The horns are rulers who are in charge of parts of these tribes; maybe even specific nations. The tribes in Genesis 10 are still around according to God, and this is one way that He sees them.

The tribes or languages gradually became nations, and a number of what we see as nations today still have a common bond because of the tribe of which they are part. Tribes and even nations have common physical characteristics such as facial features and skin color. The tribes have also developed their own what we call "culture" with ancient traditions, mythology, foods, and so on.

You may not know that the modern country of Pakistan was created and split off from India because of Muslim troublemakers. The problems in Serbia, Bosnia and Kosovo are between different tribes with different religions but the same behavior (mostly between Muslims and others). The so-called Palestinians are really the remains of people groups from Syria, Jordan and surrounding countries who tried to move into Israel and keep it from becoming a nation around 1948. When Israel was born anyway, they tried to flee back to their home countries but their home countries wouldn't take them back, wanting to use them as a wedge against Israel. Adherents of Islam claim it is a religion of peace, yet as a group, it has consistently been at war since Mohammed created it.

Some tribes like warmer climates and migrated to southern locations, while others preferred cooler climates and wandered north. Some are more adventurous and some are more inclined to stay put. The nations or tribes even have their own temperaments. Some are belligerent and warlike; others are more likely to get along with each other, and some have merged.

Throw the deceiver into this mix, and most nations not wanting to follow God instead follow the deceiver. Some of the groups, such as the ancient Canaanites, were more pliable and responsive to the enticements offered by the father of lies. They plunged so far into corruption so fast that God surgically removed them (remember Sodom and Gomorrah). Some nations, such as Babylon, He allowed to grow and conquer others.

Over time, however, the deceiver has wanted to overcome the problems God created for him at Babel and get everyone back together. He wants a kingdom ruling everybody, not just a few stray nations here or there. The evil one wants it all, but having so many different groups, languages and cultures has made it tough. This is one of the reasons God scrambled things in the first place.

The deceiver almost has what he wants now. The confusion from the Tower of Babel is smoothed over, with English as pretty much a common language the world over. Such things as cars, airplanes, TV, and the Internet have homogenized the culture, and politically the elites are trying to erase borders so they can rule everybody and make a lot of money. Like Babylon in Revelation.

These ideas come into focus when looking at, for instance, Revelation 13 and the appearance of the beast. According to verses one through three of that chapter, the beast rises out of the sea, which is symbolic of nations in general, probably those around the Mediterranean. It has seven heads, which are the kingdoms of seven tribes that have now developed into nations.

In Revelation 17, we get some more information on this subject from a conversation John has with an angel explaining the Prostitute. The scarlet beast providing the ride for the Prostitute (meaning support and cooperation) "was, and is not, and is about to rise from the bottomless pit and go to destruction." The word "about" as in "about to rise" we can also understand as "is on his way to rising" or even "going to rise."

If we look at the beast as a kingdom, this statement makes sense. The deceiver keeps trying to make a kingdom to challenge or replace God's kingdom, and he hasn't had much success except temporarily. So he "had a kingdom with one strong king, but doesn't have one now," perhaps because he was knocked out of heaven at the time, "and is on his way to rise again" (with a strong king called the beast). The deceiver is the power behind all the world's kingdoms, but he is most effective with a single leader to control who isn't hampered by others in a government.

When we contemplate the heads of the scarlet beast, the angel says "they are also seven kings, five of whom have fallen, one is, and the other has not yet come, and when he does come he must remain only a little while." A king and a kingdom are synonymous, even though there may be several kings over one kingdom.

Again, looking at the heads as kingdoms, and knowing that kings are equated to kingdoms, the heads represent the kingdoms as described several times by Daniel. Five of the kingdoms at the time John was seeing the vision have come and gone. Depending on how you count them, it could be Babel, Assyria, Babylon, Persia/Media, and Greece. One exists at the time of John, which might be the Roman kingdom, except it didn't have a single dictator/king. The head or kingdom to come, which remains only a little while, will be the final try by the deceiver using the beast or little horn.

The ten horns are also authorities, kings, individual nations or heads of governments coming out of the seven families or tribes. One of the heads has a mortal wound but is miraculously healed, which in other texts we find out is the political leader the Bible calls the bad shepherd, the little horn and the beast. This leader is also representative of the entire beast or coalition of nations. John lists traits of the coalition which has parts of the former nations or tribes included such as the speed of a leopard (remember from Daniel's visions this is Greece), feet like a bear's (Medes and

Persians or modern day Turkey), and mouth like a lion (remnants of Babylon, perhaps including Iraq and Iran).

Knowing the history recorded for us in the Bible, we get a better grasp of the visions not only of John in the Revelation, but also the prophets in general.

4 The Apple of God's Eye

Zechariah 2:8 ESV. For thus said the LORD of hosts, after his glory sent me to the nations who plundered you, for he who touches you touches the apple of his eye:

As you might've guessed from the pages read so far and those you've read in His Book, Israel is and always has been God's plan and focus. They have not always participated with Him, and He's had to judge them on too many occasions. But as a group and as the point people for His kingdom on earth, He has not let them go. When God called Israel out of Egypt and set up housekeeping in their midst, it wasn't just a sometime thing. As Paul says later, God doesn't go back on His Word or change His plans just because He has to deal with some obstinate people here and there.

Romans 11:29 ESV. For the gifts and the calling of God are irrevocable.

God gave a system of government to Israel (and all children of Israel such as we) centered around the Tabernacle (later the Temple) and the priesthood. In Leviticus 23, we are given holidays by God, not just for some fun every so often, but for learning His ways and participating in rehearsals of prophetic events.

Physical or visible Israel is made up of children of Jacob as well as those who have chosen to convert to Judaism. However, just like the Church, not all of these people actually follow God or do what He says. Frequently there is more loyalty to genetics or religion than there is to God and His Word. Not all who are descended from Israel are Israel as Paul says. Those who commit to live the Words of God are members of the Israel olive tree, regardless of genetics or doctrines of men.

The people at the Tower of Babel (egged on by the deceiver no doubt) wanted to make an eternal name by building a structure they thought would keep them united and keep their kingdom going in defiance of God. God, on the other hand, is making a name for Himself by building believers into a kingdom united by His Spirit of love. This kingdom is also called the Body of Christ, the Bride, the elect, and so on.

The Church is man-made, similar to the Tower of Babel. It is built by men for men and with man at the center, having the same goal as the Tower builders and not all that different from visible Israel.

Genesis 11:4 ESV. Then they said, "Come, let us build ourselves a city and a tower with its top in the heavens, and let us make a name for ourselves, lest we be dispersed over the face of the whole earth."

The Tower was usurpation by those people of God's will and an attempt to replace His kingdom with their own. Israel has done the same thing with Judaism, and The Church has created a kingdom with their doctrines of men too. Each positions itself as "the chosen people" without actual, unqualified submission to God. Both groups excel in doing what is right in their own eyes rather than eating and drinking the living oracles to sustain the soul.

The Church has built a monument to itself for a name and for unity, in similar fashion as those who built the Tower. You'll find many pastors even promote this unity (unity of man) by enforcing a strict code of adherence to doctrines of men. These doctrines were made up by those who built The Church (statements of faith, writings of the "church fathers," Creeds, Confessions, etc.). Some of those things are not bad, but many get in the way of simply reading and doing the Word. Judaism has history and the Talmud which functions in the same way.

The Church claims to follow God, and even uses His Book. But just like the Pharisees, it has covered over the simple teachings of God's living oracles with a smothering collection of the philosophies of men. Towers built by men are empty, bereft of the obedience of the gospel and the fruit of the Spirit. At the very best, leaders dole out only tiny slices of God's life giving Word, keeping followers malnourished and unable to reach full maturity in Christ.

Hate for Israel

Obadiah 10–11 ESV. Because of the violence done to your brother Jacob, shame shall cover you, and you shall be cut off forever. On the day that you stood aloof, on the day that strangers carried off his wealth and foreigners entered his gates and cast lots for Jerusalem, you were like one of them.

A sure-fire mark of the deceiver and his minions is hate for Israel. The deceiver hates God, and he has it in for Israel because God chooses them as the focus for His plans on earth. In the past, the deceiver tried to destroy Israel because they were the apple of God's eye, and because she was going to give birth to our Messiah Jesus the Christ. The reason the deceiver still hates Israel is that they are still in existence, just as God promised, and are the focus of the Messiah's coming kingdom. He wants to derail God's plans, but just can't seem to get a handle on victory.

The Church thinks that they are the focus of God's promises. This isn't true because the Church isn't even in the Bible (only in translations made by churches), and they do not follow what it says. Individuals who accept the sacrifice of Jesus and do what He says are grafted into an existing olive tree consisting of all redeemed people everywhere. Judaism and The Church in contrast are constructs of man, self-appointed to speak for God and doing a very poor job. God's olive tree or kingdom is alive and well, and we are still the focus along with physical Israel.

Hate for Israel is evident all over the world in modern times. Most Muslim peoples claim that Israel consists of "people of the Book" as they say also of Christians. But in actuality, most of them hate and actively work to destroy both (although many of them have recently started to leave Islam). Democrats (and many Republicans that act like Democrats) in the United States routinely vote for aid to Israel-hating countries and try to make agreements that force Israel to give up more and more land. This hate will be the driving emotion in attacking Israel on the Day of the Lord, culminating in the wipeout at Armageddon.

Obadiah 15 ESV. For the day of the LORD is near upon all the nations. As you have done, it shall be done to you; your deeds shall return on your own head.

The Adulteress Redeemed

Hosea 1:10 ESV. Yet the number of the children of Israel shall be like the sand of the sea, which cannot be measured or numbered. And in the place where it was said to them, "You are not my people," it shall be said to them, "Children of the living God."

God hasn't forgotten Israel, nor has He permanently rejected her. She has always been the foundation for His kingdom on earth, and will always be so. He's had some issues with Israel from time to time, and chastised them accordingly, but will not forsake her forever. She may not embrace the position by doing what God says all the time, but Israel's faithlessness does not mean that God is faithless.

2 Samuel 7:23–24 ESV. And who is like your people Israel, the one nation on earth whom God went to redeem to be his people, making himself a name and doing for them great and awesome things by driving out before your people, whom you redeemed for yourself from Egypt, a nation and its gods? And you established for yourself your people Israel to be your people forever. And you, O LORD, became their God.

God's continuing work with Israel doesn't mean that everything Israel does is okay with God. They have in the past, and still do, fall short of what God requires on a regular basis (don't we all). "Not all who are descended from Israel belong to Israel, and not all are children of Abraham because they are his offspring" as Paul says in Romans 9:6-8. The people who do all of what God says are Israel. This is "believing Israel" or believers.

In the Bible, Jerusalem is called nearly everything from the Holy City and the place where God puts His name, to Sodom and Gomorrah or Sodom and Egypt (Revelation 11:8). The city earns these names alternately either because of righteousness in following God's Law, or wickedness because they turn from it.

Jeremiah 23:14 ESV. But in the prophets of Jerusalem I have seen a horrible thing: they commit adultery and walk in lies; they strengthen the hands of evildoers, so that no one turns from his evil; all of them have become like Sodom to me, and its inhabitants like Gomorrah."

Revelation 11:7–8 ESV. And when they have finished their testimony, the beast that rises from the bottomless pit will make war on them and conquer them and kill them, and their dead bodies will lie in the street of the great city that symbolically is called Sodom and Egypt, where their Lord was crucified.

Israel has different names depending on what they are doing in relation to God's Law. If they follow God's voice and do what He says, they live in a land of promise flowing with milk and honey. If they don't follow God's Word, they are warned, and if they keep ignoring God, they are "not my people" (Hosea 1:10).

Sadly, visible Israel in the past consistently slid into idolatry and disobedience. God finally had to execute judgment on them, destroy the land and send them into captivity in other nations. But happily, Ezekiel delivers a prophecy of dry bones coming to life that speaks of Israel's return to the land and ultimate blessing.

Ezekiel 37:4–6 ESV. Then he said to me, "Prophesy over these bones, and say to them, O dry bones, hear the word of the LORD. Thus says the Lord GOD to these bones: Behold, I will cause breath to enter you, and you shall live. And I will lay sinews upon you, and will cause flesh to come upon you, and cover you with skin, and put breath in you, and you shall live, and you shall know that I am the Lord."

Miraculously, those of us living today have seen this literally begin to come to fruition. Israel is established as a nation in her own land again, against impossible odds. No other nation, tribe or other group of people in history can claim to spring back into existence after being scattered for centuries. We are seeing the development of Israel as bones, sinews and flesh are knit together and covered with skin. We are still waiting for the breath of God to enter them and complete the resurgence. This will probably be after the unbelievers are winnowed out.

Isaiah 1:27–28 ESV. Zion shall be redeemed by justice, and those in her who repent, by righteousness. But rebels and sinners shall be broken together, and those who forsake the Lord shall be consumed.

The "rebels and sinners" will not only be cleaned out of the nations, but also out of Israel, with Israel judged first.

Ezekiel 20:33–39 ESV. "As I live, declares the Lord God, surely with a mighty hand and an outstretched arm and with wrath poured out I will be king over you. I will bring you out from the peoples and gather you out of the countries where you are scattered, with a mighty hand and an outstretched arm, and with wrath poured out. And I will bring you into the wilderness of the peoples, and there I will enter into judgment with you face to face. As I entered into judgment with your fathers in the wilderness of the land of Egypt, so I will enter into judgment with you, declares the Lord God. I will make you pass under the rod, and I will bring you into the bond of the covenant. I will purge out the rebels from among you, and those who transgress against me. I will bring them out of the land where they sojourn, but they shall not enter the land of Israel. Then you will know that I am the Lord. "As for you, O house of Israel, thus says the Lord God: Go serve every one of you his idols, now and hereafter, if you will not listen to me; but my holy name you shall no more profane with your gifts and your idols.

"Passing under the rod" is a figure of speech for discipline and sorting or counting. A shepherd has a rod or staff, and he uses it to separate and count sheep. They need separating in this case because there are some bad ones mixed in to the flock. As God says, He will purge from Israel the rebels and those who transgress against Him.

It's a little hard to say when this will happen. Jesus says in Matthew 25:31-46 that He will separate sheep and goats from "all the nations" after He is on the throne of David, and John in Revelation 20:11-15 tells us about a separation at the "great white throne." Zechariah 14:5 speaks of a valley formed by Jesus splitting the Mount of Olives, through which people will "flee to the valley of my mountains," implying some sort of separation also. These actions will probably be at different times for different reasons. Suffice it to say that those who persevere in following God will inherit eternal life, while those who decide they don't want all of God won't have to stay with Him.

All people who are truly part of Israel will return to God, and all her remaining living believers along with resurrected dead believers will be collected and returned to the land. There is a little bit of confusion because physical Israel, or "Jewish people," in modern times are the only ones who are called Israel and who think of themselves as Israel. But God's kingdom is not based on genetics alone. He is working with the descendants of Jacob to bring out a people and a kingdom whose whole heart is devoted to Him. Genetic Israel can certainly be a part, but only as each one repents and is reborn.

Hosea 14:1–2 ESV. Return, O Israel, to the LORD your God, for you have stumbled because of your iniquity. Take with you words and return to the LORD; say to him, "Take away all iniquity; accept what is good, and we will pay with bulls the vows of our lips.

The restoration of all Israel will result in endless blessings because of the "prince" or leader that will dare approach God. This prince is none other than Yeshua haMashiach or Jesus the Christ.

Jeremiah 30:18–22 ESV. "Thus says the LORD: Behold, I will restore the fortunes of the tents of Jacob and have compassion on his dwellings; the city shall be rebuilt on its mound, and the palace shall stand where it used to be. Out of them shall come songs of thanksgiving, and the voices of those who celebrate. I will multiply them, and they shall not be few; I will make them honored, and they shall not be small. Their children shall be as they were of old, and their congregation shall be established before me, and I will punish all who oppress them. Their prince shall be one of themselves; their ruler shall come out from their midst; I will make him draw near, and he shall approach me, for who would dare of himself to approach me? declares the LORD. And you shall be my people, and I will be your God."

Part of this prophecy was fulfilled when Israel returned from exile during the time of Nehemiah. More is being fulfilled in our present time, except such things as the palace standing where it used to be and accepting their prince. But Jerusalem will be rebuilt even better than it is now during the 1,000 year reign of Yeshua. At the end of that time, we'll get the final, best and perfect version which is the New Jerusalem coming down from heaven.

Jeremiah 31:38–40 ESV. "Behold, the days are coming, declares the LORD, when the city shall be rebuilt for the LORD from the Tower of Hananel to the Corner Gate. And the measuring line shall go out farther, straight to the hill Gareb, and shall then turn to Goah. The whole valley of the dead bodies and the ashes, and all the fields as far as the brook Kidron, to the corner of the Horse Gate toward the east, shall be sacred to the LORD. It shall not be plucked up or overthrown anymore forever."

Many, many blessings will accompany the gathering of Israel and the rebuilding of Jerusalem. Speaking of songs of thanksgiving, there's a song based on a Scripture from Jeremiah that expresses it well.

Jeremiah 31:11–14 ESV. For the LORD has ransomed Jacob and has redeemed him from hands too strong for him. They shall come and sing aloud on the height of Zion, and they shall be radiant over the goodness of the LORD, over the grain, the wine, and the oil, and over the young of the flock and the herd; their life shall be like a watered garden, and they shall languish no more. Then shall the young women rejoice in the dance, and the young men and the old shall be merry. I will turn their mourning into joy; I will comfort them, and give them gladness for sorrow. I will feast the soul of the priests with abundance, and my people shall be satisfied with my goodness, declares the LORD."

Seek wisdom and understanding, and these things will become plain to you as well if you don't understand them already. "The Church" is not Israel, has not replaced Israel, and will never be Israel.

Hosea 14:9 ESV. Whoever is wise, let him understand these things; whoever is discerning, let him know them; for the ways of the LORD are right, and the upright walk in them, but transgressors stumble in them.

Prophecy in God's Holidays

Leviticus 23:1–2, ESV. The LORD spoke to Moses, saying, "Speak to the people of Israel and say to them, These are the appointed feasts of the LORD that you shall proclaim as holy convocations; they are my appointed feasts.

God's feasts or holy days are intricately associated with prophecy. There are three perspectives wrapped up in the practice of God's feasts listed in Leviticus 23: past, present and future. They are God's holidays; they are not "Jewish" but are presented in this chapter because Israel is the leader in them (when they stick with the Word). God specifically says that they are "the appointed feasts of the Lord" or "my appointed feasts" though they were delivered first to Israel.

These appointed times or holidays are a roadmap for the events of the end of the age and the inauguration of the millennial kingdom of Yeshua. Believers follow the holidays as best as they are able, and in doing so discover more of the mind and Spirit of God, gaining wisdom and understanding in God's Word.

The first perspective in the feasts or holy days is the past, where His people remember what happened. Then there's the present, where we apply His truths to daily living and speak (or witness) to others of what He has done and the wonderful riches in God's Word. Finally, there's the future perspective of a rehearsal for upcoming events. His holy days figure in with prophecy and speak to us of the need for repentance, if we would only listen.

The real Sabbath (not the Church's fake one) teaches us rest and oneness with God, just as it was in the Garden and will be again. We learn what it really means to "rest in Him" now, and get a glimmer of what it will be like soon (hopefully). Sabbath also teaches us to put God first in everything.

The Day of Blowing or Awakening Blast (Trumpets or Yom Teruah) has the present aspect of sweetness and good things coming from God, and a future aspect of warning for the coming judgment (related to the trumpet judgments). The plagues suffered by Egypt bear a remarkable resemblance to the plagues in the book of the Revelation, and for those who have eyes to see both processes appear to be nearly identical.

Yom Kippur or Day of Atonement in the past was the only day the High Priest could enter the Holy of Holies and put the blood of the sacrifice on the Ark of the Covenant (a picture of the atoning work of Yeshua). It is also called "a day of smoke and burning" and the "the day of the Lord." Through this holy day, God gives us a picture of the future judgment of a world without Him which continues to reject the payment of Yeshua for sin.

The feast of Tabernacles or Booths includes the memory of Israel tabernacling with God in the wilderness. It also has the fun of connecting with Him again in our own tabernacles (our bodies and our tents or booths), and the rehearsal for the future 1,000 year kingdom, called the millennial kingdom. At that time, Yeshua will reign and there will be rest from our labors.

The blood of the lamb in the Passover sacrifice covers over the sin of all who accept it in the person of the Messiah Yeshua. His blood causes the Destroying angel to "pass over" all who take refuge under it, and will continue to function that way during the awful events of the Day of Judgment, also known as the Day of the Lord or the Tribulation.

The feast of Unleavened Bread is a symbol of obedience, related to eating the unleavened Bread from Heaven, which is obedience to God and His Son. This is the true definition of faith: trust God, do what He says, and live out the Words of God daily.

God's holidays summarized in Leviticus are not only relevant for daily living, but are intricately woven into prophecy. Many don't understand how, because they reject the holy days as a part of a believer's walk, relegating them to 'ceremonial' or 'shadow' things that Christians don't "have" to do. At most, some regard them as novelties and play around with them a little.

Well, Churchgoers may not "have" to do them, but believers who love Him, who hunger and thirst for every word from Him in every part of our being, sure desire them. His holidays are jammed full of instruction for daily living and for learning other parts of His Word. They're like kindergarten instructions similar to learning the alphabet before you can read. If we can't follow the easiest and most basic instructions from Him, how will we ever figure out the more difficult instructions? How will we know if He speaks to us for a specific event in our lives, telling us what we need to overcome it? How will people recognize the sound of His voice, when those who wear His name spend so much time stopping their ears so they can't hear it? He gave the holy days to us for teaching, so if you do not avail yourself of His teaching it goes without saying you will not understand prophecy. Yeshua says something related to this to Nicodemus in John 3.

John 3:10–13, ESV. Jesus answered him, "Are you the teacher of Israel and yet you do not understand these things? Truly, truly, I say to you, we speak of what we know, and bear witness to what we have seen, but you do not receive our testimony. If I have told you earthly things and you do not believe, how can you believe if I tell you heavenly things? No one has ascended into heaven except he who descended from heaven, the Son of Man.

If we do not understand earthly things, simple things like God's holidays or being born again, how will we understand heavenly things such as prophecy? Either we take in all of what God has, or we just flounder around trying to fake it. What if events were to happen in an entirely different fashion than that popularized in current so-called "Christian" fiction (like the Left Behind books)?

Times and Seasons

Mo'ed is a Hebrew word meaning literally "appointed time" or appointment (1 Samuel 20:35); appointed place (Joshua 8:14); appointed sign (Joshua 20:38); or appointed day (1 Samuel 13:11). This word is also sometimes translated "times and seasons" or "set time," (2 Samuel 20:5) and was first used in Genesis 1:14.

Genesis 1:14–15 ESV, parenthesis added. And God said, "Let there be lights in the expanse of the heavens to separate the day from the night. And let them be for signs and for seasons (or appointed times), and for days and years, and let them be lights in the expanse of the heavens to give light upon the earth." And it was so.

Mo'edim (moe-a-deem) is the plural form. God set the stars and planets in place specifically to help us regulate our relationship with Him through the times and seasons. There is every scriptural reason to believe that God also uses the "set times" as markers for intervention into the affairs of men.

Psalm 75:2-3 NASB. "When I select an appointed time, it is I who judge with equity. The earth and all who dwell in it melt; it is I who have firmly set its pillars." Selah.

Psalm 102:13 NASB. You will arise and have compassion on Zion; for it is time to be gracious to her, for the appointed time has come.

Going back to what was presented earlier, three of the aspects of the mo'edim or "appointments" are past, present, and future. We remember what God did for His people, what He is doing for us, and especially what He will do for us. The word "remember" means "to speak or act on behalf of" so we speak and act on behalf of what He has done, is doing, and will do for His people. Ain't it great? We can actually "remember" the future! We remind ourselves and teach others of His past actions in history and comfort one another with what He will do. And we personally apply the messages from both past and future in daily living.

One of the many grievous errors of the Church is to set aside God's holidays as "ceremonial" and so "we don't have to do them anymore." This is a mark of the beast and the deceiver.

Daniel 7:23–25 ESV (underline added). "Thus he said: 'As for the fourth beast, there shall be a fourth kingdom on earth, which shall be different from all the kingdoms, and it shall devour the whole earth, and trample it down, and break it to pieces. As for the ten horns, out of this kingdom ten kings shall arise, and another shall arise after them; he shall be different from the former ones, and shall put down three kings. He shall speak words against the Most High, and shall wear out the saints of the Most High, <u>and shall think to change the times and the law</u>; and they shall be given into his hand for a time, times, and half a time.

The eleventh horn or the beast will "think to change the times and the Law" and is exactly what the Church has done already. They have declared the "set times" or God's feasts and the law are no longer in effect. This will also be what the beast wants to do. You might see now why The Church as a whole will be right in line with the plans of the deceiver at the end.

Another word to describe what we do in the holy days is "rehearse." By "acting out" the elements of His plans that are yet to come, we teach our children and witness to the world of His coming intervention. We give glory to Him because of His love, wisdom and power displayed for us when He intervened in the affairs of men, and for His promises to intervene in a more permanent fashion soon. These appointments are part of His Word we proclaim so others "hear and fear."

Deuteronomy 4:10 NASB. "Remember the day you stood before the Lord your God at Horeb, when the Lord said to me, 'Assemble the people to Me, that I may let them hear My words so they may learn to fear Me all the days they live on the earth, and that they may teach their children.'

Jeremiah 33:9 NASB. 'It will be to Me a name of joy, praise and glory before all the nations of the earth which will hear of all the good that I do for them, and they will fear and tremble because of all the good and all the peace that I make for it.'

Another term for the mo'edim is "holy convocation." Gathering together in a holy convocation is one of the activities included in the practice of the mo'edim. The Hebrew words are *mi'qrah qodesh* (mee-kraw koe-desh), meaning literally an "assembly of sanctified ones." God instructs us to gather together for specific appointments with Him - Sabbath, first and seventh day of Passover, Pentecost, Trumpets, Day of Atonement, first and eighth day of Tabernacles – about 59 days a year normally. These holidays are probably one of the things the writer of Hebrews was referring to when he said not to forsake assembling together.

Hebrews 10:25 NASB. Let us hold fast the confession of our hope without wavering, for He who promised is faithful; and let us consider how to stimulate one another to love and good deeds, not forsaking our own assembling together, as is the habit of some, but encouraging one another; and all the more as you see the day drawing near.

This gathering or assembling does not mean "church." Part of the gathering was traveling to Jerusalem three times a year - Passover, Pentecost and Tabernacles. The other part was gathering in family groups. When the Sabbath instructions were given during the Exodus, everyone was supposed to remain in place.

Exodus 16:29 ESV. See! The LORD has given you the Sabbath; therefore on the sixth day he gives you bread for two days. Remain each of you in his place; let no one go out of his place on the seventh day."

The word "gathering" (similar to assembly) also means "harvesting," which applies to both crops and people. It applies, for instance, to those who belong to Him at the end of the age.

Isaiah 17:5 NASB. It will be even like the reaper gathering the standing grain, as his arm harvests the ears, Or it will be like one gleaning ears of grain in the valley of Rephaim.

2 Thessalonians 2:1 NASB. Now we request you, brethren, with regard to the coming of our Lord Jesus Christ and our gathering together to Him, that you not be quickly shaken from your composure or be disturbed either by a spirit or a message or a letter as if from us, to the effect that the day of the Lord has come.

So when we gather we are not only fulfilling His holy day instructions but foreshadowing our eventual, permanent gathering also. The prophetic rehearsal portion of the mo'edim continues to forewarn unbelievers of God's intentions and comfort His people with promises of continued care and protection.

Daniel 8:19 NASB. He said, "Behold, I am going to let you know what will occur at the final period of the indignation, for it pertains to the appointed time of the end. (compare also Daniel 11:27,29)

Daniel 11:35 NASB. "Some of those who have insight will fall, in order to refine, purge and make them pure until the end time; because it is still to come at the appointed time.

Habakkuk 2:3 NASB. "For the vision is yet for the appointed time; it hastens toward the goal and it will not fail. Though it tarries, wait for it; for it will certainly come, it will not delay."

One day soon God has made an appointment to visit the kingdoms of the world in fury. He will not miss it or delay.

Faith-Filling

A critical factor in receiving any benefit from the holy days, or the whole Word for that matter, is our motivation. Without trusting obedience (faith), it is impossible to please God (Hebrews 11:6), and therefore receive any benefit from what He tells us to do. Trusting means that the one we place our trust in is worthy of that trust, and can and will follow through on His Word to us. Obedience springs from that trust, because if God IS as He says He is, it would follow that we should DO what He says to do. Do not think that we can follow the holy days to the letter, but then act any way that seems right in our own eyes, and expect to please God with our practice.

In the following reference, the Father reminds us that just following a few rules will not please Him. If we follow every single rule He made for a holy day, but harbor iniquity in our hearts, then observing the day is useless. Sodom and Gomorrah in the reference below are other names for people who "honor him with their lips but their hearts are far from him" (Isaiah 29:13), in this instance applying to hypocritical Isra'el.

Isaiah 1:10-15 NASB. Hear the word of the Lord, you rulers of Sodom; give ear to the instruction of our God, You people of Gomorrah. "What are your multiplied sacrifices to Me?" Says the Lord. "I have had enough of burnt offerings of rams and the fat of fed cattle; and I take no pleasure in the blood of bulls, lambs or goats. When you come to appear before Me, who requires of you this trampling of My courts? Bring your worthless offerings no longer; incense is an abomination to Me. New moon and Sabbath, the calling of assemblies— I cannot endure iniquity and the solemn assembly. I hate your new moon festivals and your appointed feasts, they have become a burden to Me; I am weary of bearing them. So when you spread out your hands in prayer, I will hide My eyes from you; yes, even though you multiply prayers, I will not listen. Your hands are covered with blood."

Why does the Father hate the offerings, sacrifices, and appointed times (holy days)? Does this mean we are to eliminate the Torah? Or is it that people corrupted the practice of the Law with presuming on His grace by including the filth of evil deeds? Hear what the Lord says to us in the same chapter.

Isaiah 1:16-23 NASB. "Wash yourselves, make yourselves clean; remove the evil of your deeds from My sight. Cease to do evil, learn to do good; seek justice, reprove the ruthless, defend the orphan, plead for the widow. Come now, and let us reason together," says the Lord, "Though your sins are as scarlet, they will be as white as snow; though they are red like crimson, they will be like wool. If you consent and obey, you will eat the best of the land; but if you refuse and rebel, you will be devoured by the sword." Truly, the mouth of the Lord has spoken. How the faithful city has become a harlot, she who was full of justice! Righteousness once lodged in her, but now murderers. Your silver has become dross, your drink diluted with water. Your rulers are rebels and companions of thieves; everyone loves a bribe and chases after rewards. They do not defend the orphan, nor does the widow's plea come before them.

Our Father is not kidding around here. The outward observance of the holy days could be perfect and still not pleasing to God, because we forget to observe ALL of His Word in perfect balance without showing any partiality.

Much More

Expanding on each of the appointments, we can learn more from the themes associated with them. The themes have become an integrated part of the celebrations, built up by association with the first use of a term, meanings of words, the first events, the time of year, and subsequent related events happening at the same time. For instance, when the Father says that Yom Teruah (Trumpets) is a "day of blowing," then sounding the shofar for fun or warning at other times becomes associated with this action or holiday. One of those times is probably at the blowing of the seven trumpets of judgment or warnings in Revelation.

The Pesach (or Passover) Lamb is an example that is understood first, to be an actual fuzzy offspring of a ewe, but also Yeshua (Jesus) the Lamb of God. Our Father uses these types of things to illustrate His spiritual realities for us (see John 3).

Another way that themes become associated with the mo'edim is through prophecy. Our Father makes and fulfills prophecy around the holy days, using the elements of each holy day to inform His people about what is going to happen, helping us to persevere in times of adversity. He reminds us that He is always in control, knowing (and declaring) the end from the beginning, and encouraging us to overcome. Through the recurring pattern of annual appointments with Him, salted throughout with various themes relating to His character and attributes, He reveals Himself to His people. He is the Center, the Rock, and our Redeemer; on Him, we can rely. We trust and obey with full confidence that He doesn't fail. He will never leave nor forsake those who place that confidence unreservedly in Him.

The major themes for **Passover** are redemption, renewal, salvation, and freedom. God gives a picture to us of the people of God being released from Egypt to worship Him through a series of plagues visited on the Egyptians. The final plague was the death of all first-born children in houses (literally) that were not protected through obedience by marking the doorframe with the blood of a lamb. Egypt is symbolic of the evil world system (or sin), the blood of the lamb was foreshadowing the Blood of the Messiah (the Lamb of God), and the meal is symbolic of the flesh of the Messiah, which Yeshua declares to be His Word in John 6.

At first, the appointment was for remembering Egypt and freedom, and to look forward to the Messiah. After the resurrection, the feast reminds us of His sacrifice (Luke 22:19) that saved us from the curses of sin. There may also be an element of "passing over" believers in the Tribulation (see the section on **Hidden From Wrath** in chapter 9). In the meantime, through this appointment we celebrate our present release from captivity and rejoice in the freedom of bond service to our Father. This is part of our sanctification process, forgetting what lies behind and reaching forward to what lies ahead, pressing on toward the prize of the upward calling of God in Yeshua the Messiah (Philippians 3:13,14).

Themes associated with **Unleavened Bread** include cleansing (baptism); sanctification; purity; removing sin and Yeshua as our *mikveh* (baptism). All yeast (or leaven, which symbolizes sin in this instance) is removed from the house, which teaches us about purification, sanctification, and leaving sin behind (in Egypt, as it were). In place of sin, we live on the Word of God, the Bread of Life, Yeshua our Messiah (the unleavened bread). There is also a baptism (symbolized by going through the Red Sea), which helps us understand cleansing and identification with God. The Sea is a *mikveh* (Hebrew for literally "a gathering of waters," the place where baptisms take place) which IS Yeshua. He is our baptism, our identity, our cleansing. One of these days, we will experience a final cleansing and entry into the eternal reality of the Kingdom.

First Fruits starts the beginning of counting the weeks until Pentecost; and includes the offering to God of the first fruits of the spring harvest. Yeshua offered Himself as the first fruits of the resurrection according to Paul (I Corinthians 15:23). Those of us who belong to Him are also a sort of "first fruits" according to James 1:18.

Pentecost gives us the themes of reception of instructions for holy living (His Word) from the "breath" (Holy Spirit) of God (man does not live by bread alone); the Akeidah (ah-kay-daw or the binding of Isaac) and what rabbis call the first (or left) trump of redemption. The first Pentecost in Exodus 19 and the Pentecost in Acts chapter 2 are very similar. Both have flames (or lightnings) symbolizing purification, both have the Spirit of God moving (breath = wind = words), and at both the Words of God were delivered for us to live by. At the first Pentecost, people died; in Acts 2 people lived. The Word at the first one was delivered on stone tablets; in the book of Acts, it was written on the heart. This holy day is also called the Feast of Weeks because we count seven weeks between it and First Fruits.

The Akeidah is the story of the binding of Isaac, and of Abraham's obedience in offering him as a sacrifice (Genesis 22). It figures into both Pentecost and Trumpets, but its association with Pentecost comes from the voice of God represented as a shofar sounding louder and louder (Exodus 19:16, 19). Horns are also reminders of the sin of the golden calf worship (Exodus 32, idolatry). It is a picture of the sacrifice made by the Father using His Son for our redemption. The ram caught by its horns (both of them, which rabbis identify as two stages of redemption - the body and the soul) was the substitute, just as Yeshua was the substitute for us. The first horn (left horn) symbolizes the first redemption.

The **Feast of Trumpets** (Yom Teruah) has a veritable plethora (a way of saying a whole bunch) of themes. There is a king's coronation (who is our king, the calf or God?) perhaps best pictured in Daniel 7:9,10,13,14 (related to Revelation 4:1,2), where books are opened and judgment is made (that's why this scene is associated with this holy day), and the Son of Man is given a kingdom (dominion and glory). The meaning of the word Teruah means "awake" or "shout" and Yom Teruah literally means "Day of Awakening Blast" (or shout). So we wake up from the sleep of sin to repentance or from spiritual lack of awareness to resurrection. Waking up might also be associated with the seven trumpet judgments described for us in the book of Revelation.

Other themes recommended for further investigation are marriage; concealment, and the last (or right) trump of the Akeidah (redemption of the soul). Sweetness is prominent in the food we eat; my wife likes to call this the "feast of Sugar." Scripture includes Isaiah 27:13; Isaiah 52:1 and I Corinthians 15:52. These are prophetic of resurrection, our gathering together with Him, our "wedding" with Him, and being hidden on the Day of Wrath (Yom Kippur or day of Atonement). (See the section on **Hidden from Wrath** later in the book for further development of this idea.) Remember that God switched this month with the month of Pesach. Even though many call this the "head of the year" (Rosh HaShanah), it really is in the seventh month. Also, even though now it is a two-day event (because it starts right smack on the new moon), it is supposed to be only one day long.

Yom Kippur (yohm-key-poor, Day of Atonement), although solemn, has only a few but very important themes. The main theme is Atonement/Judgment. For believers there is atonement, and for those who do not have a sacrifice (Yeshua the Messiah) there is only judgment. Those who do not repent before this day can only see "smoke and burning," but believers have access to His presence through the Messiah. This holy day not only has a current application for believers but also looks forward to the Day of the Lord or Tribulation.

The shofar is sounded on this day but with a different meaning, in the same way that this day is different from the others. It's called the *shofar haGadol*, "the Great Trump." You might recognize this from a statement of Yeshua (Jesus) in Matthew 24:31 and perhaps 1 Thessalonians 4:16.

We can fast for many reasons and at any time, but doing this fast on this day brings with it a special relationship with God. We specifically do what He tells us to do, and we connect intimately with Him on this "fast day." The constant desire for food and water teaches us about fasting from the tendency to go our own way or do our own thing. It is a minute by minute resistance to giving in to temptation. His people learn from this that resisting temptation on a daily basis is a trial and a fight.

The **Feast of Tabernacles** themes are: resurrection; rewards; rest; thanksgiving; rejoicing; celebration; also called the Season of Our Joy and the Feast of Nations. Some scriptures that are associated with this holiday are Isaiah 26:17-21; Psalm 27:5; and Psalm 47:5 (ascended = coronation, shouts of joy, trumpets). This could be called God's Camping Trip because of traveling to Jerusalem and living in tents. We live in tents or booths during this time to remind us that Yeshua dwelt with us for a while, and we will dwell with Him when He sets up His Kingdom and reigns from Jerusalem for 1,000 years. We have joy now because we are free in Him, and we will be completely free when He comes again.

The eighth appointment with God is the Sabbath, which has strong themes of rest and fellowship. The first Sabbath was observed by God Himself and recorded for us in Genesis 2:1-3. The millennial kingdom looks like it will be the "seventh day" of a seven-thousand year "week." In the millennial kingdom, the world will be at rest from fighting, war and other conflict.

Isaiah 11:6–9 ESV. The wolf shall dwell with the lamb, and the leopard shall lie down with the young goat, and the calf and the lion and the fattened calf together; and a little child shall lead them. The cow and the bear shall graze; their young shall lie down together; and the lion shall eat straw like the ox. The nursing child shall play over the hole of the cobra, and the weaned child shall put his hand on the adder's den. They shall not hurt or destroy in all my holy mountain; for the earth shall be full of the knowledge of the LORD as the waters cover the sea.

There is something supernatural in obeying the Father's instructions on this day. This is true for all of His instructions or Torah, but we "feel" it more on this day. Resting on this particular day has peculiar far-reaching aspects to it. It reaches deep into your soul, and unwinds you in a way that brings peace and contentment to every fiber of your being. Part of this could be from "resonating" with the Father's Spirit because of obedience. Part of it could be that we "do" what we see the Father "do," and that creates a spiritual bond with Abba (our "daddy") through which flows His presence or peace (shalom). Or part of it could be that your own physical rhythms move at the same rhythm that the Father set with an end of the week rest. Hmm. It couldn't be that He built you and knows what you need, could it?

Appointments with Yeshua

Yeshua is the focus of the mo'edim, or appointments. He is the beginning and the goal. In the mo'edim, we are privileged to physically connect with our Redeemer. To worship God with all our mind, soul and strength includes anything we can physically change in our lives to honor His Word to us.

Zephaniah 3:17-18 NASB. "The Lord your God is in your midst, a victorious warrior. He will exult over you with joy, He will be quiet in His love, He will rejoice over you with shouts of joy. "I will gather those who grieve about the appointed feasts— they came from you, O Zion; the reproach of exile is a burden on them."

Some of the ways that Yeshua is found in the holy days have already been highlighted, but here is a summary. Yeshua is our Passover lamb, the unleavened bread we live on, the promise of our eventual resurrection (First Fruits). He is the one who gives us His Word to live by through the power of His Torah and His Spirit (Pentecost). We blow shofars to wake people up to repent and come to Him, and He is the bridegroom that will come for His bride and also the soon to be crowned King (Yom Teruah).

We remember the atonement He makes for us. We fast and pray that the judgment is postponed as long as possible, so as many as possible will accept His blood for payment of sins and come to Him (Yom Kippur). He lived in a human body, or tabernacled among us sharing our temptations, trials, and afflictions. We know that we also dwell in tabernacles (our bodies), and we are only here for a little while, and will eventually dwell in a place that will be so harmless we will not need houses (Tabernacles) or walled cities.

The events of the earthly ministry of Yeshua followed closely the first three holidays (spring feasts) in His death (Passover), resurrection (First Fruits), and the pouring out of the Spirit (Shavuot or Pentecost). We can see that the last four also provide a road map for the termination of worldly kingdoms and His reign on the throne of David.

Jerusalem

Zechariah 12:2–3 ESV. "Behold, I am about to make Jerusalem a cup of staggering to all the surrounding peoples. The siege of Jerusalem will also be against Judah. On that day I will make Jerusalem a heavy stone for all the peoples. All who lift it will surely hurt themselves. And all the nations of the earth will gather against it.

Did you ever wonder why Jerusalem is so important? Why doesn't the deceiver just pack it in and go to some other planet and start a kingdom? Is he planet bound, as C.S. Lewis says in his wonderful three-volume fiction book series starting with Out of the Silent Planet? Or is he just not that bright?

Obviously, he can't go to another planet, because he would have to be able to create a paradise such as Earth. This planet might be a wrecked planet (because of the flood and the curse), but it is still fruitful and beautiful and populated with people easy to sucker into following the deceiver. The deceiver cannot create; he can only corrupt, so that's one reason.

Another reason is that God has established the battle lines. He is the one that set His Name in and on Jerusalem and said, in essence, this is where my kingdom will be centered.

Romans 11:29 ESV. For the gifts and the calling of God are irrevocable.

So of course Jerusalem is where the deceiver is going to directly challenge "the LORD, who stretched out the heavens and founded the earth and formed the spirit of man within him" (Zechariah 12:1).

The deceiver did his best to sidetrack and corrupt the physical line of descent of our Messiah Yeshua. Yeshua was born at exactly the right time and in exactly the right place anyway. The deceiver thought he'd won when he managed to get the Son of God crucified, until Yeshua broke the power of hell. The deceiver took several shots at wiping out Jerusalem, one of which seemed to succeed in 135 A.D. when the people of the prince who is to come destroyed it and plowed it with salt. But he didn't accomplish anything that wasn't in the will of the Father at the time. In using people to try and destroy God's kingdom, the deceiver was in fact used by God as a discipline tool.

Jerusalem is back on the world's scene again, and it has indeed become a "cup of trembling" (or staggering) to all the surrounding peoples. These peoples are sold out to the deceiver and fixated on destroying Jerusalem again. Whatever you may know of world politics or religion, know that the single most important objective now and in history is the desire of the deceiver and his minions to eliminate Jerusalem once and for all. They think they will do it with the beast or little horn in partnership with the false christ and the dragon, but they are sorely mistaken.

If anything, they are going to trigger the full wrath of God coming to the defense of Israel. If they thought they had seen the full extent of His wrath with the flood or with Egypt, they will soon find out how wrong they are. When the followers of the deceiver threaten Jerusalem with destruction again, as the warning trumpets are blown and the bowls of His wrath are poured out, God will be making sure everyone gets an advanced education in what He can do when He is isn't holding back. If you'll excuse the language, a bumper sticker seen one time that conveyed the sentiment perfectly said, "Jesus is coming, and boy is He pissed."

The Temple

Proverbs 16:6 ESV. By steadfast love and faithfulness iniquity is atoned for, and by the fear of the LORD one turns away from evil.

There were two Jewish temples (and at least one tabernacle) so far. One was constructed by Solomon with most material collected and contributed by David, and one was rebuilt after the Babylonian captivity described for us in the books of Ezra and Nehemiah which wasn't nearly as beautiful. This second one was remodeled by Herod (the guy who killed the babies of Bethlehem trying to get Yeshua) and is frequently called Herod's or the second temple.

A side note here is that Herod is an excellent example of a "religious" person doing something like remodeling a temple, and at the same time killing babies trying to destroy God's plan in the Christ. We've still got a lot of these types around, even now. Religious people build huge, expensive temples, mosques and churches all over the world, while at the same time they ignore the whole of God's Word. This, in essence, is the Babylon of Revelation 18: people who make a great show of looking religious without actually doing what God says.

In 70 A.D, during the Jewish War (67 A.D. to about 73 A.D.) the second temple was destroyed. Jerusalem itself was destroyed in 135 A.D., plowed under, and sown with salt. The destruction of the Temple is reminiscent of the glory of the Lord departing the Temple in Ezekiel chapter 10. We have been without a temple for several thousand years, but not because the systems around the Temple were no longer needed due to the sacrifice of our Messiah. It is because God's glory has withdrawn from the world by that much due to its rejection of Him. When Yeshua ascended into heaven, it was also similar to the glory of the Lord leaving the Temple. After-images of His glory are still evident in the hearts of believers everywhere, as we live and breathe His Words. We have His promise that He will return, take up the throne of David, and build a new Temple that lasts until the world doesn't need one anymore.

Muslims removed a huge amount of debris from around the general area of the temple in 691 A. D. and built the Dome of the

Rock, attempting to erase all signs of God from Jerusalem. No archeology has been allowed in the area by the godless ever since (a little was allowed underneath after Israel took over again), so we don't really know where the temple was actually situated. The holy of holies for Solomon's temple is believed to have been built on the rock on top of Mount Moriah which is now thought to be under the Dome of the Rock. The Western or Wailing Wall is believed to be a part of a retaining wall built by Herod and is said to be the only surviving part of the second temple.

Solomon's temple was smaller than Herod's temple complex, about 30 feet by 90 feet. The tabernacle wasn't very big either, measuring about 15 or so feet wide and 45 feet long. Solomon's temple had extra rooms for various purposes and courtyards that added to the size of the whole area, but the temple itself was rather small. So it could fit into a small space.

It seems plain from Scripture that a third temple will be built (and perhaps even a fourth, if you literally believe Ezekiel). Some people think it is impossible because the Dome of the Rock is sitting on the apparent Temple site. But there are several possibilities for constructing a third temple.

One is that the Dome is destroyed supernaturally, or even by an earthquake or something. The second possibility, and the one that seems most likely, is that the Dome is not in the way, because it isn't on the spot of the Temple. There are scholars who think instead that the actual site of the Temple was a little south of the traditional Temple Mount, nearer what we now know as the City of David. This is in the neighborhood of the Gihon spring, which would provide a source of water for cleansing.

In line with this second possibility is the discovery of foundation stones, apparently of Herod's temple about 150 feet or so north of the Muslim abomination in a tunnel 200 feet under the

Temple Mount called the Rabbi's tunnel. This tunnel is about 900 feet long running along the Western (or Wailing) wall from a spot called Wilson's arch. Archeologists ran into stones measuring 10 by 10 by 46 feet and weighing up to 400 tons. This means that the Dome of the Rock would *not* be in the way of a Jewish Temple.

It is possible that a third temple could be located in the area of the Dome of the Rock without disturbing that blight on the beauty of Jerusalem. The Dome could be sitting in the "court outside the temple" and allowed to stay there by God for the 42 months described in Revelation 11.

Another, less likely building site, is the Mount of Olives. David is said to have climbed the Mount of Olives "where God was worshipped" (2 Samuel 15:30-32). Yeshua prayed there, was arrested there, will set foot there again (Zechariah 14:4) and a temple on that site seems like it could work. A fourth possibility is that Israel stops shaking in their shoes, as their army did in the incident with Goliath, and just bulldozes the Dome, daring the Muslims to do anything about it. Or God could neutralize the Muslims as He has done many times with enemies of His people.

A fifth option is building a tabernacle to house the Ark of the Covenant instead of a huge building, and a tent would have an even smaller footprint than a temple. This is perhaps the least likely possibility, but not terribly far out of the range of consideration. Sometimes it seems that tabernacle and temple are interchangeable terms (see for instance Revelation 15:5), so perhaps a tent wouldn't be out of the question. Tabernacle and temple, along with "sanctuary" and others words such as "dwelling" or "house," mean pretty much the same thing.

Psalm 27:5 ESV. For he will hide me in his shelter in the day of trouble; he will conceal me under the cover of his tent; he will lift me high upon a rock.

Scripture seems to indicate strongly that some sort of third temple or perhaps tabernacle built in Jerusalem in the near future. It might be that allowing Israel to build a temple or tabernacle on the temple mount would be included in the "agreement with many for one week" spoken of by Daniel. This would give the little horn something to use to claim to be God, and a reason for many nations to attack Israel (probably several times) culminating in the final battle of Armageddon.

There's plenty of precedent for having at least a tabernacle in different places. For a long time the tent was at Shiloh. The Ark was captured by the Philistines and after getting hit with lots of trouble returned it to Beth-shemesh (1 Samuel 6) who in turn relayed it to Kiriath-jearim where it stayed 20 years. Offerings were made at various places also, which you can read about in the rest of Samuel and Kings among other books. David brought the Ark up from Baale-judah to Jerusalem where he put it in a tent, the exact spot unknown. It looks like there were two tents for a while (1 Kings 1:39 and 2:28, compare to 1 Chronicles 1:1-6), one for the Ark in Jerusalem and the other was the formal Tabernacle, which was a close by at Gibeon according to 1 Chronicles 1:1-6.

David purchased the threshing floor of Araunah (2 Samuel 24) which is where the angel stopped his destruction of Israel due to David's sin in the census. There David built an altar. Later, Solomon brings it all together (parts assembled by David, the threshing floor, and the Ark) and builds the first Temple. The Ark finally finds a resting place, for a while, in the temple built by Solomon (1 Kings 8).

There's also an obvious precedent for altars in different places than where the temple was located. Elijah, for instance, used an altar on Mount Carmel to fight with the 450 prophets of Jezebel's god Baal (1 Kings 18). God consumed it when He "answered by fire" and accepted the water-drenched sacrifice offered by Elijah. That altar was in existence at the same time as the temple, and there were others too. Ezra records for us the building of an altar along with the resumption of sacrifices before the second Temple was started (Ezra 3:1-3). At one time, altars were common, and anyone could build one.

Exodus 20:24–25 ESV. An altar of earth you shall make for me and sacrifice on it your burnt offerings and your peace offerings, your sheep and your oxen. In every place where I cause my name to be remembered I will come to you and bless you. If you make me an altar of stone, you shall not build it of hewn stones, for if you wield your tool on it you profane it.

The problem with anyone building an altar anywhere was that the overwhelming tendency was to drift away after other gods and ignore the only true God. After Israel was established in the Land, God didn't want people sacrificing just anywhere, because of that tendency to drift.

Leviticus 17:8–9 ESV. "And you shall say to them, Any one of the house of Israel, or of the strangers who sojourn among them, who offers a burnt offering or sacrifice and does not bring it to the entrance of the tent of meeting to offer it to the LORD, that man shall be cut off from his people.

Deuteronomy 12:26–27 ESV. But the holy things that are due from you, and your vow offerings, you shall take, and you shall go to the place that the LORD will choose, and offer your burnt offerings, the flesh and the blood, on the altar of the LORD your God. The blood of your sacrifices shall be poured out on the altar of the LORD your God, but the flesh you may eat.

The question is, if we build an altar now in our back yard and offer sacrifices on it (particularly thanksgiving, freewill, fellowship and peace offerings) and stay true to God, would that be okay? Especially when we don't have a Temple? It seems apparent from Scripture that this would be acceptable. We don't have altars now, and we don't offer sacrifices, and man is still heavily into idolatry anyway. So perhaps trying to follow all of what God says, including sacrifices, loving God with all of our hearts, mind and strength would be the antidote to the world's idolatry.

In response to a statement from the woman at the well in John 4 about only "worshipping" in Jerusalem, He says that the day will come when God is worshipped in spirit and truth.

John 4:21–24 ESV. Jesus said to her, "Woman, believe me, the hour is coming when neither on this mountain nor in Jerusalem will you worship the Father. You worship what you do not know; we worship what we know, for salvation is from the Jews. But the hour is coming, and is now here, when the true worshipers will worship the Father in spirit and truth, for the Father is seeking such people to worship him. God is spirit, and those who worship him must worship in spirit and truth."

This means, of course, that worshipping is the same as doing all the words that God speaks. If we obey by building an altar in our back yard and have a barbecue with God, it seems reasonable we would also be worshipping in spirit and truth. If God dwells in us, and we are a tabernacle for Him, does that mean that the "place where He puts His name" is wherever His people live?

John 14:15–17 ESV. "If you love me, you will keep my commandments. And I will ask the Father, and he will give you another Helper, to be with you forever, even the Spirit of truth, whom the world cannot receive, because it neither sees him nor knows him. You know him, for he dwells with you and will be in you.

So at one time we weren't supposed to sacrifice just anywhere, we were supposed to do it at "the place that the LORD would choose." It seems that this "place" was Jerusalem. It would be nice if we could build on the same spot that was chosen by David, but God didn't indicate an exact spot for a temple.

Some people are fixated on having to have a temple on the temple mount. But other than tradition, there is no command anywhere to require a temple on a certain spot. There's also no reason for hesitating to build just because a certain favorite spot is seemingly off-limits. God put His name on Jerusalem, but He also put His name on or at Shiloh (Jeremiah 7:12). On the other hand, He also told Jeremiah that He was going to do to Jerusalem what He did to Shiloh. You may recognize part of this reference, quoted by Yeshua in places like Matthew 21:13.

Jeremiah 7:8–15 ESV. "Behold, you trust in deceptive words to no avail. Will you steal, murder, commit adultery, swear falsely, make offerings to Baal, and go after other gods that you have not known, and then come and stand before me in this house, which is called by my name, and say, 'We are delivered!'—only to go on doing all these abominations? Has this house, which is called by my name, become a den of robbers in your eyes? Behold, I myself have seen it, declares the LORD. Go now to my place that was in Shiloh, where I made my name dwell at first, and see what I did to it because of the evil of my people Israel. And now, because you have done all these things, declares the LORD, and when I spoke to you persistently you did not listen, and when I called you, you did not answer, therefore I will do to the house that is called by my name, and in which you trust, and to the place that I gave to you and to your fathers, as I did to Shiloh. And I will cast you out of my sight, as I cast out all your kinsmen, all the offspring of Ephraim.

The exact placement of a temple is not an issue according to the Word. Ezekiel tells us that the millennial temple is built "on a very high mountain" (Ezekiel 40:2) but doesn't name the mountain or location (probably Jerusalem). It is more important to be faithful to all the Father commands. If Israel chose to build a temple on the Mount of Olives, it would show the world that the heart is more important than real estate. The godless world systems would shake in their shoes and be amazed at the blessings that would flow to Israel, if they would worship God in spirit and truth.

Whatever temple we build now is going to probably be leveled in that last earthquake where islands sink, mountains become valleys, and valleys mountains (Isaiah 40:3-4; Revelation 16:20). (A side note: the Isaiah passage may just be referring metaphorically to repentance, because it is said of John the Baptist that he would preach "make straight paths for the Lord.") Or whatever temple we built might fall when Yeshua sets foot on the Mount of Olives at the end of the tribulation period, and it splits in two. So in a way the temple is not a big deal one way or the other, except for trying our level best to love Him in every way possible.

The temple described in Ezekiel 40 through 47 is the millennial Temple built at the direction of Yeshua. It will be real because too much of the description belongs to the kingdom ruled by Yeshua after the Tribulation, such as the river and trees of healing. This will be the center of worship for a thousand years.

One of the big sins by The Church is not only in attempting to block the nation of Israel from forming again, but in blocking the building of a temple. The philosophy of men that "ceremonial laws" were fulfilled and eliminated by the sacrifice of Yeshua has been instrumental in forestalling construction of the temple. While it is true that Yeshua paid the price for sin, and there is no longer a sacrifice for sin, that has been true since the beginning of time as far as the Father is concerned. The death of His Son had to be demonstrated in due time in our physical world, but Yeshua was the lamb slain from the foundation of the world. Otherwise, believers would not have their names written in Yeshua's book of life from the foundation of the world (Revelation 13:8).

If it were true that the destruction of the temple (or the death of Yeshua) meant that the ceremonial laws were eliminated, then when the first temple was destroyed did that mean that Yeshua eliminated them at that time too? How did all those people living *before* the Tabernacle or Solomon's Temple get by without ceremonial laws? What did believers do in the three decades between the Resurrection and the Temple destruction? The answers are self-evident. Tabernacles and temples, along with ceremonial laws, were instituted so that God could live among His people, and they could in turn be a witness to the rest of the world.

The Temple was a symbol of "God with us," so when it was destroyed it meant that God had departed. Of course, God had departed long before the destruction of Solomon's temple because the people had departed from Him (Ezekiel 10-11). Obviously, the men who created these "fulfilled and eliminated" philosophies didn't think them all the way through.

Animal sacrifices have always been memorials of the death of God's Son. Never were they sufficient for the payment of sin. Even the burnt offering and sin offering were not adequate legal tender for permanent payment. There were also four other types of sacrifices that didn't have anything to do with sin. These are the fellowship, peace, thanksgiving and freewill offerings. The Church has always been willfully blind to many truths (like Israel) because of the insistence that they are somehow separate, unique and apart from Israel. This is why they come up with these ridiculous philosophies and have sidetracked the building of a temple.

In some ways, focusing on the temple mount as the only possible building site lets people off the hook for fellow-shipping with God as He instructed. It's an excuse for not having a temple (or tabernacle), because there's an idolatrous unholy shrine holding things up. A case is made by perverse men who claim to want to follow God, but also allow some stupid geography to keep them from it. The Mount of Olives could be a perfect spot for either a temple or a tabernacle. What's more important? A temple in a certain spot, or a home for the Ark in a place where sacrifices can resume, and perhaps even the glory of the Lord would find a resting place as in days of old?

The Ark

Jeremiah 3:15–17 ESV. "'And I will give you shepherds after my own heart, who will feed you with knowledge and understanding. And when you have multiplied and been fruitful in the land, in those days, declares the LORD, they shall no more say, "The ark of the covenant of the LORD." It shall not come to mind or be remembered or missed; it shall not be made again. At that time Jerusalem shall be called the throne of the LORD, and all nations shall gather to it, to the presence of the LORD in Jerusalem, and they shall no more stubbornly follow their own evil heart.'"

The Ark disappears in the biblical accounts somewhere before the time of Nebuchadnezzar's siege of Jerusalem. It isn't listed among the items that the Babylonians took from the temple, and it wasn't in the second temple.

We covered a little about the Ark of the Covenant in the preceding chapters, but perhaps more perspective wouldn't be a bad idea considering some of the modern stories surrounding it. For instance, an Ethiopian sect claims to be guarding a small building housing the Ark. Lots of stories locate the Ark in countries such as Egypt, Jordan, South Africa, France and Italy.

In other testimony, Ron Wyatt (God rest his soul) claimed to have discovered the Ark in 1982 under a hill that looked like a skull in Jerusalem. He thought the hill might have been Golgotha, the hill where Yeshua was crucified. He says the Antiquities Department of the Israeli government gave him permission to do some digging, but made him keep some of his findings secret. Some people think that it's because the Israeli government would see the Ark as a threat to their power, which makes sense.

The problem with many of these stories claiming that the Ark has been located is that the Ark has not actually surfaced. The stories usually claim that there is some type of conspiracy to keep it hidden, which might be true. The unveiling of the Ark would be the biggest news since Noah's announcement of a coming flood.

If you think about it, there is an odd commonality to the stories of the Ark as well as those about such things as Israel crossing the sea, the Tower of Babel, Noah's ark and the destruction of Sodom and Gomorrah. It is that while much archeological evidence has confirmed many Bible stories, and none has contradicted it, evidence for some of the major finds that should have been discovered has not surfaced. Archeological evidence for the momentous stories is missing. It isn't because there is none. It seems plain that the evidence is suppressed.

Clear evidence for the Exodus for instance has been dismissed because it doesn't fit the expected timeline. So-called "experts" have decided that the Bible's description of Pharaoh matches one 400 years later than the actual date of the Exodus, and they claim there is no evidence (400 years later) of a colony of Hebrews living in Egypt. The evidence is actually there, they just have made a 400-year error. They simply refuse to consider looking at the evidence of a Hebrew community in Egypt that existed 400 years earlier than they expect to see it. It's apparent that they do it deliberately.

The Saudi's have fenced off areas and won't allow visits to what is probably the mountain where God gave Moses the Law (called by them Jebel-al-lawz). The question is: why? Surely if they didn't think it was Mt. Sinai, they would allow examination? But it seems Arabs have been trying to bury evidence of God's involvement with men for a long time. The Dome of the Rock was built to hide the location of the temple. Turkey won't allow exploration or archeology on what seems to be the location of Noah's Ark. And on and on it goes.

The lack of archeological evidence for these major events could mean they didn't happen, as the godless claim. Or, and this is more certain, the very lack of some of the evidence is proof that the events did indeed happen. All other archeological evidence that has been uncovered points to an unerring Biblical account. Nothing discovered has disproved any of God's Word. It's obvious that the reason something like the Ark of the Covenant hasn't been discovered is that there is a conspiracy to cover up the evidence for political and religious reasons.

Some (including Mr. Wyatt) think that the Ark won't see the light of day, and that the temple won't be rebuilt because the sacrifice of Yeshua replaced any and all animal sacrifices. The sacrifice of Yeshua, for these people, is equated to animal sacrifices, which were never meant for salvation. There is a faulty logic in the reasoning, because if animal sacrifices were eliminated due to the cross, then that makes animal sacrifices equal to the death of Yeshua, which is an impossibility. Animal sacrifice was never about salvation, ever. Animal sacrifices were stopped by God because of disobedience, not the death of Yeshua. Besides, the sacrifices weren't the point. The heart of flesh obedient to God's Word was the point.

Jeremiah 7:21–24 ESV. Thus says the LORD of hosts, the God of Israel: "Add your burnt offerings to your sacrifices, and eat the flesh. For in the day that I brought them out of the land of Egypt, I did not speak to your fathers or command them concerning burnt offerings and sacrifices. But this command I gave them: 'Obey my voice, and I will be your God, and you shall be my people. And walk in all the way that I command you, that it may be well with you.' But they did not obey or incline their ear, but walked in their own counsels and the stubbornness of their evil hearts, and went backward and not forward.

One of those huge inconsistencies between the philosophies of men and the Bible is that if animal sacrifices are eliminated because of the death and resurrection of Yeshua, then why, in the millennial temple described by Ezekiel, do animal sacrifices resume? (Ezekiel 43:18ff.) The answer is that the death and resurrection of Yeshua doesn't have anything to do with animal sacrifices. The writer of Hebrews tells us that it is impossible for the blood of bulls and goats to take away sin. Animal sacrifices have many other good purposes, but never paid for eternal life.

Equating the sacrifice of Yeshua to animal sacrifices in the matter of salvation, and rejecting the rebuilding of the temple because of it, is, to put it as kindly as possible, ignorant. It necessarily means that sections of the Bible such as Ezekiel 40 through 47 must be explained away in some "spiritual" fashion, ignoring the literal meaning. If we just take God at His Word then Ezekiel's temple will in fact be built by Yeshua after He gets back here from His extended stay in heaven.

Gathering the Outcasts of Israel

There are hints and outright blunt statements in several places in Scripture of God gathering Israel together. Almost all the prophets have at least a few statements pointing to a future restoration of the nation. Ezekiel in particular has a number of good things to say about this event.

Ezekiel 20:33–38 ESV. "As I live, declares the Lord GOD, surely with a mighty hand and an outstretched arm and with wrath poured out I will be king over you. I will bring you out from the peoples and gather you out of the countries where you are scattered, with a mighty hand and an outstretched arm, and with wrath poured out. And I will bring you into the wilderness of the peoples, and there I will enter into judgment with you face to face. As I entered into judgment with your fathers in the wilderness of the land of Egypt, so I will enter into judgment with you, declares the Lord GOD. I will make you pass under the rod, and I will bring you into the bond of the covenant. I will purge out the rebels from among you, and those who transgress against me. I will bring them out of the land where they sojourn, but they shall not enter the land of Israel. Then you will know that I am the LORD.

It seems that this gathering happens in stages, at least when we compare Scriptures with historical migrations. There are starts and stops, but ultimately God will do it. Israel came back after the Babylonian captivity and rebuilt in times of trouble, as it was told to Daniel. But they rejected Yeshua the Messiah and tried to regain their land by their own hand from the Romans, which resulted in another expulsion. After about 2,000 years, they are again in the process of regaining and rebuilding the Land, but many of them are still thinking they are doing it by their own hand.

Some of what the prophets tell us for Israel coming together has come to pass, but some hasn't. For instance, Ezekiel in chapter 37 of his book records dry bones revitalized into whole people, representative of the renewed nation today. But God also tells Ezekiel that he will open graves and raise Israel from them, that He will set His sanctuary in their midst, and that they shall walk in His rules and be careful to obey His statues. None of this has happened yet, which probably means we are waiting for the breath of God to enter them.

Zechariah was a co-worker with Haggai and prophesied to the exiles returning to Jerusalem from the Babylonian captivity.

Zechariah 2:6–9 ESV. Up! Up! Flee from the land of the north, declares the LORD. For I have spread you abroad as the four winds of the heavens, declares the LORD. Up! Escape to Zion, you who dwell with the daughter of Babylon. For thus said the LORD of hosts, after his glory sent me to the nations who plundered you, for he who touches you touches the apple of his eye: "Behold, I will shake my hand over them, and they shall become plunder for those who served them. Then you will know that the LORD of hosts has sent me.

This prophecy from Zechariah is likely in reference to the return of the exiles after the Babylonian captivity, but it also is an example of partial immediate fulfillment and a permanent future fulfillment. Not all of the Jewish exiles returned after Babylon, and the "daughter of Babylon" has not become plunder for the Jews quite yet. Even now, the Jews are gathering in Israel, but many remain outside of Israel. The reason that the gathering has had fits and starts is that the hearts of the people are not completely His. Israel has not followed His Word as they should, and still isn't.

Soon this Scripture will be completely realized along with the previously mentioned Ezekiel passages and others. God will cause Israel to "pass under the rod" of the discipline of His Word and bring all believers into His promised mountain or kingdom on earth. Unbelievers or "rebels" will be winnowed out and those who are really Israel (believing Gentiles included, Isaiah 56:6-8) will take up residence in the Land. This will probably be after the first resurrection (and rapture) as the Kingdom of our Lord and Savior on earth begins, also known as the Millennial Kingdom. The current partial gathering of Israel is just the start.

5 Tribulation Like No Other

Deuteronomy 4:25–31 ESV. "When you father children and children's children, and have grown old in the land, if you act corruptly by making a carved image in the form of anything, and by doing what is evil in the sight of the LORD your God, so as to provoke him to anger, I call heaven and earth to witness against you today, that you will soon utterly perish from the land that you are going over the Jordan to possess. You will not live long in it, but will be utterly destroyed. And the LORD will scatter you among the peoples, and you will be left few in number among the nations where the LORD will drive you. And there you will serve gods of wood and stone, the work of human hands, that neither see, nor hear, nor eat, nor smell. But from there you will seek the LORD your God and you will find him, if you search after him with all your heart and with all your soul. When you are in tribulation, and all these things come upon you in the latter days, you will return to the LORD your God and obey his voice. For the LORD your God is a merciful God. He will not leave you or destroy you or forget the covenant with your fathers that he swore to them."

As already mentioned, there have always been troubles or tribulations of one form or another since our mom and dad got booted out of the Garden. Some of them have been pretty terrible, and some by comparison have been mild. Some were local (a drought, disease or plague) and some worldwide (such as the flood). There have been events that God said would never happen again, such as the cries over the death of the Egyptian firstborn (Exodus 11:6) or the flood (Genesis 9:11).

Once God tells us that war will be abolished, which obviously has not come to pass.

Isaiah 2:4 NASB95. And He will judge between the nations, And will render decisions for many peoples; And they will hammer their swords into plowshares and their spears into pruning hooks. Nation will not lift up sword against nation, And never again will they learn war.

But there is a period of trouble, described in the Bible, which is different from all the others. In fact, Yeshua tells us there has never been one like it and there never will be one like it again. Considering all the terrible things that have happened in the world, this makes for a very scary proposition.

Matthew 24:21–22 ESV. For then there will be great tribulation, such as has not been from the beginning of the world until now, no, and never will be. And if those days had not been cut short, no human being would be saved. But for the sake of the elect those days will be cut short.

This particular time of trouble is so unique we call it The Tribulation, although the Bible calls it The Day of the Lord, and it is the culmination of a lot of plans.

Isaiah 13:9 ESV. Behold, the day of the LORD comes, cruel, with wrath and fierce anger, to make the land a desolation and to destroy its sinners from it.

It's also a transition of sorts. It marks the changeover from kingdoms ruled by men (and mostly Godless men at that) to a kingdom on earth ruled by the Son of God. Some of the other names for this time of trouble reflect this changeover, such as "labor pains," and "the time of Jacob's trouble." We also hear other names for it such as "the day of wrath," "the day," "that day," "latter days" and "a day of smoke and burning."

The day of the Lord is not necessarily a 24-hour day. Compared to the last 6,000 years though, it is a short time on the calendar, probably three and a half years, 1,290 days (Daniel 12:11) or 1,335 days (Daniel 12:12) spoken of by Daniel.

It will hit unexpectedly - surprising everyone, even the Church, because like Israel, it, as a whole, has forsaken God's ways delivered to believers in His Law. The letters to the seven congregations at the beginning of Revelation tell us that all is not well within groups that call themselves by His name at that time, and it still holds true today. Read the letters, and remember that they applied at the time they were written but also to congregations since then. Does it sound like any of the congregations then or now are without the need for preparation or repentance?

- Ephesus (2:5) I will remove your lampstand.
- Smyrna (2:10) be faithful unto death.
- Pergamum (2:16) I will come and war against them with the sword of my mouth.
- Thyatira (2:26) those who commit adultery with Jezebel I will throw into great tribulation.
- Sardis (3:3) I will come like a thief.
- Philadelphia (3:10) keep you from the hour of trial.
- Laodicea (3:20) stand at the door and knock.

The Four Beast Kingdoms

Daniel in chapter 7 of his book sees visions of four great beasts. We know that these beasts represent four world empires: Babylon or Chaldea, Media/Persia, Greek, and Terrible or Roman. Each of the beasts representing the four empires have characteristics specific to the kings or governments leading them. Babylon is like a lion with eagle's wings, swift and mighty like a lion, but later he turns into a man (probably because he acknowledges God, Daniel 4). A bear, lumbering yet ferocious and deadly, represents the Medo-Persian Empire. Greece is a fast leopard with four wings indicating rapid conquest. The fourth beast has iron teeth (presumably the Romans), chewing up other kingdoms and stamping on what it doesn't chomp. This last beast has ten horns which later are said to be ten kings or kingdoms. An eleventh horn comes up after those and destroys three of the first ten kingdoms. This "little horn" has "eyes like the eyes of a man and a mouth speaking great things." It is identified later

(Revelation 13) as the beast, making war with the saints and prevailing against them until the arrival of one like a son of man (Yeshua).

Daniel 7:25 ESV. He shall speak words against the Most High, and shall wear out the saints of the Most High, and shall think to change the times and the law; and they shall be given into his hand for a time, times, and half a time.

The statement, "shall think to change the times and the law" is one of the reasons it is clear that the Church (as a whole) will be right in there with the programs of the little horn, at least until the little horn destroys it. The Church is very anti-Law, anti-Israel, and has changed or attempted to change many of the Law's stipulations.

We recognize the agents of the little horn by their actions, not by their wool clothing. The Church has worn out those who really want to follow God and continually teach that the Law has been changed to where they don't have to follow it. The Church has changed "the times" which include God's "appointed times" (Leviticus 23:2) also known as holidays such as Passover, and they cherry-pick which Laws they want to follow, if they follow any at all. Mostly they are modern-day versions of unrepentant Pharisees, Sadducees, scribes and Nicolaitans.

In Revelation 13:2 the beast is described as having parts of three beasts: looks like a leopard, feet like a bear's, and mouth like a lion. This indicates that either he has mixed ancestry or he is leading a kingdom that has parts of the three former empires of Greece, Persia and Babylon or Chaldean. He could even operate with similar characteristics such as speed, ferociousness and speak "great things." The three colors on the body armor of the army of Revelation 9:17 (red, yellow and purple or blue) could also indicate a coalition consisting of remnants of the three kingdoms.

The final king of the north seen in Daniel 11 is from the area having a heavy Chaldean, Greek and Persian cultural mix. Don't forget too that the Roman Empire was actually a coalition of many nations, with an army made up of soldiers from many different countries or tribes. The same tribal and cultural influences from ancient times are still evident in the area of Turkey and Syria, so it's no surprise that the last king of the north, the little horn or the beast, has parts of those ancient cultures in his kingdom too.

Babylon

Nimrod established Babylon way back in the times of Genesis 11. You might not recognize it because the name was slightly different. At first, the name was Babel, as in the Tower of Babel. But both Babel and Babylon are the same word and mean "confusion" or "mixing." Babylon is the name of a city; it is the name of a religion, a kingdom, and the name of a deceiver-inspired government system. They are all devised and driven by the deceiver through his henchmen (various kings and governments).

The Babylon government system is the deceiver's attempt to establish his own kingdom, and his kingdom is opposed to God and God's ways of doing things. It's a kingdom that is both political (because he wants to rule) and religious (because he wants worship). We can see some of the goals of this kingdom or government in Genesis 11:1-9. Nimrod and the other servants of the deceiver wanted to build a city and a tower with its top in the heavens, perhaps to avoid the drowning in another flood. They attempted to make it permanent by building with fired bricks and bitumen mortar. By this, they were going to "make a name" and stay unified in opposition to God with one language and common interests. As we see throughout Scripture, these interests included gaining wealth and power by cheating and theft, stealing worship rightfully belonging to God, and challenging the authority of God in every way they could think of with a heaping helping of sexual immorality.

Babylon is a fitting symbol of world kingdoms in general. Like that fourth beast kingdom shown to Nebuchadnezzar, anytime men get together in a government, they build without regard for God, destroy what they can't consume, and lust after wealth plundered from God and other people. The golden statue built by Nebuchadnezzar in defiance of the dream given by God is an excellent symbol of every anti-God, idolatrous government and religious practice. All of men's efforts at kingdoms are, at their root, a worship of self (doing what is right in their own eyes).

The city kingdom of Tyre in Ezekiel 27 and 28 is spoken of in a way similar to ancient Babylon, because they are both fronts for the real power behind them. Ezekiel's lament for Tyre applies not only to the then-current king of Tyre and to the city itself, but also to the fallen angelic power that drove its formation. The lament resonates throughout history because of repetition. Ezekiel 28:11-19 describes a being that, similar to Isaiah's description in Isaiah 14:12-20 of the king of Babylon, has to apply to the power behind the king. We know this one to be the deceiver, serpent, or dragon.

People have tried to identify a city or a particular country as the Babylon of Revelation, and there might be a particular city of that name eventually, but the concept of Babylon is not confined to one city. Our entire world system, all the individual countries and governments, have the very same motivations and goals as Babylon. To modify a popular phrase, we are all Babylon now.

Babylon includes every anti-God economic and religious global system ever thought up by man or the deceiver. The world is Babylon. Every world-wide empire or attempt at an empire, as with the Germans and Japanese in the '30's and '40's or China and Russia currently, are Babylon. The "globalists" of our present time are agents of the deceiver and part of Babylon.

This Babylonian world system includes the group that crucified Yeshua, though we call them Romans. Representatives from the (at the time of the Incarnation) world religious-government and their momentary allies from Judaism conspired together to get Yeshua executed and out of their hair. They thought. The commonality between these groups is their membership in Babylon. All anti-God religions and government systems are a part of Babylon; they just have different names and slightly different features throughout history.

Babylon, or the land of the Chaldeans, is said to be a "trading land" according to Ezekiel.

Ezekiel 16:29 ESV. You multiplied your whoring also with the trading land of Chaldea, and even with this you were not satisfied.

Ezekiel again calls it a "land of trade" and a "city of merchants" in Ezekiel 17:4. Zephaniah 1:11 says that at some point "traders are no more." Assyria (in power before Babylon) "increased your merchants more than the stars of the heavens" (Nahum 3:16) which seems to be a bad thing because the trading wasn't often honest or fair. It's clear that there is a connection between the land of the Chaldeans and Babylon of Revelation. A chief distinction is that of merchants; probably those merchants who were dishonest or only out for gain at the expense of others.

Revelation 18:11–13 ESV. And the merchants of the earth weep and mourn for her, since no one buys their cargo anymore, cargo of gold, silver, jewels, pearls, fine linen, purple cloth, silk, scarlet cloth, all kinds of scented wood, all kinds of articles of ivory, all kinds of articles of costly wood, bronze, iron and marble, cinnamon, spice, incense, myrrh, frankincense, wine, oil, fine flour, wheat, cattle and sheep, horses and chariots, and slaves, that is, human souls.

Babylon is not capitalism, although the two are frequently associated. Babylon features central control, as in a king or emperor or tyrannical government such as that desired by Stalin, Hitler, Castro, and U.S. democrats. Socialism, communism, fascism, and totalitarianism are different names for Babylon because of the desire of the people in those anti-God systems for control over others. Slavery is when the state or government (or an individual) either controls the means of a person's production or owns it outright. That describes all modern governments.

If you don't think slavery is active in modern times, you aren't paying attention. There was a story that swept the internet in April 2021 concerning a container ship named Evergreen blocking the Suez Canal. Supposedly, 3,000 children (a little less than half of them still alive) were found in the containers. The cargo ship left from Malaysia (think China) and was headed to Rotterdam in the Netherlands. Trading in human souls? This is Babylon at its worst. Some say that this never happened, and claim there is no evidence. Most of us weren't there so we don't know, and we can't trust most of the journalists anymore. But the circumstances are extremely suspicious, and even if not true that doesn't mean the selling of children isn't going on. Just ask the people around Jeffrey Epstein, if you can get them to talk. There's also reporting on child pornography rings and (overwhelmingly Democrat) politicians involved in pedophilia. Muslim groups in African nations routinely kidnap and sell members of other tribal groups, especially those that are Christian.

Slavery is also from debt. Whether you know it or not, or are personally in debt, all the different kinds of debt are enslaving you. Government debt in particular affects everything from the value of paper money to prices we pay for gas and food. The entire world population right now is in slavery to debt whether they know it or not. Wars are fought using debt to buy or build weapons and move armies around. Interest expense on debt demands that we work our fingers to the bone in order to pay back a home mortgage at four to five times the value of the original loan.

Amos 8:4–6 ESV. Hear this, you who trample on the needy and bring the poor of the land to an end, saying, "When will the new moon be over, that we may sell grain? And the Sabbath, that we may offer wheat for sale, that we may make the ephah small and the shekel great and deal deceitfully with false balances, that we may buy the poor for silver and the needy for a pair of sandals and sell the chaff of the wheat?"

Capitalism, especially as practiced in the best way in the United States, is control over yourself and the freedom to keep the gain of your own hands. Capitalism can be defined in one way as "you keep what you earn." Socialism/communism then is defined as "<u>they</u> keep what you earn," "they" being the people in control. In American capitalism, the individual has the freedom to own land or come up with a service or product that is sold to people who want to buy, and keep the proceeds. Babylonian communism or socialism dictates what the individual is allowed to earn and sees the proceeds of any effort as the property of the state. Just like slavery.

Capitalism gets a bad name because many people, who gain a large amount of money through it, turn around and use money to control or attempt to control others. A lot of money concentrated in the hands of a few people encourages fascism or socialism, because power corrupts. These people think they know better and want to force their views on others.

Wealthy individuals usually get "fascism fever" after they accumulate a lot of money. They use their money to bribe or influence governments to make regulations helping their money-grabbing lust. Control is the issue, and has always been that way with governments/empires. The lust for control is evident in all the works of the deceiver. These people might protest that they are trying to do good things or even what's good for everybody. They are lying, because God is not a part of their plans except perhaps using His name like a lucky rabbit's foot.

Israel had what should have been the best government because God was at the top, working through priests and elders using His Laws. The United States is unique in history (other than Israel at its best) because of the subordination of the government to the freedom of the individual. Rights in the U.S. are granted by God and (are supposed to be) protected by the government.

Babylonian communism/fascism/socialism on the other hand keeps all the power (money, privilege) centralized with a few rulers who take what money they want to furnish their lavish lifestyles from those who labored to gain the money. The government systems of Babylon don't like the freedom, independence and power of the United States citizens within pure capitalism, and have been trying for decades to knock the United States down and bring us under their control.

We can tell that Revelation 18 is not talking about money alone because of the mention of slaves. Slavery, which is the control of people willingly or even unwillingly, is the heartbeat of Babylon. Ancient Babylon wanted to control its destiny by uniting people against God and forcing other kingdoms (or tribes) to go along. Nebuchadnezzar made his statue and forced (or tried to force) everyone to worship it (him). It was a preview of the image of the beast in Revelation 13:11-18, and has been the desire of the deceiver since the beginning.

The deceiver wants control over people, whether he gets it by lies and trickery or force, he doesn't care which. God wants voluntary conversions back to His kingdom based on love. The deceiver uses the fear of death to control, but God has removed the sting of death by the blood of His Son Yeshua haMashiach.

Dress for Action

You might think it a little weird to talk about clothing in a book on prophecy, or when talking about the Tribulation. But garments play an important role, and it isn't actual cotton and polyester off-the-rack tee shirts and jeans. Decoding prophecies is easier when we study and personally apply the whole of the Word. If we look up words like garment, robe, or fine linen, we find that for believers, garments are salvation and righteousness.

Isaiah 61:10 ESV. I will greatly rejoice in the LORD; my soul shall exult in my God, for he has clothed me with the garments of salvation; he has covered me with the robe of righteousness, as a bridegroom decks himself like a priest with a beautiful headdress, and as a bride adorns herself with her jewels.

Revelation 19:7–8 ESV. Let us rejoice and exult and give him the glory, for the marriage of the Lamb has come, and his Bride has made herself ready; it was granted her to clothe herself with fine linen, bright and pure"— for the fine linen is the righteous deeds of the saints.

For unbelievers, garments are something quite different.

Psalm 73:6 ESV. Therefore pride is their necklace; violence covers them as a garment.

Psalm 109:18–19 ESV. He clothed himself with cursing as his coat; may it soak into his body like water, like oil into his bones! May it be like a garment that he wraps around him, like a belt that he puts on every day!

God has robes and garments, but figuratively ours are similar to His, because we get our garments from Him. The first (good) garments were made by Yeshua when He made garments of skin for Adam and Eve. Garments that God makes for us are much better than the works of our own hands.

Psalm 104:1–2 ESV. Bless the LORD, O my soul! O LORD my God, you are very great! You are clothed with splendor and majesty, covering yourself with light as with a garment, stretching out the heavens like a tent.

Garments also describe the heavens and earth, which are rolled up like a scroll or garment at the end of the 1,000 year kingdom.

Psalm 102:25–27 ESV. Of old you laid the foundation of the earth, and the heavens are the work of your hands. They will perish, but you will remain; they will all wear out like a garment. You will change them like a robe, and they will pass away, but you are the same, and your years have no end.

Hebrews 1:10–12 ESV. And, "You, Lord, laid the foundation of the earth in the beginning, and the heavens are the work of your hands; they will perish, but you remain; they will all wear out like a garment, like a robe you will roll them up, like a garment they will be changed. But you are the same, and your years will have no end."

Revelation 6:12–14 ESV. When he opened the sixth seal, I looked, and behold, there was a great earthquake, and the sun became black as sackcloth, the full moon became like blood, and the stars of the sky fell to the earth as the fig tree sheds its winter fruit when shaken by a gale. The sky vanished like a scroll that is being rolled up, and every mountain and island was removed from its place.

Yeshua tells us in Revelation 3 that Sardis still had "names," or "people who have not soiled their garments." Those who persevere or conquer (the world or the flesh) "will be clothed thus in white garments" and "walk with me in white, for they are worthy." So garments are the efforts of believers who cling to the Words of God and "work out their salvation with fear and trembling" as Paul says in Philippians 2:12. They cover themselves with good works which result from following the whole of God's instructions to His people, including His Law.

Malachi 3:16–18 ESV. Then those who feared the LORD spoke with one another. The LORD paid attention and heard them, and a book of remembrance was written before him of those who feared the LORD and esteemed his name. "They shall be mine, says the LORD of hosts, in the day when I make up my treasured possession, and I will spare them as a man spares his son who serves him. Then once more you shall see the distinction between the righteous and the wicked, between one who serves God and one who does not serve him.

In Luke 12:35 Yeshua tells believers to "dress for action."

Luke 12:35–38 ESV. "Stay dressed for action and keep your lamps burning, and be like men who are waiting for their master to come home from the wedding feast, so that they may open the door to him at once when he comes and knocks. Blessed are those servants whom the master finds awake when he comes. Truly, I say to you, he will dress himself for service and have them recline at table, and he will come and serve them. If he comes in the second watch, or in the third, and finds them awake, blessed are those servants!"

Garments in this case are also "good deeds" connected with doing what Yeshua tells us to do. We are supposed to stay dressed for action, ready for His return, doing what He told us at all times. Matthew (chapter 25) records for us the parable told by Yeshua of ten virgins and oil for lamps. This is an illustration of having the Spirit of God, and is another way of describing good deeds (following God's Word).

The Earthquake

Isaiah 24:19–20 ESV. The earth is utterly broken, the earth is split apart, the earth is violently shaken. The earth staggers like a drunken man; it sways like a hut; its transgression lies heavy upon it, and it falls, and will not rise again.

Isaiah 13:13 ESV. Therefore I will make the heavens tremble, and the earth will be shaken out of its place, at the wrath of the LORD of hosts in the day of his fierce anger.

Ezekiel 38:19–20 ESV. For in my jealousy and in my blazing wrath I declare, On that day there shall be a great earthquake in the land of Israel. The fish of the sea and the birds of the heavens and the beasts of the field and all creeping things that creep on the ground, and all the people who are on the face of the earth, shall quake at my presence. And the mountains shall be thrown down, and the cliffs shall fall, and every wall shall tumble to the ground.

Revelation 6:14 ESV. The sky vanished like a scroll that is being rolled up, and every mountain and island was removed from its place.

Revelation 16:20 ESV. And every island fled away, and no mountains were to be found.

This section is labeled "The Earthquake" because there have always been earthquakes, but there is one prophesied that is more destructive than all others. Mountains become valleys; valleys become mountains (Isaiah 40:3-5). Cities are broken down, Jerusalem splits into three parts, and the whole earth staggers like a drunken man.

Six times earthquakes are mentioned in Revelation (6:12, 8:5, 11:13, 19, 16:18 and 16:20). It looks like the one at 6:12 (or 6:14) and the one at 16:18 (or 16:20) are the same. Three of the six earthquakes (besides the earthquake at the 6th seal and 7th bowl) seem like regular earthquakes. One is at the opening of the seventh seal (just "an earthquake" 8:5). Another is after the resurrection of the two witnesses at the sixth trumpet, in which 7,000 people were killed and a tenth of "the city" (Jerusalem) falls (a "great earthquake," 11:13). There's also one after the seventh trumpet ("an earthquake" 11:19). Revelation 16:20 doesn't have the word "earthquake" but that "every mountain and island was removed from its place" which relates it to "the big one."

There are other earthquakes recorded for us in the Bible (1 Kings 19:11; Amos 1:1), but one in particular stands out in Revelation 16:18. This one is "such as there had never been since man was on the earth." It appears to be the same one mentioned in Isaiah, violently shaking the earth, making it sway like a hut. This earthquake also appears by the description in Ezekiel to be the one that causes mountains to flatten (Revelation 16:20). It might also cause valleys to rise up and make the uneven ground level as Isaiah says in chapter 40 of his book (or his statement might just be a metaphor for repentance, or both).

There are two places in the Bible where people say to mountains "cover us." One is at the sixth seal in Revelation. The other is in Hosea. Both are related to idolatry which is also known as abandoning or "cheating on" God.

Hosea 10:8 ESV. The high places of Aven, the sin of Israel, shall be destroyed. Thorn and thistle shall grow up on their altars, and they shall say to the mountains, "Cover us," and to the hills, "Fall on us."

This seems more like a generic statement of people who are seeing God coming after them. His fury will be so formidable and intense that those rejecting Him will try to hide any way they can, even by groveling in dirt or wishing mountains would bury them.

So it's as Yeshua said. There "will be famines and earthquakes in various places. All these are the beginning of birth pains." Earthquakes come and go, but in recent history, they have been increasing in frequency and intensity, just like labor for a woman about to give birth. The Big One is the pinnacle of earthquakes and shakes the whole earth, just before Yeshua shows up to clean house on the kingdom of the deceiver and the little horn.

Stars

In the Bible, there are stars, and then there are stars. As in modern movies, you have your A-list stars (Yeshua) and your B-list stars. Sometimes stars are human leaders of families (Genesis 37:9; Revelation 12:1), or congregations (angels, Revelation 1:16). Kings can be stars, and sometimes the word refers to angels (Job 38:7) and fallen angels (Daniel 8:10). Other times stars are just the lights we see in the heavens or even idols (Amos 5:26; Acts 7:43).

The Messiah is said to be a star (Numbers 24:17) or the "bright morning star" (Revelation 22:16), and Lucifer is said to be a Day Star or son of Dawn (Isaiah 14:12) and was the power behind the king of Babylon and all other earthly kingdoms.

The "stars of the sky that fall to earth" in Revelation 6:13, and the stars that the dragon sweeps out of heaven and casts to the earth by his tail (Revelation 12:4), are probably angels or what we call demons now.

Physical stars that we see in the sky apparently are angels, or celestial bodies controlled by them. Some angels have job titles, like the watchers of Daniel 4 (although there is no direct mention of stars there) or cherubim (guardians like the angel at the entrance to the garden of Eden Genesis 3:24). Others of them have names, such as Michael and Gabriel, Wormwood in Revelation 8:11, Abaddon (Apollyon in Greek, a.k.a. destruction or destroyer) the king of the stinging locusts from the bottomless pit in Revelation 9, or the Destroyer of Exodus 12:23.

These instances give us insight into the "prince of the power of the air" (Ephesians 2:2) and "the cosmic powers of this present darkness" (Ephesians 6:12) Paul talks about. These are directly connected to Pergamum, a city in the same area as Ephesus. Yeshua says that this part of what is now western Turkey (Pergamum) is the place "where Satan's throne is" (Revelation

2:13). The deceiver might've moved his throne location by now, but probably not (because of proximity to Israel). Even though his throne might be in one particular spot, that doesn't mean he doesn't still arrogantly "roam to and fro on the earth" (Job 1:7, 2:2) as God allows. The former Day Star is still at work trying to force his kingdom on everyone else, and other "stars" are going right along with him (see the section titled **The Hot Spot** later in this chapter).

Numbering the Days

Five places in the Bible have a specific number of days listed in connection with the Tribulation or Day of the Lord. Three are in Daniel: 8:14 (2,300 evenings and mornings or about 76 months plus 20 days or 6 years 4 months and 20 days), 12:11 (1,290 days or 3 1/2 years plus a month) and 12:12 (1,335 days or 3 1/2 years plus 75 days or about 10 1/2 weeks). One is in Revelation 11:3 where two witnesses prophesy for 42 months (1,260 days or 3 1/2 years) and the other is in Revelation 12:6 where the woman hides out in the wilderness for 1,260 days.

If we use the 30 day month common in the period before the Incarnation (before the Romans changed the calendar), 42 months equals 1,260 days or three and a half years. Another way of saying 42 months or 1,260 days is "time, times and half a time" (Daniel 7:25, 12:7 and Revelation 12:14) meaning one year plus two years plus a half a year, or 3 and a half years (again with 30 day months). If one month is added to 1,260 days, we get 1,290 days. Six more weeks gives us 1,335 days. It is not certain how these numbers all add up, but possibilities are presented here and elsewhere in this book.

One other important time reference is in Daniel 9:27 where the prince who is to come "shall make a strong covenant with many for one week. This period is most likely a week of years or 7 years, given the context of 70 years for the exile. For half of the week (42 months or 1,260 days) the prince shall put an end to sacrifice and offering." However, just because the little horn makes an agreement for one week doesn't mean the time of Jacob's Trouble will go the full seven years.

The "strong covenant for one week" occurs after "the people of the prince who is to come" destroy the city and the sanctuary, and we know that the people who destroyed the Temple and Jerusalem were the Romans. It follows that the prince who is to come will come from part of the old Roman Empire, and perhaps wants to revive it. It is indicated in Scripture that this prince will come from western Turkey or Syria (the king of the north - see the next section).

Some think that the 2,300 evenings and morning applies to the time of the Maccabees (around 173 years before the Christ) when the offerings and sacrifices ceased. But first, it doesn't really fit, and second the angel says this applies to the time of the end. An additional philosophy from men tries to correct for this by including the time of the Maccabees and calling the last 2,000 years the "time of the end." But that is stretching the time way too much. See the section **Prophetic Timing** for additional insight. It is more likely that 2,300 evenings and mornings is the actual length of time of the time of Jacob's Trouble or Tribulation. It is shorter than seven years perhaps because as Yeshua said those days are cut short for the sake of the elect.

We know the Daniel 8:14 reference is for the Tribulation because of Daniel 8:26 - "The vision of the evenings and the mornings that has been told is true, but seal up the vision, for it refers to many days from now," and Daniel 8:19 "it refers to the appointed time of the end." It's also because it applies to the "little horn" of Daniel 8:9, and the angel in Daniel 12:9 says that "the words are shut up and sealed until the time of the end."

Daniel 12:11 informs us that the time after the taking away of the regular burnt offering and the setup of the abomination that makes desolate (it seems we should take these two events as happening together) is 1,290 days. Taken together, we get a picture with the following points.

Three sections of weeks are decreed (7, 62, and 1), and they are not end to end: batches of 49 years, 434 years, and 7 years. Depending on how you set up the start points (according to Scripture) it took 49 years to rebuild Jerusalem and the Temple. Then there's the next batch of 434 years after which the Messiah shows up and is "cut off." There remains still one batch of seven or 7-year period "to finish the transgression, put an end to sin, atone for iniquity, bring in everlasting righteousness, seal both vision and prophet and anoint a most holy place" (Daniel 9:24).

The people of the prince who is to come who destroy the sanctuary and Jerusalem are the Romans. Their empire was composed of many conquered nations, and their armies had lots of conscripts from these nations. The prince who is to come from the Roman Empire (the beast) signs, or makes a seven-year "covenant" with many, indicating some sort of democratic vote in Israel.

We know from Revelation that two witnesses testify for 1,260 days, probably in the first half of the seven-year Tribulation to about the half-way point. The trumpet judgments are probably being dropped on the world during this time. But it could also be that the 42 months is a stand-alone time, happening within the week of years instead of starting at the beginning. The woman of Revelation 12 may hide out at the same time or perhaps an overlapping period.

In the middle of the beast's agreement week (the time frame may not be exact) the beast or little horn gains power from the deceiver or dragon, kills the two witnesses, puts an end to sacrifice and offering, and sets himself up as God with a talking image of himself. The bowl judgments occur during this period.

For 1,290 days or 43 months, the regular sacrifice is stopped and the image of the beast is in place. Six weeks or 45 days after that (1,335 days) is perhaps the end of Armageddon.

Yeshua says that the days of the Tribulation are cut short for the sake of the elect. This may be why 2,300 evenings and mornings (six years four months twenty days) come up short of seven years.

Matthew 24:22 ESV. And if those days had not been cut short, no human being would be saved. But for the sake of the elect those days will be cut short.

Another three and a half year time worth mentioning is described in 1 Kings 17 and 18 where a drought falls on the land at Elijah's command.

Luke 4:25–26 ESV. But in truth, I tell you, there were many widows in Israel in the days of Elijah, when the heavens were shut up three years and six months, and a great famine came over all the land, and Elijah was sent to none of them but only to Zarephath, in the land of Sidon, to a woman who was a widow.

James 5:17 ESV. Elijah was a man with a nature like ours, and he prayed fervently that it might not rain, and for three years and six months it did not rain on the earth.

If Elijah is one of the two witnesses of Revelation, and he prophesies for the first half of the seven year tribulation, then it could be that the famines mentioned with the third seal (black horse rider) are due at least in part to Elijah preventing the rain from falling during that time.

Revelation 11:6 ESV. They have the power to shut the sky, that no rain may fall during the days of their prophesying, and they have power over the waters to turn them into blood and to strike the earth with every kind of plague, as often as they desire.

Mostly, though, we just need to watch and be ready. As we get closer to the changeover from man's kingdoms back to God's, we will be better able to see the alignment of the days with events.

Kings of the North & South

Much of the prophecies in the book of Daniel are so accurate that unbelievers say they could not actually have been given *before* the events took place. Chapters 10 and 11 in particular are an exact account of the time between the rebuilding of Jerusalem and the Incarnation of the Messiah. Unbelieving historians' claim the prophecies must have been written *after* the events foretold rather than before. This denial is an excellent example of people ignoring God even when presented with direct, irrefutable evidence of His power and knowledge. No wonder they will be groveling in the dirt when what they think is a fantasy God or "flying spaghetti monster" is visiting the earth in wrath and fury.

After the Greek ruler Alexander suddenly died, he of the four-winged leopard indicating speed in conquering (Daniel 7:6), four of his generals divided the newly-acquired kingdom between them. The northern kingdom, what we now call Syria and other parts north of Israel such as Turkey, and east of Israel such as Babylon, ended up in the hands of what historians call the Seleucid (say-loo-kid or sa-lay-oo-kid) kings, which took their names after one of Alexander's generals (Seleucus 1 Nicator). The south kingdom, (Egypt and surrounding areas) was ruled for quite a while by the Ptolemy (toll-ah-me) dynasty, also named after another of Alexander's generals (Ptolemy 1 Lagi Soter). Notice that the names of the kingdoms (north and south) connect to their geographic location in relation to Israel.

Daniel's prophecies are a very precise account of the intrigues and wars that go back and forth between the Greek Ptolemaic kings (south) and the Seleucids (north). Israel was hammered between these two kingdoms for hundreds of years after Daniel's day.

One of the Seleucid kings was Antiochus the fourth. He was a king of "the North" or Seleucid empire (Syria, Babylon, Turkey) around the time of the Maccabees (175-164 BC). He called himself "Epiphanes" meaning "manifest" (as a god), but ancient historians, in a play on words, called him "Epimanes" which sounds similar but means "utterly mad."

This guy was a crackpot (albeit a very powerful crackpot), adding to his territory by force without permission from Rome. He made Jewish people take on Greek cultural practices and attacked Jerusalem twice, killing a lot of people. He ransacked the Temple and sacrificed to Zeus on a new altar, which is why some think he is the "abomination of desolation" from Daniel 11 and 12. He is a *type* of abomination, but not The Abomination (the little horn), and is another example of the cyclic nature of the deceiver's and men's attempts to overthrow God.

Antiochus did cause the sacrifices to cease, and he commanded the Jews to stop following the Law and offer pigs to other gods. But there is no record of an agreement with many for one week of years, and then stopping the sacrifices in the middle of the week. He also didn't lose the use of his right eye and (presumably) right arm (Zechariah 11:17). He didn't proclaim himself God, but "a god." He had actions close to the actions of the little horn in the Day of the Lord, but he doesn't follow prophecy exactly, as we know to expect from our Father.

Isaiah 48:3 ESV. "The former things I declared of old; they went out from my mouth, and I announced them; then suddenly I did them, and they came to pass."

Antiochus is an example of cycles of fulfillment. He did many of the things the little horn or beast will do, because the deceiver keeps trying the same strategy and tactics repeatedly. Satan sets up a guy ruling a kingdom, tries to expand it around the whole globe, and uses the same tactics each time such as corrupting the practice of the Word. God robs him of success (to this point) by always knocking him down a couple of pegs.

But in the Day of the Lord, the deceiver again tries to set up his kingdom one more time using the little horn and false prophet or anti-Christ. The events will be like a ghostly repeat of his efforts in the past. Or perhaps the former efforts were like a rehearsal for the main show. At the time of the end, however, God allows the deceiver a little more leeway to get the job done. The effort will fail yet again, and God will drop the final hammer on all the attempts to set up a kingdom, in opposition to His, once and for all. The deceiver will be able to get things off the ground for a short while in the Tribulation, only to be semi-permanently decked by God. This lasts until his final rebellion at the end of a thousand-year jail sentence.

The Hot Spot

It's probable that the scope or the area affected most by the Great Tribulation is the Middle East. This doesn't mean that the whole globe isn't affected; it just means that the main battle action is in and around Israel.

Evidence for this is that first, most of history centers in an are called the "Fertile Crescent." This is a large sort of crescent shaped area arcing from the Persian Gulf and Caspian Sea in the east, westward through Babylon and Persia (Turkey) and covering an area down through Israel and continuing down the Nile River through Lower Egypt.

Most every important event and kingdom up until just a little while after the Christ resurrected was in this area. Babel and/or Babylon, Assyria, Media, Persia, Greece and Egypt were "the world" and got their starts in this area. Although Greece is a little north and west of it, as is Rome, most of their focus was in the Crescent. Europe, North America, South America, Russia, India, China and other areas are historically just suburbs formed by migration from the great civilizations birthed in the Fertile Crescent. When John got the Revelation, this area was still the happening place or the hot spot. It still is.

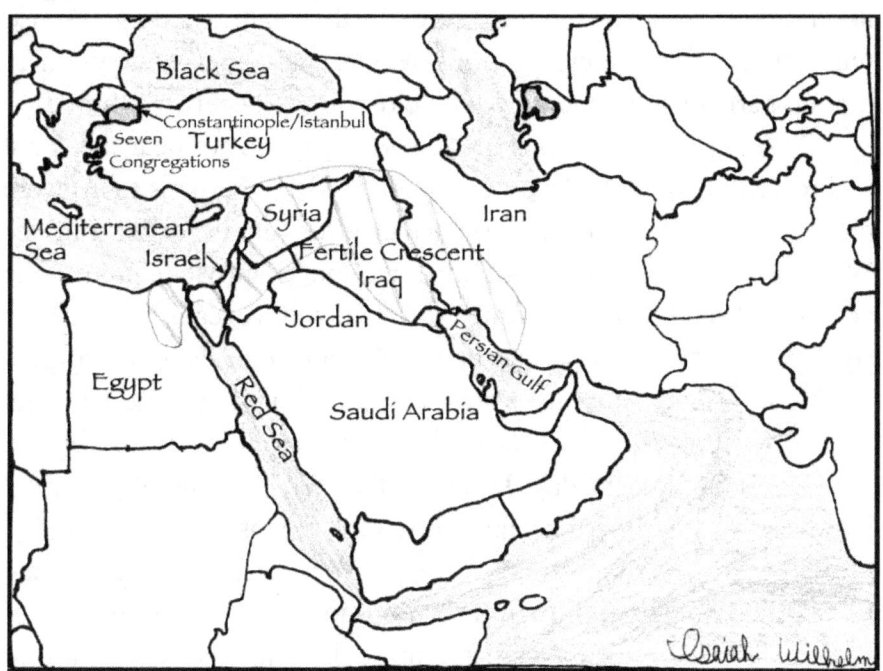

Image of The Fertile Crescent

The second piece of evidence that the action in Revelation is centered in the Fertile Crescent is the letters of Revelation 2 and 3. They are addressed to seven congregations of believers in the part of the Fertile Crescent called Asia, and we now call western Turkey. Out of all the many congregations in existence at the time, Yeshua dictated letters directly only to these seven. Seven other books (Ephesians, Galatians, Colossians, 1 Timothy, 2 Timothy, 1 Peter, 2 Peter), are addressed to leaders or congregations in Asia (part of the Persian empire), indicating a lot of problems there.

A related major clue to answer the question of why, is that Yeshua says the deceiver has his throne in Pergamum (Revelation 2:13) right in the middle of western Turkey. The seven congregations addressed by Yeshua were in the hot spot of where the deceiver operated then and now. In their natures, they are also representative of congregations everywhere and every-when, though perhaps not geographically close to the deceiver's throne.

A supporting clue is in Acts 16:6, where we hear that Paul is directed away from Asia or western Turkey. Perhaps there were greater needs elsewhere, or God had other plans for getting the Word to that area. It could also be that Paul challenging the deceiver directly on his home turf would have caused a greater conflict than the world could handle at that time. Paul is also kept from going into Bithynia (also now part of Turkey). He later got around to some parts of Asia when he lived in Ephesus (on the west coast of present day Turkey). The Word eventually did get into Asia by other, perhaps more low-key, means.

Another supporting series of clues is that after the Revelation was given, in the next thousand years or so, the city of Byzantium (later called Constantinople) in the northern part of Bithynia, would be the cradle and sort-of capitol (for a while) of The Church. It was also the capitol of the eastern (and sometimes the whole) Roman Empire. Byzantium was renamed Constantinople by Emperor Constantine (a major evangelist for the Roman Church), and later Istanbul by the Muslims. It is only a few days foot travel just north and east of Pergamum, the city where the deceiver has (or had) his throne. A half-dozen or more "Church" conferences were held in and around Constantinople over hundreds of years. Islam got its start around this area, the Church was formed next door, and Israel is just to the south.

All the major kingdoms of the world were born and/or ruled in the Fertile Crescent and surrounding areas. None of this is coincidental. Taken together, it points to the area of Turkey/Syria as a place where the deceiver has his TOC (tactical operations center) and has a great deal of influence.

Revelation 13:2 ESV. And the beast that I saw was like a leopard; its feet were like a bear's, and its mouth was like a lion's mouth. And to it the dragon gave his power and his throne and great authority.

As mentioned previously, this verse compared to the context of Daniel means that the kingdom of the beast is made up of parts from Greece, Persia (modern Turkey and Iran), and the older Babylonian and Assyrian empires, which were all around the hot spot. It is not coincidental that the center of anti-God, anti-Jew and anti-Israel power and thought was (and is) in Istanbul, right next door to the location of the deceiver's throne (Pergamum).

It makes sense that the deceiver would set up his throne as near as he could get to Israel and yet still control the big kingdoms, because Israel is representative of God's kingdom. Jerusalem is God's line-of-death in the sand. The dragon or deceiver gives the beast his throne, which is in the area north of Israel, so it makes tactical and strategic sense that the hot spot is in the same area.

The non-biblical construct called the Church has believers in it, but also many Nicolaitans and other followers of Jezebel and

Balaam. The Church (the whole thing) has invested a lot of effort carrying out some of the deceiver's plans. This is shown by their history of ignoring God's Word, immorality, idolatry, mixing pagan things with Bible things and martyring real believers. All while striving to look innocent covered in wool clothing.

The Church (again, as a whole) is against Israel (though some individuals correctly defend it), the majority of Muslims are against Israel, and other anti-God nations will join them in blaming Israel for the world's problems. These will make up the religious part of the little horn's kingdom, which we see riding the beast as the prostitute mystery religion Babylon in Revelation.

A final argument (for now) is that Daniel seems to point to the geographic location of the rise of the beast. In Daniel 7 and 8, we get the outline of world history as it concerns kingdoms of the world and Israel. The little horn, or beast, is said to come out of the north or what we now know as the Seleucid kingdom of Alexander's broken empire (Daniel 8:9). Directions in these chapters are using Israel as a reference point, so the north kingdom is, you guessed it, Syria and Western Turkey. This part of the Old Persian and Greek Empire is the same area Yeshua addresses in His Revelation letters. His strengthening is for those congregations and for local troubles at the time of John, but also for future troubles in which believers in general would be found.

The Endurance of the Saints

There are two main players besides God and the angels in the Great Tribulation. As you might expect, they are believers, represented by those who hold to the commandments and the testimony of Yeshua, and unbelievers or those who hold to the enemy of God. The beast and his followers are marked by behavior or with the number of man. Believers, or those who hold to the commands and the testimony of Yeshua, are marked with the seal of God (the Holy Spirit Ephesians 1:13, 4:30). Believers spend their time during the Tribulation witnessing, hiding out in a place prepared for them or perhaps dying for the faith.

This subject always arrests the attention of the thoughtful disciple when reading Revelation and trying to figure out prophecy. Endurance and conquering seem to be regular encouragements for believers when we are hearing of tribulation. It was mentioned in the last section, but more in depth coverage is needed here because it should literally scare the hell out of people (hopefully). The misunderstanding of this is a core reason for many who try to explain that what is happening in the Tribulation isn't really happening.

Revelation 13:10 ESV. If anyone is to be taken captive, to captivity he goes; if anyone is to be slain with the sword, with the sword must he be slain. Here is a call for the endurance and faith of the saints.

Some think that this verse must be referring to converted Jews only, because of a philosophy of men that "the Church" is gone in a so-called "rapture." These people think that there are two bodies, instead of one like Paul said in Ephesians 4

However, after reading the Bible many times, and taking it in its plain meaning (the one the author intended), it is obvious that Paul was right and there is only one body. Believers are grafted in to one, already existing, olive tree, and there is no Church in the Bible (except as illustrated by mystery religion Babylon).

This verse has to refer to both believers (Jewish or non-Jewish) and non-believers. We can see first that it is a general statement of God ordaining who will go where. Some of the other places this concept is mentioned might help with our understanding here (or might scare us even further).

Jeremiah 15:2 ESV. And when they ask you, 'Where shall we go?' you shall say to them, 'Thus says the LORD: " 'Those who are for pestilence, to pestilence, and those who are for the sword, to the sword; those who are for famine, to famine, and those who are for captivity, to captivity.'

Jeremiah 43:11 ESV. He shall come and strike the land of Egypt, giving over to the pestilence those who are doomed to the pestilence, to captivity those who are doomed to captivity, and to the sword those who are doomed to the sword.

The first Jeremiah reference is directed at Israel, disciplined by God and dispersed from the Land. The second is for Egypt, and for those of Israel that went there against God's specific command not to go. A similar passage is in Jeremiah 48:44 where a person fleeing from terror will fall into a pit, and when he climbs out of the pit he'll be caught in a snare. The Revelation 13:10 passage is delivered to believers concerning the bad stuff that is happening to the kingdom of the little horn, but in which believers may also be caught because the deceiver hates us. Revelation 13:7 says the beast will be "allowed to make war on the saints and conquer them," which indicates that believers will either be thrown in jail or enslaved or slain in war.

The people who wish to limit this to "the Jews" would prefer to think that believers are whisked away in an extra-biblical "rapture" and only Jews are affected here. This thought begs the question of the identity of John and of the people to which he is delivering these words. John is Jewish, yet he is still a believer in Yeshua as the Messiah. Yeshua is very much Jewish, and belief in the Messiah is a Jewish concept even if the Jews in general don't accept Yeshua as the Messiah. John is speaking to people of similar persuasion as he, along with some Gentile believers. The Gentile believers are grafted into the one body of Messiah believers.

Something God told Ezekiel might also contribute to illuminating our understanding here. In chapter 5 of his book, Ezekiel is told to shave his hair, burn a third, strike a third with the sword, hide a small number in his robe, and then take some of the hidden hairs to burn them. This illustrated the fate of the people in Jerusalem and surrounding areas as Babylon attacked. Verse 12 of that chapter gives us clarification that a third part of Israel would die of pestilence and famine, a third would fall by the sword, and a third would be scattered to other nations chased by the sword.

Of the scattered group, Ezekiel was to take a representative number and hide them in the skirts of his robe, and again of this number he was to take another small amount and burn them with fire. From this "fired" group a fire will come out into all the house of Israel. This illustration is to represent those who persevere in following God and are hidden from God's judgments at the time, but also at the Tribulation. Some of these hidden ones will also "forth tell" God's Words, even if it kills them, so that other people are inflamed with passion for God. More on the idea of believers "hidden" on the day of smoke and burning is in the section of this book on the resurrection and rapture.

God counts every hair on everyone's head and not a sparrow falls to the ground but that He knows. Some of us will suffer from man's wrath, but we will all be protected from His judgments falling on the kingdom of the little horn.

The seven letters at the beginning of Revelation contain warnings to people who might wear His name but have strayed from what God commanded, just as Israel has done many times throughout history. Smyrna is told that some will be imprisoned, have tribulation, and is encouraged to "be faithful unto death." Yet Yeshua also tells those in Philadelphia who "kept my word about patient endurance" that He will "keep you from the hour of trial that is coming on the whole world." This hour might have been already experienced, but it is also appropriate encouragement for believers at any time, such as those in the Big Hour of Trial coming soon to Israel.

John here gives a "call for the endurance and faith of the saints," indicating that there will be a need for perseverance through difficult times. If much of the trouble is occurring around Israel, then the persecution is likely local to that area, but I'm sure the trouble will also spread to other nations. Believer's trust has to be in God and we need to continue to stay true to His word in all things.

Mix all these things together in balance and it's apparent that while God has determined some for sword and some for captivity, this will mostly apply to unbelievers only. Believers might suffer on the edges, but most of our suffering will come from the wrath of people aligned with the deceiver.

Believers even now are being persecuted and killed for no other reason except that they follow the God of Abraham, Isaac and Jacob. Muslims, Chinese, Democrats, Democrats masquerading as Republicans, and many other despotic and tyrannical people hound, rape, torture, enslave, rob, block us from assembling or worshipping together, and kill us out of hand by the thousands. We are a threat to the deceiver, his plans, and his people. Plus he just hates us because we are the evidence that God's kingdom wins and will always win.

God is watching, and He will not forget the treatment of His people by the enemy. We might suffer from man's wrath but they will suffer God's. Believers have only a little power but we keep His word and will not deny His name or the name of His Son Yeshua, the true and only Anointed savior of us all. He will protect us. We need to listen in all humility to everything He says, so we will not miss His direction and go into hiding to avoid what trouble we can when it comes.

God's Wrath and Man's Wrath

There's a huge difference between the wrath of God and the wrath of man. The wrath of man is driven by the wrath of the deceiver's hate for all of God's works. The wrath of man is merely an extension of the deceiver's wrath and both are relatively superficial (though painful and horrible), in that they can only affect us in the physical realm. God's wrath is much more intense, more creative, more powerful, more effective and more complete. He has control over all creation, from diseases and insects all the way up to planetary bodies such as the sun and the moon. The worst that a man can do is destroy the body, but God can destroy both body and soul in hell.

Matthew 10:28 ESV. And do not fear those who kill the body but cannot kill the soul. Rather fear him who can destroy both soul and body in hell.

In the meantime, God can make it extremely miserable on earth too. He hates sin, and without the sacrifice of our Messiah, we would have to face His wrath. Yeshua paid the price for our sin. That way we can become part of God's kingdom and receive God's love instead of His justified wrath. He has no pleasure in the death of the wicked (Ezekiel 33:11). But His wrath will be poured out in the Day of the Lord on all those who reject that ultimate act of sacrifice and love from God and Yeshua.

However, when we accept the sacrifice of Yeshua, believers then have to endure the wrath of the deceiver and those who follow him. The deceiver has some power, and can fake some miracles to make it look like his agents are acting on behalf of God, but only in a limited way allowed by God.

Matthew 24:23–24 ESV. Then if anyone says to you, 'Look, here is the Christ!' or 'There he is!' do not believe it. For false christs and false prophets will arise and perform great signs and wonders, so as to lead astray, if possible, even the elect.

The telling difference is that the deceiver's agents always lead away from the Word of God, even if only a little bit at a time (remember the concept of gradualism). Believers might lose their physical body, but God rescues our eternal souls. The worst the deceiver can do to believers is limited to the physical realm, unless a person gives in to temptation and worships the deceiver or his agents. Then that person ends up in the same place with the people he obeyed or worshipped.

Anointing

You might think this is another odd subject for a book on prophecy, but in fact, it is very important. Anointing in its simplest meaning is just putting some oil on something or someone. In the Bible, wounds or sick people are anointed with oil as an aid to healing, for instance (Mark 6:13). Frankincense and myrrh are added to the oil because they are anti-bacterial and bolster the immune system, and are very effective medicines used for centuries. This explains the association with gold, because good medicine was very valuable too.

Jacob anointed a couple of pillars (Genesis 28:18 and 35:14) and made offerings to God. Oil was used for the sacrifices at the Tabernacle and Temple, and presumably for pagan sacrifices as well. Oil was also used for sprucing up the outside of a person in the hair or beard, similar to hair gel (Matthew 6:17), cosmetics or deodorant. The way anointing is mostly used in the Bible, however, can mean a great deal more.

Anointing was a common action in ancient times. It symbolizes the blessing of God, or in copycat paganism, perhaps gods. The first people anointed in the Bible were Aaron and his sons for the work of the priesthood (Exodus 28). The articles of the Tabernacle were also anointed. Later, kings were anointed (Judges 9) such as Saul, David and Solomon. Prophets were anointed too, and did it to transfer the authority of the prophet that was leaving this earth to his successor.

Lots of people and things are anointed, but without God's blessing and presence, it just means they were a little slippery. The purpose of oil with God's blessing symbolizes the Holy Spirit. If God is in the anointing, then a person's actions are consistent with God's will. Cyrus, for instance, was "the lord's anointed" (Isaiah 45:1) because he carried out the will of God in his decree to rebuild Jerusalem and the Temple.

The Holy Spirit anointed Yeshua, when it descended on Him in the form of dove at His water baptism by the hand of John (Matthew 3:16; Luke 3:22). Mary also anointed Him with expensive nard oil perfume (John 12:3), apparently for burial. More on this subject will be revealed in the following pages (because the little horn works with a "false anointed").

Believers are anointed with the Holy Spirit according to Paul (and John, 1 John 2:20 and 27).

2 Corinthians 1:21–22 ESV. And it is God who establishes us with you in Christ, and has anointed us, and who has also put his seal on us and given us his Spirit in our hearts as a guarantee.

We act in accordance with our anointing by following every Word from our Shepherd, going through the Door He opened for us which no one can shut. Lots of people claim anointing by God, but their teachings are not in line with the whole of the Word. These false anointed, using part of the Word just as the deceiver does, are one of the reasons that the deception he fosters (Matthew 24:24) is very successful during the last days.

Except the truly anointed or elect will not be deceived, because we happily hear only His voice and follow all of His Words.

The 70 Weeks of Daniel

Another name for the Day of the Lord (though not quite in the Word this way) is the 70th week of Daniel. As we discussed before, this is from information given to Daniel of 70 weeks concerning events in Israel's future.

Daniel 9:24 ESV. "Seventy weeks are decreed about your people and your holy city, to finish the transgression, to put an end to sin, and to atone for iniquity, to bring in everlasting righteousness, to seal both vision and prophet, and to anoint a most holy place.

In Daniel 9, we have recorded for us Daniel's prayer for Israel. He knew from Jeremiah that the "desolation of Jerusalem" would last for 70 years (Jeremiah 25:11), and he knew that time was at an end. So he prays to God about it, and gets a surprising answer. Seventy periods of seven weeks (a week means a week of years from the context) are decreed.

Literally, Daniel is told "seventy sevens are decreed about your people." The angel who gives Daniel this timeline also breaks it down for him into periods of seven sevens (49 years) 62 sevens (434 years) and a final seven or week of years. The groups of sevens are not one right after the other. They are separate chunks of time starting and ending with a specific event. Each interval ends with the arrival of an anointed one (twice) and a prince (once). A prince can also be an anointed one, but in the case of Daniel 9, this prince isn't marked as anointed.

The first group of seven sevens (49 years) ends with the coming of an anointed one, a prince. This could be Zerubbabel (governor of Judah at the return of Jews from Babylon) because he is in the genealogy of Yeshua (Matthew 1:13). (See the books of Ezra, Nehemiah, and Haggai).

During the second group of 62 sevens (434 years), the city and sanctuary will be an ongoing building project in times of trouble. This batch of seven ends with the arrival of another prince or anointed one, who is cut off or killed and has nothing (doesn't get the kingship or kingdom). This person is Yeshua, who is a son of Zerubbabel legally through His foster or stepfather Joseph and was crucified without ascending to the throne of David.

After the second group of sevens the people (mix of nations governed by Rome) of the prince who is to come destroy the city and sanctuary again. The Temple was destroyed in 70 A. D., and the city in 135 A. D. All Yeshua was doing when He said "not one stone will be left on another" (Mark 13:2; Luke 19:44, 21:6) was confirming this prophecy from Daniel.

The prince "who is to come" is not said to have an anointing. There shall be war and desolations after the destruction of Jerusalem until the last group of seven. Then the prince who is to come (the little horn or beast) arrives and makes a strong agreement with many for that seven. Halfway through the prince stops the sacrifice and offering.

Understand that biblical timelines are not figured out necessarily to the exact day (although they can be). For instance, Daniel knew from reading Jeremiah (see for instance Jeremiah 25:11) that the Babylonian captivity was supposed to last 70 years. But it was actually a little longer than that, and God might've been waiting for Israel to request an end (as Daniel did in chapter 9). Another example is when Yeshua says no one knows the day or the hour of the appearing of the son of man in Matthew 24. More on this is in the section **The Ripe Time** earlier in the book.

Matthew 24:36 ESV. "But concerning that day and hour no one knows, not even the angels of heaven, nor the Son, but the Father only.

A third example is in the same chapter of Matthew when Yeshua says "those days will be cut short." Apparently, God ends the plans of the deceiver and the little horn early because of His elect.

Matthew 24:21–22 ESV. For then there will be great tribulation, such as has not been from the beginning of the world until now, no, and never will be. And if those days had not been cut short, no human being would be saved. But for the sake of the elect those days will be cut short.

Understand too that the calendar God is using might be different from what we expect. Israel's calendar went according to the lunar cycle (12 months of 30 days each for a 360 day year) instead of the solar cycle (365.25 days per year). Every 13 years a month was added to stay in line with the seasons. Or God might be using a different method of calculation. This frustrates the western mind because we want something more specific.

It is not as though God is messing with us though. It's that He has different ways of thinking than we do and we sometimes have trouble adjusting.

Isaiah 55:8–9 ESV. For my thoughts are not your thoughts, neither are your ways my ways, declares the LORD. For as the heavens are higher than the earth, so are my ways higher than your ways and my thoughts than your thoughts.

Daniel had no problem with the 70 year timing but believed it completely, and other people have taken God at His Word with no problems either.

Daniel 9:26 indicates the people of the prince who is to come (who are apparently the Romans) will destroy the city (135 C.E.) and the sanctuary or temple (70 C.E.). Remember that the Roman armies were made up of soldiers from many different nations. This is important because the people of the prince who is to come are not just Italian. After they destroy Jerusalem, more war and desolation is determined, speaking of Israel and Jerusalem in particular. The fact that more war and desolation is determined means obviously that events continue into the final "seven."

The Agreement for One Seven

Daniel 9:26–27 ESV. And after the sixty-two weeks, an anointed one shall be cut off and shall have nothing. And the people of the prince who is to come shall destroy the city and the sanctuary. Its end shall come with a flood, and to the end there shall be war. Desolations are decreed. And he shall make a strong covenant with many for one week, and for half of the week he shall put an end to sacrifice and offering. And on the wing of abominations shall come one who makes desolate, until the decreed end is poured out on the desolator."

The last "week" or week of years of Daniel 9:27 is special due to an agreement or "strong covenant" for seven years between "many" in Israel and the prince who is to come. The phrase "a strong covenant with many" implies a democratic vote, something that wouldn't happen unless Israel is back in the land and has a democratic government, which is obviously now present. The "years" we get from the context of 70 years of dispersion for Israel earlier in Daniel's book.

This last week of years doesn't seem to have played out yet. The "prince who is to come" is from those who destroy the city of Jerusalem. Since the Romans destroyed the Temple (70 A.D.) and the city (135 A.D.), this suggests that the prince is a descendant of Romans. The Roman Empire included many different nations, tribes and cultures, so it doesn't mean the little horn is an Italian.

We have no record of a strong agreement by a Roman prince made with many (probably 'voted on' as free countries do in modern times) in the middle of which he puts an end to sacrifice and offering. Since the city and the sanctuary were destroyed, how can sacrifice and offerings cease except if they first somehow resume? A resumption of sacrifice and offerings implies that Israel is back in the land and has finally rebuilt the Temple. Israel is back now, but still hasn't built a temple, which is another indication that the final seven has not run its course.

There have been many candidates for the office of the beast throughout history. Remember, this is because the deceiver keeps trying the same plans over and over and is only partly successful each time. The candidates (such as various Roman emperors, Muslim army leaders, popes and people like Stalin and Hitler) have been terrible people and have acted without very much mercy towards Israel, yet none of them have managed to work out a seven-year agreement with an Israel who (presumably) gets possession of a temple. Much less have they even had a chance of standing in the Temple and proclaiming they are God (not "a god" but big "G" God). Some have thought a particular candidate was close, but none of them did what the prophets and Paul said the "man of lawlessness" should.

2 Thessalonians 2:3–4 ESV. Let no one deceive you in any way. For that day will not come, unless the rebellion comes first, and the man of lawlessness is revealed, the son of destruction, who opposes and exalts himself against every so-called god or object of worship, so that he takes his seat in the temple of God, proclaiming himself to be God.

Another thing is that just because the agreement or covenant is for seven years it does not mean that the Tribulation is only seven years long. When Yeshua says "except those days should be shortened" He is talking about a time of trouble that is not necessarily limited to seven years, or that "shortened" would mean shorter than seven years. The judgments of God might last longer than seven years if they are not shortened, or if the power of the little horn was not removed before his plans were finished.

The Temple Rebuilt

Adding to the Temple thoughts already listed previously, and speaking of the resumption of sacrifices and offerings, it appears Israel builds another temple before the Tribulation. Remember, the earthly temple is just a copy of the Temple in heaven. We get to see glimpses of the heavenly original many times in the accounts of Revelation. The place where God resides or focuses His presence is also the location of the Temple.

The heavenly Temple was the pattern for the Tabernacle and the two (and maybe four) earthly temples. It has an altar with fire that is used in some of God's judgments on people of the earth. The heavenly temple also has an ark of His covenant which, curiously, can be seen within His temple, meaning that there is no veil hiding it from view.

A third temple (or temple substitute) is built or partially built probably in or around the week of years called the Tribulation. A fourth temple will be completed soon after the slaughter of the world's armies at Armageddon, and after Yeshua takes David's throne. The third one will probably be destroyed by the once-in-history earthquake which levels mountains and elevates valleys.

Some people think there are only three temples, and that the third one is the one described by Ezekiel in chapters 40 through 47 of his book. But Yeshua sets foot on the Mount of Olives and it splits in two, and this is after there is an earthquake so severe that Jerusalem is split into three chunks. That's a lot of seismic activity shaking things up. It's possible that God would protect the third temple, if it is Ezekiel's, but it is more likely that a temple built by people will be destroyed (the third temple). A fourth one built by Yeshua will be the one in place during the millennial kingdom.

Besides, if you read Ezekiel, there are too many things such as a river of cleansing and trees of life that are part of the new Temple that are not part of a human-constructed building.

A Tale of Three Women

Wrapped up in the end times stuff is a tale of three women: one in Revelation 12 (Israel), one in Revelation 17 and 18 (prostitute, mystery religion Babylon), and one in Revelation 19:7 (the bride of the Lamb). The woman in Revelation 12 is described in such a way that it strongly suggests believing Israel, and probably is part of the Bride of the Lamb. The description John gives harkens back to Joseph's dream in Genesis 37, where Israel and sons are described as sun, moon and eleven stars.

The similarly clad woman in Revelation gives birth to a male child who is undoubtedly Yeshua the Messiah. "The rest of her offspring" would be those who "keep the commandments and hold to the testimony of Jesus" (Revelation 12:17). The woman who gives birth to the Messiah ("one who is to rule all the nations with a rod of iron" 12:5) is also part of the bride. The Bride is composed of those who follow God's instructions or Law and accept Yeshua as God in the flesh who "freed us from our sins by his blood" (Revelation 1:5).

Revelation 17 and 18 describes the prostitute dressed in scarlet and purple (colors of royalty) wearing gold and jewels and pearls. In contrast, the bride of the Lamb is dressed in plain white garments which are righteous deeds of the saints (Revelation 19:8).

Two of the women are also called "great" cities, not necessarily for size but more probably for importance or influence.

The prostitute is called Babylon, and the New Jerusalem is called a bride (Revelation 21:2). Israel too was a bride at one time.

Jeremiah 2:2 ESV. "Go and proclaim in the hearing of Jerusalem, Thus says the LORD, "I remember the devotion of your youth, your love as a bride, how you followed me in the wilderness, in a land not sown.

It's interesting that John pictures a "dear lady" or the "elect lady and her children" in 2 John. In that letter he's obviously writing to believers about loving one another, which is a command we've had from the beginning. But he also warns about many deceivers and antichrists who deny that Yeshua is God in the flesh.

His encouragement to love one another is for those who "know the truth" and are "walking in the truth," which we are "commanded by the Father." The truth to which he refers is the "teaching of Christ" and includes an admonishment to continue the love by walking "according to his (the Father's) commandments." This carries over to the Revelation when John speaks of the deceiver making war "on the rest of her offspring, on those who keep the commandments of God and hold to the testimony of Jesus" (Revelation 12:17).

The second woman or "mother of prostitutes" is a murdering seductress working in concert with the dragon and the beast, who takes life from the people of God rather than giving life to anything. She is a combination of all fertility goddesses such as Asherah or Ashtaroth, Ishtar, or that invoked by the pagan feast of Easter, and other similar false gods such as the Goddess of Reason. She looks on the surface as if she is beautiful royalty, but in reality drinks the blood of those who follow God and is full of abominations, sexual immorality and impurities: very much like United States Democrats, The Church, and other tyrants in modern times. She rides the scarlet beast with seven heads and ten horns but they all hate her and can't wait to destroy her.

It could be that the woman of Revelation 12 is exactly what it says she is: "a great sign appeared in heaven." God made the "lights" of the heavens for signs, telling a story that He wants told.

Genesis 1:14–15 ESV. And God said, "Let there be lights in the expanse of the heavens to separate the day from the night. And let them be for signs and for seasons, and for days and years, and let them be lights in the expanse of the heavens to give light upon the earth." And it was so.

Astrology is a pile of something that comes out of the south end of a north-bound cow. Astronomy is God speaking to the world of His plans and works. The stars, constellations and planets were studied for thousands of years before astrology corrupted the meanings. The magi from the east who were looking for the king of the Jews read the meaning in the heavens and followed a star to His birthplace. Astronomy is not a bad thing, unless it is misused. When the stars and constellations are perverted into a method of trying to tell the future, it becomes bad. God puts His message in the heavens as signs and seasons for us to read of His glory. We don't worship the signs, we worship the signer.

The sign in heaven of a woman "clothed with the sun, with the moon under her feet and on her head a crown of twelve stars" could very well be one of God's heavenly messages. The constellation of the Virgin, which some call Virgo, is a woman, and in ancient times represented Israel. If the regular motion of the heavenly bodies (relative to us) the moon is positioned at her feet with the sun at the side, as it would be just before dawn, it would look like it was near and she would be, "clothed with the sun".

With other stars aligned in a crown of twelve, then it might have been the sign seen by the magi that led them to the Christ child. It might be seen at the time of the end as an evangelistic message too. This constellation can be seen in the night sky even now, except not exactly lined up as in Revelation 12. However, given the natural progression of the nightly celestial dance, everything could have lined up at the time of the birth of Yeshua. They may also line up exactly during the tribulation as another witness to God's plans and glory.

Image: Scroll of Authority

Scroll of Authority — Outline of The Time of the End

White Horse Bow/crown	**Red Horse** Sword/wars/ rumors/no peace	**Black Horse** Scale/ Famines	**Pale Horse** 1/4 dead from sword/famine/ pestilence/beast	**Martyrs under altar** White robes

Beast gets authority

⟶ **Agreement w/many for one week of years** ⟶

4 angels hold winds, 144,000 sealed. Multitude from resurrection seen.

2 Witnesses with powers like trumpets for 1,260 days.

Angel w/censer, prayers, fire.

Woman hides for 1,260 days.

Trumpet One Fire, blood, hail mixed, 1/3 of earth/trees + all grass burned.

Trumpet Two Burning mountain 1/3 sea blood, 1/3 dead critters, 1/3 ships destroyed.

Trumpet Three Wormwood in 1/3 of waters kills many.

Trumpet Four Light from 1/3 of sun, moon, stars gone

Trumpet Five First Woe: Poisonous locusts, 5 months no death.

Trumpet Six Second Woe: 4 angels released, army of 200m kills 1/3 of people.

Trumpet Seven Mystery of God fulfilled, earthquake, thunder, hail Third Woe: war in heaven. Dragon evicted from heaven.

Middle of Week Deceiver gives power to little horn/beast. Two witnesses killed and resurrected. Little horn says he is God, sets up image. Sacrifices cease.

Bowl One Painful sores on marked people.

Bowl Two Sea is blood, all critters die.

Bowl Three Springs are blood.

Bowl Four Scorching sun.

Bowl Five Felt darkness on beast kingdom.

Bowl Six Dry Euphrates, frog spirits gather armies.

Bowl Seven Great earthquake, 100 pound hailstones.

Seal Seven Silence; Resurrection, Armageddon

Earthquake like no other, Blood Moon, Black Sun

1,260 days → 1,260 days till shattering of holy people power ends
1,290 days → +30 days → 1,290 days regular offering taken away and image set up
1,335 days → +45 days → 1,335 days, end of Armageddon/time of Jacobs Trouble

Total time for most of the events is 2,300 evenings and mornings. Time cut short for the sake of the elect.

234

6 Scroll of Authority

Psalm 110:1-7 NASB95. ¹A Psalm of David. The LORD says to my Lord: "Sit at My right hand Until I make Your enemies a footstool for Your feet." ²The LORD will stretch forth Your strong scepter from Zion, *saying,* "Rule in the midst of Your enemies." ³Your people will volunteer freely in the day of Your power; In holy array, from the womb of the dawn, Your youth are to You *as* the dew. ⁴The LORD has sworn and will not change His mind, "You are a priest forever According to the order of Melchizedek." ⁵The Lord is at Your right hand; He will shatter kings in the day of His wrath. ⁶He will judge among the nations, He will fill *them* with corpses, He will shatter the chief men over a broad country. ⁷He will drink from the brook by the wayside; Therefore He will lift up *His* head.

John in Revelation 4 describes the throne room with God on the throne and a scroll in His hand. In chapter 5, John weeps because no one in heaven, on earth or under the earth is worthy to open the scroll or look into it. This means the scroll must be very important. Indeed, it gives the bearer "dominion and glory and a kingdom."

Daniel 7:13–14 ESV. "I saw in the night visions, and behold, with the clouds of heaven there came one like a son of man, and he came to the Ancient of Days and was presented before him. And to him was given dominion and glory and a kingdom, that all peoples, nations, and languages should serve him; his dominion is an everlasting dominion, which shall not pass away, and his kingdom one that shall not be destroyed.

After a lot of prayer, contemplation and study of the Word, the description of this scroll appears to be an outline of the time of the end in very general terms. It also gives the "worthy one" authority to destroy the kingdoms of the world and establish the Kingdom of God.

Revelation 5:9–10 ESV. And they sang a new song, saying, "Worthy are you to take the scroll and to open its seals, for you were slain, and by your blood you ransomed people for God from every tribe and language and people and nation, and you have made them a kingdom and priests to our God, and they shall reign on the earth."

The scroll looks like an outline mostly because of the earthquake at the sixth seal in Revelation 6:14. See the image for the scroll before this chapter for a visual on rough timing of events. On one hand, we have a certain earthquake (The Earthquake as was mentioned before) that is like no other. On the other hand, the sixth seal earthquake seems to be the same as The Earthquake of Revelation 16:18. Both prophecies describe the same cataclysmic earthquake that only happens once in history.

In addition, the chapter 8 break is in the wrong place (technically not needed at all). It should be after verse one and before verse two (if used at all). The seventh trumpet results in silence in heaven, then the Lord's trumpet section begins to blow, and they are in a separate vision from the scroll happening at a different time.

The seals of this scroll also match Matthew 24 and Luke 21. In those chapters, Yeshua says (summarizing) that there would be false Christs (white horse rider), wars and rumors of wars (red horse rider), famines (black horse rider), and pestilence or death (pale horse rider). He also told the apostles (as representative believers) that "they will deliver you up to tribulation and put you to death," (fifth seal of martyrs). To wrap it all up, Yeshua said that the sun would be darkened, the moon would not give its light and the powers of heaven will be shaken (sixth seal).

As mentioned before, a curious feature of the scroll vision is that there are four groups of believers represented (elders, martyrs, 144,000, multitude), but they are out of sequence. For instance, the number of martyrs is yet to be completed and the 144,000 are being prepped for a future job. If the elders are the same as the names on the pearls and foundation stones of the New Jerusalem, at this point they have passed away, and the multitude comes "out of the great tribulation" which presumably hasn't started yet. This further suggests that the scroll is an outline of the whole tribulation picture.

The scroll is addressed to someone "worthy." No one else could open it because that would be like opening someone else's mail and stealing what was in it. Only a worthy person could take this scroll and open it. A search is made and no one is found worthy; the only worthy person is the Lamb looking like He was slain, who takes it and opens the seals.

John's vision is conveyed in symbolism, but it is nevertheless very real. This scroll is very important; much more so than a mere letter or book. At the very least, the scroll communicates to us the solemnity and magnitude of the giving of authority to our Messiah. Yeshua is given the Scroll of Authority so "The kingdom of the world (will) become the kingdom of our Lord and of his Christ, and he shall reign forever and ever" (Revelation 11:15). The Scroll is an overview of Yeshua taking possession of His kingdom, one of the purposes of the seventieth week of Daniel.

Daniel 9:24 ESV. "Seventy weeks are decreed about your people and your holy city, to finish the transgression, to put an end to sin, and to atone for iniquity, to bring in everlasting righteousness, to seal both vision and prophet, and to anoint a most holy place.

The seals inaugurate phases of possession over the course of the time of the end at least, meaning that as each seal is opened judgments are made and Yeshua gets closer and closer to taking His place on the throne of David. It might be limited to the seventieth week, or opening the seals might begin sooner. Matching the earthquakes of the sixth seal and the seventh bowl reinforces the idea that the prophecies in Revelation are not chronological and need to be evaluated individually. John's prophecies are more event oriented than calendar or clock oriented.

John's visions communicate specific principles rather than a minute-by-minute detailed account. So the seals on the first scroll tell us that, as Yeshua wrests control of His kingdom from the deceiver, there will be conquerors fighting back and forth, peace will disappear (war will increase), many people will die from famines and so on. Martyrs will increase but will find a place of protection during this time (fifth seal), and then the really bad stuff hits (sixth seal).

In one way, false messiahs and war and such like have always been around. In another way, these types of events will intensify and become more common until we reach the climax of God's judgment on everything anti-God. As Yeshua phases in direct control of events on earth as they are in heaven, the forces of the deceiver grow more panicked, desperate and violent in order to prevent Him.

This scroll is associated with all the other scrolls mentioned in the Bible that come from the Lord. In every case, such a scroll contains the Word of God, either for life or judgment. It is like a decree from an earthly king such as Nebuchadnezzar which cannot be altered. In this case, the scroll is for authority and judgment.

A scroll is also called a book, and sometimes the Word of the Lord is inscribed on a tablet such as the Ten Words or Ten Commandments. A king of Israel was supposed to write a copy of the Law on his own scroll (Deuteronomy 17:18). Whatever the form, however it is delivered; His Word will never be old or outdated.

On this "sealed book" or scroll, the seals could be all across the first edge, or they could be spaced throughout the scroll.

Yeshua could open the first seal, unroll part of the scroll, then break a second seal and unroll another portion and so on. The first idea is more likely, that there are seven seals keeping the whole scroll closed, because John can see all the seals at the start.

If this is an overview of the entire tribulation, then this scene can be compared to the "back story." As the movie unfolds, we are shown how individual details fit into the whole.

Judgment Belongs to Yeshua

The person to whom a scroll was addressed was the only one who could open it. Apparently, this scroll was addressed to someone so worthy that at first no one was found who could open it. Angels couldn't do it. No person anywhere could do it except One. The Lamb standing as though it had been slain is the only one worthy to take the scroll and open the seals.

It's not as if God doesn't know who is going to take and open the scroll. This scene intends to show that only one person could, anytime or anywhere, open this scroll. They do the search to demonstrate no one other than Yeshua haMashiach could do it. Ezekiel says something very interesting that is connected with this scroll.

Ezekiel 21:27 ESV. A ruin, ruin, ruin I will make it. This also shall not be, until he comes, the one to whom judgment belongs, and I will give it to him.

"The one to whom judgment belongs" is our Messiah Yeshua. We see this stated a little bit differently here and there in the Scriptures. Genesis 49:10 tells us "the scepter shall not depart from Judah, nor the ruler's staff from between his feet until Shiloh comes, and to him the obedience of the peoples." The word "Shiloh" means "rest," "peace" or "tranquility" and is another name for Yeshua. Balaam also sees the scepter or "a star."

Numbers 24:17 ESV. I see him, but not now; I behold him, but not near: a star shall come out of Jacob, and a scepter shall rise out of Israel; it shall crush the forehead of Moab and break down all the sons of Sheth. (See also Zechariah 10.)

The word "scepter," indicating a ruler, is used of others in the Bible. But only one scepter like this comes from Judah. There were other, temporary scepters in the kings of Judah, but only one is a "star." He is the son of David, the morning star, the only one worthy to take the scroll of judgment and open its seals.

Seven Seals

The four horsemen of the apocalypse are revealed at the opening of the first four seals of the scroll in Revelation chapter 5. Four is the number of the earth, as in four directions, four winds, and four corners. Horses are symbols of speed and strength. Four riders swiftly carry their assignment out all over the earth. Each rider has a specific task and has the tools to do it. Keep in mind too that they might be released one at a time, but they are all working at the same time. In other words, all the riders are riding together.

Many people are in awe of the four horsemen, but they really aren't that big of a deal as far as the events of Revelation. They are no doubt harbingers of death and destruction, but the events they initiate are just a warm-up for the trumpets and bowls. Yeshua calls them beginning birth pains. War, death, pestilence, and famine have always been around, and Yeshua alludes to them.

Matthew 24:4–8 ESV. And Jesus answered them, "See that no one leads you astray. For many will come in my name, saying, 'I am the Christ,' and they will lead many astray. And you will hear of wars and rumors of wars. See that you are not alarmed, for this must take place, but the end is not yet. For nation will rise against nation, and kingdom against kingdom, and there will be famines and earthquakes in various places. All these are but the beginning of the birth pains.

However, these horsemen seem to be an accelerated version of birth pangs, perhaps increasing in intensity in comparison to the normal pace of wars, rumors of wars, famines and death that have been around since Adam. They also seem to be merely phases of one judgment. In other words, they are a visual representation or symbols of God's whole judgment rather than stages or chronological events. They are four parts of one, larger proclamation. Three of them (red, black and pale) are associated directly with death on a large scale. The white horse rider is not specifically said to be killing people, but the act of conquering has a lot of collateral damage and death.

You might be surprised to learn that there are other places in the Bible that talk about a horse of a different color, other than those in Revelation chapter 6. These other instances seem to be more like examples of using colored horses as a metaphor rather than a direct association.

Zechariah tells us about visions he had with different colored horses in chapters one and six of his book. In chapter one there are no specific riders mentioned. It appears that the horsemen are gathering information on the condition of the earth. It is not a good thing that the kingdoms of the earth are at rest while Jerusalem lies in ruins. In chapter six, the horses are drawing chariots. Black and white horses each pull a chariot to the north, and a dappled (spotted) pair draws a chariot to the south. The chariots that patrol to the north are said to "set my Spirit at rest" (Zechariah 6:8) in that area. Curiously, there is no mention made of the red horse chariot's mission. Perhaps it is because it stays put in Israel.

This is an example of the "just because it looks the same, doesn't mean it is the same" principle as well as showing the failure of expositional constancy. The four horsemen in Revelation are probably not setting His Spirit at rest. That is, unless we look at the judgments as God releasing His anger at sin in a sort of cathartic way. But it does show us that the colors of the horses relate to the tasks of the riders. The four horsemen of Revelation are not directly related to Zechariah's horses that can be seen from the text. Horses and horsemen are just a visual way of representing the job assignments.

We might have trouble identifying exactly what happens with the horsemen and when, but those of us who are believers and prepared with the Word of God will recognize what is going on at the time. With God's grace, we will take steps to persevere. Keep in mind that John saw this vision about 2,000 years ago, which bears on the time table. Yeshua could have taken this scroll a long time ago, or there could be a long time between each seal. We also have this statement from Yeshua to work into the equation.

Matthew 28:18 ESV. And Jesus came and said to them, "All authority in heaven and on earth has been given to me.

If Yeshua already has all the authority, then the timing for this vision might be covering an event that has already happened. Or there could be a reenactment in the vision to emphasize that no one else could take the scroll.

The riders are riding all through the Tribulation. They don't just take a weekend ride in the country for fun. Conquering, war, famine and death are all packed into the seven-year period (and even outside of this period). We know that this time is when the deceiver's (and man's) wrath against God reaches a peak and God in turn drops the hammer to stop it. There is lots of conquering, war, famine and death wherever man sets up kingdoms. But this time is special and much more concentrated.

Yeshua tells us that "unless those days were cut short, no flesh would be saved" (Matthew 24:22). These four horse riders show us four different ways that people will die in the Tribulation. The sixth trumpet gives us another way, speaking of 1/3 of mankind dying by fire, smoke and sulfur from the mouths of horses in a huge army (Revelation 9:18). This does not count the deaths from the two witnesses (Revelation 11:5-6) or the large number of deaths at Armageddon, either, but they could be combined.

Seal 1: The White Horse Rider

The breaking of the first seal releases a white horse with a rider having a bow. The rider is not white, the horse is white. The rider already has a bow as standard equipment but is given a crown, going forth "conquering and to conquer." This guy is not the Church as some think, and it isn't Yeshua, because the conquering he does is with a weapon of war and not the Word of God. God shows that the crown is "given" to him, signifying that authority is granted (and controlled) by Him. This rider is not specifically war, although war is part of his makeup, because the next rider is the one who causes people to slay one another.

A bow is a powerful weapon that kills from a distance. A sword is an up-close, personal weapon. A bow doesn't mean this person is going to use arrows to kill, but it does mean that he will wage war or threaten to wage war on those around him, possibly from a distance or with more powerful weapons than swords. Some say that the rider doesn't have arrows, and so he wages war with something else like vaccines, but this is what is called an "argument from silence" and doesn't hold much water. If he has a bow, it is assumed he also has arrows. His crown means he has authority to do the conquering, at least in a limited way.

Because of these facts, believers can immediately identify this rider as the little horn or beast. Some people call both the beast and the false prophet "anti-christ" which in a sense is true because both are "instead of" the true Anointed or Christ. But we need to keep in mind there are many "anti-christs" and false prophets. Many less famous agents of the deceiver also get supporting roles throughout history in his efforts to unseat God from His throne.

The opening of this seal kicks off the rise of the beast (or many anti-Christs), and allows him to start building his short-lived kingdom. According to Daniel's prediction, the beast is also the "little horn" on the beast with iron teeth (Daniel 7:8) that plucks up three of the other horns. Remember that the word "horn" is a symbol of a king or kingdom's strength or authority. "Pluck up" is a figure of speech for destruction or conquering.

In conquering, there are many side effects besides people dying directly from conflict. Supply chains are disrupted, which contributes to famines and death. Water for crops, especially doled out from government dams, can be stopped. Sewage treatment projects can be shut down, increasing disease and pollution.

There are many ways to wage war, and not all of them use artillery and rifles. Population control with abortion and vaccines is at the top of the list. Selective taxation, shutdown of pipelines and fracking, and denial of medical treatment are close seconds. The manipulation of elections such as that of the 2020 election in the United States, stealing political office for a dictator, is on that list too because totalitarian measures contribute to the death toll. Conquering doesn't openly have to use explosives and ammunition.

We see another rider on a white horse later in Revelation 19. This second rider is much different from the seal horseman. This one has a name of "Faithful and True, and in righteousness judges and makes war." He wears a robe dipped in blood that is perhaps is own (or maybe not), eyes like a flame of fire, and many diadems or crowns on His head. His other name is The Word of

God. He has still another name only He knows, which is one of the reasons the "sacred name" controversy is not helping people. A fourth name on His robe and thigh is King of Kings and Lord of Lords, more of a title than a name, but it is the same as a name.

Isaiah 63:1–6 ESV. Who is this who comes from Edom, in crimsoned garments from Bozrah, he who is splendid in his apparel, marching in the greatness of his strength? "It is I, speaking in righteousness, mighty to save." Why is your apparel red, and your garments like his who treads in the winepress? "I have trodden the winepress alone, and from the peoples no one was with me; I trod them in my anger and trampled them in my wrath; their lifeblood spattered on my garments, and stained all my apparel. For the day of vengeance was in my heart, and my year of redemption had come. I looked, but there was no one to help; I was appalled, but there was no one to uphold; so my own arm brought me salvation, and my wrath upheld me. I trampled down the peoples in my anger; I made them drunk in my wrath, and I poured out their lifeblood on the earth."

Obviously, this rider is our Messiah (Yeshua has many names or titles). The armies of heaven, dressed in "fine linen, white and pure" and also riding white horses follows him. Just before these riders, we get a description of the Bride wearing "fine linen, bright and pure" (Revelation 19:8). So it seems the armies are also the Bride of Christ, "for the fine linen is the righteous deeds of the saints." In order for these armies to be the saints or the Bride, they would have to be resurrected sometime before this.

The first white-horse rider conquers with force and unrighteousness. The second rider on a white horse judges and makes war on the first rider, and his minions, in righteousness. Out of the mouth of Yeshua comes a sharp sword which is the Word of God. He rules with a rod of iron which is also the Word of God.

The Word doesn't change, but the people change according to how they react to the Word. If we behave like sheep towards

God, His Word is a gentle thing like a shepherd's crook, leading and guiding. If we resist or challenge God, then the Word is like a sword or rod of iron that breaks the nations in pieces. Are you getting the picture that the Word of God is the key around which all things revolve?

Seal 2: The Red Horse Rider

Cracking the second seal introduces a bright red horse with a rider who is given a great sword and is permitted to take peace from the earth, so that people should "slay one another." This means that war in general will be all over the world. The red horse rider is in partnership with the pale horse riders Death and Hades because they all kill a lot of people. In a sense, the horsemen are all one. God is telling John concepts and ideas like a movie trailer instead of, in this instance, actual horsemen. Although it could be both and we just can't see the horsemen.

The beast apparently has some wars, because as the "little horn" he is supposed to take out three kings or kingdoms. War is a hallmark of the dragon and the beast in the Tribulation. They take what they want by theft and force, just like tyrants, communists, socialists, and Democrats of modern times. Communism and socialism are strategies of the deceiver, and all who practice these belief systems are agents of the deceiver. Some agents disguise themselves with good-sounding names like "black lives matter" or "anti-fascist," but can be recognized by their fruit. Their murderous, tyrannical and fascist actions give them away.

Seal 3: The Black Horse Rider

Amos 8:11 ESV. "Behold, the days are coming," declares the Lord GOD, "when I will send a famine on the land— not a famine of bread, nor a thirst for water, but of hearing the words of the LORD.

At the opening of the third seal, a black horse is called forth and its rider has a pair of scales. A voice is heard from the midst of the four living creatures saying, "A quart of wheat for a denarius, and three quarts of barley for a denarius, and do not harm the oil and wine!"

This rider causes food shortages and probably famines (other than a famine for the Word as told to us by Amos). The scales are used to measure and weigh food, indicating scarcity. The black horse rider is only allowed to affect the wheat and barley (and presumably other grain) harvests, reducing them. The price of bread goes up because of damage to either the crops or people to do the harvesting, but the oil and wine are not harmed.

Grains in Israel are generally harvested in the spring, perhaps about May or so. At times in the past wealthy people ate wheat, while the poor ate barley. In modern times, the availability of bread is not marked by wealth but by government policies. Babylonian governments, also known as totalitarian, communist, Democrat and socialist, tend to run shy of food because of their command and control economic practices (and they are frequently wrong on forecasts and control). Nations that have freedom, such as the United States, end up feeding the rest of the world. Wheat and barley shortages could mean that all people are suffering from lack of bread, or that government stupidity is more rampant.

Some think that the command to avoid harming the oil and wine means the wealthy don't suffer. This is not necessarily the case, because wine and oil are easy to make and are inexpensive. This could mean that trees and vines are not harmed at this time, but only grain crops are affected. Bread is a common food, while wine and oil are perhaps a little less common. A denarius was a day's wages at the time. A quart of wheat makes enough bread for maybe a meal or two. So this rider causes the price of a loaf of bread to "rise," (sorry, couldn't resist the pun) to a high level while the oil and wine prices stay even.

The oil and wine could be salad dressing, or it could be just that the wheat and barley crops are affected. Psalm 104:15 says that wine "gladdens the heart of man" and "oil make(s) his face shine." It also says "bread to strengthen man's heart." So it seems people during the judgments will be able to drown their fears in alcohol and keep themselves looking good to hide it. But their hearts will not be strengthened as easily.

Oil and wine are used for grain offerings and drink offerings, so this could be another indicator that a Temple is rebuilt and operating. Olive oil and wine are easy to make. Just crush the fruit and with a little sifting you'll get your wine or oil right away. So the idea that wine and oil are for rich people doesn't really make complete sense.

What does make sense, however, is that harming only the grain would be a definite sign of the hand of God. Usually a pestilence that would harm grain crops would also harm olives and grapes. Excessive rain might do it. An insect would just eat them all. Drought, floods, tornados, hurricanes or fire would also be indiscriminate in their destruction. Selective destruction of grains only would be like a neon sign to those with the willingness to see.

Another possibility is that the destruction of crops is local. As a for instance, take a look at California of the United States. The government is denying irrigation water to farmers in the central valley (San Joaquin) using the lame excuse of saving a stupid fish (the snail darter) that isn't a separate species at all. Food production in the area is declining rapidly and farmers are going out of business faster than you can say "black horse rider." It doesn't take a lot of imagination to see the parallel between famines caused by the breaking of the third seal and the actions of tyrannical governments. Tyrants are God-deniers, and those who cut themselves off from God are unable to avail themselves of His wisdom in any area, especially in governing.

Seal 4: The Pale Horse Rider

When Yeshua cracks the fourth seal, a pale horse is revealed with Death for a rider and Hades tagging along. Together they are given authority over a fourth of the earth to kill with sword, famine, pestilence and wild beasts. This indicates that the rider of this horse is working in concert with the others.

These types of deaths are typical of people without God. They are judgments for ignoring Him and doing what is right in their own eyes. There are at least three ways to look at the "fourth of the earth" figure, two by population and one by geography. If we use geography, then the people occupying about a quarter of the land or the equivalent will die. If we use seven billion as the earth's current population, then about 1.75 billion go into the grave early. This could be one out of four people all over, or it could be large chunks in small areas all over the globe.

It takes time for people to die from famine and pestilence, and unless wild beasts attack all at once, the deaths from wild beasts are spread out over time. Death from war is quicker, but even wars overall take a while. People die all the time and others are born to replace them, so this rider and his shadow Hades take a while to do their work, or a whole lot of people will die quickly.

It is interesting to note that attacks by beasts have increased quite a bit over the last couple of decades. Usually animals avoid humans if they can, so death by beast attack was rare before our current time. Famines are increasing, even though crop yields are higher than ever. Some of the famines are self-inflicted, such as those in central California caused by the government refusing to give taxpayer-funded water to farmers, or African government leaders who hoard donations of food to sell for personal gain.

Pestilence or disease, doctors tell us, used to be under control due to vaccines. This is a fiction, because death by disease was declining long before vaccines were introduced due to improved water treatment, sanitation and nutrition. So in recent years, drug-resistant strains of bacteria and viruses have begun to show up. Vaccines are partly responsible, because they program the immune system only slightly and only for specific strains (research the concept of "original sin" which doesn't have anything to do with the Bible). If the virus mutates, there will be no defense. Plus, vaccine production is faulty and contributes to helping new drug-resistant strains mutate. Side-effects from vaccines are numerous and, if not killing us outright at the time, seriously attack and weaken our bodies in other ways for the rest of our lives. Nevertheless, people want a security blanket and don't want it taken away from them. Vaccines (and intramuscular injections that claim to be vaccines such as the so-called Covid-19 jab) cause more problems than they solve, and will be entirely ineffective when increased pestilence is released by the pale horse rider.

Revelation 18:23 ESV (parenthesis added). ...for your merchants were the great ones of the earth, and all nations were deceived by your sorcery (Greek word φαρμακεία transliterated *pharmakeia* (farm-a-kay-e-ah) where we get our words pharmacy and pharmaceutical).

According to surveys done by the American Medical Association, the third leading cause of death after cancer and heart disease in the United States (and without a doubt worldwide) now is medical "mistakes." Somewhere around 250,000 people a year die from complications with drugs or just outright screw-ups by the medical establishment in the United States alone. Yet these same people try to convince us that they are "expert" medical people, all knowing and all powerful.

Many good medical people out there are truly concerned and are the best examples of the medical ideal. They lay their personal reputations and financial well-being on the line everyday to educate and actually heal. But overall and in general, we are being played by governments, medical establishment people, and huge corporations who have agendas other than health care, such as money or population control. These agents of the pale horse rider, if not directly involved, are at the very least advance soldiers helping establish the beast's kingdom.

Another leading cause of unnecessary death is abortion. About 54 million babies as of this date have been killed since the 1973 United States Supreme Court ruling legalized baby-killing, or over 1 million a year. And that's just in the U.S. That ruling has been reversed, but many still want to kill babies for convenience.

The pale horse rider may already be at work. If he isn't, one shudders to think about the scale of death and destruction to come on the earth. Even so, these types of indicators are only a warm up for the big show of God's wrath in the trumpets and bowls. Truly, the love of many is waxing cold.

Seal 5: Martyrs Under the Altar

In keeping with the idea that this scroll is a general description of the entire 70th week of Daniel, the fifth seal is a comfort to all whose lives were and are cut short by unbelievers because they "hold to the commands and the testimony of Jesus." John had to be encouraged too.

Revelation 1:9 ESV. I, John, your brother and partner in the tribulation and the kingdom and the patient endurance that are in Jesus, was on the island called Patmos on account of the word of God and the testimony of Jesus.

Revelation 12:17 ESV. Then the dragon became furious with the woman and went off to make war on the rest of her offspring, on those who keep the commandments of God and hold to the testimony of Jesus. And he stood on the sand of the sea.

Revelation 19:10 ESV. Then I fell down at his feet to worship him, but he said to me, "You must not do that! I am a fellow servant with you and your brothers who hold to the testimony of Jesus. Worship God." For the testimony of Jesus is the spirit of prophecy.

Revelation 20:4 ESV. Then I saw thrones, and seated on them were those to whom the authority to judge was committed. Also I saw the souls of those who had been beheaded for the testimony of Jesus and for the word of God, and those who had not worshiped the beast or its image and had not received its mark on their foreheads or their hands. They came to life and reigned with Christ for a thousand years.

The martyrs are identified as those who have been "slain for the word of God and for the witness they had borne" (Revelation 6:9). They want to know "how long before you will judge and avenge our blood on those who dwell on the earth?" Presumably, the avenging will be at the time of Armageddon, so they are told to rest a little longer in their white robes, because the slaughter of worldly empires is not going to take place quite yet.

A way to identify the additional martyrs, those who will complete their number, is those who have patient endurance. All believers need to be patient and endure, but some of us will patiently endure till death. Three congregations are encouraged by Yeshua in Revelation 2:2, 2:3 (Ephesus), 2:19 (Thyatira) and 3:10 (Philadelphia) for their "enduring" or "patient endurance." Smyrna is told to "be faithful unto death" (Revelation 2:10).

The text in Revelation chapter six just tells us that the additional martyrs will be killed. It doesn't say how. But later, in Revelation 20:4, it is added that at least some of the martyrs have been beheaded. Beheading is a favorite pastime of Muslims when dealing with those who will not accept the false god of Islam. This hints that the little horn or false prophet are adherents of Islam. When they are allowed to wage open war against believers, and prevail for a little while, they will use beheading as one way to trim down the population of those who won't worship Allah.

Some limit the verses speaking of holding to the commands in combination with the testimony of Yeshua to just the Jewish believers. The "Church" doesn't follow "The Law" or "commands" (what an indictment!), so they think that this couldn't be "the Church." It is true that this description doesn't apply to the Church, because as already noted the Church doesn't exist in Scripture!

According to tradition, John was exiled to Patmos after the failure of Rome to kill him by boiling in oil. We don't know for sure, but it is sure that martyrdom was at the top of his thinking, at the least because death was close at hand. He had heard of, and perhaps witnessed, the persecution of believers such as those in Nero's time (about A. D. 54 to 68). Nero, in his murderous quest to transfer blame for a huge fire in Rome to the Christians, used them as human torches to light his parties. So an encouragement in the form of the fifth seal would have been a great comfort to believers.

The standard Church theology is that those "under the altar" had to be Jews because the Church doesn't have anything to do with the altar. In the same vein, it is taught that those who hold to the testimony of Yeshua and keep the commandments (The Law) must be Jews because the Church doesn't follow the "old covenant." But this altar is in heaven, the bronze altar is in fact a symbol for the sacrifice of Yeshua, there is only one Body, and all men everywhere are supposed to follow God's Law or living oracles but do not do so. Those who hold to the testimony of Yeshua also keep the commandments if they are really believers.

Some believers might be blocked from following all of the Law due to Church teachings, but such as they know, they keep.

In John's book are many encouragements for those who face tribulation and perhaps death. In 1:9, John says he is our "brother and partner in the tribulation and the kingdom and the patient endurance that are in Jesus," which tells us that tribulation (and martyrdom) for believers has been going on for a long time. Ephesus (twice), Thyatira, and Philadelphia are all directly commended for patient endurance. All seven congregations are told that those who "conquer" will receive blessings such as eating of the tree of life, avoiding the second death, gaining hidden manna and a new name, assuming authority over the nations, and gaining the morning star along with white garments. In addition, they will not get blotted out of the book of life, and Yeshua confesses their names before the Father and His angels.

Two other direct encouragements for believers to keep on keeping on (as was said in the '70's) are in 13:10 and 14:12 where we are told directly to persevere or endure. Other perhaps more indirect encouragements are in 7:9-17 (the great multitude out of the tribulation) and 11:15-18 (twenty-four elders on thrones). Also 14:1-4 (the 144,000), 16:15 (Jesus comes like a thief, blessed are those who stay awake), 20:4-6 (first resurrection), 21:1-8 (new heaven and new earth), and 22:1-4 (river of life). In fact, it may be said that the entire Revelation was written to encourage believers to stay faithful and continue to do what God says.

These encouragements to endure or persevere imply that believers are suffering through painful events. The martyrs under the altar are a reminder that God watches over believers and has a place for them. The fifth seal tells us also that there are going to be more believers during the tribulation that experience an unwanted yet God-known demise.

Revelation 13:9–10 ESV. If anyone has an ear, let him hear: If anyone is to be taken captive, to captivity he goes; if anyone is to be slain with the sword, with the sword must he be slain. Here is a call for the endurance and faith of the saints.

There are philosophies of men that try to pawn the death of believers off on the Jews, meaning that any believers in the Tribulation must be Jews and Jews are the only ones dying. They develop fairy tales such as a "church age" with a "rapture" where churchgoers are supposed to escape all the trouble but Jews are stuck with it. I'm sorry to say those people are not reading the Bible, and not paying attention to much of anything God says.

Seal 6: Earthquake, Blood Moon, Black Sun

Ezekiel 32:7 ESV. When I blot you out, I will cover the heavens and make their stars dark; I will cover the sun with a cloud, and the moon shall not give its light.

Joel 2:31 ESV. The sun shall be turned to darkness, and the moon to blood, before the great and awesome day of the LORD comes.

Acts 2:19–20 ESV. And I will show wonders in the heavens above and signs on the earth below, blood, and fire, and vapor of smoke; the sun shall be turned to darkness and the moon to blood, before the day of the Lord comes, the great and magnificent day.

Revelation 6:12–14 ESV. When he opened the sixth seal, I looked, and behold, there was a great earthquake, and the sun became black as sackcloth, the full moon became like blood, and the stars of the sky fell to the earth as the fig tree sheds its winter fruit when shaken by a gale. The sky vanished like a scroll that is being rolled up, and every mountain and island was removed from its place.

Joel says that the sun will be darkened and the moon turned to blood before the day of the Lord, which Peter quotes in Acts 2. Ezekiel says something a little different, that the light from both will be blocked. Isaiah agrees with Ezekiel.

Isaiah 13:10 ESV. For the stars of the heavens and their constellations will not give their light; the sun will be dark at its rising, and the moon will not shed its light.

It could be that Isaiah and Ezekiel are talking about a different occurrence, Isaiah for Babylon and Ezekiel for Egypt. But the context of both references point to the day of the Lord also (and Isaiah even says it directly in verse 6 of the chapter). Yeshua says concerning the moon and sun that they will be darkened.

Matthew 24:29 ESV. "Immediately after the tribulation of those days the sun will be darkened, and the moon will not give its light, and the stars will fall from heaven, and the powers of the heavens will be shaken.

We don't know for sure how God is going to darken the lights in the sky or make them like blood. Maybe it will be a cloud from volcanoes. Maybe He'll just turn off the lights in a way we can't see (pun intended). It will be something unnatural so that it is unmistakable that it is God. The sixth seal lines up with the seventh bowl judgment because of the "earthquake like no other" in history, along with the darkening of the sun and moon.

Ezekiel 38:19–20 ESV. For in my jealousy and in my blazing wrath I declare, On that day there shall be a great earthquake in the land of Israel. The fish of the sea and the birds of the heavens and the beasts of the field and all creeping things that creep on the ground, and all the people who are on the face of the earth, shall quake at my presence. And the mountains shall be thrown down, and the cliffs shall fall, and every wall shall tumble to the ground.

Revelation 16:17–21 ESV. The seventh angel poured out his bowl into the air, and a loud voice came out of the temple, from the throne, saying, "It is done!" And there were flashes of lightning, rumblings, peals of thunder, and a great earthquake such as there had never been since man was on the earth, so great was that earthquake. The great city was split into three parts, and the cities of the nations fell, and God remembered Babylon the great, to make her drain the cup of the wine of the fury of his wrath. And every island fled away, and no mountains were to be found. And great hailstones, about one hundred pounds each, fell from heaven on people; and they cursed God for the plague of the hail, because the plague was so severe.

If this is true, then it follows that the scenes in the next few verses of Revelation (elders, 144,000, a great multitude) are from just before (or perhaps just after) Jesus comes back with armies to fight in Armageddon.

Elders

John describes the scene around the throne in Revelation 4 as having 24 elders. They are seated on thrones, dressed in white garments and have golden crowns. The 24 elders are probably 12 elders from the tribes of Israel (Revelation 21:12) and the 12 apostles (Revelation 21:14). This comes from the foundation stones (Revelation 21:14) of the New Jerusalem and the "pearly gates" (Revelation 21:21).

Also remember the words of Yeshua promising the apostles that they would sit on thrones judging Israel (Matthew 19:28, Luke 22:30). It's funny to think that John is probably one of those elders at the same time he is describing them. But he doesn't make a point of it. Several times John has to ask the identity of a group of people, but he does not have to ask about the elders. I'm guessing it's because he knew whom they were. It must've been odd to see himself in the elders, because he is certainly one of the 24.

144,000 Sealed from 12 Tribes

An interesting association is apparent when reading this section. In Revelation 7:1 four angels are standing at the four corners of the earth holding back the four winds of the earth, waiting for the 144,000 to be sealed. Sealing means that the people sealed are protected from God's wrath or judgment. One other group of sealed individuals mentioned in Scripture might give us some insight into this group.

Ezekiel 9:1–6 ESV. Then he cried in my ears with a loud voice, saying, "Bring near the executioners of the city, each with his destroying weapon in his hand." And behold, six men came from the direction of the upper gate, which faces north, each with his weapon for slaughter in his hand, and with them was a man clothed in linen, with a writing case at his waist. And they went in and stood beside the bronze altar. Now the glory of the God of Israel had gone up from the cherub on which it rested to the threshold of the house. And he called to the man clothed in linen, who had the writing case at his waist. And the LORD said to him, "Pass through the city, through Jerusalem, and put a mark on the foreheads of the men who sigh and groan over all the abominations that are committed in it." And to the others he said in my hearing, "Pass through the city after him, and strike. Your eye shall not spare, and you shall show no pity. Kill old men outright, young men and maidens, little children and women, but touch no one on whom is the mark. And begin at my sanctuary." So they began with the elders who were before the house.

Those who "sigh(ed) and groan(ed) over all the abominations" were marked by God in Ezekiel 9:4. The marked sigh-ers and groaners of Jerusalem were saved from the destruction instigated by God when He commanded the six "executioners of the city" (Ezekiel 9:1-2) to kill everyone not marked by Him (all the idolaters). So the seal protected them from the destruction ordered by God, and presumably sealing protects the 144,000 also. Remember that refusing the mark of the beast is also a "sealing."

Compare Daniel 7:2 where "the four winds of heaven were stirring up the great sea" with the four angels in this passage. This is a figure of speech illustrating how the nations are always stirred up and restless (not at peace). So it could be that while these men are being marked there is a momentary calm of sorts in the nations.

Maybe this is what Paul conveys to the Thessalonians about the "day of the Lord" and "peace and security."

> 1 Thessalonians 5:1–3 ESV. Now concerning the times and the seasons, brothers, you have no need to have anything written to you. For you yourselves are fully aware that the day of the Lord will come like a thief in the night. While people are saying, "There is peace and security," then sudden destruction will come upon them as labor pains come upon a pregnant woman, and they will not escape.

Later (Revelation 9:14), there are another four angels that are bound at the river Euphrates who are released to kill a third of mankind. This river goes through modern Syria and Iraq, which means that the "kings of the east" that come over the dry river (on horses) are mostly descendants of Ishmael, who have always had it in for Israel.

This group is made up of male virgins with no lie in their mouths (Revelation 14:4-5) from the 12 tribes. This is very specific, and unmistakably certifies these people as being from physical Israel. Some try to connect these to The Church, but there was no Church at the time John was writing, and as stated already The Church now is definitely not the Body of Christ. Jehovah's Witnesses try to connect themselves to this group, and they too are wrong (not young, male virgins with no lies). People in the modern Church just try to horn their way in and shove Israel aside.

It is interesting that God says a number of times in prophecy that He will "gather His elect from the four winds, from one end of heaven to the other" (Ezekiel 37:9; Matthew 24:31; Mark 13:27). He also says that He scatters Israel to the four winds (Jeremiah 49:36). So the imagery differs in prophecy sometimes, depending on context. Four is the critical point, meaning from all over the world or every direction.

The tribe of Judah is first in the list, probably reinforcing the idea that Reuben lost the place of firstborn. Levi is included in this list, but is usually excluded from lists of this nature because they were actually a thirteenth tribe (counting the two sons of Joseph, Ephraim and Manasseh, as two tribes) set aside for the service of the Tabernacle and Temple. Ephraim is missing by name, but Joseph could be another name for Ephraim. Dan is missing entirely, bur referring to Genesis 49 perhaps it is due to verse 17.

Genesis 49:16–17 ESV. "Dan shall judge his people as one of the tribes of Israel. Dan shall be a serpent in the way, a viper by the path, that bites the horse's heels so that his rider falls backward.

It might simply be that God chooses not to include Dan for some reason or other. The tribe is listed in Ezekiel 48 as having an allotment of land with the other tribes in the millennial kingdom, so apparently they are still around at that time. Maybe the intent of the list is just to show that Dan won't be included in the sealing.

The seal is apparently the name of the Lamb and the Father written on their foreheads. Blameless generally means according to the Law (like Paul in Philippians 3:6), but it also means as John says that "in their mouth no lie was found" (Revelation 14:5). They are "redeemed from mankind as firstfruits for God and the Lamb" and sing a new song only they can sing. This vision is meant to reassure believers that God has a plan for everyone, and those who believe and follow Him will live forever.

We don't know much about the activities of this group during the Tribulation. Some have speculated that they are evangelists, preaching the gospel. Others have guessed that perhaps they lead believers to hiding places away from God's wrath and protect them. It could be, but it could also be that they hold fast to God and His Law, which is a strong testimony in itself.

These people know the reason for being sealed. They will, it seems, eventually die for their Messiah by the hand of the beast. However, like Azariah, Mishael and Hananiah of Nebuchadnezzar's furnace fame, these young men refuse the mark of the beast and accept the mark of God, knowing what it means. In light of semi-humorous scenes in modern movies where characters claim they don't want to die virgins, then set about trying to rectify the condition, these men instead stick to their guns and refuse to give in. They maintain their status even to the end. This illustration just goes to show the different motivations of those who follow their own passions or flesh, and those who stick with the Word of God.

Another valid association from Scripture is the seven thousand that God reserved for Himself at the time of Elijah (1 Kings 19:18; Romans 11:4). The 7,000 people had not bowed the knee to Baal, or kissed him with the mouth. The text does not say they were sealed, but it seems they were protected like the 144,000. Kissing may be an actual kiss on an idol, or a way of referring to swearing obedience or worship. Believers are those who believe in their hearts and confess with their mouth, for instance. Kissing Baal was probably a confession of belief in that worthless idol.

Romans 10:8–10 ESV. But what does it say? "The word is near you, in your mouth and in your heart" (that is, the word of faith that we proclaim); because, if you confess with your mouth that Jesus is Lord and believe in your heart that God raised him from the dead, you will be saved. For with the heart one believes and is justified, and with the mouth one confesses and is saved.

Most modern Jews do not know their genealogy. They can guess, and there's supposed to be a genetic marker for Levites, but no one knows for sure. In some ways, what we see in Israel now is a fulfillment of Ezekiel's prophecy of the two sticks (Ezekiel 37). Jews have all become one nation again. So why now does God seal people from each tribe? We know they are "first fruits for God and the Lamb" but not much else. These young men are marked all at once, due to the holding back of the winds.

John sees the 144,000 on Mount Zion with the Lamb (Revelation 14:1) and "they follow Him wherever He goes." Then in 14:13, we are told "Blessed are the dead who die in the Lord from now on." So it looks like the 144,000 are all executed but have eternal life.

The mark utilized by the little horn or beast could be an attempt to copy the marking of the 144,000 (Revelation 7:1-3). It looks like he tries to convince his followers that, as God's mark protects this group of the Lamb's from the judgments of God, the mark of the beast will protect his followers from judgments too. He's trying real hard to look like God, and the anti-Christ is supporting him with lying signs and wonders designed to bolster that claim. It's not too hard to see that part of the selling point for the mark of the beast is protection from the judgments of an evil god, in keeping with the Scripture informing us that wrong becomes right and right becomes wrong (Isaiah 5:20). Instead, the mark of the little horn makes one a target for the wrath of God.

A Great Multitude

Included in the vision of the sixth seal, along with the vision of the 144,000, we see, through John, a great multitude no one could number, from every nation, from all tribes and peoples and languages. John is told they come out of the great tribulation, dressed in robes washed white in the blood of the Lamb.

These are obviously believers, and resurrected before, during or after the sixth seal and seventh bowl. This is another reason the vision of the scroll and the seals is giving us sort of an outline of certain events over the course of the whole Tribulation. The resurrection of the righteous occurs at the return of our Messiah, at the end of the Tribulation, and before Yeshua takes His seat on His throne in Jerusalem. We hear from them again in Revelation 19:1-4 singing a song.

Revelation 19:1–4 ESV. After this I heard what seemed to be the loud voice of a great multitude in heaven, crying out, "Hallelujah! Salvation and glory and power belong to our God, for his judgments are true and just; for he has judged the great prostitute who corrupted the earth with her immorality, and has avenged on her the blood of his servants." Once more they cried out, "Hallelujah! The smoke from her goes up forever and ever." And the twenty-four elders and the four living creatures fell down and worshiped God who was seated on the throne, saying, "Amen. Hallelujah!"

This victory song comes from the multitude shown in Revelation 7:9-17 and is similar to their shout in Revelation 7:10 "Salvation belongs to our God who sits on the throne, and to the Lamb!" This multitude of people is "coming out of" the great tribulation standing around the throne and praising the Lamb.

Revelation 7:14 ESV. I said to him, "Sir, you know." And he said to me, "These are the ones coming out of the great tribulation. They have washed their robes and made them white in the blood of the Lamb.

John is asked by one of the elders about the identity of the great multitude no one could number clothed in white robes standing around the throne. The text doesn't say they died, and "out of the great tribulation" could just as well be translated "out of (that) great affliction." The word "tribulation" is used five times in Revelation, four in the letters to the seven congregations speaking of general persecution and one (2:22) speaking of throwing the followers of Jezebel into "great tribulation." But the followers of

Jezebel, like those of the little horn or beast, are not a part of this group of multitudes.

The multitude is not composed of Jews only, but is "from every nation, from all tribes and peoples and languages." We don't know if this is a separate event, not in time sequence with the other parts of the vision. Each part of this series of visions may be a separate event happening over a widely spaced timeline.

Reinforcing this thought, and picking up a thread from the first part of this chapter, the four groups of believers (elders, 144,000, martyrs and multitude) have different timing. The elders at the time of the vision are already passed away. The number of martyrs isn't completed. The 144,000 are gearing up for the task set for them by Yeshua. The multitude comes out of "the great tribulation," which isn't completed yet, whether we consider it the historical and general affliction or The Tribulation. So John's vision of Revelation 4 through 7 reinforces the idea that just because he writes events down one after the other doesn't mean they actually occur in that order.

It could be that the multitude in Revelation 7:14 is from general persecution throughout history. If they come out of the period we call "the great tribulation," then many millions of believers are killed during that time ("a great multitude no one could number") which is possible but seems to be quite a stretch. The period between the sixth and seventh seals is after the "earthquake like no other" and before Armageddon. This multitude seems to be all the saints collected together by resurrection and rapture, waiting to return with Yeshua to clean house on the armies gathered by the three frog spirits.

Since the word "tribulation" isn't used to describe the seven-year period of judgment, and means "affliction," it makes more sense that the angel is saying "these are the ones coming out of that great affliction." The multitude is probably the body or bride of Christ, collected throughout history. It is a picture of all believers throughout the ages afflicted because of their belief. The martyrs under the altar of the fifth seal are likely included. A Scripture that might bear on this picture is Revelation 1:9.

Revelation 1:9 ESV. I, John, your brother and partner in the tribulation and the kingdom and the patient endurance that are in Jesus, was on the island called Patmos on account of the word of God and the testimony of Jesus.

John says to the seven congregations (not churches) in Asia that he is "your brother and partner in the tribulation," which he puts together with the kingdom and patient endurance that are in Yeshua. So "the tribulation" is probably referring to the general great affliction all believers suffer at the hands of the world because of our faith. But even if this group is limited to those who die during the week of years we call the Tribulation, the multitudes in this part of the vision are collected towards the end. Yeshua will gather all those who are part of His body or bride, living or dead, just before He comes back to destroy the armies of the little horn at Armageddon.

Two thousand years ago, John sees a vision of elders and those coming out of great tribulation (affliction, trouble, anguish Strong's 2347) far in the future. His encouragement is meant for believers who cling to God and His Word no matter the cost.

Seal 7: Eye of the Storm

After the seventh seal is broken, heaven is silent for half an hour. It's almost as if creation is holding its collective breath because of the magnitude of what is going to happen next. Perhaps with the idea of an outline this is also the time of the resurrection, where Yeshua is gathering His saints for the final assault on the kingdoms of the world. Again, the chapter 8 break should be after verse one and before verse two, if we have one at all, because the seals are grouped together and the coming trumpets are also grouped together in a separate vision or prophecy.

If the sixth seal lines up with the seventh bowl because of the earthquake like no other, then the silence would be a pause before the Messiah returns to earth and destroys the world's armies at Armageddon. John waits in silence, and then it seems apparent that he takes up his account going back to an earlier time, with a different vision giving details about the seven trumpets.

7 Day of the Awakening Blast

Leviticus 26:14–20 ESV. "But if you will not listen to me and will not do all these commandments, if you spurn my statutes, and if your soul abhors my rules, so that you will not do all my commandments, but break my covenant, then I will do this to you: I will visit you with panic, with wasting disease and fever that consume the eyes and make the heart ache. And you shall sow your seed in vain, for your enemies shall eat it. I will set my face against you, and you shall be struck down before your enemies. Those who hate you shall rule over you, and you shall flee when none pursues you. And if in spite of this you will not listen to me, then I will discipline you again sevenfold for your sins, and I will break the pride of your power, and I will make your heavens like iron and your earth like bronze. And your strength shall be spent in vain, for your land shall not yield its increase, and the trees of the land shall not yield their fruit.

The trumpets in Revelation chapter 8 through 11 herald events that are a fraction less intense than the bowl judgments soon to follow. These trumpets are related to the Feast of Trumpets, also called "the day of blowing," and "the day of the awakening blast." This holy day or appointment with Yeshua contains a warning to wake up and repent before the Day of Judgment or Yom Kippur (also known as the day of smoke and burning). This is one application of God's holy days and their importance in prophecy.

As mentioned before, the eighth chapter should start after verse one and the half-hour of silence instead of before. It's obvious that verse two begins another vision instead of looking like its part of the scroll seals. God lays out the blessings due to Israel if they follow all of His instructions in Leviticus 26. He also forcefully informs them of the downside if they do not. "I will discipline you again sevenfold for your sins" is a recurring theme (Verses 18, 21, 24, 28). Israel already mostly went through this process, so do you think any of the rest of the world will escape the same (or worse) judgment for ignoring His Words? Obviously, they will not, because John in Revelation gives us the first horrible round of sevenfold judgment on the kingdoms of the world with the seven trumpets.

Jeremiah 25:27–29 ESV. "Then you shall say to them, 'Thus says the LORD of hosts, the God of Israel: Drink, be drunk and vomit, fall and rise no more, because of the sword that I am sending among you.' "And if they refuse to accept the cup from your hand to drink, then you shall say to them, 'Thus says the LORD of hosts: You must drink! For behold, I begin to work disaster at the city that is called by my name, and shall you go unpunished? You shall not go unpunished, for I am summoning a sword against all the inhabitants of the earth, declares the LORD of hosts.'

These are literal trumpets, and it will be interesting to hear the blasts. The judgments at least will be literally experienced by the world population. You might want to get to know the sounds these horns make, because you might be hearing them calling or warning sooner than you think.

They are also time markers and markers for the next judgment. Imagine hearing them and at about the third or fourth trumpet blast you would start wincing and thinking, "Oh great (or something more emphatic and profane). What's next?"

Two types or styles of trumpets are mentioned a good bit in Scripture. One is a curved animal horn such as that of a sheep, goat or a kudzu (which has a horn 30 or 40 inches long with several twists) and in Hebrew is generally called a *shofar*. Shofar can mean any trumpet, but usually it's the name for the curved animal horn variety. The other trumpet is straight and silver, called in Hebrew a hasosrah (guttural "h" as in khats-oh-sraw or also Chanukah). In the Greek of Revelation, there are several words for trumpet, or blowing a trumpet, but trumpet as an instrument is transliterated *salpinx,* a word which is related to a wavering sound.

Two silver trumpets in Numbers 10 summoned the congregation for an assembly (a long blast) and kicked off the moving of the camp (an alarm). When both were blown, everybody gathered at the tent of meeting (Tabernacle). When one was blown, it was only for the heads of the tribes to gather at the tent. A third type of call or alarm reminded God to save Israel from their enemies in war. Perhaps this last sound is what we will hear.

Other important uses of trumpets or shofars were for the feast of Trumpets and the Day of Atonement, the day of gladness (when we are happy), other feasts or holidays, over burnt offerings and peace offerings, and the beginning of months. The priests blew the silver trumpets, and everyone else could blow shofars.

Trumpets are used a bunch in Bible history. Joshua was told to have the people of Israel march around the city of Jericho. He had seven priests blow shofars (ram's horns) while the people of Israel walked around the city once each day for seven days. On the seventh day, they walked around seven times. All those walks with trumpets sounding were intended as warnings. The people of Jericho were smug in the thought that their walls would protect them, but their arrogance turned to stark raving terror when the walls fell down. It wasn't the sound of the trumpets that collapsed the walls; God used the shofars as a warning, which went unheeded, and then knocked down the walls by His own power. In the Tribulation, the trumpets again are unheeded, and walls are flattened again.

Gideon had the 300 men attacking the Midianites blow their shofars (Judges 7). Priests of Judah with silver trumpets show up in a battle between Israel and Judah in 2 Chronicles 13, which Judah won. God uses trumpets to get people's attention, and to unify His people for action, if they are paying attention to Him.

Jeremiah 6:17 ESV. I set watchmen over you, saying, 'Pay attention to the sound of the trumpet!' But they said, 'We will not pay attention.'

God is said to sound a trumpet in Zechariah 9:14, and John in Revelation says that the voice of Yeshua sounds like a loud trumpet (Revelation 1:10; 4:1). Isaiah speaks of a great trumpet calling people to worship "in that day," which is probably during the millennial kingdom. But it might also connect with the reaping of Revelation 14:14-16, the gathering of the elect mentioned by Isaiah in 27:12-13, and the gathering mentioned later by Yeshua in Matthew 24:31.

Isaiah 27:12–13 ESV. In that day from the river Euphrates to the Brook of Egypt the LORD will thresh out the grain, and you will be gleaned one by one, O people of Israel. And in that day a great trumpet will be blown, and those who were lost in the land of Assyria and those who were driven out to the land of Egypt will come and worship the LORD on the holy mountain at Jerusalem.

The first time in the Bible that we hear of a series of judgments such as the trumpet and bowl judgments is way back in Egypt with the Exodus. Maybe there weren't trumpet blasts or bowls, but there were angels in charge of different parts of the whole thing (Exodus 12:23). Maybe from God's point of view it looked something like the way the plagues are initiated in the Revelation accounts.

Verbal warnings preceded the ten plagues, but there are no warnings with each of the trumpets or the bowls (except for the eagle of Revelation 8:13, the two witnesses and the three angels of Revelation 14). That's if we don't count the many general warnings from God in the Bible to repent. We could also consider that the trumpets are warnings of what is to come with the bowls.

The trumpet and bowl judgments have some things in common with the plagues leveled on Egypt such as blood, darkness, hail, lightening, famine and death, but the Revelation scenes are much more intense. There is still opportunity to repent at these judgments, but as with Pharaoh, instead of repentance there are only hard hearts and refusal to follow God.

It is also interesting to note that the trumpet and bowl judgments are associated with pagan gods. For instance, the Moabite god Chemosh, the ancient Syrian god Kamish, and Mesopotamian god Nergal were associated with famine, drought, plague, and death. Milcom was the Ammonite version, and Molech was another name for him. The names might change but the abominations are all the same. It looks like God is raining down His judgment with the trumpets and bowls as a condemnation of the false gods perhaps once again worshipped during this time.

The plagues released by the trumpet blasts will be considered by many to be natural (or from pagan gods) and not from God. God may be blamed anyway, just as He is blamed now for anything bad that happens. But most of it will be passed off as "nature" or perhaps "global warming" or even "climate change." The problem with this type of characterization is that man won't be able to change the warming no matter how hard he tries.

In a message given to a former congregation a few years ago, I said that knowing and following God's feasts or holy days is like knowing the bus schedule. If you want to take the bus, you consult the schedule and show up at the appointed time and place. Otherwise, you miss the bus. Ignoring much of the Word of God, such as the holy days, and substituting your own inventions of days such as Christmas and Easter, is a sure sign that you are missing the bus. Churchgoers now are not checking the schedule, and it is probable most will miss God's bus when the time comes. The point was (and is) that we need to repent and return to the whole of

God's Word. This will help us know what to do when the time comes.

With that message, though speaking to people who allegedly wore His name, the reaction was anger and hatred instead of contrition and repentance. There was no "receiving the word with all eagerness, examining the Scriptures daily to see if these things were true" (Acts 17:11). Soon after, I was asked to stop teaching or even participating, and eventually had no choice but to leave. Like the people spoken to by Jeremiah, they didn't want to listen for the sound of the trumpet calling people back to His ways (I was even blowing a shofar back then). Instead, they stopped their ears, threw metaphorical stones, and acted like those who already had the mark of the beast.

Nehemiah 9:29 ESV. And you warned them in order to turn them back to your law. Yet they acted presumptuously and did not obey your commandments, but sinned against your rules, which if a person does them, he shall live by them, and they turned a stubborn shoulder and stiffened their neck and would not obey.

The first four trumpets initiate judgments on a third of trees and grass (first), sea (second), rivers and springs of water (third), and sun, moon and stars (fourth). The fifth is a judgment on individual physical health (the locusts). The sixth trumpet heralds the slaying of a third of men. Heaven and earth both are affected, but only part. Later, the bowls will affect everything.

These trumpet blasts are warnings from God letting everyone know that His wrath has finally reached critical mass and more is coming. Yet even in wrath, God still holds out the option of repentance. Only a third of everything is affected at first, so God is giving the people of the earth a chance to change their ways and acknowledge their Maker. Sadly, they don't take the offer.

Revelation 9:20–21 ESV. The rest of mankind, who were not killed by these plagues, did not repent of the works of their hands nor give up worshiping demons and idols of gold and silver and bronze and stone and wood, which cannot see or hear or walk, nor did they repent of their murders or their sorceries or their sexual immorality or their thefts.

The seventh seal of the scroll Yeshua opens results in silence in heaven for about half an hour. This is kind of like a rest period. After this rest, the visions shown to John back up to give an account of events happening during the opening of the first six seals. In other words, the seven trumpet judgments occur while Yeshua is breaking at least the first four seals. The visions of the first four (and perhaps five) of the seals closely track the trumpet judgments as well as the events listed by Yeshua in Matthew 24. Seal one is false christs/prophets. Seal two is wars and rumors of wars. Seals three (famines) and four (Death and Hades) are the direct results of burning, wormwood poisoning, locusts and war.

To kick the trumpet concert off, an angel with a golden censer comes and stands at the altar. If you don't know, a censer is kind of like a plate or bowl which hangs from chains, because it is filled with coals from a fire and it gets hot. The angel with the censer gets a lot of incense to lie on the altar fire, which combines with the prayers of all the saints (implying they are living), and the smoke rises before God. Then the angel puts fire from the altar in the censer and hurls it to the earth. Fire or coals from the altar is a sign of judgment. Then the seven trumpet-carrying angels get ready to sound the trumpets.

We don't know the timing of the trumpets such as when they start, if they sound one right after the other, or if there are days, weeks or months in between. The fifth trumpet (the first woe) does have a period of five months at least. The sixth trumpet (the second woe) has a general period specified, because the army of 200,000,000 kills a third of men, which would take a while. It also has one other more specific period: 42 months or 1,260 days for the two witnesses. A marker is also given (though we don't know what it is) in the release of the four angels at the Euphrates who have waited for the exact hour, day, month and year for their parole.

Yet another clue to the timing of the trumpets is in Revelation 10:7 where the angel with the scroll standing on the sea and land says that "in the days of the trumpet call to be sounded by the seventh angel, the mystery of God would be fulfilled." The phrase "in the days" means that the events take more time than just the time for the sounding. However, we can't nail down the exact timing of all the events. The two witnesses prophesy in the first half of the seven year "agreement with many for one week," and the trumpets also sound in the first half of the week.

The "mystery of God fulfilled" is a bit of a poser, because the bowl judgments are still to come and are poured out in the Day of the Lord. More about this is a little later in the chapter when we examine the seventh trumpet in depth. Suffice it to say here that the mystery of God is the kingdom of God which destroys all of the anti-God earthly kingdoms. Each trumpet is like a bell tolling the deceiver's funeral march.

God's Feast of Trumpets points us to these trumpet judgments, because like that holy day the trumpets here are warnings. As bad as the trumpet judgments are, there are more severe plagues coming with the seven bowls on the Day of the Lord or Day of Atonement. This "day" is at the last half of the seven-year period. Whole Bible believers observe the holy days of God as a sign to unbelievers of what is coming, and are a constant reminder that the Day will in fact come, and everyone needs to repent before then.

Jeremiah 6:16–19 ESV. Thus says the LORD: "Stand by the roads, and look, and ask for the ancient paths, where the good way is; and walk in it, and find rest for your souls. But they said, 'We will not walk in it.' I set watchmen over you, saying, 'Pay attention to the sound of the trumpet!' But they said, 'We will not pay attention.' Therefore hear, O nations, and know, O congregation, what will happen to them. Hear, O earth; behold, I am bringing disaster upon this people, the fruit of their devices, because they have not paid attention to my words; and as for my law, they have rejected it.

Jeremiah said this about Israel, but it applies to anyone with the same behavior. Remember that there are cycles of events both because the deceiver keeps trying the same plan over and over, and also because people will not listen. Instead, they keep "doing what is right in their own eyes." God does not want anyone to perish, and in His love, He gives people space to amend their ways and follow His instead.

2 Peter 3:9–10 ESV. The Lord is not slow to fulfill his promise as some count slowness, but is patient toward you, not wishing that any should perish, but that all should reach repentance. But the day of the Lord will come like a thief, and then the heavens will pass away with a roar, and the heavenly bodies will be burned up and dissolved, and the earth and the works that are done on it will be exposed.

Trumpet 1: Mix of Fire, Blood & Hail

Hail, fire and blood thrown on the earth follow the first trumpet blast, which results in a third of trees, earth, and all green grass burning up.

Revelation 8:7 ESV. The first angel blew his trumpet, and there followed hail and fire, mixed with blood, and these were thrown upon the earth. And a third of the earth was burned up, and a third of the trees were burned up, and all green grass was burned up.

Other Scripture tells us that the fire part of hail and fire could be lightening, or coals.

Psalm 18:13 ESV. The LORD also thundered in the heavens, and the Most High uttered his voice, hailstones and coals of fire.

Hail combined with fire is mentioned several times in the Bible, the main time being the plagues on Egypt. The addition of the blood part is only mentioned here. Blood from the sacrifices was thrown against the altar to atone for different sins, but this is not from an offering.

A side effect of a third of trees and all the grass burning up is that it reduces the amount of available oxygen. We don't know if every third tree the world over is destroyed, or the trees on a particular third part of the world. Blood properly applied to the altar or Ark of the Covenant is for atonement, but other blood defiles or makes things unclean. In this case, people who delight in shedding innocent blood are covered with more corruption.

One way God could use nature to shower the earth with hail, fire and blood could be after volcanic eruptions. Fire is obvious, and hail could come from large volumes of moisture being forced into the upper atmosphere where it condenses into hail. Blood could come from people who live around the volcanoes. Or God could just start chucking from heaven, too.

Volcanic activity could also be a way of affecting only a third of the trees, earth and all the grass. We know eruptions produce clouds that would block the sun and moon such as in the plague released by the fourth trumpet. Volcanoes also produce something called a pyroclastic flow or cloud. This flow is a fast moving collection of very hot gas and matter destroying nearly everything in its path, like a massive freight train that has left the tracks. Volcanic activity would also contribute to the sea becoming blood and fresh waters becoming bitter at the sounding of the second and third trumpets.

Trumpet 2: Burning Mountain

Revelation 8:8–9 ESV. The second angel blew his trumpet, and something like a great mountain, burning with fire, was thrown into the sea, and a third of the sea became blood. A third of the living creatures in the sea died, and a third of the ships were destroyed.

Speaking of volcanoes, the second trumpet heralds a burning mountain thrown into the sea. When we are trying to figure out symbolic language, which at the same time is literally true, we have to look at the nature of what is communicated. On the one hand, this is probably something like an actual burning mountain, but on the other hand, it could represent a volcano or even an asteroid. We don't know how it is thrown, so it could come from space, be ejected through a volcanic eruption, or actually tossed in the ocean by an angel.

The earth's population will fail to catch the connection to God and judgment. The lack of eyesight in making connections will be a factor in refusing to repent. Whichever way it happens, a third of the sea becomes blood. Of course, this will kill probably a third of the inhabitants of the affected areas, those who get their food from the sea.

Oceans cover about 70% of the earth's surface, but we don't know if this passage is referring to all of the oceans or just the Mediterranean Sea. If the center of all this action is what we call the Middle East with Israel as the hub, then it follows that "the sea" is limited to the sea right next to Israel. If all the oceans are the target, then it would be a much bigger disaster.

We also don't know the size of the burning mountain. In Colorado we have about 53 mountains that are 14,000 feet tall or more. The Himalayas have peaks well above that size. Some people think a hill is a mountain. So the burning mountain might be as small as a hill, or as big as Mt. Everest or K2. If the

Mediterranean is the target, it would still have to be a pretty big mountain to turn a third of it into blood.

However, in the recent movie Sahara, the plot revolves around heavy metal toxins leaching into ground water and traveling to the ocean. The toxins create a red-tide type of effect, robbing the water of oxygen and killing people. At one point they show a computer simulation where the toxic effect spreads through the oceans very quickly, killing everything. Of course, this is movie magic, but it does suggest how quickly toxins in the oceans could spread. If a burning mountain falls into the sea, it is not hard to imagine that it might have heavy metals and toxic effects that spread quickly.

At this trumpet one-third of the ships are destroyed, contributing to famines because a lot of the world's food moves by ship. The cruise ship industry will also go down the tubes.

Trumpet 3: Wormwood

With the third trumpet a star falls from heaven that is called Wormwood. A third part of the rivers and fountains of waters or springs turn bitter enough to kill many men. The terms "wormwood" and "bitter" are both associated with idolatry and sexual immorality. This could mean new diseases or old ones making a comeback.

Deuteronomy 29:18–19 ESV. Beware lest there be among you a man or woman or clan or tribe whose heart is turning away today from the LORD our God to go and serve the gods of those nations. Beware lest there be among you a root bearing poisonous and bitter fruit, one who, when he hears the words of this sworn covenant, blesses himself in his heart, saying, 'I shall be safe, though I walk in the stubbornness of my heart.' This will lead to the sweeping away of moist and dry alike.

In the King James or Authorized version of the Bible, "poisonous and bitter fruit" is "gall and wormwood." In Proverbs

5:4, a forbidden woman is "bitter as wormwood." So the star called Wormwood probably makes the waters bitter because of people turning away from God's Law to idolatry and sexual immorality.

Jeremiah 9:13–15 ESV. And the LORD says: "Because they have forsaken my law that I set before them, and have not obeyed my voice or walked in accord with it, but have stubbornly followed their own hearts and have gone after the Baals, as their fathers taught them. Therefore thus says the LORD of hosts, the God of Israel: Behold, I will feed this people with bitter food, and give them poisonous water to drink.

This isn't just Israel, by the way. It is all those who ignore the Law of God and turn to their own ways and knowledge.

Amos 5:6–7 ESV. Seek the LORD and live, lest he break out like fire in the house of Joseph, and it devour, with none to quench it for Bethel, O you who turn justice to wormwood and cast down righteousness to the earth!

Three times in Jeremiah God tells Israel that He will give them poisonous water to drink. He certainly did this when He removed His presence and gave them up to war, disease and captivity. So wormwood could be a metaphor, or it could actually be that one-third of the waters become bitter. Both are good possibilities. Those who reject the source of living water deserve the poisonous or bitter water reserved for them.

Every day and in many ways the people on earth dispense bitterness instead of justice, and throw righteousness into the landfill. God is going to give them the poisonous fruit of their labors at the sounding of the third trumpet. This could just be imagery trying to describe perhaps an asteroid, or it could literally be an angel.

It would be odd that only one-third of the rivers and fountains are affected, if it was a stellar event like a hit from an asteroid. You would think there would be more destruction than just some fresh water turning bitter. So it is more probably a supernatural event. A controlled descent by an angel called in by God for making some of the fresh water bitter sounds reasonable.

Trumpet 4: Third of Sun, Moon, Stars

Revelation 8:12 ESV. The fourth angel blew his trumpet, and a third of the sun was struck, and a third of the moon, and a third of the stars, so that a third of their light might be darkened, and a third of the day might be kept from shining, and likewise a third of the night.

We don't know exactly how this is going to play out. Will the sun go dark for a third of the day, sort of like a strobe light? Since the moon doesn't rotate but keeps the same face toward the earth all the time, will a third of it be covered, or because the moon gets its light from the sun, does it just mean that when the sun isn't shining the moon isn't either? Does it mean that nights will be longer, or that the sun's output will be reduced by a third? (Probably not a reduction in output or our planet would freeze.) What about the stars? Will every third star go dark, or a third of the sky be covered? Could this be related to Revelation 12:4, where the dragon sweeps down a third of the stars of heaven with his tail and casts them to earth? If angels are swept down, that would be a permanent situation. Otherwise, we don't know if this is a permanent condition, or just for a short while.

We have this tidbit of information from Ezekiel, speaking at the time of Pharaoh and Egypt. But it seems to me it is also applicable here. It suggests one of the ways that God could control only a third of the sun.

Ezekiel 32:7–8 ESV. When I blot you out, I will cover the heavens and make their stars dark; I will cover the sun with a cloud, and the moon shall not give its light. All the bright lights of heaven will I make dark over you, and put darkness on your land, declares the Lord God.

But if you read the rest of the chapter, it sounds as if the blotting out has not happened yet. Instead, it sounds terribly like Armageddon, and will more likely take place in the latter days or Day of the Lord.

Whatever method God uses, natural or supernatural, a third of the day and night won't have any light. This would probably impact the growing season for everything from grain to grapes. At the very least, the lack of light for a third of the day will slow growth and reduce the yield per acre, contributing to famines.

Trumpet 5/First Woe: Poisonous Locusts

Revelation chapter 9, verses 1 through 11 tells us of the first of three woes after the trumpet of the fifth angel sounds. A star falls to earth, which is apparently an angel, and he is given a key to the shaft of the bottomless pit. He opens the shaft and really thick dark smoke billows forth, and out of the smoke come something called locusts with the power of scorpions. No grass, green plant or trees are to be harmed (which would be the normal diet of locusts). Only those without the seal of God on their foreheads will be affected. The harm would not cause death, but people are going to wish they were dead for five months. This is where the phrase "death takes a holiday" comes from.

We don't know where the shaft of the bottomless pit lies. At a guess, this shaft is probably hidden somewhere in the mountains of northern Turkey, one of which is called Ararat. If it is correct that the last king of the north is from the area of western Turkey, near the throne of the deceiver which is still in or near Pergamum (maybe Istanbul), then it makes sense that the bottomless pit shaft is in the same neighborhood.

These locusts look like horses prepared for battle. An interesting parallel is in Jeremiah, where he likens horses to "bristling locusts," probably because they are very numerous and weapons they carry stick out all over them. It is quoted here, not because they are the same, but because the language is similar.

Jeremiah 51:27 ESV. "Set up a standard on the earth; blow the trumpet among the nations; prepare the nations for war against her; summon against her the kingdoms, Ararat, Minni, and Ashkenaz; appoint a marshal against her; bring up horses like bristling locusts.

This doesn't mean the locusts are the size of horses. It just means they have armor like a war horse. What looks like (emphasis on "looks like") crowns of gold are on their heads. They have faces like humans, hair like a woman's, teeth like a lion, and breastplates like iron. The noise of their wings is like chariots going into battle. Notice all of the "likes" or "looked like" words and phrases. John is describing the appearance of something that has no exact equivalent that we know of in nature. So he uses similes to convey an impression of the warlike looks and behavior of these locusts. Joel makes similar comparisons when describing a plague of locusts in his time.

Joel 2:3–5 ESV. Fire devours before them, and behind them a flame burns. The land is like the garden of Eden before them, but behind them a desolate wilderness, and nothing escapes them. Their appearance is like the appearance of horses, and like war horses they run. As with the rumbling of chariots, they leap on the tops of the mountains, like the crackling of a flame of fire devouring the stubble, like a powerful army drawn up for battle.

The closest comparison to insects we know might be the Asian giant hornet. If you think the locusts are simply John's imagination, you haven't looked up this hornet in an encyclopedia or on the internet. They can grow up to two inches long, with a quarter-inch long stinger which they can use repeatedly. Their sting is extremely painful, and if enough of them attack a human, they can kill. Right now, they are common in Japan and routinely kill about 40 humans a year.

An interesting tidbit about the Asian giant hornet is that it attacks honey bees. If enough bees die, then crops needing bees for pollination will die also. These locusts are ordered not to harm any green plant, tree or grass, so they are not the same insect. These are related to the "hornets" of Exodus 23:28, Deuteronomy 7:20 and Joshua 24:12. God said He would send these before Israel to drive out those who hated God and Israel.

Deuteronomy 7:20, ESV. Moreover, the LORD your God will send hornets among them, until those who are left and hide themselves from you are destroyed.

They are just "amped up" versions God is using as a judgment and torment for all those who have signed up with the beast. The description sounds too unnatural for them to be simply prophetic imagery. They are real and probably very close to actual insects or beings from the pit. Breastplates of iron mean they are difficult or impossible to kill. No one will be able to just swat them or wave them away.

Some, such as Robert Morris, pastor of Gateway Church in Texas, have suggested that the locusts could in fact be demons (from his video "Symbols - More Than Words" on YouTube). It's possible because they have a demon king whose name is "Destroyer" in English, or Abaddon in Hebrew and Apollyon in Greek. This king coordinates the attacks of these insects (or demons), which explains how they are able to distinguish those without the seal of God on the forehead from those who have it. It also explains why they avoid harming grass, green plants or trees. But even if they are demons, there's no difference. It's still the same effect. If not insects, why stings and why only five months?

I'm sure the nations will panic with this plague just as they do with regular pestilence or disease. If you remember the Covid 19 or China virus hoax in 2020, governments were frantically searching for a vaccine and hoarding medicines for relieving symptoms. Travel was restricted, healthy people quarantined, billions of dollars thrown at the problem, and there were all kinds of lies and stupid panic. Just wait until this plague of locusts descends on the Middle East (and it seems the locusts might be centered in that area). The people of the anti-God nations will be running and hiding, screaming in pain, unable to find relief, and nothing will work. Even if you had a pharmacy full of pain killers, it wouldn't help. The only thing that would work is repentance and worship of God, and they will not do it.

Joel 2:10–11 ESV. The earth quakes before them; the heavens tremble. The sun and the moon are darkened, and the stars withdraw their shining. The LORD utters his voice before his army, for his camp is exceedingly great; he who executes his word is powerful. For the day of the LORD is great and very awesome; who can endure it?

Revelation 9:20 and 21 says that the survivors of this woe and the next woe (sixth trumpet) "did not repent of the works of their hands nor give up worshipping demons and idols...nor their murders or sorceries or sexual immorality or thefts." As with the behavior of the world with the China Virus in 2020, media outlets or internet websites will similarly be lying about the cause of the tribulations. The rebels will seek to justify every anti-God action as "natural" or "diverse" or "tolerant," and even invoke the Goddess of Reason or Science for excuses to continue their selfish and self-destructive notions. They will disguise hate as love, lies as truth, and many other wrongs as right, just as they are doing now. The trumpets are warnings to repent but will, as always, go unheeded by the bulk of the world's population.

Trumpet 6/Second Woe: Army, Witnesses

The sixth trumpet angel sounds off in Revelation 9:13 and kick starts the second woe. There are four main events between 9:13 and 11:14 when we get the statement "the second woe has passed," so all four parts together might constitute the second woe. The four events are the large army killing a third of mankind, the mighty angel with the scroll, the two witnesses, and an earthquake that kills 7,000 people. It might be that all four constitute the second woe, or perhaps the second woe is just the last event of the two witnesses and the earthquake.

It's not clear from the text exactly where the four angels are confined at the Euphrates. One would presume that they are at the headwaters of The River, which are in northern Turkey, but they could be anywhere. There are anecdotal stories of screams and groans coming from under the Haditha dam in Iraq and soldiers not wanting to guard the area. This dam is about halfway down The River Euphrates, near the original location of the city of Babylon, and might be a good place for angels to be confined.

The four angels were probably each once in charge of the four kingdoms of Babylon, Persia, Greece and Rome. They might symbolize that remnants of those nations make up the huge army. This, however, is just supposition and a guess. The only possibility that supports this is in Daniel, where a prince of Persia withstands what are possibly Jesus and Michael.

Daniel 10:13–14 ESV. The prince of the kingdom of Persia withstood me twenty-one days, but Michael, one of the chief princes, came to help me, for I was left there with the kings of Persia, and came to make you understand what is to happen to your people in the latter days. For the vision is for days yet to come."

If princes or angels are behind kingdoms, then the four locked up at The River could actually be those behind the four big kingdoms of Nebuchadnezzar's image. This suggests a possible location of the prison (near Babylon).

The Euphrates does not dry up at this time as the text describes at the sixth bowl judgment of Revelation 16. Modern armies have engineers who can build bridges in a hurry, so maybe a dry river bed is not necessary. It may not be necessary anyway because the army doesn't cross the River to invade Israel. In fact, the Euphrates doesn't seem to figure in here at all except as a location for the angelic prison.

John in 11:1 is "given a measuring rod like a staff" and told to measure the temple of God, the altar and those who worship there, but exclude the court outside the temple because the nations were going to trample it for 42 months. John doesn't tell us if he actually did the measuring but he probably did. It is this verse that makes some people think the book of Revelation was written before the destruction of the temple in 70 A.D. However, John is seeing the temple in a vision. The Temple could easily be rebuilt by the time of the events in the vision.

We don't know if the trampling of the court by the nations took place when the Roman armies destroyed the temple way back when, or if a temple is built in the future (from John's perspective) that has the outside court trampled. If a Temple is rebuilt, it could be that the Dome of the Rock is sitting on the location of the Temple court, symbolic of Gentiles trampling on the court. It's more probable, however, that the Temple will be built in the modern City of David which is the location of the Gihon spring and could provide water for washing.

Measuring is a way to state that whatever is measured really exists or will exist. Dimensions, like the numbering of hairs on our heads, reassure us that God knows exactly what is going on and has taken steps to either judge the situation or protect the subject. Measuring indicates exact knowledge of things in a way that man cannot. Isaiah records some rhetorical questions showing us that God measures and knows far outside of man's abilities.

Isaiah 40:12–15 ESV. Who has measured the waters in the hollow of his hand and marked off the heavens with a span, enclosed the dust of the earth in a measure and weighed the mountains in scales and the hills in a balance? Who has measured the Spirit of the LORD, or what man shows him his counsel? Whom did he consult, and who made him understand? Who taught him the path of justice, and taught him knowledge, and showed him the way of understanding? Behold, the nations are like a drop from a bucket, and are accounted as the dust on the scales; behold, he takes up the coastlands like fine dust.

Belshazzar the Chaldean king was "weighed in the balance and found wanting" (Daniel 5:27). The millennial Temple is measured in Ezekiel 40 through 47 to show us that it will indeed be built and it will be built to exact dimensions according to God's plan. By the time we get to John measuring the temple of God in Revelation 11, we understand that the measuring is very specific and according to God's plan and knowledge in His blueprints.

The four angels, bound at the great river Euphrates, have been waiting for the exact day, hour and month and are released to kill a third of mankind. They do it with mounted troops numbering 200,000,000. This seems like a fantastic number, but not so fantastic for a world population of eight billion. These mounted troops kill with the mouths of their horses, spewing out three plagues of fire, smoke and sulfur. As an added bonus, the tails of the horses are like serpents with heads and give wounds.

Going back to Joel for a minute, we are reminded that he gives us a picture that helps understand this prophecy.

Joel 2:4–5 ESV. Their appearance is like the appearance of horses, and like war horses they run. As with the rumbling of chariots, they leap on the tops of the mountains, like the crackling of a flame of fire devouring the stubble, like a powerful army drawn up for battle.

He says that an army on the day of the Lord will look like "the appearance of horses." Using the words "like" or "as" is a way of describing the nature of the armies by comparing them to horses. So it may not be that the horses are actual horses, but merely "like" horses, strong and fierce and fast. The individual soldiers might have weapons, such as flame throwers and explosives, or might simply be destructive "like" a horse that breathes "as" a dragon. The horses, or more likely soldiers, can destroy from both the front and the back (tails). Another reference that illustrates "like" or "as" descriptions is in Chronicles.

1 Chronicles 12:8 ESV. From the Gadites there went over to David at the stronghold in the wilderness mighty and experienced warriors, expert with shield and spear, whose faces were like the faces of lions and who were swift as gazelles upon the mountains:

The comparison to gazelles is obvious, because the warriors or mighty men were fast. "Faces of lions" could mean that they had shaggy hair or more likely a fierce countenance. Either way one wouldn't want to be on the wrong side of them in a battle.

An interesting note is that the breastplates of the horse riders are the colors red (fire), sapphire (blue) or more likely hyacinth (a purple flower native to the eastern Mediterranean) and sulfur which we might think of as a dirty or dull yellow. These could be the colors of a particular nation, or perhaps colors of a confederacy of nations making up the 200,000,000 man army. Breastplates sounds out of place to us, like medieval knights, but considering that many modern soldiers wear body armor it isn't that strange.

This doesn't seem to be a battle as much as it is a huge army just killing a lot of people. There is a difference. In a battle, both sides are armed and work at killing each other. The army with the purple/red/yellow flag (from the colors on the breastplates) is operating in other places than Israel. A third of mankind, at the present number of about 8 billion, is around 2.66 billion. That's a lot of people for an army to kill, even an army of 200 million, and it's more than the current population of Israel. Liberal despots like Bill Gates, who want the world's population reduced, will get their wish. You first, Bill.

It's probable that this is the army of the little horn or beast, and the killing is part of three horns or kingdoms that he "uproots" or destroys (Daniel 7:8). The population of India is about one and a half billion, with an army of a little over one million. China has easily the same (standing army of 1.6 million). Throw in the Muslim nations, Russia, Greece, northern Africa, and a few others in the area, along with navies, air forces and ballistic missiles, and it's easy to see how united armed forces of the little horn could mow down a third of the world's population.

Mouths

Isaiah 5:24 ESV. Therefore, as the tongue of fire devours the stubble, and as dry grass sinks down in the flame, so their root will be as rottenness, and their blossom go up like dust; for they have rejected the law of the LORD of hosts, and have despised the word of the Holy One of Israel.

Before we get to the other two parts of the third woe (the big angel and the two witnesses), there's an interesting thing about mouths in the book of Revelation that is worth reviewing. Yeshua is said to have a sword coming out of His mouth (Revelation 1:16, 2:16, 19:15, 19:21), and He "spews" lukewarm people out of His mouth (Revelation 3:16). The sixth trumpet tells us about horses that have fire, smoke and sulfur coming out of their mouths, killing a third of mankind (Revelation 9:17-19). The two witnesses of Revelation 11 are able to defend themselves against those who would kill them with fire pouring from their mouths. Perhaps this fire is God's Word, as Jeremiah described in the distant past.

Jeremiah 5:14 ESV. Therefore thus says the LORD, the God of hosts: "Because you have spoken this word, behold, I am making my words in your mouth a fire, and this people wood, and the fire shall consume them.

God's Word is full of power, love and mercy for those who follow Him, but destructive to those who are separated from Him and choose to go their own way. In the beginning, He speaks and His Word creates fantastic, beautiful life. The witnesses here are preaching God's Words, which if accepted in humility and submission, also create life. If the Word is rejected, we are apart from Him and we spend eternity that way, burning with fire. United with God (and His Word) we are ultimately resurrected or bodies recreated and live eternally. If people want to try and stop the message by destroying these witnesses, the Word works the opposite way.

Another metaphor is given to us by James for the tongue.

James 3:3–6 ESV. If we put bits into the mouths of horses so that they obey us, we guide their whole bodies as well. Look at the ships also: though they are so large and are driven by strong winds, they are guided by a very small rudder wherever the will of the pilot directs. So also the tongue is a small member, yet it boasts of great things. How great a forest is set ablaze by such a small fire! And the tongue is a fire, a world of unrighteousness. The tongue is set among our members, staining the whole body, setting on fire the entire course of life, and set on fire by hell.

The serpent pours water from his mouth to try and kill the woman of Revelation 12, and the earth opens its mouth to defend her. The beast or little horn has a mouth like a lion that utters blasphemies (Revelation 13:2-6). No lie is found in the mouths of the 144,000 of Revelation 14:5, but out of the mouths of the little horn, false prophet and serpent we are told that unclean spirits looking like frogs jump out (Revelation 16:13).

In the case of the sword, we know this to be another picture of the Word of God, which is likened to a sword in Hebrews.

Hebrews 4:12–13 ESV. For the word of God is living and active, sharper than any two-edged sword, piercing to the division of soul and of spirit, of joints and of marrow, and discerning the thoughts and intentions of the heart. And no creature is hidden from his sight, but all are naked and exposed to the eyes of him to whom we must give account.

This sword of the Word is sharper than a physical sword. It can slay or destroy, it holds the universe together, and it can create.

Hebrews 1:1–4 ESV. Long ago, at many times and in many ways, God spoke to our fathers by the prophets, but in these last days he has spoken to us by his Son, whom he appointed the heir of all things, through whom also he created the world. He is the radiance of the glory of God and the exact imprint of his nature, and he upholds the universe by the word of his power. After making purification for sins, he sat down at the right hand of the Majesty on high, having become as much superior to angels as the name he has inherited is more excellent than theirs.

For the two witnesses it might be the same thing (the fire is the Word), or perhaps they will literally breathe fire like a mythical dragon.

Hosea 6:5 ESV. Therefore I have hewn them by the prophets; I have slain them by the words of my mouth, and my judgment goes forth as the light.

The water from the mouth of the serpent that pursues the "woman" or Israel we can most likely interpret as godless nations persecuting the Jewish people, perhaps the same as the 200,000,000 soldier army of the little horn. Waters or floods like this have been used to describe armies several times in Scripture.

Jeremiah 46:7–8 ESV. "Who is this, rising like the Nile, like rivers whose waters surge? Egypt rises like the Nile, like rivers whose waters surge. He said, 'I will rise, I will cover the earth, I will destroy cities and their inhabitants.'

Isaiah 8:5–8 ESV. The LORD spoke to me again: "Because this people has refused the waters of Shiloah that flow gently, and rejoice over Rezin and the son of Remaliah, therefore, behold, the Lord is bringing up against them the waters of the River, mighty and many, the king of Assyria and all his glory. And it will rise over all its channels and go over all its banks, and it will sweep on into Judah, it will overflow and pass on, reaching even to the neck, and its outspread wings will fill the breadth of your land, O Immanuel."

This time with the woman is different in that the armies are flooding after Israel but God causes the earth to swallow them.

The Word can also be sweet in the mouth but bitter in the stomach, as it was for John in Revelation 10, and honey-sweet, as it was for Ezekiel a few centuries earlier (Ezekiel 3:3). God's Word is sweet initially, but as it works its way through our thoughts and the world system, it develops a bitter aspect of judgment. It makes sense then that the fire pouring from the mouths of the two witnesses is also the Word of God, although it could be actual pyrotechnics too. The Word of God can give life, or destroy those opposed to it.

Isaiah 29:5–6 ESV. But the multitude of your foreign foes shall be like small dust, and the multitude of the ruthless like passing chaff. And in an instant, suddenly, you will be visited by the LORD of hosts with thunder and with earthquake and great noise, with whirlwind and tempest, and the flame of a devouring fire.

Mighty Big Angel, Little Sweet Scroll

Revelation 10:5–7 ESV. And the angel whom I saw standing on the sea and on the land raised his right hand to heaven and swore by him who lives forever and ever, who created heaven and what is in it, the earth and what is in it, and the sea and what is in it, that there would be no more delay, but that in the days of the trumpet call to be sounded by the seventh angel, the mystery of God would be fulfilled, just as he announced to his servants the prophets.

The third part of what seems to be the second woe is another scroll. The scroll in the angel's hand described for us in Revelation 10 is related to the scroll of Revelation 6 in that it is the Word of God. They might even be the same scroll, and the angel bears a strong resemblance to Yeshua. John is instructed to take the scroll and eat it, and it will be sweet as honey in his mouth but bitter in his stomach. The Word of the Lord here is at first sweet, as all words from God are sweet to those who are sweet, but in this case also contains judgment, so when it settles in the stomach it is not so sweet.

Psalm 119:103 ESV. How sweet are your words to my taste, sweeter than honey to my mouth!

Ezekiel does something similar with a scroll (Ezekiel 3:1-3). He also eats, and in his mouth, it was sweet. He doesn't say it was bitter in the stomach, but given what he has to tell Israel it would seem that it was not so sweet later.

The seven thunders answer the angel who roars with a loud voice like a lion roaring. John understands the thunders, but he is not allowed to write down what they say. Believers at the time the angel stands with a foot on the land and the other on the sea might be able to hear the thunders and understand. John is able to write down the words of the angel, however, which are to the effect that there will be no more delay.

The angel swears by "him who lives forever and ever, who created heaven and what is in it, the earth and what is in it, and the sea and what is in it, that there would be no more delay, but that in the days of the trumpet call to be sounded by the seventh angel, the mystery of God would be fulfilled, just as he announced to his servants the prophets." John picks up the description of this mystery in the text right after a vision of the two witnesses.

The Two Witnesses

Zechariah 4:11–14 ESV. Then I said to him, "What are these two olive trees on the right and the left of the lampstand?" And a second time I answered and said to him, "What are these two branches of the olive trees, which are beside the two golden pipes from which the golden oil is poured out?" He said to me, "Do you not know what these are?" I said, "No, my lord." Then he said, "These are the two anointed ones who stand by the Lord of the whole earth."

Revelation 11:3–4 ESV. And I will grant authority to my two witnesses, and they will prophesy for 1,260 days, clothed in sackcloth." These are the two olive trees and the two lampstands that stand before the Lord of the earth.

The fourth or remaining part of the sixth trumpet or second woe is the testimony of the two witnesses. Actually, we don't know if the sixth trumpet starts the ministry of the witnesses, or we just find out that they've been doing their thing during the time of the trumpet judgments. They work for three and a half years, so their preaching covers a longer period that it would take to blow a horn.

But in Deuteronomy (17:6 and 19:15), God gives us a court procedure for bringing charges against anyone for a crime. At least two witnesses are required for a charge to be established. The two witnesses mentioned in the verses above are likely God's witnesses against the people of the earth for the crimes they have committed.

Moses uses the concept of two witnesses when he calls "heaven and earth" to testify that he told Israel what would happen should they (or more accurately when they) "act corruptly and turn aside from the way that I have commanded you" (Deuteronomy 4:26, 30:19, 31:28).

Deuteronomy 30:19 ESV. I call heaven and earth to witness against you today, that I have set before you life and death, blessing and curse. Therefore choose life, that you and your offspring may live,

The two witnesses from Zechariah and Revelation are most probably the two people listed in the Word as having avoided death so far: Enoch (Genesis 5:24) and Elijah (2 Kings 2:11). Enoch is a witness from before the flood and Elijah for the time after the flood. Since it is appointed for a man to die once (Hebrews 9:27) and after that the judgment, it seems plain that Enoch and Elijah will show up in Jerusalem to witness for God and then die and resurrect at the end of their three and a half year task.

Some think that Enoch isn't eligible because he isn't "Jewish." This is not backed up by Scripture, because this requirement is not listed anywhere. Many churchgoers are used to splitting things apart and separating Scripture that should be kept together, so maybe they also have some secret way of qualifying the two witnesses. It sure isn't from the Word.

Another philosophy of men is that one witness is from the "old testament" and one from the "new testament." Old and New Testament labels are pasted on the Bible by the Church and not applied by the Word itself. Old and new testaments in the Word are connected with the condition of the heart. Since the labels were given by the Church long after the apostles departed, one has to wonder why the witnesses would be chosen this way. The old covenant (or "testament") was old because it was written on stone. The new or "renewed" covenant (or "testament") of Jeremiah 31:31-34 is written on a heart of flesh, and all will abide by its terms eventually. Applying a philosophy of man over the Word is sure to bring about skewed interpretation results.

All flesh has to die once. Even those who are translated (or changed) after the resurrection can be considered to have died. As

Paul says, the perishable must put on the imperishable (1 Corinthians 15:50-58). Neither Enoch nor Elijah died, and seems to me that they have to come back so they can go the way of all flesh like the rest of us.

It is interesting that the powers these two witnesses have are very similar to the trumpets and the four horsemen. In addition to destroying anyone with a fiery breath, they can shut the sky so no rain falls (drought which brings on famine, black horse rider (Revelation 6:5), they can turn water to blood (second trumpet, Revelation 8:8) and strike the earth with every kind of plague (fourth rider, death, pestilence Revelation 7:8). Perhaps the two witnesses are working in concert with the trumpets and within the domain of the four horsemen. Or perhaps in their prophesying they are warning of what is to come with the bowl judgments.

God tells John that the two witnesses testify for 1,260 days, which works out to 42 months of 30 days each. The boys here are doing their thing for the first half of the covenant week between the little horn and Israel. The little horn or beast wants to kill them but can't, which means his power is still limited. He's on the scene, and ruling somewhere, but cannot take out the two really big pains in his posterior until after the 42 months are up.

Compare this to Scripture such as Revelation 13:5 where the beast is "allowed to exercise authority for forty-two months" and 13:7 "it (the beast) was allowed to make war on the saints to conquer them." The timing of this section of 42 months appears to be different from the 42 months of the witness ministry. First, the witnesses have their ministry, and then the dragon gives the beast "his power and his throne and great authority." When we hear in Revelation 13:5 that the beast is "allowed to exercise authority for 42 months," the conclusion is it must be the second half of the 70th week of years, kicked off by the death of the two witnesses.

So the witnesses frustrate the beast for 42 months after he signs the seven year agreement (the first half of the seven), and while the trumpets are announcing judgments. At the halfway point, the beast finally gets all the power he needs from the deceiver or dragon to kill the witnesses, set up the talking image and start marking people. Their deaths in turn bring on the period of the seven bowl judgments of the Day of the Lord (the last half of the seven-year covenant period).

It seems apparent that the two men who haven't yet died are in heaven "witnessing" all that transpires of the evil of men throughout history, and will return for a short while to tell us about it. Then, like many such witnesses, they too are murdered, as the deceiver keeps trying to silence the testimony from God against him. But not for three and a half years, which will bug the deceiver and his minions to no end.

2 Chronicles 36:16 ESV. But they kept mocking the messengers of God, despising his words and scoffing at his prophets, until the wrath of the LORD rose against his people, until there was no remedy.

Trumpet 7: Mystery of God Fulfilled

The seventh trumpet announces "the mystery of God fulfilled." Part of the mystery of God referred to here, and by the mighty big angel previously, is the kingdom of God. This kingdom was promised to Adam and Eve and the promise repeated to Noah, Abraham, King David, and so on through the prophets and apostles to us. The mystery was shown to king Nebuchadnezzar and illuminated for us in Daniel, which was of world kingdoms getting smashed by the stone cut from a mountain by no human hand. Nebuchadnezzar sees the mystery of God in a dream, but doesn't understand it. He can't even remember the exact description of his dream and has to have the dream and the meaning explained.

The mystery of God (Daniel 2:47) was the progression of earthly empires, with the "stone cut out by no human hand" (the kingdom of God) destroying all of them at the appointed time. The stone is the kingdom of Yeshua, the virgin-born only begotten Son of God, king of kings and lord of lords. The blast of trumpet seven starts the final process of blowing away all earthly, deceiver-inspired, anti-God kingdoms.

Revelation 11:15 ESV. Then the seventh angel blew his trumpet, and there were loud voices in heaven, saying, "The kingdom of the world has become the kingdom of our Lord and of his Christ, and he shall reign forever and ever."

Revelation 11:19 ESV. Then God's temple in heaven was opened, and the ark of his covenant was seen within his temple. There were flashes of lightning, rumblings, peals of thunder, an earthquake, and heavy hail.

In rapid order, the bowls will finish what was started by the trumpets; that is, destroying "the new world order." This is really the old world order having a slightly different marketing approach. The seven trumpets soften up the world and invite repentance; the bowls crush the kingdom of the deceiver.

Yeshua teaches in parables because believers will understand the secrets of the kingdom of heaven, but unbelievers will not (Matthew 13:11; Mark 4:11; Luke 8:10).

Luke 8:9–10 ESV. And when his disciples asked him what this parable meant, he said, "To you it has been given to know the secrets of the kingdom of God, but for others they are in parables, so that 'seeing they may not see, and hearing they may not understand.'

Paul says part of the mystery is that a partial hardening is on Israel until the fullness of the Gentiles is come in (Romans 11:25). In another place, Paul says the mystery is disclosed to all nations, specifically to bring about the obedience of faith (see also Colossians 1:26).

Romans 16:25–27 ESV. Now to him who is able to strengthen you according to my gospel and the preaching of Jesus Christ, according to the revelation of the mystery that was kept secret for long ages but has now been disclosed and through the prophetic writings has been made known to all nations, according to the command of the eternal God, to bring about the obedience of faith— to the only wise God be glory forevermore through Jesus Christ! Amen.

Paul also says that part of the mystery is that Gentiles are "fellow heirs, members of the same body" in Ephesians 3:6 and another part is that "we shall not all sleep" in 1 Corinthians 15:51. Yet another part of the mystery is that marriage is a picture of Christ and His One Body (not the Church, as the translations have it). There is also a "mystery of lawlessness" and the mystery of the woman riding the beast in Revelation 17. The mystery spoken of by the angel in Revelation 10 is all of these parts wrapped up into the kingdom of God in and through Yeshua our Messiah.

The mystery of God's kingdom in Yeshua, to some people, is only a mystery because they are not tuned into God's Word. They tune out because they don't want either the Word or the Kingdom. The different parts of the mystery are plain to believers because God has shown them to us. We have accepted His kingdom and live by its rules, statutes, commands and directions.

Third Woe: Dragon, Beasts, Messages

Isaiah 24:5–6 ESV. The earth lies defiled under its inhabitants; for they have transgressed the laws, violated the statutes, broken the everlasting covenant. Therefore a curse devours the earth, and its inhabitants suffer for their guilt; therefore the inhabitants of the earth are scorched, and few men are left.

Revelation 12:12 ESV. Therefore, rejoice, O heavens and you who dwell in them! But woe to you, O earth and sea, for the devil has come down to you in great wrath, because he knows that his time is short!"

The sixth trumpet kind of leaves us hanging because there is no direct association with a third woe. John doesn't specifically say this is the third woe, but he does record a voice from heaven that says something about a woe. So the eviction of the evil one is probably the third woe, which would make sense because he has always been angry and destructive of anything good, trying to hinder the plans of God. Remember that John is recording pictures for us of images that mean something in addition to their simple appearance. For instance, the river that pours from the dragon's mouth is probably a symbol of an army or armies (Revelation 12:15). The earth swallowing the watery attack (verse 16) might actually be an earthquake fault such as what happened to Korah in Numbers 16, or it could symbolize many centuries of persecution derailed by God as He protects His people.

It could be both because the end-of chapter prophecy (Revelation 12:6), where the woman would go to a place prepared for her and be nourished for 1,260 days, has not happened yet. As pointed out before, sometimes there are large gaps of time between items in a single vision, sometimes even in the same sentence. This is because the scene described by the prophet is telling a story with a specific purpose, not recounting a minute-by-minute timeline.

Some prophecies about Yeshua, for instance, confused rabbis for a long time because they spoke of a suffering servant and almost in the same breath a conquering king. Rabbis tried to resolve the confusion by postulating two Messiahs, but even at that, they didn't see the two thousand-year gap between the visits. The prophecies ended up being about one Messiah and two trips.

So John in this vision is given a story recounting the birth and ascension of Yeshua, there is a 2,000 year gap (so far), either while the woman evades the watery attack or when she does evade it. Eventually she finds the place prepared for her for a time, times and half a time (3 1/2 years, 1,260 days). Perhaps this is during the Day of the Lord.

Many bad guys are revealed for us in the Word. God describes false teachers of every size, shape and language, as well as bad kings, nations, prophets, tribes, and fallen angels we call demons. The serpent, also called the deceiver, is the major bad guy and the person who is responsible for seducing, teaching and developing most of the other bad guys and girls. Of course, men are very capable of mayhem all on their own too.

The book of Revelation features three main bad guys: the dragon, the beast and the anti-christ or false prophet. We see them all in chapter 13 of Revelation. Bad guys are in opposition to God, promising wonderful riches and power, but delivering only death and destruction. Sometimes they are allowed to succeed in building a kingdom or gathering wealth to themselves, but ultimately they are divided against themselves (Matthew 12:25; Mark 3:24-25; Luke 11:17) and their kingdoms fall. Anyone who opposes God will end up in a place suitable for those who don't want Him.

Signs in the Heavens

Continuing with the sign associated with trumpet seven, the first thing to notice is that it is a "great sign that appeared in heaven" (Revelation 12:1). It is possible that at least part of this vision is a constellation, and a conjunction of the sun and the moon (our thanks to Avi ben Mordechai from cominghome.co.il who suggested this to us). God put the heavenly bodies above in order to tell a story.

Genesis 1:14–15 ESV. And God said, "Let there be lights in the expanse of the heavens to separate the day from the night. And let them be for signs and for seasons, and for days and years, and let them be lights in the expanse of the heavens to give light upon the earth." And it was so.

The woman could be the Virgin or Virgo, known in Hebrew as Bethulah. This would explain why John sees her "clothed with the sun," the "moon under her feet," and "on her head a crown of twelve stars." The sun could be to the side of the constellation (perhaps in the hour before dawn), the moon lower down under her feet, and a group of stars at the top of her head.

It is worth considering that God is communicating His story to those with the wisdom of the Magi (wise men). They traveled to Bethlehem because they saw a sign in the heavens or "His star in the east" (Matthew 2:1-2).

Of course, John could also have literally seen, as in a movie against the backdrop of space, an actual woman with interesting clothes and a crown, who is in a delivery room for babies. It is sort of confusing because the sign is in heaven, and in Revelation 12:6 the woman "fled into the wilderness," with "the two wings of a great eagle." The serpent tries to get her with a river out of his mouth which is swallowed by the earth. So the sign starts in heaven but transitions to the earth. This makes the idea of a constellation representing the woman to be a stretch perhaps. But it could be both a sign in star or constellation form, as well as a "movie trailer" for the time of the end.

Another possibility is that this sign is a history lesson to start with (the part in heaven), and then a look at the future (the earth and fleeing part). If so, then the deceiver's tail sweeping a third of the stars from the sky could simply be a historical note for fallen angels (even "fallen" from heaven) who follow the dragon.

The story that starts in the stars and ends on earth is one complete story showing past and future. In 12:1-5 we get some history (from John's viewpoint). The fallen stars or angels are swept from the sky sometime in the past, and then the birth of the Messiah is recounted. So the first part of the story goes something like this: Stars swept, Messiah birth, dragon tries an ambush, Messiah caught up to heaven, woman flees (verse 6). Next, we try to understand the throwing down of the dragon.

The Dragon Thrown Down

Revelation 12 (verses 7-13) seems to switch perspective to a future war in heaven (from John's time). The dragon loses and is thrown down to earth with his demons. But Yeshua seems to say a casting out happened close to the crucifixion.

John 12:31 ESV. Now is the judgment of this world; now will the ruler of this world be cast out.

If we look at His statement closely, He could be making a prophecy that the deceiver will be cast out eventually. He doesn't say "is cast out," he says effectively "will be cast out." Yeshua says in another place that He saw the deceiver fall.

Luke 10:18–19 ESV. And he said to them, "I saw Satan fall like lightning from heaven. Behold, I have given you authority to tread on serpents and scorpions, and over all the power of the enemy, and nothing shall hurt you.

Yeshua could have been talking about an emergency exit of the deceiver from heaven at that time, as the deceiver was trying to deal with the losses inflicted by the 72 disciples announcing the kingdom of God. Or Yeshua could have been looking ahead, perhaps towards the end time when the kingdom of God destroys the kingdom of the deceiver. Peter says he is still hunting for victims on the earth.

1 Peter 5:8 ESV. Be sober-minded; be watchful. Your adversary the devil prowls around like a roaring lion, seeking someone to devour.

Most probably these two events (Satan falling like lightening and war in heaven) are separate, because the "loud voice in heaven" (12:10) after the war in heaven says, "woe to you, O earth and sea, for the devil has come down to you in great wrath, because he knows that his time is short!" (Revelation 12:12.) The deceiver's plans are dead; he just doesn't know it yet. The key phrase is in Revelation 12:8 where it says "there was no longer any place for them in heaven" (the dragon and his angels).

So the path of the deceiver changes from "going to and fro on the earth, and from walking up and down on it" (Job 1:7 and 2:4) in arrogance as he wills, to "no longer any place" in heaven.

Yeshua tells us that the deceiver's throne is in Pergamum in Revelation 2:13, and by Revelation 12 he is permanently kicked out of heaven from that point on. The last we hear of him is in Revelation 20 where he is released from the (earthly) pit and even then foments another rebellion on earth.

In the beginning, it was said of the serpent that he was "more crafty than any beast of the field." This doesn't mean (although it could) that he was actually a snake, but it does characterize him like a beast. He's sneaky, quick, and an opportunistic predator. He's out for himself, cold, voracious, vicious and intelligent.

Genesis 3:1 NASB95. Now the serpent was more crafty than any beast of the field which the LORD God had made. And he said to the woman, "Indeed, has God said, 'You shall not eat from any tree of the garden'?"

Sometimes God describes people, especially in visions, by their internal character and actions. Daniel for instance sees a series of beasts representing kingdoms of the world (Daniel 7) because their nature is beastly. This is why the deceiver has the titles The Serpent and The Dragon. God sees him as he is inside.

2 Thessalonians 2:1-12 NASB95. ¹Now we request you, brethren, with regard to the coming of our Lord Jesus Christ and our gathering together to Him, ²that you not be quickly shaken from your composure or be

disturbed either by a spirit or a message or a letter as if from us, to the effect that the day of the Lord has come. ³Let no one in any way deceive you, for *it will not come* unless the apostasy comes first, and the man of lawlessness is revealed, the son of destruction, ⁴who opposes and exalts himself above every so-called god or object of worship, so that he takes his seat in the temple of God, displaying himself as being God. ⁵Do you not remember that while I was still with you, I was telling you these things? ⁶And you know what restrains him now, so that in his time he will be revealed. ⁷For the mystery of lawlessness is already at work; only he who now restrains *will do so* until he is taken out of the way. ⁸Then that lawless one will be revealed whom the Lord will slay with the breath of His mouth and bring to an end by the appearance of His coming; ⁹*that is,* the one whose coming is in accord with the activity of Satan, with all power and signs and false wonders, ¹⁰and with all the deception of wickedness for those who perish, because they did not receive the love of the truth so as to be saved. ¹¹For this reason God will send upon them a deluding influence so that they will believe what is false, ¹²in order that they all may be judged who did not believe the truth, but took pleasure in wickedness.

Here, among other teachings, is a plain text argument against a rapture before the Tribulation. In 2 Thessalonians 2:3-4 the "man of lawlessness" or "son of destruction" has to be revealed first. Some offer the theory that "he who now restrains" is the Holy Spirit, who will be taken out of the way and will take believers with him. But this ignores the first part of the section where Paul tells us "our gathering together to Him" is on "the day of the Lord," which will not come until *after* the lawless one is revealed. It is more likely that "he who now restrains" is an angel (such as Michael) or even our Messiah Yeshua haMashiach. "Taken out of the way" most probably means that the angel moves aside. This relates to Daniel's visit with the angel who contended with the prince of Persia and was delayed.

The man of lawlessness "takes his seat in the temple of God displaying himself as being God." Some people think this was the Roman emperor Nero (we'll talk more about this in the section on the little horn). Others think it was Antiochus Epiphanes, who ran around persecuting the Jews a couple hundred years before the Incarnation. These rulers (and others) perhaps, claimed to be "a god," but did not claim to be capital G "God." The son of destruction takes the claim up a couple notches and directly challenges the Father. Because of the cyclical nature of human events, the others were also-rans or wannabe men of lawlessness, but not THE man of lawlessness.

At this point John picks up the story from the woman fleeing (back in verse 6) for 1,260 days and continues with her plight. The dragon, kicked out of heaven, chases her (verse 13) but she is given speed (wings of an eagle) to reach safety and is nourished for a "time, times and half a time" (verses 14-16). Again, using a 30 day month, three and a half years is 42 months. That lines up with the 1,260 days of verse six. Furious, the dragon makes war on the "rest of her offspring" (verse 17) which are most likely or at least including believers going through the Tribulation.

An Unholy Trinity

The combination of the little horn, false prophet, and the dragon is said by some to be an unholy trinity, modeled after the Father, Son, and Holy Spirit. There are similarities in that, but the comparison to Moses and Aaron (with God) is probably more accurate. Aaron ended up being a prophet in partnership with Moses (Exodus 7:1) acting to relay God's Words coming through Moses to Israel.

The beast, or "little horn," is the coming ruler spoken of in the Bible who will sway nearly the whole world to follow his lead. As a token of appreciation, the false prophet will make an image of the beast. This image speaks and will cause all who worship the beast to receive a mark on the hand or forehead, without which no one can buy or sell (see the section on **Buying and Selling**). The false prophet is one who looks like a lamb and is called the anti-Christ or 'instead of' Christ. This helper of the beast is the one who causes all to receive the mark. The dragon will back these two.

This unholy trinity will unite much of the world population in a rebellion against God and His Christ. They will not succeed, but while they have their run, there will be much death, destruction and wrath poured out by both God and the deceiver.

The Blasphemous "Little Horn" or Worthless Shepherd

A person with the title of "the little horn" or beast is mentioned many places in the Bible. He is a man having magnetic charisma, amazing the world with his wit and knowledge. He's literally without God's Law (remember Paul calls him the "man of lawlessness" in 2 Thessalonians 2:3), and consequently he exalts himself above every other object of worship. *He* thinks he's wonderful anyway (Daniel 8:25), but so do those who take his mark. Daniel 7:8 is the first time the little horn makes an appearance in Scripture.

Daniel 7:8 ESV. I considered the horns, and behold, there came up among them another horn, a little one, before which three of the first horns were plucked up by the roots. And behold, in this horn were eyes like the eyes of a man, and a mouth speaking great things.

Some say that this little horn is Antiochus Epiphanes IV, who has been mentioned a few times already. He was a Roman ruler who tried to increase his kingdom against the wishes of the Roman emperor, and persecuted Israel about 175 years before the Incarnation of the Messiah Yeshua. He did a lot of bad things, but he is not the little horn. He was a type of the little horn, and there have been many of these throughout history, but not THE little horn. Proof of this is in the statements that the little horn "became great, even as great as the Prince of the host" (who is Yeshua, not the high priest at the time of Antiochus IV), and "some of the stars it threw down to the ground and trampled on them." There are some other reasons to disqualify Antiochus covered later.

Daniel goes on to ask about this little horn after he sees it "made war on the saints and prevailed over them" (7:21, see also Revelation 13:7). In Daniel 7:25, he records for us that the little horn will succeed for a little while.

Daniel 7:25 ESV. He shall speak words against the Most High, and shall wear out the saints of the Most High, and shall think to change the times and the law; and they shall be given into his hand for a time, times, and half a time.

The Church has sought to "change the times and the law," and do so thinking they are somehow special and apart. These actions, however, mark them as "the people of the prince who is to come" (Daniel 9:26). At the appointed time the little horn is defeated and his dominion taken away.

Daniel 7:26 ESV. But the court shall sit in judgment, and his dominion shall be taken away, to be consumed and destroyed to the end.

Daniel sees the little horn again in 8:9, and this time he more specifically comes from part of the Greek empire, divided into four pieces by Alexander's generals after Alexander died suddenly. The part he comes from is the north, because the little horn grows exceedingly great towards the south, the east and Israel (the glorious land). He can't grow west because of the Mediterranean, which is an indication that this is western Turkey and Syria.

We are told twice in chapter 8 that the vision is for the "appointed time of the end" and once "for it refers to many days from now." Gabriel explains to Daniel that this little horn is "a king of bold face, one who understands riddles" and whose "power shall be great, but not by his own power" and will cause "fearful destruction" and "succeed in what he does" even to killing "mighty men and the people who are saints" without warning. Little horn will appear at the latter end of the Greek north kingdom, (again, modern day Syria or Turkey) "when the transgressors have reached their limit" (8:23).

The little horn will be very persuasive, and the "great signs and wonders" he uses (Matthew 24:24) will have such an impact that if it were possible they would even deceive the elect. His signs and wonders, however, don't work on those who know God and His Son and follow all of their commands.

As discussed before, the technical term for the north kingdom is the Seleucid dynasty, now called Syria and western Turkey. Little horn will rise up against the Prince of princes (the Messiah, Yeshua HaMashiach) and shall be broken "but by no human hand" (literally without human power). This is a specific comment on how the little horn is defeated.

It is written that the little horn has blasphemous names on its heads and is given a mouth uttering haughty and blasphemous words (Revelation 13). A comprehensive word study will show that blasphemy is mocking, reviling or insulting God. Eli's sons were "worthless men" (1 Samuel 2) who "did not know the Lord" and blasphemed or despised God by treating the sacrifices as their personal meat locker and "lay with the women who were serving at the entrance to the tent of meeting." Knowing what God requires, yet sticking a finger in His eye, so to speak, is blaspheming. At the bottom, it is also either attributing evil to God's works or attributing the works of God to evil (Satan, the little horn, or the anti-Christ get the credit instead of God).

This means the little horn will claim that he is the author of works that are God's, and will blame God for all the evil actually coming from him and his two buddies. Right will be wrong and wrong will be painted as right. He will stick his finger in the eye of God and dare Him to do anything about it.

It's humorous that the methods used by many for identification of the little horn or beast are mostly based on personal feelings, or perhaps newspaper exegesis. If you remember, this type of Bible interpretation is by newspaper headlines. So far, these identification attempts do not come from an understanding of the Bible. The best method of identification is right there in black and white. Or black, white and red. Or whatever fruity colors used in your translation of the Bible.

Zechariah 11:16–17, ESV. For behold, I am raising up in the land a shepherd who does not care for those being destroyed, or seek the young or heal the maimed or nourish the healthy, but devours the flesh of the fat ones, tearing off even their hoofs. "Woe to my worthless shepherd, who deserts the flock! May the sword strike his arm and his right eye! Let his arm be wholly withered, his right eye utterly blinded!"

The little horn has been identified as Hitler, or rulers/kings like him. Several Roman emperors such as the previously mentioned Antiochus Epiphanes (a couple hundred years give or take before the Incarnation) or Nero (a few decades after the Ascension) have seemed to fit the bill in some ways. Some pegged President Obama as the beast. As bad as Obama was as a president of the United States, he wasn't fungus on the big toe of the beast.

The beast is described by John in Revelation 13 as having ten horns and seven heads. This shows that the beast is most likely a confederation of kingdoms, with one of the leaders being foremost and representative of all of them (the little horn). It could be too that the heads and crowns are a series of rulers with the little horn being the latest.

Right now, we have examples of this type of organization in what is known as the G7 or group of seven and others. This informal group of nations economically represents over half of the global net wealth and consists of the United States, Germany, France, Japan, Canada, Italy and the United Kingdom.

There is also the G8 (which had Russia also until it illegally annexed the Crimea in 2014), the G10 (a group of 11 with similar economic interests and which funds the International Monetary Fund) and the G12. These last two are variations on the G10 and have different combinations of countries which number more than the group designation. In other words, the G10 has more than just ten nations. So it's not hard to make the connection to a deceiver-inspired G7 beast with seven heads and ten crowns.

Various other leaders from time to time have been, sometimes hysterically, identified as the little horn or worthless shepherd. A lot of these leaders may appear similar to, or faint echoes of, the little horn, but that's because it's the same deceiver behind them all, and he keeps trying the same tactics. The little horn or beast has a mortal wound but recovers, and ends up with (probably) losing his right eye and his right arm becomes useless. None of the previous candidates mentioned have those particular deformities. His wounds should kill him, but he miraculously recovers, which adds to his mystique and attractiveness to the rest of the world.

At one time people in the Calvary Chapel denomination along with many others in the early '80's were all excited about a computer in Belgium called "the beast." At the time, it could have numbered every person on the planet. Lately some are pointing to a smooth-talking atheist in Greece that has got them worried. Some are, again hysterically, concerned about tattoos or embedded chips that supposedly herald the arrival of the little horn. None have panned out because none of the hysteria was, or is, based on knowledge of Scripture.

For these kinds of ignorant behavior and a few other reasons it is probable that the beast will look a lot like a mega-Church pastor (except for the eye and arm thing), and teach many of the same things. He will be so very acceptable to the majority of the Church because He will look and act just as they do. The Church looks the same as the world, acts the same, and believes the same except for a little Jesus flavoring. The beast will bridge the (very small) gap between the world and the Church very easily. That might sound hard to some people. But truth only continues to be hard to the unrepentant hard-hearted.

Identifying the beast is kind of an exercise in futility for the Church. You can't very well find his hiding place when you're looking everywhere but in the Church building. This guy will indeed be a ravenous beast. He will speak beguiling words; words that are close to God's but just a little bit off at first. Just like the words of most Church leaders and followers of today. He will say things that sound good and appeal to self-seeking pride, and he will be suave and debonair.

The average Churchgoer is not grounded in the Word of God, so they will be willing to accept him and his instead-of-Christ prophet, even to receiving the mark of the beast. They will believe in him so much they will gladly do whatever he says. They will be enamored of his teachings on sexual immorality, tolerance and unconditional love because these teachings will mirror their own. He will be able to quote the Bible better than most Christians, albeit with his own twisted slant, and will match almost word for word the text of many sermons. He will mix science with sorcery and maybe claim to be the next evolutionary step for all mankind. He might even be like a super hero.

The lack of grounding in the Bible for the majority of self-named Christians will contribute to the acceptance of the beast. The blasphemy practiced by the Church (calling most of God's Law irrelevant for instance) along with sexual immorality (adultery, divorce, fornication, homosexuality) and watered-down teaching from the Balaams, Jezebels and Nicolaitans among them, will combine to allow easy acceptance by stone-hearted people.

2 Thessalonians 2:11-12 ESV. Therefore God sends them a strong delusion, so that they may believe what is false, in order that all may be condemned who did not believe the truth but had pleasure in unrighteousness.

For confirmation of this, read the letters to the seven congregations in Revelation 1-3. Types of those congregations have always been around. The door that Yeshua is standing at and knocking (Revelation 3:20) is the door of a congregation that claims to know Him. It's just that in modern times a greater percentage of wolves in sheep's clothing are present and the corruption is more prevalent than in the past. It's a situation like the one at the time of Yeshua, where the Jewish establishment was so corrupt they wouldn't listen to God Himself standing right in front of them. They crucified the Lord of Glory much as the current religious establishment metaphorically does to believers every day now in a thousand small ways.

The worthless shepherd is opposite of the Good Shepherd, who is Yeshua haMashiach or Jesus the Christ.

John 10:11–16 ESV. I am the good shepherd. The good shepherd lays down his life for the sheep. He who is a hired hand and not a shepherd, who does not own the sheep, sees the wolf coming and leaves the sheep and flees, and the wolf snatches them and scatters them. He flees because he is a hired hand and cares nothing for the sheep. I am the good shepherd. I know my own and my own know me, just as the Father knows me and I know the Father; and I lay down my life for the sheep. And I have other sheep that are not of this fold. I must bring them also, and they will listen to my voice. So there will be one flock, one shepherd.

The beast/little horn/bad shepherd will come to power slightly in advance of making a strong covenant with many for one week or seven years. Around the same time, he will receive a mortal wounding that leaves its mark on his right eye and right arm. The two witnesses of Revelation 9 will oppose him for the first three and a half years or 42 months or 1,260 days. At this half-way mark of the covenant period, he gets all of the power, throne and great authority of the dragon and finally manages to kill the witnesses. Then he sets himself up at the reconstructed (or partially reconstructed) Temple, causes the sacrifice and offerings to cease, and declares that he is the God of Abraham, Isaac and Jacob. The false prophet assists by forming an image and giving it power to speak, which causes all heaven to break loose at the bowl judgments.

The Abomination(s) Causing Desolation

Yeshua tells us about someone or something He calls the abomination of desolation (AoD) in Matthew 24 and Mark 13.

Matthew 24:15–18 ESV. "So when you see the abomination of desolation spoken of by the prophet Daniel, standing in the holy place (let the reader understand), then let those who are in Judea flee to the mountains. Let the one who is on the housetop not go down to take what is in his house, and let the one who is in the field not turn back to take his cloak.

At the time, Yeshua says this will be the person or thing spoken of by the prophet Daniel (Daniel 9:27, 11:31, and 12:11 ESV). Daniel in Daniel 12:11 calls it or him "the abomination that causes desolation." Theories abound as to what, or who, this thing or person is. Some think it is the image of the beast from Revelation 13. Some think it is the beast. Others think it already happened when that guy Antiochus Epiphanes IV sacrificed a pig on the Temple altar a few hundred years before the Incarnation. Still others think that Yeshua is speaking of the destruction of the Temple which took place about 40 years after the crucifixion, and the Romans were the abomination.

Obviously, the little horn isn't Antiochus, because Yeshua (and Paul in 2 Thessalonians 2:3) speaks of it as a future event. Also, it is a person because Yeshua says "standing in the holy place" in Matthew 24:15. The holy place is the middle of the Temple. There was indeed an AoD standing in the holy place when the Romans destroyed the Temple. Remember the cycles of fulfillment mentioned earlier.

However, there have been, and are, lots of abominations. Shoot, Israel put all kinds of abominations in the Temple (Ezekiel 8). The word from God's perspective means something like a dirty, detestable idol, a pile of stinky something you don't want to step in, or anything that goes against His will or Word.

The abominations of desolation in these cases are people, kings or emperors or political leaders, who are very un-godly. Many of the Roman emperors were abominations such as Caligula and Nero. There have also been abominations that caused desolation, meaning destruction of some area or people.

But the one of these talked about by Yeshua was an AoD that He said would stand in the Temple claiming to be God. Not just "a god," but God Himself. A dry run for this happened in 70 A. D. when the Roman general Titus destroyed the Temple and sacrificed to other gods in the Holy of Holies. Yeshua was trying to tell the Jews that the Temple would be destroyed and instead of fighting, the believers should run for the hills and get away.

The warning stays true for all the cycles of fulfillment and any time the deceiver tries using any abomination of desolation. The deceiver keeps trying throughout history to set up his kingdom using various people we can call an "abomination of desolation." He will finally succeed with the little horn, the last AoD. Other abominations (kings, government leaders, etc.) only got part of the way to setting up a worldwide kingdom. God does not tell us to fight the abominations. He tells us that He will take care of it.

The warning from Yeshua tells believers that there will be hardship along with attempts by the deceiver to destroy using whatever abomination he can raise up, but not to fight it ourselves. God will take care of the deceiver's plans, ultimately rendering judgment on all his efforts in the Day of the Lord.

The title of "abomination that causes desolation" is a generic title for all of the deceiver's agents who have risen to the head or almost head of a government, country, army or empire. It is also a specific title for THE abomination of desolation, otherwise known as the little horn or the beast.

The deceiver keeps trying to destroy God's people and steal God's kingdom for himself, so he keeps coming up with all sorts of "abominations" that cause desolation. Some of these rulers were just abominations. Some of them caused desolation, especially of the Jewish people or land of Israel. Hitler and Stalin were a couple of the most recent AoD's, though neither stood in the Temple (mostly because there wasn't one). They might have claimed to be doing God's work, but didn't claim to be God.

The final cycle of fulfillment with an abomination causing desolation will be the little horn a.k.a. the beast. This beast will

The Second Beast: Antichrist

The definition of antichrist comes to us from John, the disciple who wrote the gospel, the epistles of John, and the Revelation.

1 John 2:22, ESV. Who is the liar but he who denies that Jesus is the Christ? This is the antichrist, he who denies the Father and the Son.

2 John 7, ESV. For many deceivers have gone out into the world, those who do not confess the coming of Jesus Christ in the flesh. Such a one is the deceiver and the antichrist.

There are in fact many, many anti-Christ's (anointeds), deceivers or false prophets. Whoever denies that Yeshua is the Anointed of God and God in the flesh is a liar and shares the spirit of the antichrist. The words "came in the flesh" imply that Yeshua was pre-existent before the incarnation, and of course that would mean that Yeshua is God (there are many other proofs too). The group of deniers includes atheists, Jehovah's Witnesses, pagans, Mormons, many Jewish people, and many self-named "Christian" Church denominations and para-Church organizations.

Matthew 24:3–5 ESV. As he sat on the Mount of Olives, the disciples came to him privately, saying, "Tell us, when will these things be, and what will be the sign of your coming and of the end of the age?" And Yeshua answered them, "See that no one leads you astray. For many will come in my name, saying, 'I am the Christ,' and they will lead many astray.

Who is it that "come(s) in (His) name" but those who say they "follow the Bible" or "I believe in Jesus?" Just as it was with Israel throughout history, the Church has many who claim the name of Jesus and teach and lead falsely.

Matthew 24:10–12 ESV. And then many will fall away and betray one another and hate one another. And many false prophets will arise and lead many astray. And because lawlessness will be increased, the love of many will grow cold.

Now, there are many, many antichrists in the Church and Judaism. Some we can see plainly and others simply have more sheep's wool covering them. Denying that Yeshua came in the flesh takes many forms and is disguised by a bevy of Bible words or good-sounding teaching, but it all leads astray.

Acts 20:29–30 ESV. I know that after my departure fierce wolves will come in among you, not sparing the flock; and from among your own selves will arise men speaking twisted things, to draw away the disciples after them.

The antichrists teach either that Jesus is not God and not the Messiah, or they teach that believers shouldn't follow parts of the Bible such as the Law (lawlessness). They make up all sorts of "oral laws" that cast doubt on God's Word and transfer authority to the teacher. In turn, this causes people to follow the teacher instead of the Bible. After all, Yeshua said that "lawlessness will be increased" causing the "love of many" to "grow cold," didn't He? Aren't we seeing lawlessness increased? And aren't we seeing the love of many claiming to follow Him growing cold?

Some anti-Christ groups admit that Yeshua was an actual historical figure, but dismiss Him as just another nice teacher. Others (like atheists) just go the whole route and dismiss God entirely. The denial of Yeshua as the Anointed of God (Christ) who came in the flesh is and will be the mark of the beast. Another mark is teaching against the Law and the prophets. The external mark just validates what people already believe.

Both the beast and the false prophet are anti-Christ, because both operate in the spirit of anti-Christ if nothing else. Usually the title antichrist, which means 'instead of Christ,' is applied to the Beast, but all three together are antichrist. The deceiver has always been the main antichrist.

John describes the false prophet in the Revelation as a "beast rising out of the earth. It had two horns like a lamb and it spoke like a dragon." On the outside, he resembles Yeshua, or says he follows Yeshua, but the things that he speaks come right from the deceiver, dragon or serpent. He is the sidekick of the beast.

He will be a religious leader; an authority figure intended to bring together the many religious people of Babylon (the Prostitute) to worship the beast. A guess is that he will come right from the ranks of the Church or Islam. This leader will deceive all those who merely maintain the outward appearance of following God, or a god. He will appeal to pagans, atheists, Churchgoers, Muslims and Jews, or all those who claim to be "spiritual but not religious." He might be the pope at the time, or he might be the Mahdi that the Muslims expect. The Mahdi is a redeemer figure sort of like Yeshua. The false prophet will be a combination of features such that he is acceptable to a wide swath of people who claim to worship God but do not.

The false prophet's task is to get people to worship the beast. He does this by working powerful, deceiving miracles such as calling down fire from heaven to earth in front of people (like the two witnesses), and making a talking image of the beast who was wounded by the sword and yet lived. He can only perform the wonders in the presence of the beast. The image causes people to be marked on the right hand or forehead with the name or number of the beast. Any who refuse the mark are executed. Those who accept it are allowed to buy and sell (see the section on **Buying and Selling**).

At the sixth bowl or vial judgment (Revelation 16:12-16) the false prophet along with the beast and the dragon let go of a frog spirit out of their mouths that gathers kings of the whole world to Armageddon. He is captured alive after Armageddon and then cast into the lake of fire, along with the beast.

The Image

Revelation 13 describes an image of the beast made by the false prophet or anti-christ (Revelation 13:11-18). The false prophet who looks like a lamb but speaks like a dragon will be allowed to give breath to the image of the beast. Note that he is "allowed," which is a reminder that nothing happens without God's permission. Then the image will be able to speak and cause people to worship the beast. It will also cause those people to be killed who will not worship the beast or the image. Those who worship the image and the beast will receive a mark on the right hand or forehead and will not be able to buy or sell without it. Everyone who receives the mark will end up with the beast, false prophet and the deceiver in the lake of fire which is the second death. The mark is the name of the beast or the number of its name, so it is the same mark for everyone who receives it. The mark is not an account number; it is voluntarily received and is a sign of allegiance to the beast, the deceiver, and the anti-God kingdoms they represent.

The image fashioned by the anti-Christ could very likely be a clone who will speak as the serpent did in the Garden, offering a path to be "like God." Same old story, different image. It's more likely that the image will be a mechanical construct having artificial intelligence so complex it will appear to be human.

It may seem far-fetched, but the world's elitist rich genuinely think they will be able to upload their consciousness into a machine and live forever as gods. You might think this is the plot of one of those episodes from a science fiction TV series or movie, but they really think they will soon be able to do it. Research the term "singularity" or "brain computer interface (or BCI)" for more information. A quick summary is that we are near the point where artificial intelligence, robotics, nanotechnology, computers and genetics come together to make bodies and brains (think computer chips) that will house the conscience, experiences and personalities of those who can afford it and hope to live forever.

Living forever in a machine is one of the reasons the elites want to reduce or eliminate the world's population, and why they have a "war on carbon." People are carbon-based, and we exhale a lot of CO2, so it follows that their war includes people. This could explain some of the motivation behind the death of one-third of the world population at the sixth trumpet blast (Revelation 9). Reducing the population will enable them to pursue their dream using the earth's resources, instead of having to share them with the rest of us. The image could also be an animated statue, or perhaps something from a super hero movie. Whatever it is actually, it will reinforce the message of the beast and the deceiver.

The Mark

Revelation 14:9 NASB. Then another angel, a third one, followed them, saying with a loud voice, "If anyone worships the beast and his image, and receives a mark on his forehead or on his hand, he also will drink of the wine of the wrath of God, which is mixed in full strength in the cup of His anger; and he will be tormented with fire and brimstone in the presence of the holy angels and in the presence of the Lamb."

Did you know there is a mark of God in the Scriptures? We'll look at this along with the mark of the beast so we can get a better understanding of the exact nature of the mark. For this subject we'll start by going over the references in the Bible which talk about a, or the, mark. You may be surprised to learn that marking people (even on the forehead or hand) is mentioned in the Word a few centuries before the book of Revelation was even a twinkle in John's eye (Ezekiel 9:4-6). Oh, the wonders of searching His Word by reading through it on a regular basis, or with a computer and a Bible search program!

Before that, though, it would be good for you to look at some words and make sure of the word meanings, so that when you read the verses you understand the idea the writer of the Scripture was trying to convey to us. For instance, what do you think of when you read the word 'mark?' A lot of times it's not just a smudge on a piece of paper, is it? That can be one of the meanings of 'mark,' but the normal use of the word is more along the lines of 'identification.' When someone (or something) is 'marked,' he or she (or it) is somehow identified and separated from those who are not marked the same. The 'mark' can be visible or invisible to others. Sometimes the ID can be positive, and sometimes negative, but the 'marking' is not neutral.

Why mark? The whole idea of a mark is to make some sort of statement about what is marked. Part of the time the statement could reflect ownership. Another part of the time, it could be an advertisement. Other times the statement we are trying to make with our mark could be to 'set apart' an item or a person from a group of similar items or people in order to give it (or them) special treatment. When a soldier 'marks' a target (like 'painting' it with a laser) that means he has separated it from the surrounding area in order to give it special treatment (uh-oh). A teacher might 'mark' a student as being a disruption to the class, and take steps to keep him (or her) from disrupting the class. In either of these cases no actual 'mark' is made, but there is a marking nonetheless.

An object is usually marked because it doesn't exhibit any characteristics of its' own that would help with identification. For instance, the boundary marker mentioned before is just a rock, all by itself. But plunk it down in a particular spot and place a special mark on it and the simple rock becomes a sign showing where one property stops and another starts. Very important if you want to know where to stop pulling weeds!

A person who is marked, on the other hand (in the Word), seems to exhibit behavior that leads to the marking. They are marked by their behavior long before any external mark is made. Cain is one example (Genesis 4:15). Another example is in the Ezekiel passage it's time to address.

Ezekiel 9:4-6 NASB. The LORD said to him, "Go through the midst of the city, *even* through the midst of Jerusalem, and put a mark on the foreheads of the men who sigh and groan over all the abominations which are being committed in its midst." But to the others He said in my hearing, "Go through the city after him and strike; do not let your eye have pity and do not spare. Utterly slay old men, young men, maidens, little children, and women, but do not touch any man on whom is the mark; and you shall start from My sanctuary." So they started with the elders who *were* before the temple.

This is a very important point to note about marks on people (again, in the Word). They are made <u>after the fact</u>. A person is marked after he or she exhibits behavior consistent with the (eventual) marking. We might even say, as some people do about baptism, that a physical mark is an outward sign of an inward condition. People are 'marked' by their actions, apart from any kind of a name tag, whether hung on the shirt or stamped on the skin. According to this passage, first there were people 'sighing and groaning' over all the evil being committed in Jerusalem, and only later were they marked.

Indelible marking. There is an element of permanence in biblical marking. In the case of people, it is sort of like God is putting a stamp on a person's behavior to 'lock' it in, or to say, 'so be it.' For the believer or child of God, at some point in our lives God stamps His mark on us and says, 'So be it.' For the person who takes the 'mark of the beast' described in the book of Revelation God also says, 'so be it.' In this vein the psalmist expresses relief that God does not 'mark' iniquities (meaning to make a judgment without space for repentance), which should be a great relief to all those who want to take advantage of it.

Psalm 130:1-4 NASB. Out of the depths I have cried to You, O LORD. Lord, hear my voice! Let Your ears be attentive to the voice of my supplications. If You, LORD, should mark iniquities, O Lord, who could stand? But there is forgiveness with You, that You may be feared.

The mark of pickiness in wording. If you want to do a fascinating study, look up the word "mark" in the Scriptures. When you do, you should notice that there isn't a great deal of difference in the different words for 'mark' in the Bible. While there may be different kinds of marks represented by different words (carve, impress and so on), the basic meanings are nearly the same. It doesn't appear that there is a great deal of difference between "carving" a mark or "writing" a mark, between a "banner" or a "sign," between "seal" and "impress," or whether a mark is invisible or visible. For those with wisdom to see, imparted by the Word, a mark by any other name is still obvious, especially when it comes to people.

The mark of God. God has been marking people for a long time, through following His Word (laws, statutes, commands, and instructions, whatever you want to call them).

Deuteronomy 6:4-8 NASB. "Hear, O Israel! The LORD is our God, the LORD is one! You shall love the LORD your God with all your heart and with all your soul and with all your might. These words, which I am commanding you today, shall be on your heart. You shall teach them diligently to your sons and shall talk of them when you sit in your house and when you walk by the way and when you lie down and when you rise up. You shall bind them as a sign on your hand and they shall be as frontals on your forehead." (see also Deuteronomy 11:18)

Ezekiel 20:11-12 NASB. "I gave them My statutes and informed them of My ordinances, by which, if a man observes them, he will live. Also I gave them My sabbaths to be a sign between Me and them, that they might know that I am the LORD who sanctifies them." (see also 20:19,20)

Exodus 13:9, 16 NASB, parenthesis added. "And it (Passover) shall serve as a sign to you on your hand, and as a reminder on your forehead, that the law of the LORD may be in your mouth; for with a powerful hand the LORD brought you out of Egypt."

When a person chooses to follow God's Word, he or she is marked by the Holy Spirit in that decision. It is proven or shown by actions that are in keeping with that decision. Just like in Ezekiel 9 where people were marked after they sighed and groaned over the iniquities that were committed, God's people everywhere are marked when doing what He says. By pursuing, hungering or thirsting after righteousness we are 'sealed,' 'impressed,' 'signed,' 'stamped,' 'inscribed' and 'carved.' We are 'assigned' a place with the righteous, and He 'establishes' us on the Rock of our Salvation, the Messiah Yeshua. He is our 'banner' and we are His. His Spirit signature is on us, and we couldn't be any more His if we were branded like cattle. We 'keep watch on' or 'guard' His commandments because they are our very life. As surely as if we had a mark on the forehead or hand, our actions and reactions mark us as belonging to Him.

The mark of the beast. Now we come to the 'mark of the beast.' This mark is mentioned six times in the book of Revelation (plus once in a negative sense in 20:4). The first time is not until chapter 13, after a series of judgments. Notice, however, that repentance (or lack of it) is mentioned a total of ten times, eight of those before the mark is given (leaving aside the question of whether the book is chronological or not). What's really sad is that five of those eight mentions of repentance are directed at the congregations that wear His name.

It's significant that first we are told people 'would not repent,' and later these same people are given the mark of the beast. The mark is simply a 'stamp' of approval from the little horn for the anti-God behavior that has already been exhibited. It is also received voluntarily, albeit because of deception according to 19:20. However, the mark is also connected to 'worship' of the beast (14:9, 14:11, 16:2, 19:20 and 20:4), which suggests that there is an 'eyes open' exchange – perhaps monetary gain (buying and selling, 13:17) for worship. The "buying and selling" thing points to wealthy people who throw in with the beast. This includes business people, princes, kings, sultans, and other government leaders; religious icons such as the pope, cardinals, priests, rabbis, mullahs, imams, ayatollahs or mega-church pastors; and also people like actors, musicians and news personalities.

This mark is not given (or taken) accidentally. It is not a computer chip, a bar code, vaccine, or other mundane signature. It seems to be something very specific, received knowingly, and an 'outward sign of an inward condition.' These people already follow the little horn (in fact are following the spirit of anti-Christ even now), and the mark is just a testament to a pre-existing fact. Carving a mark in their forehead or hand is just bringing it out in the open, so to speak.

Distractions. The people who are trying to identify the exact nature of the mark are throwing out, in essence, "red herrings." Some are so busy trying to spook people with tales of evil computer chips (in order to sell books) they forget that the focus is God, not the beast or the false prophet. It's a lot like the near hysteria that surrounded the year 2000 changeover. Remember how many were convinced that Y2K was going to be the end of the world, only to have the actual event fizzle like so many wet fireworks? But the real problem is that after one too many people cry 'wolf,' the rest of us have a tendency to let down on our watchfulness. Too many of us are focusing on the mark of the beast and not enough on the mark of God (following His commandments).

The deceiver counterfeits the things of God as much as he needs to in order to keep his kingdom going. It follows that if people can be 'marked' by submitting to God, they can also be 'marked' by submitting to the little horn. Even if there is an external mark, which seems likely given the meaning of *charagma* in Revelation (to carve or impress), it is most probably given after a person has made a decision to worship and follow the beast.

Obviously, this word (*charagma*) is more emphatic than merely "to mark," but equally obvious is that the word describes something more than a computer chip imbedded under the skin. It also tells us that the 'mark' is not something that one receives because they were walking down the sidewalk and accidentally fell down (or got a vaccination, or whatever), but is something deliberately taken.

Let us consider how we are marked, and take care that the marking is according to His Word and in His Spirit, not according to the 'instead of' (the meaning of 'anti') Christ. The deceiver is crafty, and will soon put forth all his power to entice the unwary into permanent disobedience. May our Father include you as one of His own "marked ones."

The first time the English word 'mark' is used is in Genesis 4:15, where Cain gets a mark from God so he won't be attacked for killing Able. The next time (in the ESV at least) that a mark is used is in Exodus 13:16, but perhaps verse 9 of the same chapter has a better picture.

Exodus 13:7–10, ESV. Unleavened bread shall be eaten for seven days; no leavened bread shall be seen with you, and no leaven shall be seen with you in all your territory. You shall tell your son on that day, 'It is because of what the LORD did for me when I came out of Egypt.' And it shall be to you as a sign on your hand and as a memorial between your eyes, that the law of the LORD may be in your mouth. For with a strong hand the LORD has brought you out of Egypt. You shall therefore keep this statute at its appointed time from year to year.

According to this set of verses, and others, a mark is the same as a "sign on your hand" and a "memorial between your eyes." This sign or mark is that the feast of Unleavened Bread is being observed, and that "the law of the LORD (is) in your mouth." In other words, the mark of the people of God is that they follow His Law with the Holy Spirit. It is in their heads and the motivation for their hands. The mark of God is on the hand, meaning what we do, and on the forehead meaning what we think and see.

So it is very possible that the mark of the people of the little horn is that they follow the law of the little horn. There might also be an actual physical mark, like a brand or a tattoo, because those passages in Revelation that describe the mark using the Greek word *charagma*. And it's not outside the realm of possibility given the present generation's tendency to show their dedication to their rock music gods or other beliefs with tattoos and piercings.

But marking does not have to be with ink or needle for God to see. The mark of the Beast may not be an actual physical mark, like a tattoo or a hand stamp at the door of a nightclub. The mark may be, primarily, behavior that marks a person one way or the other. This type of mark is visible to anyone who can see, and even people who can't see.

As stated before, the mark of the Beast is not a computer chip inserted for bank transactions or RFID marker for finding lost pets or kids. It is obviously something more formal, and the people who take it do so voluntarily and to sign up for the little horn's program. No one will accidentally take it. It won't be slipped into a drink like a mickey. You won't wake up one morning after a drunken party with a tattoo you can't remember getting.

People who receive the mark will have to do something overt to get it. It will probably be a mark of pride, like fans at a football game that paint themselves in team colors and dress up in related costumes. Or like the Goth who dresses all in black and has 46 piercings in his nose and lips. The mark of the Beast is for those who worship the Beast. Worship implies an active participation. We are also told a number of times that these people "would not repent" of their behavior. The combination of worship and "would not repent" will mark those people more surely than any tattoo or carving. They will be marked by specific actions taken to choose the Beast, the false prophet, and the serpent behind them.

The number 666 is the number of man. It denotes thinking and action that is consistent with the doctrine of men. Three sixes are significant, like using 'holy, holy, holy' three times for God. The number three is a decree set in concrete. Repeating something three times in Scripture is like pronouncing a sure judgment. The number six is the number of Man (or woman) because he was created on the sixth day of creation and is just short of the number seven, the number of completeness or perfection.

The number seven is God's number, and it is the number of completeness. So the number six is one short of completeness, and one short of God. We need God to "complete us." Three sixes mean that our incompleteness is three times short of God. It probably points to the unholy trinity of Satan, the Beast, and the false prophet too, but still even with three of them, they are three points shy of God.

Remember when Joseph was interpreting the dreams of Pharaoh? In Genesis 41:32 Joseph says that the doubling of the dream (the cows and the corn) meant that "the thing is fixed by God." This is for a prophecy given to an earthly king in a dream, but doubling and tripling are principles that nail down a title or an event with exacting certitude.

Buying and Selling

Studying the mark of the beast brought up the subject of buying and selling, so let's dive into that a little bit more.

Revelation 13:16–17, ESV. Also it causes all, both small and great, both rich and poor, both free and slave, to be marked on the right hand or the forehead, so that no one can buy or sell unless he has the mark, that is, the name of the beast or the number of its name.

It is commonly thought that the phrase 'buy and sell' refers to anyone who buys something from someone else, or who sells something. Many teachers tell us it is two separate actions. This is a very wide definition. It includes those who buy food at the market instead of growing it themselves, and those people who trade with each other on a limited basis too. This definition has led many people to think that during the Tribulation food can't be purchased at the grocery store without the mark. Therefore, if a person doesn't take the mark, they will have a tough time eating.

But buying and selling in the Bible is not that general or that separate. It more specifically applies to people who both buy and sell as a trade or business rather than to individuals buying food. The Bible mentions buying and selling a few times, and it seems to refer to merchants.

Matthew 21:12–13, NASB95. And Jesus entered the temple and drove out all those who were buying and selling in the temple, and overturned the tables of the money changers and the seats of those who were selling doves. And He said to them, "It is written, 'MY HOUSE SHALL BE CALLED A HOUSE OF PRAYER'; but you are making it a ROBBERS' DEN." (See also Mark 11:15)

James 4:13–15 ESV. Come now, you who say, "Today or tomorrow we will go into such and such a town and spend a year there and trade and make a profit"— yet you do not know what tomorrow will bring. What is your life? For you are a mist that appears for a little time and then vanishes. Instead you ought to say, "If the Lord wills, we will live and do this or that."

Zechariah 14:20–21, ESV, underline added. And on that day there shall be inscribed on the bells of the horses, "Holy to the LORD." And the pots in the house of the LORD shall be as the bowls before the altar. And every pot in Jerusalem and Judah shall be holy to the LORD of hosts, so that all who sacrifice may come and take of them and boil the meat of the sacrifice in them. And there shall no longer be a <u>trader</u> in the house of the LORD of hosts on that day.

We need to remember that for much of the earth's history people grew their own food and clothed themselves with fibers made from their own land or livestock. Buying and selling was secondary. If a person grew more than they could use for food, they could sell or trade some of the excess to buy things they couldn't grow or make themselves. For a long time, people first fed themselves and only after that did they engage in commerce.

Now it's a little different. Many people do not grow their own food, and must buy it. There are many other things we use every day we cannot make for ourselves. Even if the mark is for mundane transactions at the grocery store, it still doesn't include food you grow yourself. Nor does it preclude barter or trade.

One reference describes buying and selling not necessarily connected with merchants.

Luke 17:26–30, ESV. Just as it was in the days of Noah, so will it be in the days of the Son of Man. They were eating and drinking and marrying and being given in marriage, until the day when Noah entered the ark, and the flood came and destroyed them all. Likewise, just as it was in the days of Lot—they were eating and drinking, buying and selling, planting and building, but on the day when Lot went out from Sodom, fire and sulfur rained from heaven and destroyed them all— so will it be on the day when the Son of Man is revealed.

However, this is just saying that daily life was going on as usual, with no idea of the coming destruction. Buying and selling could just as easily be describing merchants as it could be describing what people had to do to live. In other words, this reference is general and pointing to the 'sudden destruction' rather than to a way to make a living.

One other reason buying and selling is connected to merchants is in Revelation 18:11 and 15. After Babylon is destroyed, "merchants who gained wealth from her" stand far off and mourn for her destruction.

Revelation 18:15–18, ESV. The merchants of these wares, who gained wealth from her, will stand far off, in fear of her torment, weeping and mourning aloud, "Alas, alas, for the great city that was clothed in fine linen, in purple and scarlet, adorned with gold, with jewels, and with pearls! For in a single hour all this wealth has been laid waste." And all shipmasters and seafaring men, sailors and all whose trade is on the sea, stood far off and cried out as they saw the smoke of her burning, "What city was like the great city?"

The connection is perhaps more subjective than objective. We do have to be careful when comparing things that look similar yet are very different. But it seems a reasonable view considering how the Word defines buying and selling, and the specific mention of merchants in this section.

Wealth (or Mammon) is a big goal for many people of the earth, frequently pursued to the exclusion of God's ways and words. It's not a big stretch to realize that the merchant mentality is a big part of the world's governments, a.k.a. Babylon. Most are established in defiance of God, and are going to be some of the man-created systems judged by Him.

Buying and selling is frequently associated with unjust gain. God has a lot to say about dishonest gain, interest, extortion and profit in places such as Ezekiel 22. There you will find lists of sins in which Israel was heavily involved. Included in those lists are "the sojourner suffers extortion in your midst" (verse 6), "taking interest and profit" (verse 12), "take bribes to shed blood" (verse 12 again), "dishonest gain" (verse 13) and so on. Isaiah mentions unjust gain also.

Isaiah 57:17 ESV. Because of the iniquity of his unjust gain I was angry, I struck him; I hid my face and was angry, but he went on backsliding in the way of his own heart.

God even relayed a Law against using dishonest weights and measures (Leviticus 19:35; Deuteronomy 25:15; Proverbs 20:10), which suggests this type of thing was a common practice. False prophets "have taken treasure and precious things," but God was left by the roadside and forgotten (Ezekiel 22:12). Hosea gives us another viewpoint.

Hosea 12:7 ESV. A merchant, in whose hands are false balances, he loves to oppress.

Buying and selling is not a general condemnation of having a business. It seems more obvious that it is a rebuke or judgment for the single-minded pursuit of wealth or unjust gain at the expense of others. It is one thing to sell a loaf of bread to someone who is buying dinner. A businessman or farmer who prices his wares factoring in costs such as warehousing, transport, taxes, regulations and risk is one who uses fair weights and measures.

One who profits from another's misery, on the other hand, characterizes much of modern business and government practice. Failing to give generously as God blesses, cheating customers with a thumb on the scale, weights that aren't accurate, and usurious tax and interest rates are all part of the negative meaning of buying and selling. Buying and selling characterizes governments who find all sorts of excuses to tax people or redistribute wealth by their own standards. Governments are the biggest cheats by any measure.

We see many super-rich people now such as Saudi princes, Russian oligarchs, U.S. Democrats and other communist or socialist dictators who use their wealth to enslave people and force tyrannical practices and governments on the unwilling. This is another definition of slavery or trading in the souls of men. These people think their wealth belongs to them instead of belonging to the One who makes it possible for them to accumulate it. God will not forget their idolatry or worship of self.

The mark is more like a business license. Even now, to protect profits and continue to do business, merchants will work hand in glove with governments. If the government requires a face mask be worn in public (in 2020) or force vaccines to be taken (2021), then the merchants are in lockstep and try to enforce the regulation. They are afraid of losing their business license. It doesn't matter that masks do not work at all to control things like viruses, and in fact increase health problems such as kidney failure. It doesn't matter that the misnamed "covid vaccine" is at most only 3% effective and causes all sorts of health problems and death. It's obvious that the merchants will be also working closely with the beast when the time comes.

In the United States, large retailers selling guns and related items voluntarily help the government with gun control, by not selling certain guns or magazines to states with, for instance, magazine size restrictions. This is in spite of the fact that state courts have no jurisdiction in other states and the bureau of Alcohol Tobacco and Firearms has no authority to make laws. Whatever you think about guns or gun control, it isn't much of a stretch to see that when the little horn requires a mark for buying and selling, the large merchants at least will go right along with it.

The existence of the mark of the beast will make things tougher for those who do not take the mark (believers). It may be that regular buying and selling (like food for the table) is affected. God is going to make it tough on the world and those of us in the world (but not of the world) at the time will experience some of it at least. But it seems obvious that God will be judging the world while believers are protected. One of the ways He could do this is by providing manna, as He did before with another famous group of people. This is discussed more in the chapter on the resurrection. However it falls out, our trust must stay with God.

The 144,000 Victorious

A major thing to notice about Revelation 14:1-5 is that John speaks of the group as "they," and not "us." You would think that if anyone should be included in the 144,000 it would be an apostle. But that is not the case. John knows that these men have not had relations with a woman, and are "blameless" according to the Law. John might be considered blameless but had a wife.

1 Corinthians 9:5 ESV. Do we not have the right to take along a believing wife, as do the other apostles and the brothers of the Lord and Cephas?

If you don't buy this argument, that's okay. It really doesn't matter much. This group of men are sealed in a particular way and are called "firstfruits (from among men) for God and the Lamb." As mentioned before, many people (specifically Jehovah's Witnesses) have thought they were included here, but sadly lack the purity and the mark of God. We know this because of their marriages and their refusal to follow God's Laws.

Twelve dozen (or 144) has from ancient times been considered a standard way of selling goods or materials. This amount is called a "gross" and is where we get the term "grocer." We might see an association here between a gross and this group "purchased" from among men. They are sealed in Revelation 7 after the sixth seal is opened in John's vision, and apparently hang around during the blowing of the seven trumpets, up until sometime after the little horn or beast stands in the Temple and declares himself to be God. It seems apparent that the whole time they are preaching repentance and a return to the whole of God's Word. They are also preaching about Yeshua as the anointed of God, in contrast to the false anointing of the double-horned second beast representing himself as the Christ.

This "gross" purchased by the Lamb seems to be preaching along with the two witnesses and just before the messages of the three angels. So there is a constant witness for God all the way through the trumpet judgments and up until the bowl judgments.

Listen Up! Last Chance!

In Revelation 14:6-13 we hear of three messages preached by flying angels. The timing of this preaching is probably at about the same time as the false prophet, or "instead of" Christ, makes an image of the beast and causes it to speak (in the text anyway). In the midst of the false prophet's miraculous signs and wonders, and after the two witnesses have been brought to heaven, these three angels give a final warning to choose God, your Babylon kingdom is toast, and if you insist on choosing the beast by receiving his mark you will stay with him forever.

These are gracious messages from a loving God unwilling that any should perish that go out to every nation, tribe, language and people. Sadly, all of those people will insist on following the serpent and the beast all the way to hell.

2 Peter 3:9 ESV. The Lord is not slow to fulfill his promise as some count slowness, but is patient toward you, not wishing that any should perish, but that all should reach repentance.

First Angel: Choose God

Matthew 24:14 ESV. And this gospel of the kingdom will be proclaimed throughout the whole world as a testimony to all nations, and then the end will come.

Revelation 14:6–7 ESV. Then I saw another angel flying directly overhead, with an eternal gospel to proclaim to those who dwell on earth, to every nation and tribe and language and people. And he said with a loud voice, "Fear God and give him glory, because the hour of his judgment has come, and worship him who made heaven and earth, the sea and the springs of water."

The eternal gospel, preached by the first angel, is in contradiction to the choice of Adam and Eve way back in the Garden. They decided to follow their own understanding rather than God's instruction. Instead of following our own understanding, everyone is encouraged or even commanded by the angel to choose God. This message has been preached since the beginning, but here is one more chance. God is patient, kind, long-suffering, and the source of life. When we go a different way, any way other than His way, we choose death. God doesn't want anyone to die and is immensely saddened that people reject life thinking they can go it on their own. The rejection of His fix for the sin of rejecting His love, up to and including spurning the sacrifice of His only begotten Son Yeshua the Messiah, means that hate for Him has gone past the point of redemption.

The hate will have reached its climax in the final form of kingdom Babylon, headed by the beast and powered by the deceiver. God will finally be out of patience and the hour of His judgment will come. He is going to drop the hammer on it all, and when God drops the hammer there is no question, no doubt, no turning back or changing His mind.

The point has to be made here that even though God knows no one will repent (Thyatira and Jezebel, Revelation 2:21-22; the sixth trumpet, Revelation 9:20-21; fourth and fifth bowls Revelation 16:8-11), He still extends the invitation (or actually, command) to choose Him instead. At that late hour, God holds out His hand to rescue any who choose Him. Notice too that this is a choice. All one has to do is refuse to take the mark of the beast. The refusal might cost a person some physical life, but the gain is eternal life with God. Yet even that seemingly simple action is not one that the majority of people at the time are willing to take.

We know that there are those who do choose God and refuse the mark (Revelation 12:11, 15:2, 20:4, 21:7). They "conquer" the serpent and his little horn by the word of their testimony, following only God's commands and perhaps dying in the process. All seven congregations in Revelation 2 and 3 are given encouragement to conquer. Some of these are Jews, and some are Gentiles, but all will have the heritage of "son."

Revelation 21:7 ESV. The one who conquers will have this heritage, and I will be his God and he will be my son.

There is also an indication of the types of judgments to come in the message to "worship him who made heaven and earth, the sea and the springs of water." Each of these areas will be heavily affected by the bowls full of God's wrath poured out soon.

Second Angel: Your Kingdom Babylon is Toast

Jeremiah 51:60–64 ESV. Jeremiah wrote in a book all the disaster that should come upon Babylon, all these words that are written concerning Babylon. And Jeremiah said to Seraiah: "When you come to Babylon, see that you read all these words, and say, 'O LORD, you have said concerning this place that you will cut it off, so that nothing shall dwell in it, neither man nor beast, and it shall be desolate forever.' When you finish reading this book, tie a stone to it and cast it into the midst of the Euphrates, and say, 'Thus shall Babylon sink, to rise no more, because of the disaster that I am bringing upon her, and they shall become exhausted.'" Thus far are the words of Jeremiah.

Revelation 14:8–11 ESV. Another angel, a second, followed, saying, "Fallen, fallen is Babylon the great, she who made all nations drink the wine of the passion of her sexual immorality." And another angel, a third, followed them, saying with a loud voice, "If anyone worships the beast and its image and receives a mark on his forehead or on his hand, he also will drink the wine of God's wrath, poured full strength into the cup of his anger, and he will be tormented with fire and sulfur in the presence of the holy angels and in the presence of the Lamb. And the smoke of their torment goes up forever and ever, and they have no rest, day or night, these worshipers of the beast and its image, and whoever receives the mark of its name."

Revelation 18:21 ESV. Then a mighty angel took up a stone like a great millstone and threw it into the sea, saying, "So will Babylon the great city be thrown down with violence, and will be found no more;

As mentioned previously, God calls Babylon the "land of merchants" and the "city of traders" according to Ezekiel (17:4; check the ESV and NASB). Apparently, along with trading in simple merchandise, they traded in human souls too. This is evidenced by the practice of yanking conquered people out of their homelands and relocating them.

In the verses above from Jeremiah, we have to realize that Babylon was not only a huge, powerful city at the time but also representative of the way the deceiver likes to do things in his kingdom. This means that Babylon the city was trashed way back when, but the system it represents will also be destroyed sometime just before or at Armageddon. Remember that Babylon has both religious parts and a governmental or financial part.

The deceiver has a standard plan for kingdoms that is evident in what we know of the tower of Babel, ancient Nineveh, Assyria, and all the way through Babylon, Persia, Greece, Rome and modern kingdoms such as New York, Beijing, Tokyo, and London. The finishing touches of his ideal kingdom are applied by the deceiver using the little horn and the false Christ. The world system or kingdom called Babylon is at the apex or top of the heap when regarding all the efforts of deceiver-inspired man to build kingdoms without God.

The commonality in all these worldly cities, countries or empires is sexual immorality, idolatry (worship of the Goddess of Reason), the murder of God's people (Jews and believers in Yeshua), selfishness, love of money, thefts, sorcery, witchcraft, abominations and other impurities. John says in Revelation 18:3 that "the merchants of the earth have grown rich from the power of her luxurious living," meaning there's all kinds of money in sin, which makes it difficult to give up.

Babylon the world system is both a generator of wealth and a religious system that is comprised of worship of reason or self. All the anti-God religious philosophies, from Confucianism and Taoism to Islam, Catholicism, Protestantism, so-called Scientology, outright Satanism and witchcraft are all wrapped up in self-interest and rejection of the rule of God. Since Adam and Eve decided to go their own way, mankind has continued the tradition of self rule, though it might be disguised with beautiful robes and jewelry. You can see how all these religious philosophies of men are grouped together by the rejection of some or all of God's Laws in each of them.

Third Angel: Go With the Beast, Go All the Way

Revelation 14:9–11 ESV. And another angel, a third, followed them, saying with a loud voice, "If anyone worships the beast and its image and receives a mark on his forehead or on his hand, he also will drink the wine of God's wrath, poured full strength into the cup of his anger, and he will be tormented with fire and sulfur in the presence of the holy angels and in the presence of the Lamb. And the smoke of their torment goes up forever and ever, and they have no rest, day or night, these worshipers of the beast and its image, and whoever receives the mark of its name."

Most people don't realize that the existence of people with a mark implies there are those who are not marked. These unmarked people rebel against the beast and refuse to become part of his kingdom. It's possible some people could just be refusing because they are contrary anyway, but most will refuse the mark because they choose to follow God and His Anointed instead. Those who want to be marked are given a warning, trumpeted out from heaven by an angel, that if they receive the mark they will end up in the same place as the beast.

Revelation 14:12–13 ESV. Here is a call for the endurance of the saints, those who keep the commandments of God and their faith in Jesus. And I heard a voice from heaven saying, "Write this: Blessed are the dead who die in the Lord from now on." "Blessed indeed," says the Spirit, "that they may rest from their labors, for their deeds follow them!"

Seven times in Revelation, five times in the first three chapters, believers are encouraged to endure. We need to remember that John is writing this about 2,000 years ago, and it applied to believers then as well as through the centuries to our own time and beyond.

Whenever a person decides to follow God, they go from floating with the current of the world to fighting against it. Endurance is a big part of a believer's life. We endure all sorts of abuse from culture and hateful people who don't want to follow God, and who resent anyone or anything that reminds them of it. These encouragements to endure are not just for the time of the Tribulation. They are for all of His children all the time. Those who "die in the Lord from now on" are not just those in the Day of the Lord but also everyone at anytime.

The verses above are dismissed by Church teachers as pertaining only to Yeshua-believing Jewish people, because of the phrase "those who keep the commandments of God." It is said that of course the Church doesn't follow the Mosaic Law so this passage must be referring to Jews.

This argument is nonsensical at best and downright stupid at worst. The part about the Church not following the Law is correct, because the Church, to their shame, indeed doesn't follow the commandments of God. However, the part about it only applying to Jews is not correct. The Law applies to everyone who claims to be part of the Body. In contrast, the Church teaches that in order to believe in Yeshua you have to give up Judaism (including the Law) and avoid the so-called "civil" and "ceremonial" laws. This contradicts the teaching of Yeshua.

Luke 16:10 ESV. "One who is faithful in a very little is also faithful in much, and one who is dishonest in a very little is also dishonest in much.

The verses in Revelation 14:12-13, along with Revelation 13:10 and those addressed to the congregations in the first three chapters, are encouraging all believers in these difficult situations to persevere and endure through them. The verses also characterize believers as "those who keep the commandments of God." Just because one goes to Church, or says "I believe in Jesus," does not mean they are part of the Body of Christ. A believer is one who keeps the commandments of God. They are not the commandments of Moses or the commandments of Jews. They are the commandments of God and His Son Yeshua the Messiah.

James 2:17–19 ESV. So also faith by itself, if it does not have works, is dead. But someone will say, "You have faith and I have works." Show me your faith apart from your works, and I will show you my faith by my works. You believe that God is one; you do well. Even the demons believe—and shudder!

The Hour to Reap Has Come

Micah 4:11–12 ESV. Now many nations are assembled against you, saying, "Let her be defiled, and let our eyes gaze upon Zion." But they do not know the thoughts of the LORD; they do not understand his plan, that he has gathered them as sheaves to the threshing floor.

Joel 3:13–14 ESV. Put in the sickle, for the harvest is ripe. Go in, tread, for the winepress is full. The vats overflow, for their evil is great. Multitudes, multitudes, in the valley of decision! For the day of the LORD is near in the valley of decision.

Going back to the section of this book titled "The Ripe Time," Micah, Joel, and John in Revelation 14:14-20 seem to confirm the idea. An angel with a golden crown sitting on a cloud does some reaping of the earth, presumably of grain, and another angel from the temple gathers clusters from the vine of the earth. The Micah and Joel references suggest that both the grain and grapes refer to the slaughter of nations, with the Revelation repetition meaning the event is set and will not be changed. Reinforcement for the doubling idea is in Pharaoh's dream interpretation of the cows and grain ears by Joseph (Genesis 41:32). Micah compares Armageddon to a threshing floor, while

Joel uses a winepress, yet both refer to the same event and could relate to the reaping of Revelation 14:16. God tells Joel that He will judge the nations at the valley of decision, which is also called the valley of Jehoshaphat or the valley (or plain) of Jezreel.

The Revelation passage is slightly different from Micah and Joel because it doesn't say grain and is not said to be threshed. So it's possible that this reaping has a different focus. It might be that reaping is a symbol of the resurrection or of gathering God's people into a place safe from the wrath soon to be poured out.

A sickle is a curved hand-knife for cutting grain or grapes (or anything, really). It's also called a "pruning hook" in some places in the Word, although a pruning hook might have a longer handle for cutting fruit out of trees too. In the case of grapes, with a quick motion you cut the cluster at the top, drop it in a basket and take it to the winepress. A winepress was generally a large stone container in the ground, sort of like a small pool or an oversized hot tub. The grapes go into the winepress and people stomp on them, causing the juice to flow into smaller containers for making wine. Isaiah in chapter 63 of his book describes someone who comes from Bozrah with garments stained red "like one who treads in the winepress." Isaiah seems to be referring to God (more likely, Yeshua) treading the winepress of judgment, which ties in with these verses in Revelation and to Armageddon.

Armageddon is the English word for the Hebrew name transliterated as *har-megiddone*, meaning hill of Megiddo or "hill (or place) of crowds." Megiddo was probably a city in the valley of Jezreel that has since been covered with dirt to make a hill, or was perhaps built on a hill. The name "place of crowds" is fitting, because God gathers many nations to this valley, where they are slaughtered because of their resistance to God and mistreatment of

Israel. (See also the "plain of Megiddo" in 2 Chronicles 35:22 and Zechariah 12:11.)

So this section of Revelation probably gives us a heavenly view of the slaughter of the world armies in the valley of decision. At the place of crowds, blood will flow up to the depth of a horses bridle for about 184 miles. Carrion birds will be eating their fill, and the destruction of the world's armies is devastating.

A Note on Conquering

After the reaping of the grain and pressing of grapes, in Revelation 15:2-4 we are shown a sea of glass mingled with fire, and those who had conquered the beast by refusing the mark standing beside it.

Revelation 15:2 ESV. And I saw what appeared to be a sea of glass mingled with fire—and also those who had conquered the beast and its image and the number of its name, standing beside the sea of glass with harps of God in their hands.

As the revelation continues past this point, we don't hear of any group we can call believers. Also, the reaping of Revelation 14:16 is not said to be grain and it doesn't say that what is reaped goes to the threshing floor. So as mentioned in the previous section, the reaping may be the resurrection of believers. Or it could picture the gathering of God's people to a safe place away from God's wrath. Yeshua's parable of the weeds and grain in Matthew 13:24-43 might figure in here, except He says that the weeds will be gathered first and burned while the wheat is gathered into His barn.

The word "conquered" in Revelation 15:2 recalls the words of Yeshua in the letters to the seven congregations at the beginning of the book. All seven congregations are told that if they conquer they will get lots of good things. There is one comment made by

Yeshua, after the three demonic frog spirits go to gather the nations for Armageddon, that may be an indicator of believers who are still around after the harvest.

Revelation 16:15 ESV. ("Behold, I am coming like a thief! Blessed is the one who stays awake, keeping his garments on, that he may not go about naked and be seen exposed!")

It's a little odd that believers would be falling asleep in the midst of all this chaos, but Yeshua isn't talking about a nap. Remember that these visions may not be sequential. It might just be that He is warning the reader/believer to stay alert at all times. The garments are "the righteous deeds of the saints" as explained before, so keeping the garments on means to persevere in following God's Words or doing good works.

The resurrection seems to happen just before the armies of the world are stomped in the winepress or threshing floor of God's fury. There will be a lot happening at the same time in different places, such as believers dying for refusing the mark. In any event, Yeshua encourages His people to persevere in obeying His Word and thereby conquer.

8 Yom YHVH

Isaiah 29:5–7 ESV. But the multitude of your foreign foes shall be like small dust, and the multitude of the ruthless like passing chaff. And in an instant, suddenly, you will be visited by the LORD of hosts with thunder and with earthquake and great noise, with whirlwind and tempest, and the flame of a devouring fire. And the multitude of all the nations that fight against Ariel, all that fight against her and her stronghold and distress her, shall be like a dream, a vision of the night.

Keeping with the theme of multiple seven-fold judgments established by God in Leviticus 26 for violation of His Law, He follows up the seven trumpet judgments by unloading seven even more horrible bowls full of His wrath on the earth.

Isaiah 4:3–4 ESV. And he who is left in Zion and remains in Jerusalem will be called holy, everyone who has been recorded for life in Jerusalem, when the Lord shall have washed away the filth of the daughters of Zion and cleansed the bloodstains of Jerusalem from its midst by a spirit of judgment and by a spirit of burning.

These bowls are associated with Yom Kippur or the day of smoke and burning, also known as the Day of the Lord or Yom YHVH (used five times in Joel for instance). The trumpet judgments, connected with the "day of the awakening blast" or Feast of Trumpets, are lighter, and seem to be spaced in such a way as to allow time for repentance. But the bowls are different.

These horrors happen in more of a rapid-fire order than previous judgments. Babylon, for instance, is three times said to be destroyed "in a single hour," (Revelation 18:10, 17, 19) and "her plagues will come in a single day" (Revelation 18:8). Whereas the trumpet judgments are like announcements or warnings, the bowls just get poured out. There is no pause, no space for repentance. It's too late, and anyway once at the fourth (sun scorches) and fifth (darkness on throne of the beast) bowls we are told no one repented of their deeds or gave God glory. Presumably, this is the case at the other bowls too. The only hope is for those who persevere in choosing God.

The people with the mark, those who have survived the trumpets, have hardened their hearts to the point that there is no saving them. Even though covered in painful sores, the sun is scorching, they only have bloody water to drink, and the sea is full of dead creatures, they just curse God and get ready for the big battle at Armageddon instead of turning around.

So these judgments are quick and seem to happen in a relatively short space. The pace of God's dealings with the kingdom of the deceiver and the beast is speeding up. Bowls also suggest a localized judgment, very likely just on the kingdom of the beast. You would think people would notice this and turn away from their corrupt practices but it is not to be. God knows the condition of the hearts and judges accordingly.

The Egyptian plagues had stop points. That is, Pharaoh asked Moses to stop the plague and he would let the people go (he lied). These bowl judgments don't seem to have a stop point. We also don't know how long these plagues last, or if they are just focused around Israel on the kingdom of the beast. It seems as if they all pile up together. So people will have sores, dead seas, bloody water to drink, scorching heat and darkness, which make the entire group of beast followers mad enough for Armageddon. After all this God really drops the hammer with 100 pound hailstones and an earthquake bigger than any before, destroying cities, leveling mountains, illuminating the darkness with lightning and assaulting the ears with thunder like a heavenly artillery barrage.

Revelation 16:1 ESV. Then I heard a loud voice from the temple telling the seven angels, "Go and pour out on the earth the seven bowls of the wrath of God."

Bowl 1: Painful Sores on the Mark

Revelation 16:2 ESV. So the first angel went and poured out his bowl on the earth, and harmful and painful sores came upon the people who bore the mark of the beast and worshiped its image.

The last time this happened in the Bible was in Egypt with a hard-hearted, unrepentant Pharaoh standing in for his empire.

Exodus 9:8–9 ESV. And the LORD said to Moses and Aaron, "Take handfuls of soot from the kiln, and let Moses throw them in the air in the sight of Pharaoh. It shall become fine dust over all the land of Egypt, and become boils breaking out in sores on man and beast throughout all the land of Egypt."

With the first bowl judgment, we see painful sores again only on people who have taken the mark of the beast, which implies that there are people at that point who haven't. The first time (in Egypt) should stand as a warning to the people the second time it happens (not to mention they are warned here in advance), but they are unheeding. In fact, they are arrogant and proud, cursing God instead (Revelation 16:11).

The pain from sores is reminiscent of the stinging locusts of the fifth trumpet which caused agony but not death. In this phase of judgment, God steps up the pain of the body and intensifies it. Still there is no repentance, and still only cursing of God. The self-worshipping world doesn't want anything to do with the sustainer of life, choosing instead to continue on a destructive path.

Bowl 2: Sea of Blood

Revelation 16:3 ESV. The second angel poured out his bowl into the sea, and it became like the blood of a corpse, and every living thing died that was in the sea.

It is apparent when the second bowl is poured out, and the sea becomes like the blood of a corpse, that the sea stinks to high heaven. Assuming that one-third of the sea creatures are still gone from the second trumpet, the last two-thirds of everything in it dies. Although if the second trumpet occurs closer to the middle of the seven-year period, and this bowl is dumped out closer to the end of the seven years, the sea might have recovered somewhat from the second trumpet.

The sea here might only be the Mediterranean. It's possible that it includes all of what we now call the oceans, and if so would be a very huge disaster. It's not clear how it would be limited because they are all connected. Trade will probably come to a halt (remember also that a third of the ships were already destroyed at the second trumpet), and no one will want to be around the sea. The huge trading seaports at least around the Mediterranean will shut down, contributing to famines and death. The only ships moving will be those later that carry armies to Armageddon.

In Scripture, the "abundance of the sea" indicates that many riches come from the sea, and Tyre is said to have built their wealth from the sea.

Isaiah 60:5 ESV. Then you shall see and be radiant; your heart shall thrill and exult, because the abundance of the sea shall be turned to you, the wealth of the nations shall come to you.

Ezekiel 27:33 ESV. When your wares came from the seas, you satisfied many peoples; with your abundant wealth and merchandise you enriched the kings of the earth.

When everything in the sea goes belly up, the abundance is no more. Can you imagine the other two thirds (if the sea hasn't recovered from the second trumpet) of whales, dolphins, sea lions, seals, fish, reef dwellers, sharks, orcas, deep sea denizens, and many other creatures floating dead and rotting on a sea of blood?

Not to mention other critters that live off of the sea such as polar bears and sea birds? It's a sure bet there won't be any TV commercials placing the blame on the self-seeking people worshipping the little horn. So much death and no repentance!

Bowl 3: Springs of Blood

Revelation 16:4–7 ESV. The third angel poured out his bowl into the rivers and the springs of water, and they became blood. And I heard the angel in charge of the waters say, "Just are you, O Holy One, who is and who was, for you brought these judgments. For they have shed the blood of saints and prophets, and you have given them blood to drink. It is what they deserve!" And I heard the altar saying, "Yes, Lord God the Almighty, true and just are your judgments!"

At bowl number three, the rivers and springs of water (probably in the beast's kingdom alone) become blood. No more drinking water, unless you have a really strong filter. But even if you have a filter, the water might still turn to blood after it is filtered. Rivers and springs can usually clean themselves, given time, except now they just keep running with blood and dead things. At this point, there is no getting around having to drink blood. The kingdom of the beast has made war on the saints and prevailed, killing many of us. In return, God gives them blood to drink. The altar even talks in support of this judgment, saying "true and just are your judgments."

The Egyptians just before the Exodus dug next to the Nile River for water (Exodus 7:24), which might indicate that the water was filtered. God was merciful then and did not turn all the water in Egypt to blood (although a lot of it to guess from Exodus 7:21). People might be able to dig and find filtered water, but in this instance they won't be able to get around God that easily.

Drinking blood is specifically commanded against and makes people unclean (Genesis 9:4, Leviticus 3:17, 7:26-27,

17:12). Whoever eats blood, Jew or Gentile, will be "cut off" or die. Eating or drinking blood is a sentence of death, unless one is eating or drinking the blood of Christ, which is actually not red corpuscles but is the Word of God. God is handing out a judgment of bloody water here because the people have shed innocent blood. They kill believers simply because they hate what is God's and want to destroy it.

All the fresh water creatures join their brethren from salt water in death. If there's no fish to eat then other creatures that feed on them will not survive either. So at that time there is the stink of dead water creatures everywhere. Even the snow turns to blood; if not when it is frozen, surely when it thaws. Spring runoff will have a whole new meaning in the kingdom of the beast.

Bowl 4: Scorching Sun

Revelation 16:8 ESV. The fourth angel poured out his bowl on the sun, and it was allowed to scorch people with fire.

Now God really turns up the heat. You could accurately call this "man-caused global warming" at last. But man won't be able to do anything to change it. The sun, probably through solar flares or solar winds, is allowed to start cooking the earth like a huge turkey on a barbecue rotisserie. The springs and rivers are bloody, and this at a time when thirst becomes intense. Showering or swimming to keep cool won't be very appetizing, especially since the water will have the after-effects of dead stuff floating in it and a whole lotta blood. Forced to bathe and drink polluted water, plagues and disease such as dysentery, typhoid, and cholera will run rampant. Severe diarrhea and vomiting will dehydrate people, causing even more desire for water.

The heat will be fierce and even taking shelter in caves or under rocks won't help. Air conditioners will fail because they are not designed for working with heat that goes above about 120 degrees, and the demand for cooling will probably overload and cook a lot of power plants anyway. Many of the people of the beast kingdom will literally be roasting. They will squawk about global warming, and try to pass legislation for their "green new deals," yet relief will not be forthcoming except in death.

Bowl 5: Darkness They Will Feel

Revelation 16:10–11 ESV. The fifth angel poured out his bowl on the throne of the beast, and its kingdom was plunged into darkness. People gnawed their tongues in anguish and cursed the God of heaven for their pain and sores. They did not repent of their deeds.

Matthew 24:29 ESV. "Immediately after the tribulation of those days the sun will be darkened, and the moon will not give its light, and the stars will fall from heaven, and the powers of the heavens will be shaken.

Isaiah 34:4 ESV. All the host of heaven shall rot away, and the skies roll up like a scroll. All their host shall fall, as leaves fall from the vine, like leaves falling from the fig tree.

God now turns out the lights on the kingdom of the little horn. This darkness is not like a night-time dark. It is the absolute dark of no light whatsoever; the kind of dark that you find in deep caves where you can't see your hand in front of your eyes. It's probably not blindness or the text would say so. People gnaw their tongues in pain and curse God, yet still do not repent.

It's not certain how God will create darkness while at the same time the sun is so hot it is scorching everything and everybody, but if anyone can, He can. Natural explanations for this darkness don't seem to fit. It isn't an eclipse, because that's not dark enough. If it is localized, meaning just around the throne of the beast, that makes it even harder to explain naturally. It would have to be something supernatural, like being in an oven without that little light that comes on when you open the door.

Exodus 10:21–23 ESV. Then the LORD said to Moses, "Stretch out your hand toward heaven, that there may be darkness over the land of Egypt, a darkness to be felt." So Moses stretched out his hand toward heaven, and there was pitch darkness in all the land of Egypt three days. They did not see one another, nor did anyone rise from his place for three days, but all the people of Israel had light where they lived.

Darkness like this was inflicted on Egypt just before the Exodus. It was a "darkness to be felt" and could not be dispelled by artificial light. It was also only on Egypt, while Israel had light where they lived. The darkness poured out from the fifth bowl judgment is going to hang around "the throne of the beast" and make it hard for his acolytes to function. This is another indicator that the darkness of this bowl has no natural cause. It is darkness from the absence of God, who is the source of all light.

After the previous four bowls of boils, dead sea, fresh water corrupted and severe heat from the sun you'd think that people would be throwing themselves on the ground and asking for mercy from God, but not even close. Instead of softening hearts and repentance, we have hard-hearted warmongers gearing up for the next big horror.

Bowl 6: Euphrates Dry, Frog Spirits Gather Armies

Revelation 16:12–16 ESV. The sixth angel poured out his bowl on the great river Euphrates, and its water was dried up, to prepare the way for the kings from the east. And I saw, coming out of the mouth of the dragon and out of the mouth of the beast and out of the mouth of the false prophet, three unclean spirits like frogs. For they are demonic spirits, performing signs, who go abroad to the kings of the whole world, to assemble them for battle on the great day of God the Almighty. ("Behold, I am coming like a thief! Blessed is the one who stays awake, keeping his garments on, that he may not go about naked and be seen exposed!") And they assembled them at the place that in Hebrew is called Armageddon.

The river Euphrates has a long history in the Bible. The name means "fruitfulness" (Hebrew *Perath*) and is one of the rivers flowing out of Eden named in Genesis 2:14. This river was supposed to be the eastern border of the Promised Land originally gifted to Abraham (Genesis 15:18). Sometimes it is just called The River, because it was so well known it didn't need to be named.

Terah, the father of Abraham, lived on the other side of the Euphrates (Joshua 24:2) from The Land, where other gods were worshiped. Deciding to follow the one true God, Abraham crossed The River from east to west to wander the Land which would eventually be his. Later, God tells Israel they will be scattered "beyond the Euphrates" because they worshipped the Asherim, returning them to the place of the other gods once worshipped by their fathers (1 Kings 14:15).

The River originates in modern day Turkey and flows through Iraq and Syria. It is 1,750 miles long, has large areas of marshes, and waters thousands of farms. There are 22 or more dams as of this writing, and at one point in recent years, The River was in danger of drying up in some areas because of them. Iraq even now lives in fear that Turkey will use all the water before it can get to their country. Indeed, as recently as July 2020 Turkey cut the flow of water to Syria (who is before Iraq on the Euphrates), using the Alyso dam, to such an extent that The River reached record lows. So Iraq has reason to be concerned.

Islamic writings predict that the Euphrates will dry up revealing a mountain of gold, that 99 out of 100 people will die fighting over it, and that their believers are not to touch it. That doesn't mean they won't go to war with Israel anyway.

The frog-like unclean and demonic spirits will probably make stops along the way to their final destinations, performing signs for rulers to encourage their obedience. They will take some time in so doing, especially if they have to cover the globe. But it may not take them very long because most of the rulers will be primed to go already. It may also be that the Great Earthquake and 100 pound hailstones fall sometime during the recruiting, which causes fear and cursing of God but doesn't stop the armies from gathering.

Bowl 7: Great Earthquake, 100 Pound Hailstones

Revelation 16:17-21 ESV. The seventh angel poured out his bowl into the air, and a loud voice came out of the temple, from the throne, saying, "It is done!" And there were flashes of lightning, rumblings, peals of thunder, and a great earthquake such as there had never been since man was on the earth, so great was that earthquake. The great city was split into three parts, and the cities of the nations fell, and God remembered Babylon the great, to make her drain the cup of the wine of the fury of his wrath. And every island fled away, and no mountains were to be found. And great hailstones, about one hundred pounds each, fell from heaven on people; and they cursed God for the plague of the hail, because the plague was so severe.

There are a number of "great cities" named in Scripture, and eight times this combination of words is used in Revelation. Six of these refer to Babylon. Two of them are describing Jerusalem, and that is the city mentioned here that splits into three parts, instead of facing complete destruction like Babylon. Around this time, Yeshua will set foot on the Mount of Olives which will split in two, each part moving north and south to make a valley. Perhaps splitting into three parts helps with the making of the valley when the Mount of Olives splits. From the air, Jerusalem is going to look like a giant jigsaw puzzle.

When the cities of the nations fall in the earthquake like no other, it will cause a lot of death and destruction. High rises won't be so high at that time. People living in a skyscraper should sell the penthouse condo and find a place out in the country right now. Don't wait until your bird's eye view turns into a worm's eye view.

This earthquake will take some time to stop shaking. It will be so severe that the earth will stagger like a drunken man, which would make for an event that will take time to develop and to subside. This is the earthquake like no other also mentioned in Revelation 6 because both places mention that "every mountain and island is removed from its place." The seventh bowl effects don't mention anything about the sun or moon, but that could be that they were already affected at the fifth bowl (darkness).

Hailstones of 100 pounds are mentioned, which will finish the pounding of the cities if there's anything in them left standing. There are various factors affecting the speed at which the hailstones would strike, but they would probably be traveling upwards of 130 to 200 miles per hour. That is some terrific force applied to an area, sort of like very large bombs going off. The shattered ice will also act like shrapnel tearing apart anything softer in the blast zone. One other time God is said to have thrown down large hailstones from heaven (apart from the Egypt plague which had stones probably smaller). They were thrown on the armies of five kings attacking Israel, which killed more than the swords of Israel (Joshua 10).

A light show will be included in the festivities. Thunder and lightning will be all around, and it will be way more intense than is usual in thunderstorms. The overall effect will be very much like an artillery salvo in modern conventional war, except God's bombardment will be scarier.

Revelation 6:15–17 ESV. Then the kings of the earth and the great ones and the generals and the rich and the powerful, and everyone, slave and free, hid themselves in the caves and among the rocks of the mountains, calling to the mountains and rocks, "Fall on us and hide us from the face of him who is seated on the throne, and from the wrath of the Lamb, for the great day of their wrath has come, and who can stand?"

Prostitute Riding a Scarlet Beast

Part of the seventh bowl judgment is that "God remembers Babylon to make her drain the cup of wrath." So John in Revelation 17 backs up a little to cover what happens to the prostitute Babylon and her favorite refreshment (and it ain't soda pop), then covers what happens to the city. There's kind of a back and forth here between the description of the seventh bowl consequences in chapter 16, and what happens to both physical and religious parts of Babylon in chapters 17 through 19.

As mentioned before, this is probably because narratives in the Bible sometimes give the "big picture" in one chapter and then fill in details in the next chapter or two. Besides our current subject, an example of this is in Genesis chapters one and two. Chapter one covers the whole of creation, and chapter two backs up and gives details on the creation of Adam and Eve.

In Revelation 17 John is shown a woman riding on the scarlet beast who has a name of mystery on her forehead that is "Babylon the great, mother of prostitutes and of earth's abominations." In Revelation 19, we go back and pick up the thread of her story as she is destroyed at the seventh bowl.

This woman looks pretty on the outside, dressed in purple and scarlet (the colors of ruling or royalty); with jewelry to match, but inside she's as ugly as they come. Her main claims to fame are sexual immorality and murder of God's people. She is seated on many waters representing peoples, multitudes, nations and languages, so this woman represents the entire anti-God religious population of the earth that has existed since the beginning. She is riding the beast, but he and the kings who give him allegiance (the horns) hate her and destroy her. Like Hitler and many before him, the beast wants to use religion as a tool to manipulate instead of submitting to a relationship with God.

Some identify the Catholic Church as mystery religion Babylon, but that is too limited. Catholicism has only been around for about 1,800 years, and has not covered the planet that thoroughly during those centuries. The Catholic Church is certainly included with this woman, but so is every religious system created apart from God including much of what the Protestants have created. This mystery religion has been around at least since the time of the tower of Babel, a Hebrew word meaning "gate of the deity" or "confusion." Babylon is Greek for the same city/kingdom, and Babel or Babylon is where we see the first Scriptural record of idolatrous behavior (although there was probably much before the flood too).

John has to be very familiar with the pagan religions around him, and those of Scripture that Israel was involved with for many centuries. The most obvious of these older religions or gods were Baal, Asherah, and Ashtaroth. There were different spellings of the names, and sometimes the names of the idols came from a place name like Ashtaroth (Deuteronomy 1:4). As mentioned before, a more modern name is the goddess of Reason. The false gods in pagan religions are hard to tell apart, but the main two ideas in all the pagan religions were fertility (sex or sexual immorality) and lordship other than God.

Some of the religions have stories stolen from God's promise in Genesis 3:15 of a virgin birth for their god, and blasphemy in the form of giving credit for God's works to worthless idols. The deceiver is a master of this tactic called "poisoning the well." John would also be aware of the mixing of pagan religions with God's works and character. He could see firsthand the corruption of the teachings of Yeshua; which even at that time was occurring in six of the seven congregations mentioned in the book he was writing. However, he would not have seen the full-blown Catholic Church at the time of his visions. It didn't get fully established until about 325 A.D. or so. It is not a coincidence that the Prostitute is wearing purple and scarlet. John is seeing the future fashions of The Church leaders.

So when we get to Revelation 17, John knows what he is looking at. He "marvels" or "wonders greatly" (17:6) probably because he sees the full impact of the mystery religion on the world. This Goddess of Reason leads the world with a very corrupt version of false religion, mixed with teachings of Jezebel, Balaam, Nicolaitans, and the synagogue of Satan. By the time of the end, the corrupt Church will have participated in influencing many nations, tribes, peoples and tongues using the name of Jesus. But it is actually far removed from any but a superficial resemblance to Him or His Word.

It is likely that this woman is all religion combined that leads away from God with idolatry, sexual immorality and blasphemy. This includes all paganism, all idolatry, all witchcraft and voodoo and the like. It even includes the Church, Catholic or Protestant (and offshoots). Otherwise, Yeshua would not be warning the seven congregations of the teachings of Balaam, Jezebel, and the Nicolaitans in Revelation 2 and 3, which the Church has raised to an art form. Idolatry is cheating on God, with or without a statue. The modern Church is certainly cheating on God, which will put them right on the same dragon with mystery religion Babylon and the beast.

Modern day Rome is the seat of a religion that has spent a great deal of time in recent decades prostituting itself, not only in the usual areas of sexual immorality and idolatry, but in changing God's Law and trying to unite all the world's religions on the least common denominator. This lowest common denominator is "doing what is right in their own eyes." There are reports of the Catholic Church funding the construction of mosques in Europe, at a guess to try and make nice with the other people of the beast. Adherents of Islam are the fly in the ointment of that desire, however, because they are just as pagan as the rest.

Rome might be the head of the Prostitute, but it is likely that agents of Islam will be the tool for the destruction of the Prostitute in the hands of the little horn. The little horn himself is probably Muslim, because descendants of Ishmael (mostly Muslim now) have been at war with Israel since Abraham, and most are continually at war with anyone not Muslim. Something like nine out of ten current conflicts or wars involves Muslims. Their own book encourages them to lie to anyone not Muslim in order to advance their version of a tyrannical world kingdom (some of them call it The Caliphate).

Muslims want to destroy any religion not in line with it. They aren't looking to get along with anyone else unless they can further their own goals. They will probably unite with Rome, just as they united with Hitler in World War II, because they think they will ultimately be able to destroy all religions not of their own construct. The unity won't be complete because it looks like the little horn destroys the Prostitute's seat of authority. The basic premise of Islam that lying is okay as long as they can advance their false religion will cause them to look like they are cooperating with the Prostitute.

Revelation 17:16–17 ESV. And the ten horns that you saw, they and the beast will hate the prostitute. They will make her desolate and naked, and devour her flesh and burn her up with fire, for God has put it into their hearts to carry out his purpose by being of one mind and handing over their royal power to the beast, until the words of God are fulfilled.

The little horn along with ten kings who align with him for one hour (Revelation 17:12) will destroy Mystery Religion Babylon, even though it will cost them a lot of money. Just when most, if not all, of the world's religions unite and are thinking they have it all worked out, the little horn will make her "desolate and naked, and devour her flesh and burn her up with fire."

The beast is a kingdom as well as a person. God doesn't seem to make a difference as far as can be seen in the Word. Kingdoms are identified with their rulers, because the character of the leader influences the kingdom from the top down. Rulers are also identified with kingdoms because the natures of the two are the same. That's why we see prophecies of the king of Tyre (Ezekiel 28) or the king of Babylon and others applied to the whole kingdom, not just the monarch.

The beast tolerates other false religions for a while, but he wants the first place of worship. So he destroys Babylon because she's in the way. It's like that movie The Highlander, where so-called "immortals" battle it out until only one of them is left. They all use the saying throughout the movie that "there can be only one." The beast definitely thinks "there can be only one" so he destroys the competition. The Catholic Church certainly is a main part of Babylon, perhaps even the lead, but does not carry the whole burden by itself. Many other Churches, synagogues, mosques, and temples join her in immorality.

Throughout the history of the Church, she has tried to rule. The position of her leaders is that God (through them, of course) rules everything and so they (claiming to represent God) should direct the governments of whatever kingdom of which they were a part. There were lots of struggles, political intrigues and even wars fought over who was in charge (and the struggle is still going). Compromises were sometimes made where the Church would rule in things spiritual while kings would rule things physical or civil. But the Church has never given up her desire or plans to rule everything, mostly because of the power behind her. The deceiver uses the Church as long as he needs her, but her end will come when he doesn't need her anymore. "There can be only one."

Believers will need to be filled with the whole of the Word, have patient endurance, reject the teachings of Jezebel and her ilk, and hear what the Spirit says to the congregations that make up the Body. Start tuning your eyes and ears to see Him and listen for His instructions by taking in all of His Words and doing them. Now. While there's still time. "Come out of her, my people, lest you take part in her sins," says the voice from heaven in Revelation 18:4-5. This voice may be talking about the city, or the religion, but either way believers need to get away from her. Repent, find the narrow path, go through the open door, buy from Him gold refined by fire and white garments to cover the shame of nakedness, along with some salve to anoint your eyes. Be zealous and repent.

The Fall of Babylon the Great

Jeremiah 50:29 ESV. "Summon archers against Babylon, all those who bend the bow. Encamp around her; let no one escape. Repay her according to her deeds; do to her according to all that she has done. For she has proudly defied the LORD, the Holy One of Israel.

Jeremiah 51:60–64 ESV. Jeremiah wrote in a book all the disaster that should come upon Babylon, all these words that are written concerning Babylon. And Jeremiah said to Seraiah: "When you come to Babylon, see that you read all these words, and say, 'O LORD, you have said concerning this place that you will cut it off, so that nothing shall dwell in it, neither man nor beast, and it shall be desolate forever.' When you finish reading this book, tie a stone to it and cast it into the midst of the Euphrates, and say, 'Thus shall Babylon sink, to rise no more, because of the disaster that I am bringing upon her, and they shall become exhausted.' " Thus far are the words of Jeremiah.

Revelation 18:21 ESV. Then a mighty angel took up a stone like a great millstone and threw it into the sea, saying, "So will Babylon the great city be thrown down with violence, and will be found no more;

There is some confusion here, because there is Babylon the religion and Babylon the city and/or kingdom. They could be separate, but they share the same character. Babylon the religion is made to drink a cup of the wrath of God, but Babylon the beast is the one who delivers that wrath. Babylon the city is probably destroyed before all the other cities of the world are flattened in the "Earthquake like no other" at the seventh bowl. Perhaps they are both destroyed at the same time but just described differently.

Three times in Revelation the "great city" of Babylon is said to be judged in a single hour (Revelation 18:10, 17, 19) and once judgment (or plagues) comes in a single day (Revelation 18:8). The Great Prostitute and the Great City are one in the same nature, which is why the descriptions seem to blur together. It may be that the beast destroys the religion, and shortly after that, God destroys the city. Or if the beast is Muslim (or even if not), he destroys both the city of Rome and the religion of Rome.

It looks like the city is destroyed separately from the other cities in the great earthquake, because merchants have time to mourn the loss. Babylon is an actual city, said to be established on seven mountains and on seven kings. Oddly enough, the ancient city of Babylon is not built on seven hills. There are many other cities built on seven hills (or so it is claimed) but only one (and perhaps two if you include Istanbul) is associated with a major religion. Rome is built on seven hills, and so is Istanbul (formerly Constantinople and Byzantium), but mountains may also mean kings or kingdoms. If the mountains are metaphors for both kings and kingdoms, Rome is a good choice. Rome also qualifies because of the series of Roman emperors that persecuted Christians and Jews to death.

Revelation 18:24 ESV. And in her was found the blood of prophets and of saints, and of all who have been slain on earth."

There certainly is a lot of the blood of prophets, saints and many others slain in Rome or because of Rome. That location was the scene of many murders in coliseums and arenas. The emperor Nero was fond of throwing Christians to lions and dipping them in oil then lighting them on fire for his parties. And that's just the tip of the iceberg for Rome. Armies of Islam have also murdered a huge number of believers in the name of their religion.

Sure, the emperor Constantine in the eastern leg of the empire put a stop to some of the murdering when he forced a bastardized version of "Christianity" on the pagan populace. Except even he killed people who wouldn't accept his idea of Christianity. The Roman Empire (and every other empire) has a long history of killing anybody who didn't conform to the whims of the rulers, and the Catholic Church continues the tradition. Like the blood of Abel, their blood cries out from the earth to God for justice. Islam is not innocent of this murdering either.

At the time of John, five of the kings had fallen, one is, and one is yet to come. The word "kings" could refer to seven kingdoms, the five fallen being perhaps Egypt, Assyria, Babylon, Media/Persia and Greece. The one that "is" could be the Roman Empire, and the future seventh kingdom of the little horn would be composed of parts of the previous kingdoms.

The Roman emperor around the time of John was Trajan (98 to 117 A.D.) but there were many more than seven kings or emperors of Rome (and other kingdoms) in total, so just trying to match kings doesn't work. The seven kingdoms were (or will be) anti-Jewish, and mostly had a special animus or hatred for Israel.

Today's Babylon (the world system) has risen from the six kingdoms and others, so all of them could be said to have contributed to building Babylon in the present day.

The beast that was and is not and is about to (from John's perspective) rise from the bottomless pit is perhaps the deceiver who continually tries making a globe-spanning kingdom. The future try at a kingdom will be ruled briefly by the little horn or beast in the Tribulation. He might be trying to restore a Roman Empire, or trying to establish the Muslim Caliphate. If he wants to establish the Caliphate, that, along with just being Muslim, might explain his initial cooperation with the Church and later destruction of it. It might also explain his "strong covenant" with many (in Israel) for one seven" only later to cut off sacrifices and then attack Israel at Armageddon. As mentioned already, Islam favors duplicity, and a pillar of the belief system is to cooperate with enemies until strong enough to destroy them.

Rider on a White Horse

Revelation 19:11-16 reveals Yeshua in the form of a rider on a white horse. He's got some names that give added meaning to both His position and His job description. One is The Word of God, and a second is King of Kings and Lord of Lords. A third is known only to Himself, but all of these illustrate some aspect of God's will which are all embodied in our Messiah.

This rider also has a sword coming out of His mouth which hearkens back to Revelation 1:16. There Yeshua is seen another time with a sharp sword coming out of His mouth. This sword is just a way of saying that Yeshua speaks the Words of God.

Matthew 10:34, ESV. "Do not think that I have come to bring peace to the earth. I have not come to bring peace, but a sword.

Ephesians 6:17, ESV. ...and take the helmet of salvation, and the sword of the Spirit, which is the word of God,

Hebrews 4:12, ESV. For the word of God is living and active, sharper than any two-edged sword, piercing to the division of soul and of spirit, of joints and of marrow, and discerning the thoughts and intentions of the heart.

Yeshua uses the sword to "strike down the nations." Those who insist on ignoring, mocking and otherwise refusing to follow His words will feel the judgment of those words. Whatever is lifted up contrary to the will of our patient, loving and long-suffering Father will be itself laid low and buried in the dust.

The rod also mentioned in Revelation 19:15 is another way of looking at the Word of God, only in this form it is used to guide or shepherd. The staff or "shepherd's crook" used by shepherds to watch over a flock of sheep is also a "rod." God's Word can be like a sharp sword cutting to the truth of a matter, it can be used gently like a shepherd's staff or "crook," or it can be used like a staff of iron to break the disobedient.

If you remember your Psalm 23, King David, who knew something about shepherding, says, "thy rod and they staff they comfort me." That rod and staff is the Word of God. God's Words comfort and guide the believing sheep of His pasture, but they terrify the disobedient, prideful and willful. Believers are not afraid of the Word. For unbelievers it comes down like a rod of iron and cuts them off from the lies they tell themselves.

This white horse rider is different from the white horse rider of the scroll seal because of the Word of God. The scroll seal rider looks a little like Yeshua because of the horse, the crown, and he goes out "conquering and to conquer" with a bow. But looks are only skin deep. Yeshua is the true "anointed" of God, having and using the Word of God as God intends. This white horse rider has real authority, judging in righteousness and treading the winepress of the fury of God Almighty. The seal rider has only the force of arms and a few tricks, used for the task of striking down the nations with apparent success for a while.

The white horse rider has a robe "dipped in blood" where the word "dipped" is from a Greek word (βάπτω transliterated *bapto* Strongs 911) from which we also get baptize and baptism (βαπτίζω or baptizo Strong's 907). To dip, baptize or dye cloth means to immerse in a liquid which colors or identifies the cloth.

The blood on the robe is not from Armageddon, because at this point in the text He isn't there yet. The blood is more likely from His sacrifice on the cross. So His robe is dipped in His own blood, shed for the payment of the penalty for the sins of the world. It is a sharp reminder to the nations He defeats that the end did not have to be this way. He paid the penalty and most of the world spurns His gift. This refusal of the gift is the answer to the question of why there is suffering in the world.

Yeshua was perfected through suffering, and as He said before, the deceiver has nothing in (or no claim on) Him (John 14:30). Soon after this in the text, the robes of Yeshua are dipped in the blood of His enemies at Armageddon, as we see in Isaiah 63.

Armageddon: Treading the Winepress

Most of the world is familiar with the battle of Armageddon. The concept is used in movies, books, songs, and many other places so much that unless someone has been living under a rock, almost everyone is aware of the meaning. Armageddon has become synonymous with world-ending apocalypse. But it isn't world-ending, or even an apocalypse. It is a truly terrible event, but it is not the main point of Scripture, or even of the Tribulation.

Isaiah describes this huge battle as God treading a winepress. As mentioned before, a winepress is a big container, usually carved in stone, but it could also be a large tub. The container is large enough to hold many bunches of grapes, and people get into the vat or tub and stomp the grapes. Or a smaller container is used with a screw handle on top of a plate to press down the grapes. The juice flows out through the bottom and into smaller containers, which are set aside to let the yeast on the skin of the grapes consume the sugar in the juice, resulting in fermentation and eventually wine. God, of course, is not interested in the product of the vat. He is interested in payback.

Isaiah 63:1–6 ESV. Who is this who comes from Edom, in crimsoned garments from Bozrah, he who is splendid in his apparel, marching in the greatness of his strength? "It is I, speaking in righteousness, mighty to save." Why is your apparel red, and your garments like his who treads in the winepress? "I have trodden the winepress alone, and from the peoples no one was with me; I trod them in my anger and trampled them in my wrath; their lifeblood spattered on my garments, and stained all my apparel. For the day of vengeance was in my heart, and my year of redemption had come. I looked, but there was no one to help; I was appalled, but there was no one to uphold; so my own arm brought me salvation, and my wrath upheld me. I trampled down the peoples in my anger; I made them drunk in my wrath, and I poured out their lifeblood on the earth."

Countries around Israel, mostly descended from Ishmael and who've always had their eye continuously on the destruction of the people of God, will have their armies "invited" to the festivities. Micah uses another comparison of sheaves (bunches of grain just harvested) gathered to the threshing floor.

Micah 4:11–13 ESV. Now many nations are assembled against you, saying, "Let her be defiled, and let our eyes gaze upon Zion." But they do not know the thoughts of the LORD; they do not understand his plan, that he has gathered them as sheaves to the threshing floor. Arise and thresh, O daughter of Zion, for I will make your horn iron, and I will make your hoofs bronze; you shall beat in pieces many peoples; and shall devote their gain to the LORD, their wealth to the Lord of the whole earth.

A threshing floor is a flat place of hard earth or stone where the grain on the stalks is slammed against the floor to dislodge the grain and the chaff (the husk around the grain). An alternate method is to have an animal such as an ox drag around a threshing sledge (a kind of wooden sled) to separate the wheat (or other grain) from the chaff.

By either stomping or threshing, the grain or the grapes are treated rather roughly. Ezekiel tells us that the "invitation" to God's stomping is irresistible.

Ezekiel 38:1–6 ESV. The word of the LORD came to me: "Son of man, set your face toward Gog, of the land of Magog, the chief prince of Meshech and Tubal, and prophesy against him and say, Thus says the Lord GOD: Behold, I am against you, O Gog, chief prince of Meshech and Tubal. And I will turn you about and put hooks into your jaws, and I will bring you out, and all your army, horses and horsemen, all of them clothed in full armor, a great host, all of them with buckler and shield, wielding swords. Persia, Cush, and Put are with them, all of them with shield and helmet; Gomer and all his hordes; Beth-togarmah from the uttermost parts of the north with all his hordes—many peoples are with you.

As mentioned before, the Hebrew for Armageddon is *har-meggido* or hill of Megiddo. Megiddo was originally a city on a hill at the east end of the valley or plain of Megiddo which is a ways north of Jerusalem. The tribe of Manasseh gained possession of Megiddo but couldn't remove the Canaanite occupants (Judges 1:27). A lot of battles have been fought in the area because it is an access point for invasion of forces from the north of Israel.

Megiddo is mentioned a few times in Scripture as a Canaanite town that was destroyed and rebuilt (1 Kings 9:15) and eventually destroyed again. The plain of Megiddo is mentioned twice in Scripture, once when Josiah goes against the word of God and fights there (and dies 2 Kings 23:29), and once when Zechariah (12:11) mentions it as a place of mourning, most probably for Josiah's death (at Hadad-rimmon, a town near Megiddo). Zechariah also mentions that, like the mourning for Josiah who was pierced, the people of Jerusalem will look on the arriving of Yeshua to stomp on their enemies and see "Him whom they have pierced." They will mourn and "weep bitterly over him as one weeps over a firstborn" (Zechariah 12:10-11). God makes an association here between Josiah (a godly king of Judah) who was pierced and Yeshua who was pierced.

This huge battle, which isn't much of a battle really, takes place right at the end of the Tribulation because of the association with a great earthquake (Ezekiel 38:19-23). Some people think this battle is before the seventieth week, perhaps because Israel burns the weapons for seven years after the battle (Ezekiel 39:9-10). But the weapons could be burned after Armageddon and on into the kingdom of Yeshua.

There will be at least a three-pronged attack against Israel, most likely related to the fact that there are three frog demons bringing them together from all over the earth. The armies of Gog and Magog come down from the north. Another part of the armies comes over the dried-up Euphrates from the east to Jezreel. A third part will probably disembark at the west or Mediterranean end of the valley. As the armies are assembling, working out communications and a battle plan, Yeshua interrupts and destroys them all. The little horn will be thinking he is going to thresh Jerusalem, but he will instead be surprised when he is caught in the winepress of God's wrath.

Before this, somewhere in the first half of the one week covenant with many by the little horn, the two witnesses are preaching in Jerusalem and causing fits for the little horn's efforts to build his kingdom. The trumpet judgments are warnings that the little horn will blame on the witnesses.

At the half-way mark of the seven-year covenant, the deceiver pushes the little horn over the top by giving him all of his power, and the little horn is then able to kill the witnesses. This kicks off the bowl judgments pretty close to the same time.

2 Thessalonians 2:8–10 ESV. And then the lawless one will be revealed, whom the Lord Jesus will kill with the breath of his mouth and bring to nothing by the appearance of his coming. The coming of the lawless one is by the activity of Satan with all power and false signs and wonders, and with all wicked deception for those who are perishing, because they refused to love the truth and so be saved.

The bowl judgments slow the beast down quite a bit, but he finally makes his move to challenge God and consolidate his worldwide kingdom by gathering armies to squash Israel. Yeshua accepts the challenge, resurrects His army, and perhaps at this time touches down on the Mount of Olives. It splits in half, part moving north and part moving south, forming a valley apparently to allow the remaining people in Jerusalem to flee down it.

Zechariah 14:1–6 ESV. Behold, a day is coming for the LORD, when the spoil taken from you will be divided in your midst. For I will gather all the nations against Jerusalem to battle, and the city shall be taken and the houses plundered and the women raped. Half of the city shall go out into exile, but the rest of the people shall not be cut off from the city. Then the LORD will go out and fight against those nations as when he fights on a day of battle. On that day his feet shall stand on the Mount of Olives that lies before Jerusalem on the east, and the Mount of Olives shall be split in two from east to west by a very wide valley, so that one half of the Mount shall move northward, and the other half southward. And you shall flee to the valley of my mountains, for the valley of the mountains shall reach to Azal. And you shall flee as you fled from the earthquake in the days of Uzziah king of Judah. Then the LORD my God will come, and all the holy ones with him. On that day there shall be no light, cold, or frost.

There's a huge world-altering earthquake, the sun is darkened and the moon turned to blood, and Yeshua swings on over from the Mount of Olives to the Valley of Decision, executing final judgment on the world's armies, annihilating them by the breath of His coming.

Zechariah 14:12–13 ESV. And this shall be the plague with which the LORD will strike all the peoples that wage war against Jerusalem: their flesh will rot while they are still standing on their feet, their eyes will rot in their sockets, and their tongues will rot in their mouths. And on that day a great panic from the LORD shall fall on them, so that each will seize the hand of another, and the hand of the one will be raised against the hand of the other.

The blood flows as high as a horse's bridle in the Valley, probably because of bodies piled everywhere blocking the drainage. The marriage supper of the Lamb takes place in the plain of Jezreel, where all the carrion birds gather to start body disposal.

Revelation 14:20 ESV. And the winepress was trodden outside the city, and blood flowed from the winepress, as high as a horse's bridle, for 1,600 stadia.

A stadion was about 607 feet, so 1,600 stadia is about 184 miles. The height of a horse's bridle is about three and a half to four feet. That's a lot of blood. Those countries sending armies are going to think that Israel is defenseless (without walls) and full of goodies to plunder. They are going to gather in that valley north of Israel called by several names such as the Valley of Decision, the Valley of Jehoshaphat, the plain of Jezreel, and also the Valley of Vision (Isaiah 22:5).

Joel 3:14–15 ESV. Multitudes, multitudes, in the valley of decision! For the day of the LORD is near in the valley of decision. The sun and the moon are darkened, and the stars withdraw their shining.

Armageddon is the end of world governments or kingdoms, but it is not the end of God's plans. It is a huge battle, but not the last battle. It is one judgment among many judgments, and not even the most spectacular of judgments. At the end of the 1,000 year kingdom of Yeshua there is another large uprising led by the newly released-from-jail deceiver. This rebellion is put down in perhaps a more spectacular fashion when fire falls from heaven.

Refusal to Repent

A directive from Yeshua to repent marks the seven letters to congregations of believers. God starts with His own people, giving a command to straighten up and fly right as parents are wont to say. In fact, one of the major themes of the whole book is repentance, or lack of it. God gives people chances to repent all through the opening of the seals, the blowing of trumpets or the pouring out of bowls. It is so tragic that they don't.

Revelation 9:20–21 ESV. The rest of mankind, who were not killed by these plagues, did not repent of the works of their hands nor give up worshiping demons and idols of gold and silver and bronze and stone and wood, which cannot see or hear or walk, nor did they repent of their murders or their sorceries or their sexual immorality or their thefts.

God is merciful, loving and just, and keeps giving the people of the world chances to change, yet most refuse. Even in the terrible events of the Tribulation, they harden their hearts and refuse to give God glory rightfully His. They stubbornly follow their own ways instead of the wonderful, life giving, loving and holy ways of God. How sad is it that people cling to death and separation from God instead of entering into eternal life?

9 Resurrection & Rapture

Revelation 20:4-6 NASB95. [4]Then I saw thrones, and they sat on them, and judgment was given to them. And I *saw* the souls of those who had been beheaded because of their testimony of Jesus and because of the word of God, and those who had not worshiped the beast or his image, and had not received the mark on their forehead and on their hand; and they came to life and reigned with Christ for a thousand years. [5]The rest of the dead did not come to life until the thousand years were completed. This is the first resurrection. [6]Blessed and holy is the one who has a part in the first resurrection; over these the second death has no power, but they will be priests of God and of Christ and will reign with Him for a thousand years.

After going through all the possible horrible stuff that is going to happen when God's judgments fall on the kingdoms of the world, at this point you're probably looking for more hope or reassurance that God isn't going to include believers in the festivities. So in this chapter, Scripture is presented that will give you some. Just remember that our lives are hidden in Yeshua and He will take care of us, whatever happens.

In this chapter, we'll go back to fill in some details concerning the biblical position on something called the rapture, and its relation to the resurrection. The rapture is a familiar term for many Christians, but for those of you who might not know what it is here's a brief explanation.

The rapture is a minor event mentioned off-handed by Paul, as he comforts the congregation in the city of Thessalonica concerning the inclusion of dead believers in the kingdom of heaven. They were worried that Yeshua would return very soon to establish the kingdom, and believers who were dead or "fallen asleep" would not be a part of it. Paul corrects their understanding by telling them it's the other way around. He says before the kingdom is established dead believers will be resurrected first, and then living believers will get their new bodies too.

1 Thessalonians 4:13-18 NASB95. ¹³But we do not want you to be uninformed, brethren, about those who are asleep, so that you will not grieve as do the rest who have no hope. ¹⁴For if we believe that Jesus died and rose again, even so God will bring with Him those who have fallen asleep in Jesus. ¹⁵For this we say to you by the word of the Lord, that we who are alive and remain until the coming of the Lord, will not precede those who have fallen asleep. ¹⁶For the Lord Himself will descend from heaven with a shout, with the voice of *the* archangel and with the trumpet of God, and the dead in Christ will rise first. ¹⁷Then we who are alive and remain will be caught up together with them in the clouds to meet the Lord in the air, and so we shall always be with the Lord. ¹⁸Therefore comfort one another with these words.

The Greek word for "caught up" in verse 17 is *harpazo* (Strong's G726). The Latin word for *harpazo* is *rapturo* which is where we get the English word "rapture." Paul explains further in another well-known verse to the Corinthians that this "catching up" or rapture will happen quickly right *after* the dead in Christ are resurrected. As it is written:

1 Corinthians 15:50-52 NASB95. ⁵⁰Now I say this, brethren, that flesh and blood cannot inherit the kingdom of God; nor does the perishable inherit the imperishable. ⁵¹Behold, I tell you a mystery; we will not all sleep, but we will all be changed, ⁵²in a moment, in the twinkling of an eye, at the last trumpet; for the trumpet will sound, and the dead will be raised imperishable, and we will be changed.

As part of the resurrection where believers get new bodies, any believers living at the time are also changed from a flesh and blood body to a spiritual body, one like Yeshua's. He was able to walk through walls and fly, but He could also eat and be touched as if He was solid. Living believers change in the rapture suddenly, in the "twinkling of an eye," to meet Yeshua from wherever they happen to be at the time. This body change can be thought of as a sort of death.

The Day of the Lord or Tribulation is not your average, run of the mill war or series of judgments. It is a time when God judges and makes war against all those who have rejected Him, and will be like nothing ever seen before. It is a horrible time according to the Word, so the prospect of getting yanked out of here before it starts is quite appealing. But it's clearly wrong according to Scripture.

The Last Trump

Paul mentions a trumpet which announces the resurrection and the rapture, and he calls it the "last trumpet." Many people have struggled to identify this trumpet. Is it the seventh trumpet of the trumpet judgments in Revelation? Or is it the last trumpet blast of a regular daily call to worship at the temple? Perhaps it isn't even mentioned elsewhere in the Word. Most of the Church misses the meaning here because they do not know Scripture, do not practice it, and think of themselves as something special and different from Israel. It is apparent that the last trumpet is the final blast sounded on the Day of Atonement.

Leviticus 25:9 ESV. Then you shall sound the loud trumpet on the tenth day of the seventh month. On the Day of Atonement you shall sound the trumpet throughout all your land.

This trumpet call is the last one listed for the regular annual holidays of God described in Leviticus 23, and is the last of the formal holiday trumpet blasts before the year of Jubilee. Not counting, of course, trumpets sounded for the Sabbath, new moons, and just because you're happy. The events of Revelation track with the fall feasts (Trumpets, Atonement and Tabernacles), so it makes sense that the "last trump" is the last one on Yom Kippur.

As mentioned before, the Trumpets holiday is partly to announce impending doom for worldly kingdoms and give warning to repent (i.e. the Letters and Seals). Yom Kippur is a rehearsal for the Day of the Lord or day of smoke and burning, and Tabernacles reminds us of the 1,000 year kingdom reign of Yeshua on earth. Yom Teruah or feast of Trumpets is on the first day of the month, Atonement is ten days later, and Tabernacles starts five days after that. This gives us an idea of the timing between the warnings, the day of smoke and burning, and the thousand-year holiday equated to Tabernacles.

Every fiftieth year in Israel is to be a Sabbath year, as well as a year to "proclaim liberty throughout the land to all its inhabitants" (Leviticus 25:10). Property is returned to the clans, people are freed from servitude, and nobody plants or reaps. The last trump spoken of by Paul is known to those believers because no further explanation is given (although this might be dismissed by some as an "argument from silence"). It is the trumpet on the Day of Atonement, in the 49th year, which also announced the year of Jubilee. The millennial kingdom of Yeshua is like the year of Jubilee, in that freedom is proclaimed and everyone that belongs to Him rests. It's a "seventh day" of a thousand year Sabbath coming after the six thousand-year days of this age.

The Timing of the Rapture

There really isn't that much argument in most Church circles over whether believers are changed or raptured; the arguments are mostly just over the *timing*. It is a popular teaching around The Church nowadays that the rapture will take place *before* that time known as The Tribulation or The Day of the Lord. But when we actually read the Word, this philosophy of men doesn't hold water. It is used as an encouragement to repent and join The Church so one can be "saved" and miss the horrible events of the Tribulation, but this teaching wasn't used by the apostles to encourage repentance. See for instance Peter's sermon of Acts 2.

There are a number of philosophies about the timing of the rapture. The one just mentioned is the pre-trib (meaning before the seven-year tribulation). There is mid-trib (or pre-wrath) theory meaning in the middle, and the post-trib theory is for those who think it occurs after the tribulation. Some people have a theory which attempts to spread the rapture around. According to them, super righteous people get the pre-trib ticket, medium righteous people get a mid-trib slot, and the not-so-righteous get it in the end.

A tongue in cheek theory is the 'pan tribulation rapture' meaning it will all pan out in the end. All of these are built on a few verses and a whole lot of speculation. Or lame attempts at comedy implying that studying Scripture doesn't matter. Some spiritualized interpretations profess that the rapture is not really an instant change, or that it has already happened. These we can safely ignore, because they obviously aren't paying attention to the plain meaning of God's Word.

In an argument with a former friend, who was a post-tribulation person, he couldn't make any headway at the time in the discussion because he wasn't using or following the whole Bible. He was closer to the truth than many, but would have made more of an impression if he had been more complete. A whole Bible argument shows that, according to the Book, the rapture is something quite different than many have believed.

One major Scriptural truth that throws a monkey wrench in these arguments is that the rapture is definitely *after* the resurrection of the righteous, which we'll talk about in a minute. Yeshua clearly gives us the timing of the resurrection and rapture recorded for us by Luke. Yeshua says His coming is after "the powers in heaven are shaken," and *then* our redemption will occur.

> Luke 21:25–28 ESV. "And there will be signs in sun and moon and stars, and on the earth distress of nations in perplexity because of the roaring of the sea and the waves, people fainting with fear and with foreboding of what is coming on the world. For the powers of the heavens will be shaken. And then they will see the Son of Man coming in a cloud with power and great glory. Now when these things begin to take place, straighten up and raise your heads, because your redemption is drawing near."

Yeshua also tells us to "look up," which means that there are living believers at the time. Since those people do not "precede" the dead in Christ, but are "caught up after" the dead are resurrected, the so-called rapture is at the end of the Tribulation.

> 1 Thessalonians 4:15–18 ESV. For this we declare to you by a word from the Lord, that we who are alive, who are left until the coming of the Lord, will not precede those who have fallen asleep. For the Lord himself will descend from heaven with a cry of command, with the voice of an archangel, and with the sound of the trumpet of God. And the dead in Christ will rise first. Then we who are alive, who are left, will be caught up together with them in the clouds to meet the Lord in the air, and so we will always be with the Lord. Therefore encourage one another with these words.

Learning to place our faith in God and not philosophies of men, we will find comfort and protection in His Word instead of our own understanding. It is certain that most will not be happy with the biblical truth presented here about the rapture. The philosophy of a pre-tribulation rapture in particular is defended by many quite ferociously. However, if we let the Word penetrate into all areas of life, we see that all we thought we knew is not all there is.

Wrath and the Rapture

Two other references factor in to the rapture debate when Paul tells believers we are not "destined for wrath." It is written:

1 Thessalonians 1:10 NASB95. and to wait for His Son from heaven, whom He raised from the dead, *that is* Jesus, who rescues us from the wrath to come.

1 Thessalonians 5:9-11 NASB95. [9]For God has not destined us for wrath, but for obtaining salvation through our Lord Jesus Christ, [10]who died for us, so that whether we are awake or asleep, we will live together with Him. [11]Therefore encourage one another and build up one another, just as you also are doing.

Believers are delivered from a wrath that is God's, which is way scarier than man's wrath. The main wrath we are delivered from is that which is directed at unrepentant sinners in the form of the lake of fire or eternal death. The rapture theories change timing depending on how much of, and when, God's wrath is unleashed during the tribulation (at the front, in the middle, or at the end). The pre-trib rapture theory assumes that God's wrath is poured out on the earth during the entire seven-year tribulation, while the mid-trib theory postulates that the wrath of God starts in the middle (hence the other name of "pre-wrath" rapture). The post-trib theory figures on protection through the tribulation for believers, while the other theories have various mixes of these three. The complete biblical truth is that the rapture is a post-resurrection event.

God's wrath is obviously being poured out during the entire group of seven trumpet judgments, perhaps with some restraint, so His anger is not reserved only for the second half of the tribulation. It gets more intense with the bowls, but still is distributed all over (probably on the beast's kingdom). There are other ways to be protected from God's wrath, which are presented in the next pages.

Paul's reference to "Jesus, who rescues us from the wrath to come," needs a definition of "rescue" and "wrath." There are those teachers who think "rescue" means "rapture," and "wrath" means the wrath in the Tribulation. However, Paul defines "salvation" as deliverance from the wrath of God in 1 Thessalonians 5:9. So rescue from wrath most probably means rescued from God's wrath against unrepentant sinners in salvation. It does not mean rescued from the wrath of man during the Tribulation.

Believers are rescued or saved from the wrath of a holy and righteous God who will not continue to abide the presence of evil in His Kingdom forever. Yeshua will rescue us from God's wrath by the blood of His sacrifice on the cross. We still have to endure man's wrath, although Yeshua may also rescue believers by hiding them when things get really terrible on the Day of the Lord too. See the section coming up on **"Hidden from Wrath."**

The Resurrection

The rapture itself might not be mentioned in Scripture very much, but it is obviously appended to the resurrection, and the resurrection *is* mentioned a whole bunch.

Daniel 12:1-3 NASB95. ¹"Now at that time Michael, the great prince who stands *guard* over the sons of your people, will arise. And there will be a time of distress such as never occurred since there was a nation until that time; and at that time your people, everyone who is found written in the book, will be rescued. ²"Many of those who sleep in the dust of the ground will awake, these to everlasting life, but the others to disgrace *and* everlasting contempt. ³"Those who have insight will shine brightly like the brightness of the expanse of heaven, and those who lead the many to righteousness, like the stars forever and ever.

Ezekiel 37:12-14 NASB95. ¹²"Therefore prophesy and say to them, 'Thus says the Lord God, "Behold, I will open your graves and cause you to come up out of your graves, My people; and I will bring you into the land of Israel. ¹³"Then you will know that I am the Lord, when I have opened your graves and caused you to come up out of your graves, My people. ¹⁴"I will put My Spirit within you and you will come to life, and I will place you on your own land. Then you will know that I, the Lord, have spoken and done it," declares the Lord.' "

John 5:28-29 NASB95. ²⁸"Do not marvel at this; for an hour is coming, in which all who are in the tombs will hear His voice, ²⁹and will come forth; those who did the good *deeds* to a resurrection of life, those who committed the evil *deeds* to a resurrection of judgment.

Acts 24:14-15 NASB95. ¹⁴"But this I admit to you, that according to the Way which they call a sect I do serve the God of our fathers, believing everything that is in accordance with the Law and that is written in the Prophets; ¹⁵having a hope in God, which these men cherish themselves, that there shall certainly be a resurrection of both the righteous and the wicked.

Philippians 3:8-11 NASB95. ⁸More than that, I count all things to be loss in view of the surpassing value of knowing Christ Jesus my Lord, for whom I have suffered the loss of all things, and count them but rubbish so that I may gain Christ, ⁹and may be found in Him, not having a righteousness of my own derived from *the* Law, but that which is through faith in Christ, the righteousness which *comes* from God on the basis of faith, ¹⁰that I may know Him and the power of His resurrection and the fellowship of His sufferings, being conformed to His death; ¹¹in order that I may attain to the resurrection from the dead.

There have been some resurrections[2] in the Scriptures (see the footnote below for the references), but the problem was the people who were resurrected all died again. They did not receive imperishable bodies as Paul puts it in 1 Corinthians 15. After The Resurrection, no one dies again because they are given new bodies. Yeshua was the first resurrected person that went the whole way and isn't going back.

---

[2] 2 Kings 4:32 and verses following; Matthew 27:52-53 (tombs opened after crucifixion); Mark 5:41-42 (synagogue official's 12 year-old daughter; Luke 7:14-15 (an only son); John 11:1-46 (Lazarus); Acts 9:40 (Tabitha).

Three Phases of Resurrection

The resurrection has three phases summed up by Paul in Corinthians. 1 Corinthians 15 is known as the "resurrection chapter."

1 Corinthians 15:22-26 NASB95. ²²For as in Adam all die, so also in Christ all will be made alive. ²³But each in his own order: Christ the first fruits, after that those who are Christ's at His coming, ²⁴then *comes* the end, when He hands over the kingdom to the God and Father, when He has abolished all rule and all authority and power. ²⁵For He must reign until He has put all His enemies under His feet. ²⁶The last enemy that will be abolished is death.

Yeshua is called the "first fruits" and is part one of the first phase, which is the resurrection of the righteous. The resurrection of the righteous includes those who belong to the Christ and happens at His coming just before Armageddon. The second (or third) phase of the resurrection includes all the non-righteous or dead wicked people. As it is written:

Matthew 13:40-42 NASB95. ⁴⁰"So just as the tares are gathered up and burned with fire, so shall it be at the end of the age. ⁴¹"The Son of Man will send forth His angels, and they will gather out of His kingdom all stumbling blocks, and those who commit lawlessness, ⁴²and will throw them into the furnace of fire; in that place there will be weeping and gnashing of teeth. (See also Matthew 13:49-50, 22:13, 24:51, 25:30; Luke 13:28; compare to Acts 7:54)

It is important to note that everyone ever created is resurrected. Some stay with the God they love. Later, the people who hate Him go to the lake of fire. There is no annihilation, no reincarnation, and no purgatory-style second chances.

Here's a little secret: this present life *is* purgatory. Here is where we make the decision to follow or not to follow. Now is the time; today is the day. How hard is it to follow God? He is life, and without Him, we are dead. So how is following Him a hard decision? Every word He says and we follow takes us away from death. If we take too much time, if we wait too long to make a choice, the decision is made for us. What, is it really that difficult to do good things and avoid bad things as defined by Him?

People end up where they want to go, because the haters just cannot stop hating. This is the reason there is "weeping and gnashing of teeth" in the lake of fire. All three reactions (with 'wailing' in some verses) are from anger at God, and indicate anything but a repentant heart. This reaction is from the nature of hate and the pride that drives it. If people don't repent in this life they will be so hardened that it continues forever. God assigns them a place suitable for their hatred and anger. They pick the lake of fire because they completely refuse to associate with God in any way. In His kindness, He won't make anyone be with Him that doesn't want Him.

What Does 'Coming' Mean?

Notice that the resurrection of the righteous is "at His coming." The second coming of the Christ is documented in several places besides Luke 21, notably Matthew 24.

Matthew 24:26-27 NASB95. [26]"So if they say to you, 'Behold, He is in the wilderness,' do not go out, *or,* 'Behold, He is in the inner rooms,' do not believe *them.* [27]"For just as the lightning comes from the east and flashes even to the west, so will the coming of the Son of Man be.

Matthew 24:29-31 NASB95. [29]"But immediately after the tribulation of those days the sun will be darkened, and the moon will not give its light, and the stars will fall from the sky, and the powers of the heavens will be shaken. [30]"And then the sign of the Son of Man will appear in the sky, and then all the tribes of the earth will mourn, and they will see the Son of Man coming on the clouds of the sky with power and great glory. [31]"And He will send forth His angels with a great trumpet and they will gather together His elect from the four winds, from one end of the sky to the other.

The coming of the Son of Man the second time is much more visible than the first, when He showed up without much fanfare as a little baby. Lightning is a spectacular display; visible for miles and miles, so when He visits again it will be a huge event. There is no stealth mode for the second coming of Yeshua.

2 Thessalonians 2:1-12 NASB95. ¹Now we request you, brethren, with regard to the coming of our Lord Jesus Christ and our gathering together to Him, ²that you not be quickly shaken from your composure or be disturbed either by a spirit or a message or a letter as if from us, to the effect that the day of the Lord has come. ³Let no one in any way deceive you, for *it will not come* unless the apostasy comes first, and the man of lawlessness is revealed, the son of destruction, ⁴who opposes and exalts himself above every so-called god or object of worship, so that he takes his seat in the temple of God, displaying himself as being God. ⁵Do you not remember that while I was still with you, I was telling you these things? ⁶And you know what restrains him now, so that in his time he will be revealed. ⁷For the mystery of lawlessness is already at work; only he who now restrains *will do so* until he is taken out of the way. ⁸Then that lawless one will be revealed whom the Lord will slay with the breath of His mouth and bring to an end by the appearance of His coming; ⁹*that is,* the one whose coming is in accord with the activity of Satan, with all power and signs and false wonders, ¹⁰and with all the deception of wickedness for those who perish, because they did not receive the love of the truth so as to be saved. ¹¹For this reason God will send upon them a deluding influence so that they will believe what is false, ¹²in order that they all may be judged who did not believe the truth, but took pleasure in wickedness.

In Revelation 19:8 we see the Bride of Christ wearing "fine linen, bright and pure, for fine linen is the righteous deeds of the saints." Then in 19:14 we see "the armies of heaven, arrayed in fine linen, white and pure," following Yeshua. The armies of Yeshua attack the armies of the little horn in the Valley of Decision or the battle of Armageddon, so it seems the resurrection and rapture has occurred before this point.

In the Air or On the Ground

Some try to split hairs about the coming of Yeshua by making a case for different meanings out of the Greek words *parousia* (pah-roos-ee-ah G3952)[3] and *erchomai* (air-ko-my G2064).[4] They want *parousia* to mean 'in the presence of' (such as 'in the air' after rapture) and *erchomai* to mean actually setting foot back on earth. One type is said to be 'coming in the clouds' and the other is supposedly when He actually sets foot on the earth to establish His kingdom. But it is obvious that these different words (and there are others) simply mean 'return' or 'arrival' or even 'He's here.'

Mark 9:9 for instance uses *katabaino* (kah-tah-ba-ee-no G2597) which just means 'coming down' or 'descending.' *Parousia* is also used twice more in 2 Thessalonians 2:8 & 9 for both the coming of Yeshua and the coming of the man of lawlessness. There are not enough differences in these words to make separate meanings. The only reason to manufacture differences is to defend a conclusion (the timing of the rapture) that has been reached before the study is made. But if we just let the Bible speak for itself we can see the meaning clearly.

Notice another plain text argument against a pre-trib rapture in 2 Thessalonians 2:3-4 is that the "man of lawlessness" or "son of destruction" "takes his seat in the temple of God displaying himself as being God." Some people think this was the Roman emperor Nero. But while the Caesars usually claimed to be gods, none of them actually sat in the temple at Jerusalem and claimed to be God (it probably just wasn't that important to them).

---

[3] Used in 2 Thessalonians 2:1; 22 times translated 'coming' and twice 'presence' in the NT.
[4] Mark 8:38, 9:12, 10:45, 13:26, 14:41, 62; Luke 7:34, 9:56, 12:40, 17:22, 18:8, 19:10, 21:27; John 12:23 among others.

Antiochus IV Epiphanes (almost two hundred years before the Christ) had pigs sacrificed a number of times, possibly on the altar at the temple, as part of his effort to force Greek culture on all of his territories (including the Jewish ones). He put a statue of Zeus (which is who he thought he was) in the temple, but he didn't actually sit in the temple AND claim to be the God of Abraham, Isaac and Jacob. The image also didn't talk. In some thinking, the beast might not actually need a temple (perhaps only a section or "wing" of the temple") but he does in fact claim to be God. Not just a god, but God.

There are two other techniques used to explain the apparent difference between the pre-trib rapture, and what the Word plainly teaches. One is to split the Body of Christ into Israel and the Church. The other is to add an additional 3½ year period on the front of the tribulation (for a total of 10½ years). The extra time was due to a little confusion in the text (for instance Daniel seems to say there are several roughly 3½ year periods) and because that way the Church can paint the rapture as happening at the end of one of those 'tribulation sections' but before the really bad stuff got going. In the Word however, it is plain there is only one Body or Bride (remnant, etc.). Any confusion over timing is due to philosophies of men imposing a pet theory over the plain meaning of the text.

Since the rapture is appended to the resurrection of the righteous, and the resurrection of the righteous happens at His coming towards the end of the tribulation, then the rapture very obviously happens also near the end of the tribulation. Church teachers are trying to read a pre-trib position into the Scripture and splitting a lot of hairs to do it. If we just read the Word, it is plain what happens. What messes up the interpretation is when we don't want to accept the plain meaning.

So what happens after we are raptured? Do we meet Yeshua in the clouds, then return to earth? The answer is: we go wherever He wants to go! Humor aside, it would seem from the resurrection passages that He gathers us from all over the world in the clouds as He is getting ready to descend, then we come down with Him to do some work. He calls all of His people from all ages together to help with the job. Deuteronomy 33:2, Jude 14, and Revelation 19:14, 19, and 20:4, point to believers as part of the army He uses in the final battle. It makes sense that He would gather His armies before He comes back to clean house.

Taken

In Matthew 24, Luke 17 and Luke 21 Yeshua gives us an outline of what will take place at the "end of the age" as the apostles asked. At one point in the first two references Yeshua says, "Two men will be in the field, one will be taken and one left. Two women will be grinding at the mill, one will be taken and one left." Most churchgoers think these are verses about the rapture. There was a nifty song in the '70's that spoke of people being taken in the rapture (I Wish We'd All Been Ready by Larry Norman). The people remaining were "left behind." It's an attractive thought, but wrong. It is clear from the context that 'taken' means destroyed.

Yeshua compares this time to the time of the flood, when people were going about their daily living as sudden destruction came. "They were unaware until the flood came and swept them all away." If the proportion (50% or one taken the other left) is intended to be exact, that means at least half the world's population will be destroyed.

There are other places where 'taken' is obviously related to destroyed or killed, and to exile or captivity.

Jeremiah 6:11, ESV. Therefore I am full of the wrath of the Lord; I am weary of holding it in. "Pour it out upon the children in the street, and upon the gatherings of young men, also; both husband and wife shall be taken, the elderly and the very aged.

To be "taken" is not a fun thing. To be consistent with the rest of the Word, 'taken' in the context of what Yeshua is talking about is not fun at all. It is not related to the rapture, but to the winepress of God's fury.

In 1 Samuel 14, we have another example of "taken" in the negative sense. The son of Saul, by the name of Jonathan, had eaten some honey not knowing that his dad had charged Israel not to eat anything until they had vanquished the Philistines. Saul inquired of the Lord for a battle decision, but the Lord didn't answer. Saul thinks it's because of something Israel did wrong, so he has the people go through a selection process (called the "lot") to find out who did the wrong. In each phase of the process going through the tribes, clans, families and individuals, it is said that the offending group is "taken." Finally, the Lord "takes" Jonathan.

1 Samuel 14:41 ESV. Therefore Saul said, "O LORD God of Israel, why have you not answered your servant this day? If this guilt is in me or in Jonathan my son, O LORD, God of Israel, give Urim. But if this guilt is in your people Israel, give Thummim." And Jonathan and Saul were taken, but the people escaped.

So it seems that the word "taken" means those who have done wrong (even unwittingly) are destroyed. It does not mean a positive thing, such as that "taken" means "raptured." More likely, those "taken" are the wicked.

The Church in Revelation 4-19

The Church in general is defined in the first chapter of this book, but here we'll go over a big argument used for the pre-trib rapture position (and maybe the mid-trib also). The argument is that the Church isn't mentioned between Revelation chapter 4 and chapter 19. The supposition is that The Church isn't mentioned because it is gone in the rapture.

But here's a fun fact for you that was mentioned before: the Church is not only missing in those chapters, it is not mentioned anywhere in the Bible at all. It exists only in translations and the imaginations of Church Nicolaitans. The word "church" was a word coined somewhere in Catholic history to try and reinforce her control over ecclesiastical things. The King James translation of the Bible in fact was not accepted by Protestants for a long time because of the use of the word church (among other problems).

The Body, however, is mentioned a bunch in Revelation 6-18, just not by that label, and certainly not by the extra-biblical label "Church." In Revelation 12, she is just in a bit of a disguise.

Revelation 12:1-2 NASB95. [1]A great sign appeared in heaven: a woman clothed with the sun, and the moon under her feet, and on her head a crown of twelve stars; [2]and she was with child; and she cried out, being in labor and in pain to give birth.

This is Israel, but she is the Body that believes and follows Yeshua. How to tell? She gives birth to the Messiah ("who is to rule all the nations with a rod of iron" verse 5). The actual person who gave birth to Yeshua (the seed of the woman) was Mary, who is part of the Body of Christ. All the believing people to that point (prophets, patriarchs, martyrs, etc.) were glad participants in the birth either by looking forward to it or recognizing it when it was here and rejoicing. The woman's crown of twelve stars is more obviously the 12 apostles (they show up again in the foundation stones of the New Jerusalem). The next mention of the Body is in Revelation 12.

Revelation 12:17 NASB95. ¹⁷So the dragon was enraged with the woman, and went off to make war with the rest of her children, who keep the commandments of God and hold to the testimony of Jesus.

The "rest of her children" are part of the Body for two reasons. One is that they are children of the woman clothed with the sun (believing Israel) and the second is they "hold to the testimony of Yeshua." It's tempting to say that these were only converted Jews (converted after the rapture) because they "keep the commandments." But this is biblically inconsistent. Believers who hold to the testimony of Yeshua also keep the commandments. The unconverted do neither, or sometimes appear to do only one or the other. And unconverted Jews actually do not keep the commandments any more than they hold to the testimony of Yeshua. Compare Revelation 12:17 to Revelation 1:2, 9, 19:10 and 20:4 and you'll see that it is the Body of Christ being described in each situation.

In my first 20 years of life, I was part of several dozen families, from multiple step-fathers to foster homes and adoption. Part of these experiences included attendance at many different churches and schools that were using His name. By the time I started my own family I had learned a hugely important lesson. When trying to figure out who is in your family, church or otherwise, the determining factor is that *family acts like family*.

Blood or genetics is not the identifier of family. Adoption papers are not the identifier. Living with a person called mom or dad or sibling is not the identifier. It's not Judaism or Church. The identifier is that *family acts like family*. The people in the assembly, body, olive tree, grapevine, or whatever of Yeshua are known by their actions. His people act as if they are His people. When you want to know who to depend on for help in good times and bad, the people who hold to the whole of God's Word and act like it are in His family.

Another place that members of the Body are mentioned is when the fifth seal of the scroll is opened.

Revelation 6:9-11 NASB95. ⁹When the Lamb broke the fifth seal, I saw underneath the altar the souls of those who had been slain because of the word of God, and because of the testimony which they had maintained; ¹⁰and they cried out with a loud voice, saying, "How long, O Lord, holy and true, will You refrain from judging and avenging our blood on those who dwell on the earth?" ¹¹And there was given to each of them a white robe; and they were told that they should rest for a little while longer, until *the number of* their fellow servants and their brethren who were to be killed even as they had been, would be completed also.

We might think that these also must be Jews, because believers don't have anything to do with an altar. That was in the temple, and Jews were in charge of it. However, this is the Temple in heaven, not on the earth. It is God's permanent temple, not a temporary one. The souls have been killed because of the word of God and "the testimony which they had maintained." This testimony is the testimony of Yeshua with a life lived by all of His commandments.

The Word on the page and the Word in the flesh (Yeshua) are what get people killed, because the world cannot stand either one. Unbelieving Jews were killing believing Jews long before Yeshua and Acts chapter 7; also, unbelieving Gentiles kill believers when they get the chance. This picture in Revelation includes almost all of them. Apparently, there are a set number of martyrs known to God, and these souls are waiting for the remainder of their brethren. They are given white robes, just like the multitude in Revelation 7:14 who have robes that are white from washing in the blood of the Lamb.

Speaking of the multitude in Revelation 7, that group is another place where believers (the Body) are mentioned.

Revelation 7:13-14 NASB95. [13]Then one of the elders answered, saying to me, "These who are clothed in the white robes, who are they, and where have they come from?" [14]I said to him, "My lord, you know." And he said to me, "These are the ones who come out of the great tribulation, and they have washed their robes and made them white in the blood of the Lamb.

This is one of the many places in the Bible where splitting up the Word into different ages and people groups doesn't make sense. This habit of men only succeeds in disconnecting events and peoples that should be considered together. In this Scripture, we need to remember the fact that the only people who "have washed their robes and made them white in the blood of the Lamb" are believers. Remember too, that the events in Revelation are not necessarily sequential, and definitely not all chronological. The vision of the multitude appears to be a jump to the end, where we get to see what ultimately happens to the Body as a whole.

A problem with identifying the beast comes in when people, especially those in The Church, look right past the obvious. They look everywhere except in the mirror. We are so blinded by men's teachings, traditions and philosophies that we don't recognize an important fact:

The Beast will be just as acceptable to the Church as to the general populace.

That is a shocking statement to those who think that The Church is taken away by a rapture before all the really bad stuff starts, like a fairy tale princess in a flying pumpkin coach. However, as Scripture so obviously states, the rapture without question is appended to the resurrection, and that resurrection clearly doesn't happen till the end of the Tribulation.

So The Church will be here during the tribulation. It's just not described in the way expected. That's the main boo boo in the whole identification process. She's right there with the other idolatrous religions riding on the dragon in Revelation 18. Many will not realize it at first, and many will be upset when they find out their leaders have been lying.

The typical churchgoer can't now (or will not later) properly identify the beast because they are not grounded on the Word, do not read it except for a few favorite verses, and refuse to do what it says. Instead, they have crafted for themselves a seeker-friendly social gospel that only vaguely resembles anything biblical. Their instead-of-Christ is a hippie flower-child letting everyone do what is right in their own eyes, looking like a lamb but speaking like a dragon.

We have leaders telling us that hell doesn't exist, parts of God's Word are old and irrelevant, men's traditions are the new covenant, and sexual immorality is approved by God. If these teachings don't sound like "tolerating that woman Jezebel" or allowing the teaching of Balaam and the Nicolaitans (Revelation 1-3), then perhaps more studying is needed.

The Church has watered down the message of God so much that it isn't even recognizable as God's. By and large, Nicolaitans have removed the whole nutrition of His Law from the message, and are therefore not grounded on the Rock. The Church will embrace the beast because of the false prophet who looks like a lamb (a churchgoer) but speaks like a dragon (teaches philosophies of men given them by the deceiver).

Meta Tauta, "After These Things"

The Greek phrase μετα ταυτα transliterated "*meta tauta*" (may-ta tao-tah) means "after this" or "after these things." We find it at the beginning of Revelation chapter 4, when John writes in the first verse "<u>After this</u> I looked, and behold, a door standing open in heaven." John uses it a second time in chapter 4 when recording the words of Yeshua to "Come up here, and I will show you what must take place <u>after this</u>." Some teachers make a big deal out of this phrase, trying to relate it to the rapture. Their idea is that after the "Church things" of the first three chapters of Revelation, the Church is raptured through the open door in heaven, sort of like John. To these teachers *meta tauta* is a definite transition meaning something special.

The only trouble with this idea is that the phrase doesn't mean anything special. It just means something like "next." John is merely saying that after he wrote the letters to the congregations, next he saw the events of chapters 4 through 6. At the beginning of chapter 7, we see the phrase again. And it still just means "next," as in "next I saw four angels standing at the four corners of the earth..." (Revelation 7:1). It's also in 7:9, 18:1, and 19:1.

It might be that this phrase shows us more than "next." It might be a break in the sequence of visions where John sees something out of sequence. So at the beginning of chapter 7 where the 144,000 are sealed might not be right after the events of chapter 6 where Yeshua opens the first six seals of the scroll. Revelation 7:9, where John sees the "great multitude from all tribes and peoples and languages," might also be a break in the sequence and might occur later in the Tribulation. Or not.

Most other times John uses a connector like "and" or "then" as in "then I saw" or "and I saw." Teachers who try to make a special meaning out of *meta tauta* have failed to make their case adequately due to the casual use of the phrase elsewhere in Scripture. False teachers come up with all sorts of twisted things to try and make their beliefs fit the Bible, but if you know the Word and follow it, you have the eye salve that helps you avoid the quicksand of spurious teachings.

Hidden From Wrath

In the section titled **The Endurance of the Saints**, we explored some things about believers who are subject to man's wrath. Here we cover some Scripture that seems to indicate how believers are hidden from God's wrath.

It is true that Paul says believers are not subject to God's wrath. This is one of the justifications for the pre-trib and mid-trib rapture philosophies.

1 Thessalonians 5:9–10, ESV. For God has not destined us for wrath, but to obtain salvation through our Lord Jesus Christ, who died for us so that whether we are awake or asleep we might live with him.

But there are at least two ways to apply Paul's statement. One is that God won't hammer believers with earthly judgments. The other is that believers escape God's wrath at the final judgment because that wrath already fell on His Son and our Messiah Yeshua. In other words, the wrath believers avoid could be the wrath we see in the book of Revelation and other prophecy (on earth), or it could be the wrath of a final judgment (in the kingdom of heaven), or both.

If we apply the 'earthly wrath' escape, rapture is not the only way to avoid His wrath falling on the non-believing part of earth's inhabitants. God could just as easily protect us in other ways. And the Scriptures support this possibility better than the rapture escape clause. It is written:

Zephaniah 2:3 NASB95. Seek the Lord, All you humble of the earth Who have carried out His ordinances; Seek righteousness, seek humility. Perhaps you will be hidden In the day of the Lord's anger.

Isaiah 26:19-21 NASB95. ¹⁹Your dead will live; Their corpses will rise. You who lie in the dust, awake and shout for joy, For your dew *is as* the dew of the dawn, And the earth will give birth to the departed spirits. ²⁰Come, my people, enter into your rooms And close your doors behind you; Hide for a little while Until indignation runs *its* course. ²¹For behold, the Lord is about to come out from His place To punish the inhabitants of the earth for their iniquity; And the earth will reveal her bloodshed And will no longer cover her slain.

Psalm 27:4-5 NASB95. ⁴One thing I have asked from the Lord, that I shall seek: That I may dwell in the house of the Lord all the days of my life, To behold the beauty of the Lord And to meditate in His temple. ⁵For in the day of trouble He will conceal me in His tabernacle; In the secret place of His tent He will hide me; He will lift me up on a rock.

So hiding is one of the ways that God could protect us from His wrath, much like Moses was protected from God's glory on Mt. Sinai (Exodus 33:22). Another way is for God to protect us as He did with Hananiah, Mishael, and Azariah (Shadrach, Meshach, and Abednego) in the furnace in Daniel chapter 3.

Isaiah 43:2 ESV. When you pass through the waters, I will be with you; and through the rivers, they shall not overwhelm you; when you walk through fire you shall not be burned, and the flame shall not consume you.

Daniel 3:26–27 ESV. Then Nebuchadnezzar came near to the door of the burning fiery furnace; he declared, "Shadrach, Meshach, and Abednego, servants of the Most High God, come out, and come here!" Then Shadrach, Meshach, and Abednego came out from the fire. And the satraps, the prefects, the governors, and the king's counselors gathered together and saw that the fire had not had any power over the bodies of those men. The hair of their heads was not singed, their cloaks were not harmed, and no smell of fire had come upon them.

Remember, Isaiah was written long before the events of the book of Daniel. This type of fire insurance takes a lot of trust and obedience, or what we call faith. We strengthen faith by knowing

His Word and doing what He says. Believers trust God to do what He says, because we know Him intimately through taking in His Words and doing every instruction to the best of our ability.

Whole Bible believers have rejected much of the standard Church teaching telling us to ignore huge chunks of the Word in favor of their man-made doctrine, which doesn't strengthen anyone. In fact, standard Churchgoers are going to be faltering left and right (mostly left) when the Tribulation hits, because they do not know God. They know their church doctrine, creeds, statements of faith, and the résumé of their pastors or rabbis, but not the Word.

Psalm 50:14-15 ESV. [14]Offer to God a sacrifice of thanksgiving, and perform your vows to the Most High, [15] and call upon me in the day of trouble; I will deliver you, and you shall glorify me."

Malachi 3:16-18 ESV. [16]Then those who feared the Lord spoke with one another. The Lord paid attention and heard them, and a book of remembrance was written before him of those who feared the Lord and esteemed his name. [17] "They shall be mine, says the Lord of hosts, in the day when I make up my treasured possession, and I will spare them as a man spares his son who serves him. [18] Then once more you shall see the distinction between the righteous and the wicked, between one who serves God and one who does not serve him.

Then we get to a passage in Revelation which is telling.

Revelation 12:6 NASB95. Then the woman fled into the wilderness where she had a place prepared by God, so that there she would be nourished for one thousand two hundred and sixty days.

As mentioned before, this passage is usually understood to be physical Israel because of Joseph's dream in Genesis 37:9-10.

[9]Now he had still another dream, and related it to his brothers, and said, "Lo, I have had still another dream; and behold, the sun and the moon and eleven stars were bowing down to me." [10]He related *it* to his father and to his brothers; and his father rebuked him and said to him, "What is

this dream that you have had? Shall I and your mother and your brothers actually come to bow ourselves down before you to the ground?" (Genesis 37:9-10 NASB95)

However, there are some major differences. In John's vision the woman is clothed with the sun, the moon is under her feet, and she has twelve stars as a crown. The child is Yeshua (Revelation 12:5 he "is to rule all the nations with a rod of iron") so the woman is not just Israel, but believing Israel.

Another possibility for protection from man's wrath is shown in the gathering of armies for Armageddon. The deceiver, little horn, and false Christ regurgitate unclean, demonic spirits like frogs which are sent to the kings of the whole world.

Revelation 16:13–14 ESV. And I saw, coming out of the mouth of the dragon and out of the mouth of the beast and out of the mouth of the false prophet, three unclean spirits like frogs. For they are demonic spirits, performing signs, who go abroad to the kings of the whole world, to assemble them for battle on the great day of God the Almighty.

It's going to take some time to gather the world's armies and send them to the plain of Jezreel or Valley of Jehoshaphat. The gathering and shipping will take many weeks. When the armies ship out, the places they leave (and where believers live) will be at peace for a while. This is reaching quite a bit, and has no solid support from Scripture. It's just an idea, and an example of things that can happen that we don't even see yet.

If we just read the Scriptures, it's obvious that the resurrection is the main event and the rapture is a post script. The resurrection of the righteous or the just is near the end of the tribulation, while the resurrection of the wicked is at the end of the 1,000 year reign of Yeshua on the earth. During the day of smoke and burning, also known as the Day of the Lord and time of

Jacob's trouble, it seems that God will provide a way to hide from His wrath if we listen and obey.

Joel 3:16 ESV. The LORD roars from Zion, and utters his voice from Jerusalem, and the heavens and the earth quake. But the LORD is a refuge to his people, a stronghold to the people of Israel.

Falling Away

Some would-be interpreters say that "falling away" is the rapture. This comes from a short comment by Paul to the Thessalonians in his second letter to them. If you remember at the start of the second chapter of 2 Thessalonians we read some words by Paul reassuring the Thessalonians that living believers would not be alone when Yeshua comes back. First there is a resurrection of all the righteous, and the living believers would be translated and join them. In the second letter to this congregation, Paul calms their anxiety about the timing of the day of the Lord.

2 Thessalonians 2:1–4 AV. Now we beseech you, brethren, by the coming of our Lord Jesus Christ, and by our gathering together unto him, That ye be not soon shaken in mind, or be troubled, neither by spirit, nor by word, nor by letter as from us, as that the day of Christ is at hand. Let no man deceive you by any means: for that day shall not come, except there come a falling away first, and that man of sin be revealed, the son of perdition; Who opposeth and exalteth himself above all that is called God, or that is worshipped; so that he as God sitteth in the temple of God, shewing himself that he is God.

The Greek word translated by "falling away" in the KJV is Strong's 646 ἀποστασία [*apostasia* /ap·os·tas·**ee**·ah/] which you might see is where we get the English word apostasy. The ESV translates this word as "rebellion;" perhaps a better description. Paul is very clearly not talking about a rapture. He is talking about an apostasy or departure from the faith on the part of those who claim to be followers of Yeshua.

The term "falling away" doesn't really fit people who are non-believers in the first place. It does, however, fit the people who claim to follow Yeshua but only give Him lip service. The Church in general doesn't see this because of various man-made teachings such as "once saved always saved." As if "raising the hand" and "going forward" is actually salvation.

Churchgoing Nicolaitans don't want to think of a wholesale departure of their congregants from the stuff they are teaching. But Paul is saying there will be a general apostasy or rebellion against God, led by man of lawlessness or son of destruction, also known as the beast. The bulk of The Church will be "falling away" and going right along with the rebellion.

There are also a couple of other time markers here. One is that the beast will sit in the Temple of God, and the second is that Yeshua will "kill him by the breath of His mouth and bring to nothing by the appearance of His coming." Since the subject is "our being gathered together to Him" then any rapture or resurrection would be at that time. As a side note, in Revelation 19:15 and 21, Yeshua is pictured with a sharp sword coming out of His mouth which is the Word of God.

End Like a Flood

Lamentations 3:31–33 AV. For the Lord will not cast off for ever: But though he cause grief, yet will he have compassion according to the multitude of his mercies. For he doth not afflict willingly nor grieve the children of men.

Yeshua in Matthew 24:37-39 says that the coming of the Son of Man will be like the days of Noah. He tells us that people then were going about their business, unaware of the watery destruction coming. Some try to paint a picture of the rapture from this section, yet it doesn't have anything to do with the rapture. It has to do with the coming of the Son of Man, which Yeshua clearly says in 24:36 is a surprise to everyone except believers.

The flood was a surprise too, except that Noah was building his huge boat for quite a while before the flood, and probably talking with whoever would listen. The coming of the Son of Man is clearly at the end of the tribulation according to verse 29 and 30 of the same chapter as the reference says: *"But immediately after the tribulation of those days…then the sign of the Son of Man will appear…all the tribes of the earth…will see the Son of Man coming."* Notice too that the initial rains lasted 40 days and it took over a year for the water to subside, indicating that while the onset of the judgment is sudden its effects last longer than a day or two. It doesn't take a rocket scientist to figure out what is happening. Yeshua uses this analogy because of the suddenness of the destruction, which even if spread out over seven years would still be sudden depending on the expectations of the people going through it.

However, if you believe in one of the extra-biblical theologies such as dispensationalism or covenantism, you may have a hard time seeing it. That's because the theologies get in the way of the Word. Bill Perkins of Compass International, for instance, has this to say in his short article "What Jesus Said About the Timing of the Rapture." "We believe Pre-Trib is the only time Rapture can occur if you are using a dispensational approach and interpret scripture using a literal hermeneutic."[5]

The wrong thing about this statement is that a "dispensational approach" to Scripture is applied over the text contrary to a literal hermeneutic. If you understand the Bible

---

[5] Bill Perkins, Executive Director of Compass International, Inc., "What Jesus Said About the Timing of the Rapture," booklet advertising the September 19, 2019 Steeling the Mind conference in Denver, Colorado, page 10.

literally, giving the words the meaning that was intended by the author, then it is obvious the rapture is appended to the resurrection, and the resurrection of the righteous doesn't happen until just before the 1,000 year kingdom of Yeshua.

Even though Bill says he uses a literal interpretation of the Word, in typical Nicolaitan fashion he also says in order to see things his way you have to add dispensationalism. In his system of belief, you can't just use the Bible by itself; you have to add something extra-biblical. This kind of stuff affects many people in The Church and blinds them to the truth of the Word. It isn't just Mr. Perkins, however. This teaching is common in the Church.

When one first figures out that the rapture is attached to the resurrection, and that the resurrection of the righteous is toward the end of the tribulation, it can be upsetting and the tendency is to ignore it. The Tribulation will be terrible, so the lack of a rapture before the main events is a scary thought. But by continually reading and doing His Word, gradual realization will dawn that our faith is in God and not in an outside-the-Bible Church rapture doctrine. God can be trusted to inform us of actions needed at the time they are needed (for instance, if He directs us to run or hide). He will protect our families, and no matter what happens, He will be there to comfort and care for us.

So there you have a survey of the rapture. It is obviously appended to the resurrection, and after Yeshua resurrected the rest of the resurrection happens in two phases. One is for the righteous when Yeshua comes back to set up His throne on earth for 1,000 years, and the other part is at the end of the thousand years. Then the wicked are cleaned out and assigned their eternal place away from the kingdom, prior to our Father making a new heavens and new earth. The hope here is that this has helped focus your studies on the Bible and away from the teachings of men that interfere.

10 Your God Reigns

Revelation 11:15, ESV Then the seventh angel blew his trumpet, and there were loud voices in heaven, saying, "The kingdom of the world has become the kingdom of our Lord and of his Christ, and he shall reign forever and ever."

With this announcement in Revelation 11:15, Yeshua officially takes the office of "King of kings and Lord of Lords," being in charge of the kingdoms of the world. That doesn't mean He isn't already in charge, or that He is coming back to earth right at that time. But it does mean that He is beginning to use the "rod of iron" with which He will break the anti-God kingdoms or government systems in heaven and on earth. The announcement comes at the seventh trumpet, but at this point in the narrative, the seven bowls are still to come and are part of the kingdom breaking. The "mountain cut out without hands" is going to strike the kingdoms of the world and turn them to dust.

The promise of a righteous king and kingdom is all through the Bible using many different words such as "blessing," "covenant," and "promise." Ever since Adam and Eve turned their backs on the rule of God in their lives, men have been trying to build their own kingdoms. These kingdoms have had varying degrees of rightness to them, but are largely characterized by forced obedience, bloodshed, and rebellion. Some of the kingdoms had some justice and peace of a sort. By and large, they all fell apart because the foundations were inadequate to the task. Even with the assistance of the deceiver and other spiritual forces of evil in the heavenly places, those kingdoms just couldn't hold together.

Without God and His Words, the substitutes of selfishness and immorality are pitifully weak glues, unable to bind blessing and health within the realms. When Yeshua takes over, the long awaited reign of God in all things is established. The groaning of creation waiting for redemption is stilled, and peace finally fills the world. But first, we have the marriage supper of the Lamb.

Marriage Supper of the Lamb

Psalm 79:2–3 ESV. They have given the bodies of your servants to the birds of the heavens for food, the flesh of your faithful to the beasts of the earth. They have poured out their blood like water all around Jerusalem, and there was no one to bury them.

Ezekiel 39:17 ESV. "As for you, son of man, thus says the Lord God: Speak to the birds of every sort and to all beasts of the field: 'Assemble and come, gather from all around to the sacrificial feast that I am preparing for you, a great sacrificial feast on the mountains of Israel, and you shall eat flesh and drink blood.

Revelation 19:7–9 ESV. Let us rejoice and exult and give him the glory, for the marriage of the Lamb has come, and his Bride has made herself ready; it was granted her to clothe herself with fine linen, bright and pure"— for the fine linen is the righteous deeds of the saints. And the angel said to me, "Write this: Blessed are those who are invited to the marriage supper of the Lamb." And he said to me, "These are the true words of God."

Revelation 19:16–18 ESV. On his robe and on his thigh he has a name written, King of kings and Lord of lords. Then I saw an angel standing in the sun, and with a loud voice he called to all the birds that fly directly overhead, "Come, gather for the great supper of God, to eat the flesh of kings, the flesh of captains, the flesh of mighty men, the flesh of horses and their riders, and the flesh of all men, both free and slave, both small and great."

After Yeshua sets foot on the Mount of Olives, He (or His armies or both) slaughters the armies gathered together at the Valley of Decision, also known as Armageddon. This slaughter is called the marriage supper of the Lamb. When first we read of the wedding feast or marriage supper of the Lamb, it sounds like a real party. It *is* a real party, but not for the beast and his armies. The

Marriage Supper is when the birds and beasts of every sort chow down on the remains of those slain in the Valley of Decision.

Many people confuse the banquet used as a symbol in a parable by Yeshua in Luke 14 with the marriage supper, but they are not the same event. The parable was used to illustrate some principles, and might apply to an actual banquet given by Yeshua in the millennial kingdom. But the only place that the term "marriage supper" is used is in our Revelation 19 reference.

The euphemism of birds of the air and beasts of the field eating the flesh shows that the slaughter is so great (and survivors so few) bodies can't be buried fast enough to keep carrion feeders from having a huge picnic.

A number of times God decrees that this type of thing will happen to Israel because she had forsaken Him, such as in Jeremiah 7:33, 9:10, 12:4-9, 15:3 and so on. It is also said of Egypt (Ezekiel 29, 31 and 32), Edom, princes of the north, the Sidonians, Gog and Magog (Ezekiel 38 and 39), Russia, Persia, Cush, Put, Gomer and Beth-togarmah. The difference is that the slaughter of Israel already happened, while the slaughter of the other nations has not (except perhaps for a minor war or two here and there).

In the "latter years," according to Ezekiel 38:7, there will be a different yet similar slaughter, not including Israel. It will be greater and involve many nations. There will be a "great earthquake" (Ezekiel 38:19) at the same time, which is the same earthquake as at the 6th seal and 7th bowl judgments.

You don't think that God would say slaughter like this is going to happen to Israel because of its idolatry, but the nations will escape, do you? Of course not. If He did it to Israel, how much more will He do it to peoples and nations that openly defy and attack Him or the apple of His eye?

The slaughter at Armageddon will result in blood as high as a horses bridle (Revelation 14:20). This is another way to describe the marriage supper of the Lamb. It is not a happy day for the kingdom of the deceiver and the beast. But it will be a happy and blessed day for those who were and are mercilessly persecuted and killed since Cain beat Able to death.

Yeshua Touches Down

As already mentioned, Zechariah tells us that right before the marriage supper Yeshua will set foot on the Mount of Olives and it will split in two. This is before the supper because armies are threatening Jerusalem and His people need to flee.

Zechariah 14:3–5 ESV. Then the LORD will go out and fight against those nations as when he fights on a day of battle. On that day his feet shall stand on the Mount of Olives that lies before Jerusalem on the east, and the Mount of Olives shall be split in two from east to west by a very wide valley, so that one half of the Mount shall move northward, and the other half southward. And you shall flee to the valley of my mountains, for the valley of the mountains shall reach to Azal. And you shall flee as you fled from the earthquake in the days of Uzziah king of Judah. Then the LORD my God will come, and all the holy ones with him.

The whole mountain splits in two, one half moving north and the other half moving south. There is an assumption that an earthquake occurs at the same time, and it seems to be related to the one described by John that will split Jerusalem into three parts (Revelation 16:19). The valley formed will be very wide and go from east to west a very long way, probably from the Dead Sea to the Mediterranean.

It's not certain that this valley is the same valley as "the valley of my mountains" from Zechariah 14:5. It could be that His people flee "to" the new valley created by Yeshua, because He is there. No one is sure of the location of Azal (or perhaps Azel).

Azel was a Benjamite, and his clan was in the south of Israel next to Judah, and it could be that this is a comment on the width of the valley. There's another valley mentioned in connection with the Mount of Olives valley by Joel called the Valley of Shittim. But that valley was already in existence.

Joel 3:18 ESV. And in that day the mountains shall drip sweet wine, and the hills shall flow with milk, and all the streambeds of Judah shall flow with water; and a fountain shall come forth from the house of the LORD and water the Valley of Shittim.

The Valley of Shittim ("place of acacias") is a part of the area north of the Dead Sea and may include Abel-shittim or "meadow of acacias." Shittim is mentioned in Numbers 25 as a camping place where Israel stayed for a while before crossing the Jordan and beginning the cleanup of the Promised Land. This "place of acacias" is where Balaam incited the people of Midian to send women into the camp of Israel, enticing men to sexual immorality and Baal worship (Numbers 25). Later Israel warred with the Midianites who had sent the women into the camp and Balaam was killed.

Much, if not all, of the acacia wood used in the construction of the Tabernacle and the Ark of the Covenant came from this area. So there were some good things happening there, and some not-so-good things.

This valley is actually a huge area running from the Gulf of Aquaba on the Red Sea (south of Israel), all the way north to about Damascus, and includes the Jordan River, the Sea of Galilee, and the Dead Sea. The River of Life (next section) also known as the cleansing and healing river system (including the new valley made by Yeshua in the middle of the Mount of Olives), fed by the water from the southeast corner of the temple (the fountain), may fill a large part of this whole north-south valley.

West of the place of acacias (Shittim), towards the Mediterranean Sea and south-west of the Sea of Galilee, is the valley of Jezreel or Valley of Decision, probably also called the valley of Jehoshaphat or what we know more popularly as Armageddon.

Geography is important, because the splitting of the Mount of Olives is one of many examples of the specific nature of prophecy. We can see some of what is behind prophecies that may not be immediately evident. The detail is intended to show that God will do exactly as He promises, even down to the formation of a valley with (as we'll find out later in this chapter) a river of fresh water that flows to the Dead Sea, making it to where we might have to change the name to Live Sea. We also see that a lot of what God will do in the Kingdom of Yeshua is in making clean places that were defiled by immorality and idol worship.

Cleaning Up

Ezekiel describes the aftermath of the marriage supper of the Lamb, otherwise known as Armageddon.

Ezekiel 39:11–16 ESV. "On that day I will give to Gog a place for burial in Israel, the Valley of the Travelers, east of the sea. It will block the travelers, for there Gog and all his multitude will be buried. It will be called the Valley of Hamon-gog. For seven months the house of Israel will be burying them, in order to cleanse the land. All the people of the land will bury them, and it will bring them renown on the day that I show my glory, declares the Lord GOD. They will set apart men to travel through the land regularly and bury those travelers remaining on the face of the land, so as to cleanse it. At the end of seven months they will make their search. And when these travel through the land and anyone sees a human bone, then he shall set up a sign by it, till the buriers have buried it in the Valley of Hamon-gog. (Hamonah is also the name of the city.) Thus shall they cleanse the land."

Some people, such as Hal Lindsey and Chuck Missler, have theorized that this burying detail happens after nuclear war. Their thought is that the bones are radioactive, which is why there are special units that mark them and other units that bury them. They use Zechariah to bolster their position, because the plague he mentions sounds like something that might result from using nuclear weapons.

Zechariah 14:12 ESV. And this shall be the plague with which the LORD will strike all the peoples that wage war against Jerusalem: their flesh will rot while they are still standing on their feet, their eyes will rot in their sockets, and their tongues will rot in their mouths.

This is also the idea behind the ending of that famous movie Raiders of the Lost Ark. People come up with these theories because they don't read the whole of the Word, they don't want to obey the Law, and they relegate large chunks of it to "the Jews" or to a trash can labeled "outdated" (or Old Testament).

It is clear that these special groups doing the marking and burying are simply cleaning up unclean (dead) remains from the very brief war. The bones have to be buried to "cleanse" the land from the unclean human remains. Burying radioactive bones is not enough to cleanse them. Unclean doesn't have to mean radioactive, and rotting flesh could simply be an accelerated type of leprosy.

Survivor Population

A subject that is not covered very well in most commentary on end time events is the fact that some survivors of God's judgments are able to go into the kingdom of Yeshua. It is not certain how they do it. It's puzzling because it seems, from some of Revelation, that there are only two options: either the mark of the beast or death. It could be that Israel is the source of the survivors; those who didn't take the mark but also haven't fully embraced the person of Yeshua as the Messiah (until they mourn for Him as for an only son).

Zechariah 12:10 ESV. "And I will pour out on the house of David and the inhabitants of Jerusalem a spirit of grace and pleas for mercy, so that, when they look on me, on him whom they have pierced, they shall mourn for him, as one mourns for an only child, and weep bitterly over him, as one weeps over a firstborn.

Revelation 1:7 ESV. Behold, he is coming with the clouds, and every eye will see him, even those who pierced him, and all tribes of the earth will wail on account of him. Even so. Amen.

They are for God but are blind to some of His plans as Paul says in Romans 11:25. But people in the kingdom marry, and have kids, because by the end of the 1,000 years there are lots of people who go to war with God again.

If the idea that most of the Tribulation action occurs around Israel in the Fertile Crescent is correct (see **The Hot Spot**), then it may be that survivors come from all over the world. It might also be that when John talks about "the whole world" he is speaking of the known world of his time and not the entire globe. So it's possible that there are people on other continents that do not take the mark of the beast yet are not believers. This course of action isn't recommended, that is, to try and straddle the fence between the Body of Christ and the kingdom of the beast. But it is theoretically possible to do it. The recommendation from God is to repent now and avoid the chancy position of survivor.

Isaiah 4:2–6 ESV. In that day the branch of the LORD shall be beautiful and glorious, and the fruit of the land shall be the pride and honor of the survivors of Israel. And he who is left in Zion and remains in Jerusalem will be called holy, everyone who has been recorded for life in Jerusalem, when the Lord shall have washed away the filth of the daughters of Zion and cleansed the bloodstains of Jerusalem from its midst by a spirit of judgment and by a spirit of burning. Then the LORD will create over the whole site of Mount Zion and over her assemblies a cloud by day, and smoke and the shining of a flaming fire by night; for over all the glory there will be a canopy. There will be a booth for shade by day from the heat, and for a refuge and a shelter from the storm and rain.

The Spirit is Poured Out

Joel 2:28–30 ESV. "And it shall come to pass afterward, that I will pour out my Spirit on all flesh; your sons and your daughters shall prophesy, your old men shall dream dreams, and your young men shall see visions. Even on the male and female servants in those days I will pour out my Spirit. "And I will show wonders in the heavens and on the earth, blood and fire and columns of smoke.

Peter quotes this text from Joel in his first sermon, recorded for us in Acts 2:17-21, which tells us that the "last days" includes the time he was speaking. We can think of the last days as a phrase describing something like "we're on the downhill side of this age." Another way to look at this is if we count a thousand years as a "day." Six days (six thousand years) have passed, and another day will be the thousand-year millennial kingdom.

It's not known exactly when this prophecy will be completely fulfilled. Part of it happened at the renewal of the Body of Yeshua when Peter was speaking. Some happens at different times here and there with individuals. More will come when the wonders of blood, fire and columns of smoke are likewise poured out in the heavens and on the earth. The dreams and visions will help His Body weather the storms and judgments of the end of the world's kingdoms. Apparently, this pouring out of His Spirit will continue on into the kingdom of heaven during the reign of the King of Kings.

A New Name

Among the many new and renewed events that will occur with the arrival of the King of Kings is the giving to believers of gifts. According to Yeshua, believers or those who conquer will be given many gifts, one of which is a new name. John records this in Revelation 2:17 where he quotes Yeshua saying that we will get a name on a white stone. In 3:12 Yeshua says "I will write on him...my own new name." Isaiah in 62:2 relays God's statement that Israel will also get a new name. We don't know if He meant a new group name or individual name, but either way a name is a way of saying that things will be much different after the naming.

A new name is an important concept. It is a change of identity, and this change means all that was associated with the old name is gone. What was old is discarded, like Paul says in 1 Corinthians 14:42-49, and we will bear the image of Yeshua. Our bodies of flesh will be exchanged for spiritual bodies, and our souls and minds charged with spiritual health and well-being.

It's not clear when we get the new name. It might happen at the resurrection, which is most likely. It could be that the renaming comes after Yeshua takes the throne of David. Or maybe even later, but rest assured we will get a new name and identity given by our Lord and savior Yeshua HaMashiach.

A New Temple for Everyone

Isaiah 56:6–8 ESV. "And the foreigners who join themselves to the LORD, to minister to him, to love the name of the LORD, and to be his servants, everyone who keeps the Sabbath and does not profane it, and holds fast my covenant— these I will bring to my holy mountain, and make them joyful in my house of prayer; their burnt offerings and their sacrifices will be accepted on my altar; for my house shall be called a house of prayer for all peoples." The Lord GOD, who gathers the outcasts of Israel, declares, "I will gather yet others to him besides those already gathered."

The tabernacle or tent made when Israel was on their way to the Promised Land was a symbol of God dwelling in a human body in the person of Yeshua. Each part, every tiny thread, illustrated the combination of deity and humanity in the person of our Redeemer. All the activities and sacrifices were remembrances to God of the sacrifice and redemption accomplished through the death and resurrection of Yeshua haMashiach.

When the Anointed takes His earthly throne, one of His first acts will be to build (or create) a temple which will also be a representation of the simplicity and the magnificence of God with us. The sacrifices will have the same function as they did at the Tabernacle and two (or three) other earthly temples, which was to memorialize the redemptive work of Immanuel. "To remember" means to speak or act on behalf of someone or something, and this is the main idea shown in sacrifices.

This temple is described in detail in Ezekiel 40 through 47. Yeshua will build it to the exact specifications as given to Ezekiel in his 3-D blueprint. Not only will sacrifices resume, all the nations will have access to it, without the restrictions imposed by Jewish leaders in the past. From this fourth temple will flow a river of cleansing, and the banks will be lined with trees for the healing of the nations.

Return to Eden

Ezekiel 47:12 ESV. And on the banks, on both sides of the river, there will grow all kinds of trees for food. Their leaves will not wither, nor their fruit fail, but they will bear fresh fruit every month, because the water for them flows from the sanctuary. Their fruit will be for food, and their leaves for healing."

Revelation 22:1–2 ESV. Then the angel showed me the river of the water of life, bright as crystal, flowing from the throne of God and of the Lamb through the middle of the street of the city; also, on either side of the river, the tree of life with its twelve kinds of fruit, yielding its fruit each month. The leaves of the tree were for the healing of the nations.

These two sections of Scripture together are a good example of how the same scene is described differently. As stated before, Ezekiel is describing the building of a Temple that hasn't been built yet (Ezekiel 40-47), and John gives a little more specific description of the same event. Zechariah adds some detail also.

Zechariah 14:8 ESV. On that day living waters shall flow out from Jerusalem, half of them to the eastern sea and half of them to the western sea. It shall continue in summer as in winter.

Zechariah 13:1 ESV. "On that day there shall be a fountain opened for the house of David and the inhabitants of Jerusalem, to cleanse them from sin and uncleanness.

Ezekiel narrates for us that there will be water flowing from the southeast corner of a new temple (Ezekiel 47). Half of the water will flow west, and the half flowing east towards the Dead Sea will make it fresh. For about 1,500 feet the water will be ankle deep. For another 1,500 feet it will be knee-deep, waist-deep for another 1,500 feet, and finally deep enough to swim in after another 1,500 feet. There are 5,280 feet in a mile, so 6,000 feet is a little more than a mile. Apparently, the valley gets a bit narrower as the water flows, which would make the water level higher.

Everywhere this river flows, life flourishes. Fish of many kinds will live in the river and what was formerly the Dead Sea, and fishermen will have a great time catching fish. Swamps and marshes will remain salty but everywhere else will be fresh water.

Jerusalem at the present time is at an elevation of 2,400 feet above sea level (Mediterranean Sea) and the Dead Sea is 1,388 feet below sea level, a difference of about 3,800 feet or about 3/4 of a mile. The river of life flowing from the new Temple will flow very gradually to the Dead Sea which is 116 km or about 72 miles from

Jerusalem, so the river will be pretty long too. Along the banks will be all kinds of trees with fruit for food and leaves for healing.

This river may flow along the valley created by Yeshua when He sets foot on the Mount of Olives, because that valley will be very wide and very long, going from west to east. If it is, then the valley might be as long as a hundred miles or more.

It is interesting to note that in 2 Chronicles 4:10 Solomon placed the Sea, which stored 18,000 gallons of water for washing the priests and the sacrifices, at the southeast corner of the Temple. Perhaps this is not a prophecy, but it is a moving association.

Yeshua on the Throne

Zechariah 14:9 ESV. And the LORD will be king over all the earth. On that day the LORD will be one and his name one.

Zechariah 12:10 ESV. "And I will pour out on the house of David and the inhabitants of Jerusalem a spirit of grace and pleas for mercy, so that, when they look on me, on him whom they have pierced, they shall mourn for him, as one mourns for an only child, and weep bitterly over him, as one weeps over a firstborn.

After Yeshua makes a new valley at the Mount of Olives and slaughters the armies of the little horn, He ascends to the throne of David in Jerusalem. For a thousand years, He reigns with a rod of iron and the staff of the Law. Nations will come to sacrifice at the newly built Temple. If they don't then no rain falls on their land. There are at least a few survivors of the end-time terrors from the nations according to Joel and others. They are gathered in the valley of Jehoshaphat and Yeshua judges them according to their treatment of Israel (Joel 3).

The Law will go forth from the throne of Yeshua in Jerusalem. Both Isaiah (2:3) and Micah (4:2) tell us that the nations will go to the mountain of the Lord to learn of His ways and walk in His paths. This is no different than what we should be doing now. His Law is a lamp to our feet and a light to our way, and there is no reason to hold off on following it as much as we can. Might as well get a head start and do it now.

Israel Completed

God promises many times in the Bible to bring all Israel together in the Land and purge out the people who don't want God. As of the year 2022, Israel has been only partially re-gathered. There are about 6 million in the Land right now and another 6 million or so still in other areas. These numbers don't include all those who will be resurrected and raptured. Perhaps at the resurrection is the time when Israel will face the sifting as God "passes them under the rod" and purges out the rebels (Ezekiel 20:35-38). Or maybe it happens before this point. At any rate, all of those written in the book of the Lamb will be brought together and be part of the thousand-year Kingdom.

Ezekiel 36:8–11 ESV. "But you, O mountains of Israel, shall shoot forth your branches and yield your fruit to my people Israel, for they will soon come home. For behold, I am for you, and I will turn to you, and you shall be tilled and sown. And I will multiply people on you, the whole house of Israel, all of it. The cities shall be inhabited and the waste places rebuilt. And I will multiply on you man and beast, and they shall multiply and be fruitful. And I will cause you to be inhabited as in your former times, and will do more good to you than ever before. Then you will know that I am the LORD.

Not all Israel is Israel, as Paul says (Romans 9:6ff). In other words, only those who follow (or obey) God are Israel. We who are not physical descendants of Jacob are still descendants by the Promise of faith as children of Abraham (who was a non-Jew).

God's Rest

Daniel 2:31–35 ESV. "You saw, O king, and behold, a great image. This image, mighty and of exceeding brightness, stood before you, and its appearance was frightening. The head of this image was of fine gold, its chest and arms of silver, its middle and thighs of bronze, its legs of iron, its feet partly of iron and partly of clay. As you looked, a stone was cut out by no human hand, and it struck the image on its feet of iron and clay, and broke them in pieces. Then the iron, the clay, the bronze, the silver, and the gold, all together were broken in pieces, and became like the chaff of the summer threshing floors; and the wind carried them away, so that not a trace of them could be found. But the stone that struck the image became a great mountain and filled the whole earth.

You know, a lot of people want to blame God for everything going wrong in their lives or the world. They claim that God should step in and stop the wars, stop the murders, and make everything right. Well, they are going to get their wish. However, even when they get Yeshua on the throne in Jerusalem they still won't be happy, because God will actually be in charge. REALLY in charge "on earth as it is in heaven." Think about that for a minute or two.

The holidays of God start up again worldwide, and as mentioned before, if nations won't observe them, they get no rain.

Zechariah 14:16–19 ESV. Then everyone who survives of all the nations that have come against Jerusalem shall go up year after year to worship the King, the LORD of hosts, and to keep the Feast of Booths. And if any of the families of the earth do not go up to Jerusalem to worship the King, the LORD of hosts, there will be no rain on them. And if the family of Egypt does not go up and present themselves, then on them there shall be no rain; there shall be the plague with which the LORD afflicts the nations that do not go up to keep the Feast of Booths. This shall be the punishment to Egypt and the punishment to all the nations that do not go up to keep the Feast of Booths.

The new temple described by Ezekiel (40-47) is functioning. Priests will make sacrifices again. God's holidays will have to be observed, or else. Yeshua will rule by the Word of God, also known as The Law or the rod of iron; all of the Law, not just the misnamed "new testament."

> Isaiah 2:2–3 ESV. It shall come to pass in the latter days that the mountain of the house of the LORD shall be established as the highest of the mountains, and shall be lifted up above the hills; and all the nations shall flow to it, and many peoples shall come, and say: "Come, let us go up to the mountain of the LORD, to the house of the God of Jacob, that he may teach us his ways and that we may walk in his paths." For out of Zion shall go forth the law, and the word of the LORD from Jerusalem.

Remember that the word "mountain" is a figure of speech for kingdom. It might also be an actual mountain, but it points to the kingdom of Yeshua. So those of you wishing for God to step in and clean the world up can look forward to the establishment of Yeshua on the throne of David in Jerusalem. But you're not gonna like it. The complainers won't live by God's Laws now, when following is voluntary and not enforced with penalties (other than natural consequences). How much more will the complainers resist when the Father disciplines for every infraction?

> Daniel 2:44–45 ESV. And in the days of those kings the God of heaven will set up a kingdom that shall never be destroyed, nor shall the kingdom be left to another people. It shall break in pieces all these kingdoms and bring them to an end, and it shall stand forever, just as you saw that a stone was cut from a mountain by no human hand, and that it broke in pieces the iron, the bronze, the clay, the silver, and the gold. A great God has made known to the king what shall be after this. The dream is certain, and its interpretation sure."

Shalom means peace, but it isn't the peace of no conflict. It is the peace of the presence of God. In the thousand-year kingdom of Yeshua, He who is Immanuel (God with us) will be present in all ways and that presence will transform the world. The peace of God will cover the planet as water covers the dwellers in the sea.

Isaiah 61:10–11 ESV. I will greatly rejoice in the LORD; my soul shall exult in my God, for he has clothed me with the garments of salvation; he has covered me with the robe of righteousness, as a bridegroom decks himself like a priest with a beautiful headdress, and as a bride adorns herself with her jewels. For as the earth brings forth its sprouts, and as a garden causes what is sown in it to sprout up, so the Lord GOD will cause righteousness and praise to sprout up before all the nations.

The Earth Subdued

Zechariah 14:20 ESV. And on that day there shall be inscribed on the bells of the horses, "Holy to the LORD." And the pots in the house of the LORD shall be as the bowls before the altar.

Isaiah 9:6–7 ESV. For to us a child is born, to us a son is given; and the government shall be upon his shoulder, and his name shall be called Wonderful Counselor, Mighty God, Everlasting Father, Prince of Peace. Of the increase of his government and of peace there will be no end, on the throne of David and over his kingdom, to establish it and to uphold it with justice and with righteousness from this time forth and forevermore. The zeal of the LORD of hosts will do this.

Isaiah 11:6–9 ESV. The wolf shall dwell with the lamb, and the leopard shall lie down with the young goat, and the calf and the lion and the fattened calf together; and a little child shall lead them. The cow and the bear shall graze; their young shall lie down together; and the lion shall eat straw like the ox. The nursing child shall play over the hole of the cobra, and the weaned child shall put his hand on the adder's den. They shall not hurt or destroy in all my holy mountain; for the earth shall be full of the knowledge of the LORD as the waters cover the sea.

Lots of people try to envision what heaven will be like after believers are resurrected. The usual picture is of people sitting around in white robes on clouds playing harps. Like the picture of the deceiver wearing red pajamas carrying a pitchfork and waving around a pointy tail, the picture of cloud sitting is also false. Not that believers can't sit on clouds; just that the world ruled by Yeshua is far more happy and exciting.

The thousand-year reign of our King Messiah and Prince of Peace is where many of the Scriptures about "beating swords into plowshares" (Isaiah 2:4 and Micah 4:3) and "I will make the wilderness a pool of water" (Isaiah 41:18) find fulfillment.

The earth during this time will be very close to heaven and perhaps much as it was before the flood. The major difference is, instead of creation fading in glory as it did after the fall of Adam, it will be increasing in peace, prosperity, health and other glorious good things. Life will get better and better under the reign of Yeshua.

Joel 2:22–27 ESV. Fear not, you beasts of the field, for the pastures of the wilderness are green; the tree bears its fruit; the fig tree and vine give their full yield. "Be glad, O children of Zion, and rejoice in the LORD your God, for he has given the early rain for your vindication; he has poured down for you abundant rain, the early and the latter rain, as before. "The threshing floors shall be full of grain; the vats shall overflow with wine and oil. I will restore to you the years that the swarming locust has eaten, the hopper, the destroyer, and the cutter, my great army, which I sent among you. "You shall eat in plenty and be satisfied, and praise the name of the LORD your God, who has dealt wondrously with you. And my people shall never again be put to shame. You shall know that I am in the midst of Israel, and that I am the LORD your God and there is none else. And my people shall never again be put to shame.

A few survivors of God's judgment enter into the kingdom of Yeshua. The surface of the continents will be much different because of the huge earthquake. The seas might even shrink so the continents connect together again, and people will be able to walk everywhere unmolested by lions or tigers or the occasional belligerent rhinoceros.

Isaiah 65:25 ESV. The wolf and the lamb shall graze together; the lion shall eat straw like the ox, and dust shall be the serpent's food. They shall not hurt or destroy in all my holy mountain," says the LORD.

Other people groups that will be in the kingdom of Yeshua are the resurrected (and raptured) righteous ones who have new bodies that are like the post-resurrection body of Yeshua. He could walk through walls (not that we will be doing this on a regular basis), eat food, and even before His crucifixion could walk on water. Maybe we'll be able to hold onto the claws of a great bird and water ski. We might swim without air tanks next to whales.

Believers will be part of the government of the King. We will make sure that people know His Laws and teach everyone how to follow. The holidays of God will be huge celebrations and worldwide parties. Current "raves" by comparison will look like the ugly, shallow, wretched and meaningless drug-induced vomit-fests they are. On His holidays we will remember what God has done, is doing, and will do in the future with a new heaven and earth. Imagine a 1,000 year party where no one ever gets a hangover, or fouls themselves with body fluids, or wake up with a tattoo they don't want. How great is that?

Life Expectancy

Isaiah 65:19–20 ESV. I will rejoice in Jerusalem and be glad in my people; no more shall be heard in it the sound of weeping and the cry of distress. No more shall there be in it an infant who lives but a few days, or an old man who does not fill out his days, for the young man shall die a hundred years old, and the sinner a hundred years old shall be accursed.

Apparently, in the kingdom set up by Yeshua, people will go back to living a long time like people did before the flood. It could be that God sets up the water barrier in the high atmosphere again. This barrier probably existed before the flood and protected people from too much of the sun's radiation. Or it could be that the absence of cell phones, jet airplanes, automobiles and factories improves the air quality so much that it is way healthier than now.

Before the flood, with the water barrier in place above and around the earth, the barometric pressure and oxygen content of our air was theoretically higher. This would contribute to the increased life spans. In present day medical practice, for instance, it is a known fact that placing people in a chamber (called a hyperbaric chamber) with slightly higher air pressure and oxygen content helps healing. Another factor could be that corruption will be way down because almost everyone will be following the Law, especially the so-called dietary requirements of avoiding pork and shellfish. Even now, if we follow those Laws, we are much healthier than if we don't.

But we don't just avoid eating what God says not to eat because it's not healthy. We do what He says because all of His Words are loving and life-giving. Yeshua is the Word of God and we take in Yeshua by doing what He says. This is life everlasting.

Living Under the Rule of Iron

Psalm 2:7–9 ESV. I will tell of the decree: The LORD said to me, "You are my Son; today I have begotten you. Ask of me, and I will make the nations your heritage, and the ends of the earth your possession. You shall break them with a rod of iron and dash them in pieces like a potter's vessel."

Revelation 19:15 ESV. From his mouth comes a sharp sword with which to strike down the nations, and he will rule them with a rod of iron. He will tread the winepress of the fury of the wrath of God the Almighty.

With all the good stuff going on in the kingdom of Yeshua, you'd think there wouldn't be any crime. Even though life expectancy is vastly increased over what it is now, death has not been destroyed yet, and regular people will be, well, people. For instance, as presented before, anyone who doesn't observe the feast of Tabernacles will not have rain (Zechariah 14:18). Apparently, some will be obstinate and will have to be put back in their place.

Some will need a sharp sword or rod of iron (the Word of God) to break them in pieces (unless this is only for the Tribulation).

The survivors of the Tribulation will have kids, and the kids will have kids. Believers, it seems, will not marry but will be like the angels.

Matthew 22:30 ESV. For in the resurrection they neither marry nor are given in marriage, but are like angels in heaven.

We don't really know what "like the angels" means. Some think that at one time fallen angels consorted with human women and the Nephilim (or mighty men, Genesis 6) were the result. However, others (such as Dr. Walter Kaiser Jr.) interpret "sons of God" (Genesis 6:1) as rulers or kings instead of fallen angels, which makes more sense. It's possible that believers could still have kids, even though they don't marry. We know *somebody* is having kids still because "a little child shall lead them" (Isaiah 11:6) and "no more shall there be in it an infant who lives but a few days" (Isaiah 65:20).

Isaiah 65:23 ESV. They shall not labor in vain or bear children for calamity, for they shall be the offspring of the blessed of the LORD, and their descendants with them.

The subjects of the King will have enough to eat, shelter from the weather, and plenty of the things that make for a pleasant life, so there shouldn't be any crime. However, crime is not solely the result of lack. All too frequently, it is simply the result of the breaking of commandments such as "thou shall not covet."

Believers, as part of Yeshua's government, will not only be teaching the Laws, they will enforce them. Hopefully most people will see the sense of the Word of God as they experience the benefits and blessings, and so will cooperate with each other in ways unheard of now. But probably not.

The Deceiver's Final Defeat

Revelation 20:7–10 ESV. And when the thousand years are ended, Satan will be released from his prison and will come out to deceive the nations that are at the four corners of the earth, Gog and Magog, to gather them for battle; their number is like the sand of the sea. And they marched up over the broad plain of the earth and surrounded the camp of the saints and the beloved city, but fire came down from heaven and consumed them, and the devil who had deceived them was thrown into the lake of fire and sulfur where the beast and the false prophet were, and they will be tormented day and night forever and ever.

It's hard to believe, but after all the years of peace and harmony in the reign of Yeshua, where lambs and lions are lying down together and kids are playing with cobras, there is another rebellion against God. The deceiver gets out of jail, and the first thing he does is convince a bunch of people to go to war against God. Again. We expect this kind of behavior from the father of lies, but what can we say about the people who follow him? Do they just get tired of all the happiness and peace and decide they've had enough? Do they think they can do a better job than God does in running the universe? How could they build anything better when they turn their backs on the source of all light, life and love? The foundation of any kingdom these types of people build is hate, and a lasting kingdom simply cannot be built on hate. It would look like our present world system, or worse.

At the final defeat of the deceiver, fire falls from heaven and destroys Gog and Magog. This is probably the final harvest mentioned by Yeshua.

Matthew 13:24–30 ESV. He put another parable before them, saying, "The kingdom of heaven may be compared to a man who sowed good seed in his field, but while his men were sleeping, his enemy came and sowed weeds among the wheat and went away. So when the plants came up and bore grain, then the weeds appeared also. And the servants of the master of the house came and said to him, 'Master, did you not sow good seed in your field? How then does it have weeds?' He said to them, 'An enemy has done this.' So the servants said to him, 'Then do you want us to go and gather them?' But he said, 'No, lest in gathering the weeds you root up the wheat along with them. Let both grow together until the harvest, and at harvest time I will tell the reapers, "Gather the weeds first and bind them in bundles to be burned, but gather the wheat into my barn." ' "

It looks like our Messiah was being literal here. The tares in the kingdom of heaven are indeed gathered and burned at the end of the kingdom time rather than at Armageddon. Remember that Armageddon is not the end of things. It is a major battle during a terrible war. But Yeshua has one more battle before the war is really over, if you can call it a battle. As if to put a period on war, God just cuts to the chase and destroys the deceiver's army. The deceiver and all those who followed him are thrown into the lake of fire alongside the other occupants the beast and false prophet.

There are not enough words to describe the hate and stupidity of people so bereft of their intelligence and common sense that not only will they war against God, they will do so after experiencing all of the wonderful, soul-satisfying benefits of life in the kingdom of Yeshua. This action certainly gives the lie to those people who say if God would just step in and solve all the problems of a sinful world, they would gladly follow Him.

Sure, we can say that "I'm not those people," but the problem with that is people are people. From Adam to now, mankind has by and large been uninterested in God's rule and completely immersed in self-determination. In general, we don't want a relationship with God unless He allows us to do our own thing (be our own gods). If someone won't follow now, out of love for God and the immeasurable blessings He has bestowed, especially the sacrifice of His only begotten Son, then why would they be any different at any other time?

The Last Enemy is Destroyed

1 Corinthians 15:26 ESV. The last enemy to be destroyed is death.

Paul tells us that the last enemy to be destroyed is death, and this we read about in Revelation 20:14 (mentioned in the previous section). After the great white throne judging, Death and Hades are finally drop kicked into the lake of fire (next section). At the end of one thousand years of peace established by Yeshua, Death and Hades are consigned to a place created just for them and anyone else who decides that life and peace isn't their desire.

The Books Are Opened

Daniel 7:9–10 ESV. "As I looked, thrones were placed, and the Ancient of Days took his seat; his clothing was white as snow, and the hair of his head like pure wool; his throne was fiery flames; its wheels were burning fire. A stream of fire issued and came out from before him; a thousand thousands served him, and ten thousand times ten thousand stood before him; the court sat in judgment, and the books were opened.

Revelation 20:11–15 ESV. Then I saw a great white throne and him who was seated on it. From his presence earth and sky fled away, and no place was found for them. And I saw the dead, great and small, standing before the throne, and books were opened. Then another book was opened, which is the book of life. And the dead were judged by what was written in the books, according to what they had done. And the sea gave up the dead who were in it, Death and Hades gave up the dead who were in them, and they were judged, each one of them, according to what they had done. Then Death and Hades were thrown into the lake of fire. This is the second death, the lake of fire. And if anyone's name was not found written in the book of life, he was thrown into the lake of fire.

Make no mistake; we all have to answer to God for our choices and behavior in life. We all fall short of good and holy standards and we have to account for every word and deed. Either you will pay for your sin yourself, or you can allow someone else to pay the penalty. The blood of the only begotten Son of God is the only legal tender the courts will accept, but you have to get it now. You can't wait until you're in front of God and then decide to take it. You have to get your name written in the book of life before your works are published by the court.

Those who haven't taken advantage of the gift from Yeshua will have to pay with the second death after a review of their works in life. You may have done some good things; you may think of yourself as a good person and maybe you are (relatively speaking), but by themselves the works won't be enough to rescue your sorry behind from a new, fiery home. It is recommended that you don't try to pay for sin (or sins) yourself, because no matter how good you think you are, without the blood of the Christ you just won't have enough "coin" to pay the fines. The just penalty for trying to use your insufficient works to pay the balance owed will be consignment to a place apart from the God you actually hate.

The Word of God is clear: our righteousness is as filthy rags or a polluted garment (Isaiah 64:6), and the only possible way to clean us up is through the sacrifice of Immanuel. Judge yourself now or be judged later. Whether we realize it or not, all we do is actually on display for heavenly watchers and recorded in books. You might as well submit to the will of God immediately, while there is still time to establish a good relationship, than have to face an angry God on a flaming throne of justice later.

1 John 1:6–10 ESV. If we say we have fellowship with him while we walk in darkness, we lie and do not practice the truth. But if we walk in the light, as he is in the light, we have fellowship with one another, and the blood of Jesus his Son cleanses us from all sin. If we say we have no sin, we deceive ourselves, and the truth is not in us. If we confess our sins, he is faithful and just to forgive us our sins and to cleanse us from

all unrighteousness. If we say we have not sinned, we make him a liar, and his word is not in us.

The Great White Throne court is at the end of the thousand-year reign of Yeshua on earth. The last part of the resurrection is implemented and all of the unrighteous people stand before the throne of the Ancient of Days, also known as Immanuel or Yeshua the Christ. Books are opened, some showing the records of words and deeds, and one in particular is the book of life. If a person's name isn't in the book of life, the court refers to the other books.

If the works of a person (words and deeds) aren't enough to pay the death penalty for disobeying the Lamb, that person is thrown into the lake of fire which is the second death. This is a place of outer darkness (Matthew 8:12) or a fiery furnace (Matthew 13:42). It is where, as Yeshua says, "their worm does not die and the fire is not quenched" (Isaiah 66:24 and Mark 9:48) and there will be weeping and gnashing of teeth. Weeping is sadness, and gnashing teeth is a sure sign of anger. But no matter how a person cries or rages at God, they are going to stay there. Besides, this weeping and gnashing of teeth isn't from repentance. It is more like the actions of a person who has been caught in a crime and only then is sorry for their behavior, when it is too late.

Revelation 13:5–8 ESV. And the beast was given a mouth uttering haughty and blasphemous words, and it was allowed to exercise authority for forty-two months. It opened its mouth to utter blasphemies against God, blaspheming his name and his dwelling, that is, those who dwell in heaven. Also it was allowed to make war on the saints and to conquer them. And authority was given it over every tribe and people and language and nation, and all who dwell on earth will worship it, everyone whose name has not been written before the foundation of the world in the book of life of the Lamb who was slain.

Revelation 17:8 ESV. The beast that you saw was, and is not, and is about to rise from the bottomless pit and go to destruction. And the dwellers on earth whose names have not been written in the book of life from the foundation of the world will marvel to see the beast, because it was and is not and is to come.

At these court proceedings, the Lamb of God will also present the other book titled The Book of Life. So far, it is in the private library of Yeshua haMashiach, and has been since the foundation of the world. On this day it will be published, after a thousand years of His rule. In the meantime, we don't know the contents except that we hope that our own name is in it.

In Genesis 2:7, God breathes into Adam's nostrils the "breath of life." The Hebrew word for "life," transliterated *chayyim*, is plural. It seems that at the creation of Adam God breathed into him the "breath of lives," probably meaning all people were created at that time (souls along with genetic coding). Literally, God breathed into Adam part of Himself.

Another option is that God creates individuals at conception. However, this would mean that God gives each person a sin nature, which would also mean it isn't our fault that we sin and He wouldn't need a book (not that He *needs* a book). When Adam sinned, and because the law was in place where everything was supposed to reproduce "after its own kind," Adam had kids that were sinners just like dad.

It makes sense that God would know which parts of Himself would stay with Him and which wouldn't. So the names of the lives that would stay with Him are recorded in the book of Life. We might think of predestination as Paul speaks about in Romans 8, and think that people have no choice, but no one knows which names are written in the book of Life except God and His Son. Nor do we know the criteria He uses or how He exercises his foreknowledge. Each believer is tasked with living life as God directs and encouraging others to do the same. Like faithful servants, even brothers as Yeshua calls us, we do what He says. Our salvation is in His hands and has been since the beginning.

Ephesians 2:4–8 ESV. But God, being rich in mercy, because of the great love with which he loved us, even when we were dead in our trespasses, made us alive together with Christ—by grace you have been saved— and raised us up with him and seated us with him in the heavenly places in Yeshua, so that in the coming ages he might show the immeasurable riches of his grace in kindness toward us in Yeshua. For by grace you have been saved through faith. And this is not your own doing; it is the gift of God,

New Everything

Zechariah 14:6–7 ESV. On that day there shall be no light, cold, or frost. And there shall be a unique day, which is known to the LORD, neither day nor night, but at evening time there shall be light.

Dystopian is a word that is the opposite of utopia. Utopia literally means "nowhere" but has come to symbolize a paradise that is nowhere to be found on earth at the present time. So dystopian means the opposite of paradise. Most science fiction stories and movies show us a dystopian future, because they don't acknowledge God's plans for something much different. Thank God He's got a much different idea.

At the end of the 1,000 year reign of our King of Kings the Messiah Yeshua, everything is made new. From top to bottom, creation gets an in-depth makeover all the way down to the atom level. It's not just a new coat of paint, it's a complete overhaul. Our present creation is tainted by sin in all corners, and needs to be completely burned up. God will brush out the old creation and start over with completely fresh material.

Thankfully, men's ideas of a dystopian future are just nightmares. Most of our efforts at change don't change anything, because our natures are self-destructive due to sin. Every plan we make at self-improvement is doomed to failure. The best we can do is worthless, because God is not included

Yeshua Gives It Up

1 Corinthians 15:24–28 ESV. Then comes the end, when he delivers the kingdom to God the Father after destroying every rule and every authority and power. For he must reign until he has put all his enemies under his feet. The last enemy to be destroyed is death. For "God has put all things in subjection under his feet." But when it says, "all things are put in subjection," it is plain that he is excepted who put all things in subjection under him. When all things are subjected to him, then the Son himself will also be subjected to him who put all things in subjection under him, that God may be all in all.

Most people skip over this section of Scripture, and don't work it into the philosophies of men they cherish. After all the labor and sacrifice that Yeshua puts into cleaning up the world and establishing a wonderful kingdom on earth, He gives it up to the Father, so "that God may be all in all."

This means that as much as Yeshua deserves every bit of worship and adoration we can give Him, the Father is still the end all and be all of existence. Yeshua always directs us to the Father, although He accepts worship also. Since they are One, this is not a problem either practically or theologically.

The Father isn't an "old" God whose Word was eliminated by the cross. His Word and the Words of Yeshua are the same. We follow all of the Words of God whether they come from our Messiah Yeshua or the Father. Yeshua will give everything to the Father, and so must believers. We give up self-rule and make the will of the Father our will, just as Yeshua does.

11 The New Jerusalem

Revelation 21:9–11 ESV. Then came one of the seven angels who had the seven bowls full of the seven last plagues and spoke to me, saying, "Come, I will show you the Bride, the wife of the Lamb." And he carried me away in the Spirit to a great, high mountain, and showed me the holy city Jerusalem coming down out of heaven from God, having the glory of God, its radiance like a most rare jewel, like a jasper, clear as crystal.

After cleaning up from the destruction of man's kingdoms for 1,000 years, a new city descends from the new heaven to the new earth. It is a beautiful city made of pure, clear gold (Revelation 21:18) having streets also of gold and with 12 giant pearls for gates and 12 jewels for the foundation. The gates are named for the 12 tribes of Israel, and the foundation jewels are inscribed with the names of the 12 apostles.

There is no temple in this city, because God and Yeshua are the temple. The glory of the Lord will be the light, so though the sun and moon are probably present, they won't be needed for light.

Isaiah 30:26 ESV. Moreover, the light of the moon will be as the light of the sun, and the light of the sun will be sevenfold, as the light of seven days, in the day when the LORD binds up the brokenness of his people, and heals the wounds inflicted by his blow.

Almost 1,400 Miles Square

The new city from heaven is measured at 12,000 stadia on each side, which according to the ESV notes would make a cube of about 1,400 miles (1,960,000 square miles or 2,744,000,000 cubic miles). Some have suggested it is like a pyramid, which might be possible, but it wouldn't make any sense to make a pointy city, as well as giving up all that extra volume for living space.

To put this in perspective, the United States is about 2,680 miles wide east to west, and about 1,582 miles north to south. A city 1,400 miles wide would cover a little more than half the width (straight line distance from San Francisco to Omaha, Nebraska is a little over 1,400 miles) and almost all of the height, from Mexico to Canada. Currently, the world's population (perhaps 8 billion), if given, say, three cubic feet to stand on (which isn't very much space), would easily fit into just one of the larger counties in the United States.

So God's city is the biggest city ever built. Depending on the size of the homes or apartments, it will hold a mind-boggling population of people. Given that it is also made from gold so pure that it is clear, set on a foundation of expensive stones by our reckoning, it is incredibly costly. Talk about your expensive real estate. This city makes the Tower of Babel look like a child's toy, and makes a mockery of the efforts of man to build the tower and establish an eternal identity.

New Jerusalem will probably be sited on or around the current location of Jerusalem, although we don't know the size of the new earth or the shape of the continents, if any. God has worked out the physics of such a huge city on our planet, and won't let the earth wobble like an out-of-balance top.

If the 12 "pearly gates" are evenly spaced around the perimeter, there will be about 350 miles between them. The walls of the city are 216 feet thick (about two-thirds the length of a football field) and made out of jasper which reflects all kinds of different colors. So the pearls would also have to be at least 216 feet around in order to make a gate to pass through the wall of jasper. That's a big pearl. That's a big city.

Living Accommodations

The New Jerusalem is massive and must weigh millions of tons, but God handles it like a feather. He sets it down on the site of the old Jerusalem presumably. This is probably the construct completed by Yeshua when He told the apostles that He was going to prepare a place for them (us).

John 14:1–3 ESV. "Let not your hearts be troubled. Believe in God; believe also in me. In my Father's house are many rooms. If it were not so, would I have told you that I go to prepare a place for you? And if I go and prepare a place for you, I will come again and will take you to myself, that where I am you may be also.

Apparently, Yeshua has set some of this expensive real estate aside for believer's living quarters. The place He has prepared is not a cloud, although we might be able to sit on clouds. It is a real place with beautiful construction filled with the light of our Father and our Messiah. Our new home will be with Him, wherever that is, and since He is present everywhere we won't be far away.

There will be no end to the increase of His kingdom and I'm sure we will be doing a lot of traveling around the galaxy. But it will be nice to have a place to hang our garments, put up our feet and rest awhile.

Life in the Big City

Isaiah 60:19–20 ESV. The sun shall be no more your light by day, nor for brightness shall the moon give you light; but the LORD will be your everlasting light, and your God will be your glory. Your sun shall no more go down, nor your moon withdraw itself; for the LORD will be your everlasting light, and your days of mourning shall be ended.

Revelation 21:23-27 ESV. And the city has no need of sun or moon to shine on it, for the glory of God gives it light, and its lamp is the Lamb. By its light will the nations walk, and the kings of the earth will bring their glory into it, and its gates will never be shut by day—and there will be no night there. They will bring into it the glory and the honor of the nations. But nothing unclean will ever enter it, nor anyone who does what is detestable or false, but only those who are written in the Lamb's book of life.

It's worth saying again that the Word is one unified whole telling us of the plans and will of God. Isaiah speaks of not needing the sun or moon because God will be "your everlasting light" and so does John, except John adds the detail that "its lamp is the Lamb." There is no clearer statement of the unity and continuity of the Word as well as the unity of God and Yeshua.

Life in the big city will be like nothing we can really imagine now. We get ideas from God's Word, but they don't mean much if we do not follow all of His Words. For instance, when God says that He will be our everlasting light, the meaning might somewhat escape us if we do not really know Him, and we know Him by abiding in His Words. To know Him is to be intimate, such as when we "know" our spouses in the marriage act (but of course with God not in the sexual sense).

Sentiment is part of knowing God. Sentiment alone, however, is not complete. Loving Him means to humble ourselves and choose what pleases Him. He has told us many times what pleases Him, which is to do justice, mercy and care for widows and orphans. All of these things are wrapped up in His Laws. If we ignore some of what He says, thinking it is "fulfilled" and eliminated or old or some other fanciful designation, we do not really know Him and His light.

Heaven is having "God with us" and we with Him. It is no coincidence that one of the names of Yeshua is Immanuel, meaning God with us. To have God again is to have light and all the other wonderful blessings that come with Him. These blessings only flow if we submit to every jot and tittle of every Word.

No Temple

Well, it looks like during the millennial kingdom we have the Temple described by Ezekiel. At the time of the New Jerusalem, however, there is no temple because God and the Lamb is the Temple.

Revelation 21:22 ESV. And I saw no temple in the city, for its temple is the Lord God the Almighty and the Lamb.

Heaven and earth blend together after the new ones are created, with God and the Lamb providing light. It doesn't mean that there is no sun or moon, just that the city has no need of them. A crystal river, whose banks are lined with the Tree of Life bearing 12 kinds of fruit, flows down the middle of the street. The trees either bear 12 different fruits every month, or bear a different fruit every month. However it is that they fruit, the leaves are for the healing of the nations.

Gates and Jewels

There is incredible wealth in the construction of the heavenly city from the standpoint of current worldly culture. Wealth, however, is not the point. Beauty, purity, light and goodness are the point. The display of jewels and gold are to show us that wealth belongs to the Maker, and it ain't no big deal. The Maker is the real value under and through anything as mundane as gold or pearls.

God uses the things we think now are most precious, over which many men have fought wars and murdered humans like mowing grass, as building materials. Streets are paved with gold so pure it is clear, but we still walk on it. Pearls are gates, and jewels are foundation material. The whole effect is beautiful and precious and makes buildings or cities built by men look like mud huts.

Who's In, Who's Out

Revelation 20:4–6 ESV. Then I saw thrones, and seated on them were those to whom the authority to judge was committed. Also I saw the souls of those who had been beheaded for the testimony of Yeshua and for the word of God, and those who had not worshiped the beast or its image and had not received its mark on their foreheads or their hands. They came to life and reigned with Christ for a thousand years. The rest of the dead did not come to life until the thousand years were ended. This is the first resurrection. Blessed and holy is the one who shares in the first resurrection! Over such the second death has no power, but they will be priests of God and of Christ, and they will reign with him for a thousand years.

Revelation 21:8 ESV. But as for the cowardly, the faithless, the detestable, as for murderers, the sexually immoral, sorcerers, idolaters, and all liars, their portion will be in the lake that burns with fire and sulfur, which is the second death."

The purity and beauty of the building materials used for the heavenly city will not be marred by the filth of sin or sinful people. Unrepentant thieves, murderers, homosexuals, Black Lives Matter, Antifa, communists, tyrants, dictators, Bill Gates, George Soros, the crime families of Clinton, Biden and so on will be spending their eternity in a different place where there is no light and no air-conditioning.

It looks like from Scripture that the resurrection of the righteous (the first resurrection), including those who were beheaded for their testimony and the people who didn't take the mark, "come to life" somewhere before the 1,000 years starts. If they come to life, that must mean they were dead. Very possibly this means that all believers are executed during the reign of the beast. Does this mean believers have to be terrified of the future? Well, maybe a little. But our salvation doesn't depend on us, it depends on God. He will make sure we are rescued from the second death, but we may have to go "the way of all flesh."

1 Thessalonians 4:15–18 ESV. For this we declare to you by a word from the Lord, that we who are alive, who are left until the coming of the Lord, will not precede those who have fallen asleep. For the Lord himself will descend from heaven with a cry of command, with the voice of an archangel, and with the sound of the trumpet of God. And the dead in Christ will rise first. Then we who are alive, who are left, will be caught up together with them in the clouds to meet the Lord in the air, and so we will always be with the Lord. Therefore encourage one another with these words.

However, when speaking about the resurrection, Paul mentions that the dead in Christ go first, then "we who are alive and remain" will be translated (get our heavenly bodies) and join Christ also. Paul implies that there will be living believers at the time of the resurrection, so perhaps John is just saying that martyred people are present with everyone else. Or perhaps John is saying that "come to life" means getting our new bodies. We might not know for sure, so we just have to persevere and cling to God with all our heart, soul and strength.

12 Happily Ever After

Isaiah 9:6–7 ESV. For to us a child is born, to us a son is given; and the government shall be upon his shoulder, and his name shall be called Wonderful Counselor, Mighty God, Everlasting Father, Prince of Peace. Of the increase of his government and of peace there will be no end, on the throne of David and over his kingdom, to establish it and to uphold it with justice and with righteousness from this time forth and forevermore. The zeal of the LORD of hosts will do this.

The increase of His government having no end can have at least two meanings. One is that the kingdom of heaven will continue without stopping. The other is that there is a whole universe for His kingdom in which to continue expanding. The mystery is the means by which He will fill the universe with the residents of the kingdom. If we are like the angels, neither marrying nor giving in marriage, does this mean that we don't reproduce at all? Are there people in the kingdom that can have kids? Are there angels occupying much of the rest of the heavens? Or will God simply continue to create beings ad infinitum?

If, as mentioned before, God breathed the "breath of lives" into Adam, it would mean we are technically parts of God. This isn't meant to imply that the pagan, pantheistic belief of "god in everything and everything is god" has any truth, but the idea gives interesting added meaning to "created in His image." God will explain it in His own good time.

What is Certain

We may not know all the exact details of judgment, wrath and the Tribulation. It doesn't matter. Yet. What is certain is that it is going to happen very soon. This isn't because of any special knowledge, but only because the world is on a self-destructive path and God won't let it continue. If He doesn't step back and let it all come to a head, capped off by His judgment, we will destroy ourselves.

The deceiver's kingdom cannot stand because it is founded on lies, deceit, theft, trickery and murder. You know, like the governance by Democrats in the United States. He is separated from the source of life, so everything he tries to build is built on death. He promises kingdoms he can't deliver, lasting power that he doesn't have, and benefits of self-indulgence that turn deadly.

The details of God's plans will be revealed as believers need them. We are aided in good times and hard times by an understanding of the plain meaning of His Words and by humble submission to all of them. It is certain that God wants people everywhere to repent and is not willing that any should perish. It is also certain that He has given us the repentance road map to avoid the coming time of trouble if we choose to follow it. Give God the glory due Him and follow all of His Words. We can do that without having to know details of timing, severity, resurrection, rapture, symbolic language, or the identity of the players.

Matthew 25:13 ESV. Watch therefore, for you know neither the day nor the hour.

Yeshua doesn't tell us to figure out the specifics. He gives us a general idea and then assigns us the task that believers have always had in walking with Him: Do justly, love mercy, and walk humbly with our God (Micah 6:8). Hold every word He speaks in our hearts and return the fierce love He has for us by following every law or rule or statute every minute of every hour of the day.

Deuteronomy 4:6–8 ESV. Keep them and do them, for that will be your wisdom and your understanding in the sight of the peoples, who, when they hear all these statutes, will say, 'Surely this great nation is a wise and understanding people.' For what great nation is there that has a god so near to it as the LORD our God is to us, whenever we call upon him?

And what great nation is there, that has statutes and rules so righteous as all this law that I set before you today?

Some things we will have to wait to know at the time events happen. For instance, John hears the seven thunders in Revelation 10:1-4 but is told not to write down what they said. It's possible that the thunders say something that God doesn't want us to know until the time that we hear them.

Revelation 10:1–4 ESV. Then I saw another mighty angel coming down from heaven, wrapped in a cloud, with a rainbow over his head, and his face was like the sun, and his legs like pillars of fire. He had a little scroll open in his hand. And he set his right foot on the sea, and his left foot on the land, and called out with a loud voice, like a lion roaring. When he called out, the seven thunders sounded. And when the seven thunders had sounded, I was about to write, but I heard a voice from heaven saying, "Seal up what the seven thunders have said, and do not write it down."

So it will be for a lot of other events. God wants us to be in His Word and ready to go by His voice whenever tough stuff happens; the same as when good stuff is happening. We are to trust Him, be alert and prepared, and go when He says go. Or stay when He says stay.

His judgments for sin are certain. When God drops the hammer there will be no doubt His patience is at an end. Don't make the mistake of thinking that because He holds off final judgment that He is slow concerning His promises.

2 Peter 3:8–13 ESV. But do not overlook this one fact, beloved, that with the Lord one day is as a thousand years, and a thousand years as one day. The Lord is not slow to fulfill his promise as some count slowness, but is patient toward you, not wishing that any should perish, but that all should reach repentance. But the day of the Lord will come like a thief, and then the heavens will pass away with a roar, and the heavenly bodies will be burned up and dissolved, and the earth and the works that are done on it will be exposed. Since all these things are thus to be

dissolved, what sort of people ought you to be in lives of holiness and godliness, waiting for and hastening the coming of the day of God, because of which the heavens will be set on fire and dissolved, and the heavenly bodies will melt as they burn! But according to his promise we are waiting for new heavens and a new earth in which righteousness dwells.

So those of you who are sleeping: wake up and pay attention. Listen for the sound of the shofar calling you to repentance. Ask for the ancient paths, where the good way is, and walk in it, and find rest for your souls.

A Different Sort of Timeline

This section is a summary of the various parts of the future timeline as presented for us in the Bible. You've probably already figured out that the timeline presented in this book is much different from others you've seen to date. A few things are common with other timelines, because they sort of try to follow the Bible, but the difference here is in avoiding the standard philosophies of men and working hard at following all of the Word. Of course, you could say that this book is a philosophy of a man too, including the idea of following the whole of the Word. But hey, if you fill your heart with His Words, and purpose to do every one of them that you can, you will be able to see for yourself. Don't trust this book; trust God.

There is a time of trouble coming on the world where the deceiver will manage to briefly get his idea of worldwide kingdom going. God allows this kingdom to hit a high point of wickedness, control of people, and corruption, and then all heaven breaks loose during a period we call the Tribulation or Day of the Lord (although the Day of the Lord is properly the last part of the seven-year agreement). The Tribulation is different from any other period of history, where events occur that have not happened before and will not happen again. The prophet Daniel gives us a framework or a roadmap for this when he relays to us his visions, and the answer to his prayer, revealing God's timetable.

In chapter 2 of Daniel, he interprets Nebuchadnezzar's vision given by God of four world kingdoms represented by a statue. All four of these kingdoms are broken in pieces by the stone cut from a mountain without a human hand. This mountain is the kingdom of God, whose head or ruler is Yeshua the Christ.

In chapter 7, he sees the same four kingdoms described as "great beasts (that) came up out of the (great) sea," and the rise of a little horn that speaks "great things." These two dreams or visions give us an outline or overview of history from then to the end, when God's kingdom destroys all the others. We find out that the kingdoms are Babylon, Medo/Persia, Greece, and Roman. All four of these kingdoms are confederations of various tribes descended from Noah's sons that God established as what we call nations now way back in Genesis 10.

Chapter 8 focuses on the middle two kingdoms of Persia and Greece. The unicorn we know as Alexander the Great conquers the Persians but dies early, and his four generals divide the new kingdom into four pieces. Out of one of these pieces, a little horn or king arises. Here we get the first specific statement of the timing of these visions.

Daniel 8:17 ESV. So he came near where I stood. And when he came, I was frightened and fell on my face. But he said to me, "Understand, O son of man, that the vision is for the time of the end."

Chapter 9 gives us the decree of seventy sevens or weeks of years for Israel and Jerusalem divided into three groups or sections. Weeks of years comes from the context of Daniel, such as the 70 years of captivity, which is in years. These sections of time are "to finish the transgression, to put an end to sin, and to atone for iniquity, to bring in everlasting righteousness, to seal both vision and prophet, and to anoint a most holy place." None of this has happened completely yet.

The first two groups of sevens wrapped up by the time of Yeshua, and the "people of the prince who is to come" destroyed the Temple and then Jerusalem. The final group of seven has yet to play out, because the "prince who is to come" or little horn has not arisen. There have been many pretenders, but none have matched prophecy completely yet.

Daniel 9:26–27 ESV. And after the sixty-two weeks, an anointed one shall be cut off and shall have nothing. And the people of the prince who is to come shall destroy the city and the sanctuary. Its end shall come with a flood, and to the end there shall be war. Desolations are decreed. And he shall make a strong covenant with many for one week, and for half of the week he shall put an end to sacrifice and offering. And on the wing of abominations shall come one who makes desolate, until the decreed end is poured out on the desolator."

The anointed one who is cut off with nothing is identified as Yeshua. The "people of the prince who is to come" (the little horn or beast) destroy the Temple and then Jerusalem. A perspective jump seems to be involved after Gabriel says "to the end there shall be war" and "desolations are decreed." It seems that the angel makes a big time-leap from the destruction of Jerusalem to the time of the end and the strong covenant for one week. But before we get to that, we look at the events of Daniel 11 which focuses down still further on two of the kingdoms ruled at first by the Greek generals.

The king of the north controlled what we know today as Syria and Turkey (part of the Old Persian Empire), while the king of the south ruled Egypt and surrounding areas. The king of the north and king of the south are actually a series of kings. The successive rulers of these two kingdoms fought back and forth for several hundred years before the birth of Yeshua, and ground Israel between them in the process. The last king of the north is far in the future from Daniel's time and we know this one as the little horn or the beast. We get another statement of timing in Daniel 12:4 that his book is sealed (not fully understood) until the time of the end.

The little horn or beast makes a "strong covenant with many for one week" (seven years, Daniel 9:27) indicating perhaps a democratic vote in Israel, very likely to build a new temple and promising "peace and safety" (1 Thessalonians 5:3).

As we peruse the prophetic books, most of the prophets speak of this end time where iniquity abounds, kingdoms are destroyed (Isaiah 13:1-16), Israel is resurrected or regathered (Isaiah 10:20-23; 14), God's kingdom is established (Isaiah 2;), and the Messiah takes the world throne (Isaiah 4; 9:6-7; 11). Many references other than these could be quoted.

Yeshua fills in details of the time of the end in places like Matthew 24. Five times in that chapter, He warns of false Christs and false prophets (once as "the abomination of desolation"). Paul tells us that "the man of lawlessness" must be revealed and Peter says that scoffers will come in the last days saying, "Where is the promise of His coming?"

Then we get to John and his Revelation, spelling out specific events in the final group of seven weeks of years and building on all previous prophecies. He doesn't say that the visions he is given are only for a week, or even that the recorded events occur during a seven year period. He mentions several three-and-a-half year periods, but doesn't give us the sequence or place in time.

The seals on the scroll of authority Yeshua cracks in Revelation 6 are an outline of the time of the end following essentially His prophecies in Matthew 24. There will be conquering, wars, famines, pestilence, beast attacks and death.

Martyrs will be added to those under the altar. At the sixth seal, an earthquake like no other is unleashed by God with the addition of a black sun, blood moon, and stars falling, which matches events at the seventh bowl. The seventh seal features a half-hour of silence, which is the calm before the storm of Armageddon.

In between the sixth and seventh seal, the 144,000 are marked with the name of God and the Lamb, and a great multitude coming from out of the great tribulation is seen. If the sixth seal earthquake and the seventh bowl earthquake are the same, then this multitude is composed of all believers resurrected and raptured before Armageddon. These are part of the "armies of heaven" described in Revelation 19:14. The 144,000 are seen again in Revelation 14 standing with Yeshua on the Mount of Olives. Since Yeshua doesn't set foot on the Mount of Olives until Armageddon, and when He does it splits in two (Zechariah 14:4), then this event looks like it is at the same time.

After the seventh seal is broken and a half-hour of silence is observed in heaven, an angel with a golden censer sends prayers and incense smoke up to God and throws coals of fiery judgment to the earth. Then John's vision backs up some as we are introduced to the seven angels with seven trumpets in Revelation chapter 8 through chapter 10.

The rise of the beast isn't described until Revelation 13, a little over halfway through the book by chapter number. But again, the visions are not sequential, and the kicking out of the deceiver from heaven must happen before the beast kills the two witnesses and stops the sacrifices and offerings. Also, the beast must be active before the "strong covenant with many" is enacted. Sometime during the week, probably at the middle, there is war in heaven and the deceiver is kicked out.

In great anger, the deceiver begins to develop further the authority and power of the beast or little horn until he gives it all to the beast at the start of the Day of the Lord (the last three-and-a-half-year period). The beast becomes active in the politics of his country of origin, probably Turkey or Syria. He will be the king of the north. As he gains higher offices, or attains the highest office in his country, he will start to form a coalition of ten nations. These nations might not be defined by current borders, but by tribes or nations as God defined them in Genesis 10.

In the process, he will uproot or defeat three rulers of these countries. This may take him into the seventieth week, when Yeshua is breaking the seals and the little horn (white horse rider with a bow and crown) is given the go ahead to establish a kingdom with his new crown. Around this time, as he is firming up his coalition with war, he is wounded, perhaps in battle uprooting the three kings or perhaps in an assassination attempt. He loses his right eye and the use of his right arm, but in the process the world is amazed at his recovery, smooth talk and battle smarts.

As part of the little horn's building of a coalition, he makes a treaty (strong covenant with many) with Israel for seven years, perhaps with an option for renewal. This probably includes allowing or encouraging Israel to build a temple. The treaty is approved either by a democratic vote of the whole nation or maybe just the Sanhedrin (ruling politicians). As construction on the temple starts, the two witnesses appear and start causing havoc for the little horn (first half of the seven-year strong covenant).

The trumpet judgments might be part of the powers employed by the witnesses during the three-and-a-half years of their office. They could preach in concert with the blowing of the horns, or the angels might be sounding horns as backup to the music of the witnesses. Nearing the half-way point of the seven-year treaty, the deceiver gets frustrated with the lack of progress getting rid of the two witnesses and gives all of his power to the beast. The beast finally overpowers and kills the witnesses.

Flush with success, the beast with his false prophet set up shop in either a part of the uncompleted temple or actually in the holy place of a completed temple. The prophet makes an image (one wonders if it will have two eyes and two arms) of the beast and causes it to speak. Perhaps the image is a mechanical construct with artificial intelligence. The image orders everyone who buys and sells (which seems to imply merchants or business owners) to get the mark of the beast, but many others will also desire or demand the mark. Feeling pretty smug and all-powerful at this point, the little horn puts an end to sacrifice and offering.

The Great Tribulation. The second half of the seven-week period we call the Great Tribulation, where God really uncorks His wrath against the kingdom of the beast and all who wear the number of his name. The six bowl judgments seem to happen in rapid order, but it could just be that they are spread out over the whole three-an-a-half year Day of the Lord. They also appear to be focused on the kingdom of the beast.

As the little horn and his buddies move against believers, God starts to dump the bowl judgments on his kingdom. Sores, bloody water, and darkness engulf him and the people of the mark. The woman of Revelation 12 (believing Israel) flees to a place prepared for her. The little horn at some point, tired of the need for the Prostitute, destroys her and her city Babylon (probably Rome). The sixth bowl dries up the Euphrates and prepares the way for the kings of the east.

Demon frog spirits spew forth from the mouths of the three amigos, which then travel the earth performing signs and sending armies to the Valley of Jehoshaphat. The kings of the east come over the Euphrates, some come from the north (perhaps Gog and Magog) and others come over the Mediterranean and land at the mouth of the valley.

Isaiah 30:29–33 ESV. You shall have a song as in the night when a holy feast is kept, and gladness of heart, as when one sets out to the sound of the flute to go to the mountain of the LORD, to the Rock of Israel. And the LORD will cause his majestic voice to be heard and the descending blow of his arm to be seen, in furious anger and a flame of devouring fire, with a cloudburst and storm and hailstones. The Assyrians will be terror-stricken at the voice of the LORD, when he strikes with his rod. And every stroke of the appointed staff that the LORD lays on them will be to the sound of tambourines and lyres. Battling with brandished arm, he will fight with them. For a burning place has long been prepared; indeed, for the king it is made ready, its pyre made deep and wide, with fire and wood in abundance; the breath of the LORD, like a stream of sulfur, kindles it.

The seventh bowl softens up the kingdom and armies of the beast or little horn with an earthquake like no other which is also mentioned at the sixth seal of the scroll. Jerusalem splits into three parts, the cities of the nations fall, islands disappear, and mountains are flattened. Hailstones of a hundred pounds knock down whatever is still standing. The armies gathered in the valley of Decision await the marriage feast of the Lamb.

Yeshua probably gathers His elect in a resurrection and rapture just before the earthquake, and forms His army to crush the rebellion of the unholy trinity. Legions of angels join with believers, riding with Yeshua to the destruction of the next-to-last military alliance. Yeshua sets foot on the Mount of Olives probably before the battle. It splits in two creating a valley, which apparently allows many people to escape (Zechariah 14:1-5) the coming bloodbath. All armies in the Valley of Decision are destroyed, and the blood is as high as a horses bridle.

Many good things happen from this point on, after our Messiah Yeshua takes the throne. He builds a temple, water flows out of it healing the land and the nations, and for a thousand years there is life and peace and health. At the end of this time, the deceiver is released from jail and tries another war, which is put down by God without breaking a sweat.

A renewed heaven and earth are given to us, the new city of Jerusalem comes down from heaven about 1,400 miles square, and there is no end to this renewed kingdom.

Timeline in Outline Form

Here is an idea for an end-times timeline summarized from the previous section but in outline form. Remember that events listed are not always in order as presented in the Bible text.

Daniel Lays Out the Full Scope of God's Plan

I. Four beast kingdoms from the time of Daniel to the end
    A. Babylon (Daniel 7:4)
    B. Medes and Persians (Daniel 7:5)
    C. Greek (Daniel 7:6)
    D. Terrible/Roman (Daniel 7:7-8)
        1. Ten horns/kingdoms arise later
        2. A little horn/king arises, destroys three (Daniel 7:24)
        3. Little horn wears out saints for 3 1/2 years. (Dan. 7:25)
II. Focus on two of the four kingdoms (Daniel 8)
    A. Medo/Persian
    B. Greek
III. Greek kingdom splits into four, focus on north and south
    A. Seleucid in the north (Modern Syria, Turkey)
        1. Little horn comes out of this north kingdom
    B. Ptolemy in the south (Egypt)
IV. Seventy weeks are decreed for Israel (Daniel 9:24)
    A. 1st group of 7 weeks/49 years till an anointed one

B. 2nd group of 62 Weeks/434 years till another anointed one (Yeshua) who is cut off.
    1. People of prince to come destroy Temple (70 A.D.) and later destroy Jerusalem (135 A.D.).

C. Last week/7 years, time of the end (Daniel 11:29-12:13)
    1. At half-time offering stops; abomination that makes desolate set up for 1,290 days.
    2. Tens of thousands in Israel die (Daniel 11:41)
    3. Time, times and half a time, 1,290 days, Day of the Lord
    4. 1,335 days (another six weeks) (Daniel 12:11-12)

Image: Daniel Lays Out the Full Scope of God's Plan

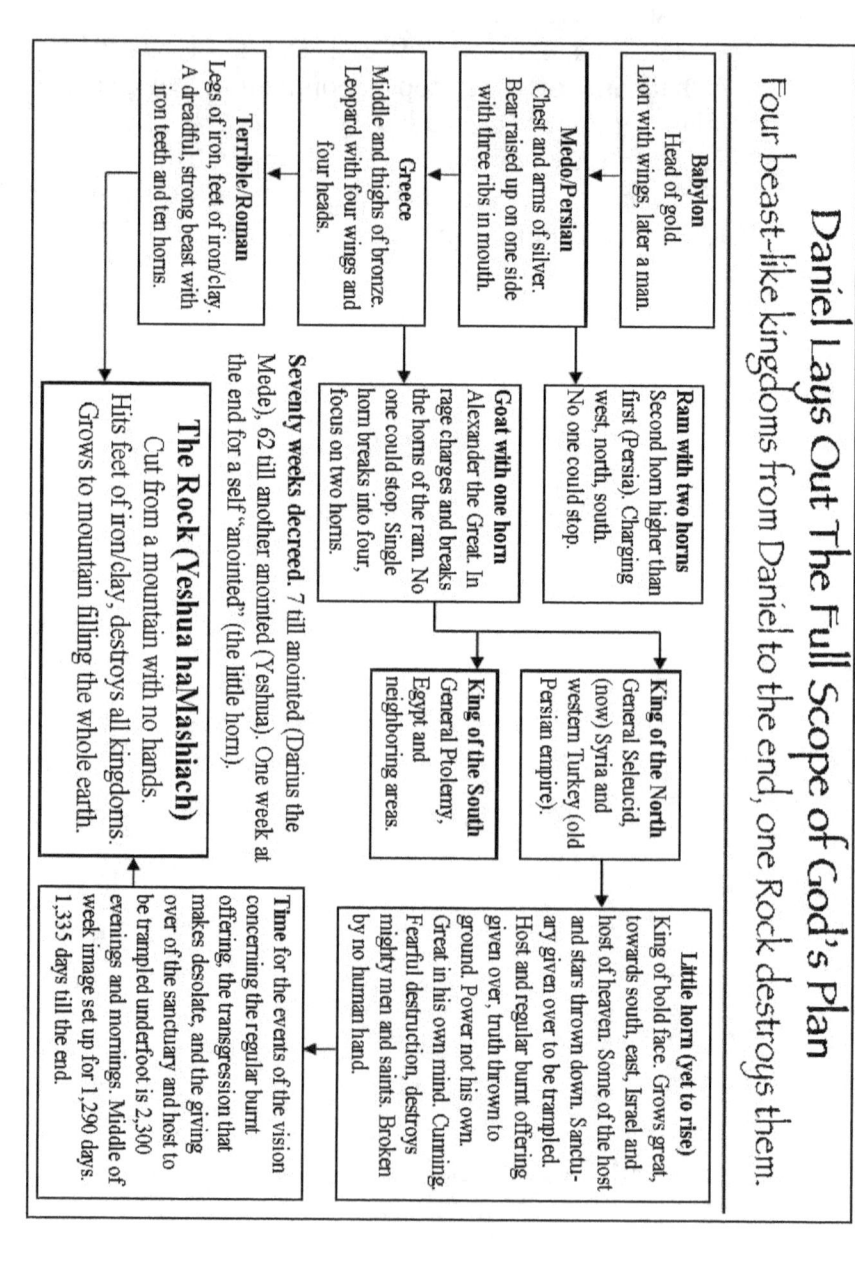

John Fills in Some Details

I. Seven congregations in the hot spot
    A. Encourages and disciplines for that time and all time.
    B. All seven encouraged to "conquer," i.e. refuse mark
    C. All in western Turkey, Satan's throne in Pergamum.
    D. Byzantium/Constantinople birth of The Church.
        1. Ultimately the religious Prostitute of Rev. 18.
            a. Probably centered in Rome.

II. Outline of the end: Scroll of Authority with seven seals
    A. Starts before 70th seven, outlines time of the end.
    B. Closely tracks with Matthew 24
    C. First seal allows rise of the little horn, not Yeshua.
    D. "Birth pangs" of war, famine and death of Tribulation.
    E. Martyrs wait for number to be completed.
    F. Earthquake of sixth seal matches seventh bowl.
        1. "Fall on us" Hosea 10:8, Luke 23:30, Revelation 6:16.
    G. 144,000 sealed before trumpets harming seas/earth/trees.

III. Rise of the little horn/beast (Rev. 13)
    A. Forms kingdom w/elements of Babylon, Persia, Greece.
    B. Mortal wound, recovers but loses use of eye & right arm
    C. Wars against saints and prevails, for a while.
    D. The false prophet jumps on the bandwagon.
        1. Perhaps Muslim Mahdi ("rightly guided one") or Pope.

IV. Strong covenant with many or seven-year treaty with Israel
    A. Seven trumpets begin sometime in first half.
    B. Temple construction starts or continues.
    C. Two witnesses slow down progress of little horn.
        1. Begin 42-month ministry.
        2. Plagues resemble those released by trumpets.

V. Seven trumpets - Fairly slow pace over at least 3 1/2 years.
    A. First trumpet hail and fire with blood.
        1. Third of earth, trees and all green grass burned up.
    B. Second trumpet, burning mountain hits sea.
        1. Probably Mediterranean, 1/3 becomes blood.
        2. 1/3 dead creatures, 1/3 ships destroyed

C. Third Trumpet, great star falls from heaven like a torch
   1. Third of rivers and springs bitter, many people die
D. Fourth trumpet lights dim.
   1. 1/3 sun, moon, stars go out, 1/3 of day and night gone.
   2. Eagle cries out three woes coming.
E. Fifth trumpet 1st woe, star/angel given key to bottomless pit
   1. Smoke from shaft darkens sun and air.
   2. Locusts with scorpion stings released.
      a. Harm only those not sealed by God.
      b. Don't eat plants like other locusts
      c. Torment doesn't kill, lasts five months, no death.
F. Sixth trumpet 2nd woe, 200,000,000 soldiers
   1. Probably little horn confederation army
   2. The deceiver hands all of his power to the little horn.
   3. Ten kings likewise hand over their power.
   4. Third of population killed in wars.
   5. Probable time three horns, kings or countries destroyed.
   6. No repentance in remaining population.
   7. Witnesses killed, finally. Celebration and holiday.
   8. Earthquake, 7,000 in Jerusalem die, tenth of city falls.
   9. Witnesses resurrect, dismay interrupts beast's party.
G. Angel with scroll, probably Yeshua, loud voice like lion
   1. "No more delay" confirms God has been holding back.
      a. At 7th trumpet mystery of God fulfilled.
   2. Temple and worshippers measured except court outside.
      a. Temple must already be built.
      b. Nations trample holy city 42 months.
H. Seventh trumpet - mystery of God fulfilled.

Image: Agreement for One Week; Middle to End

Agreement for One Week — Middle to End

2 Timothy 3:1–5 ESV. But understand this, that in the last days there will come times of difficulty. For people will be lovers of self, lovers of money, proud, arrogant, abusive, disobedient to their parents, ungrateful, unholy, heartless, unappeasable, slanderous, without self-control, brutal, not loving good, treacherous, reckless, swollen with conceit, lovers of pleasure rather than lovers of God, having the appearance of godliness, but denying its power. Avoid such people.

Little Horn ramps up operations, breaks strong covenant, declares himself God. Stops sacrifices, false prophet sets up talking image. Given 42 months.

False prophet jumps in. Forces worship of little horn using fire signs from heaven. Gives the image breath. Tramp stamp to all on right hand or forehead, buy and sell with mark only. Probably business license.

Micah 4:1–12 ESV. Now many nations are assembled against you, saying, "Let her be defiled, and let our eyes gaze upon Zion." But they do not know the thoughts of the LORD; they do not understand his plan, that he has gathered them as sheaves to the threshing floor.

First Bowl. Painful sores on marked people only.

Second Bowl. On sea, probably just Mediterranean. Becomes blood, all creatures die.

Third Bowl. On rivers and springs, they become blood. No repentance.

Fourth Bowl. On sun, people in beast kingdom scorched with the east. True, man caused, global warming.

Fifth Bowl. Dumped on beast's throne, darkness they can feel. People gnaw tongues and curse God.

Sixth Bowl. Dries up Euphrates river for the kings of the east. Unclean demon/frog spirits from gang of three go forth using signs to gather armies for battle.

"IT IS DONE!"

Seventh Bowl. Earthquake like no other, earth staggers, Jerusalem split into three parts, cities fall, islands disappear, mountains flattened, lightning, thunder. 100 pound hail. Rejoicing in heaven.

First resurrection/rapture of righteous only. Yeshua with armies of heaven. Marriage supper of the Lamb. Armageddon.

God remembers great city Babylon. Religion and city of merchants destroyed in a single day/ single hour. Weeping merchants, no sale on cargoes.

Yeshua sets foot on Mt. of Olives, splits making valley, 144,000 seen again.

2,300 evenings and mornings total, 6 years, 4 months, 20 days.

457

458

Image: Agreement for One Week; Before Start to Middle

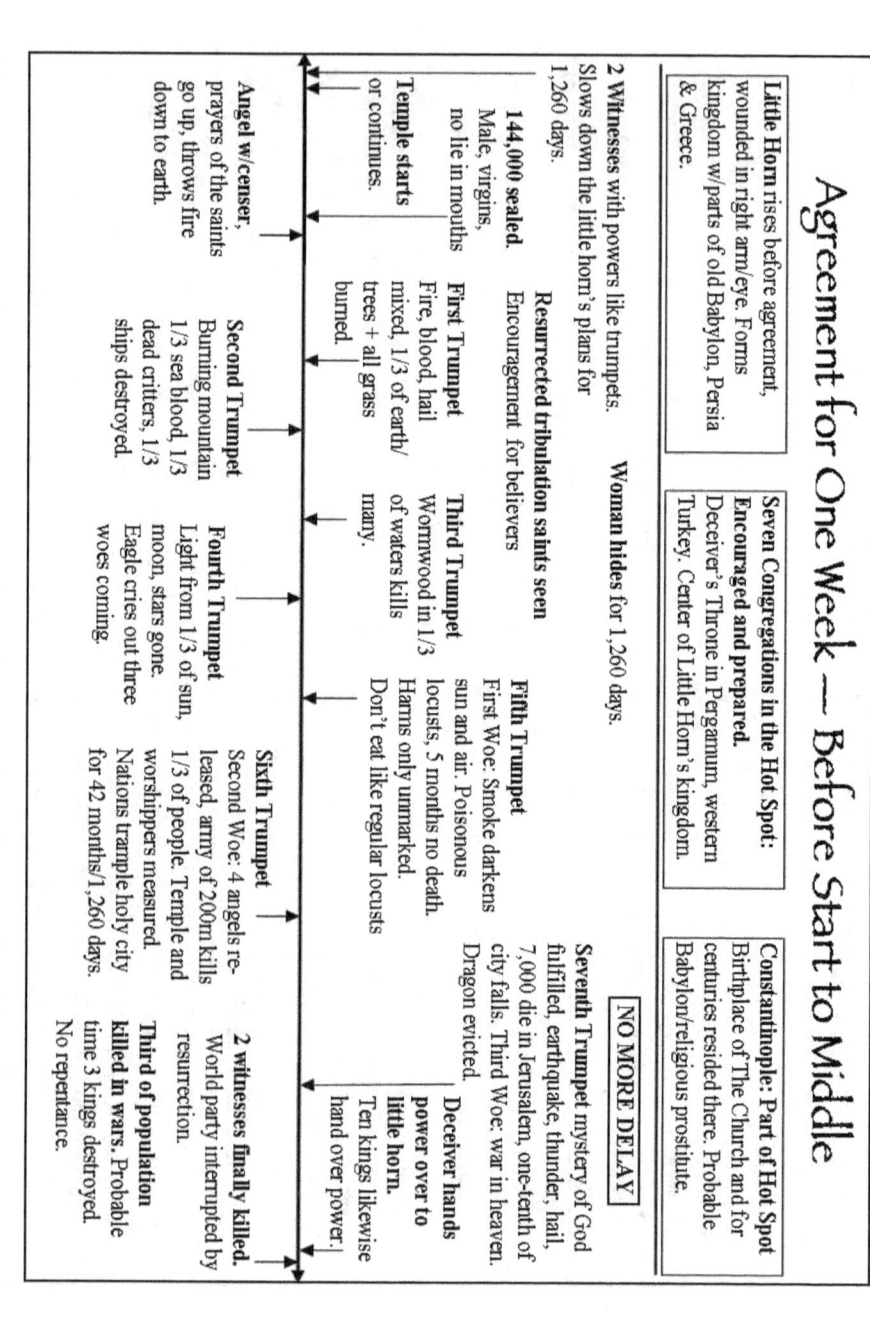

Middle of Week - Day of the Lord, War in heaven, the deceiver thrown out of heaven. Deceiver/Beast time short.

VI. Second half of seven - The Day of the Lord
    A. Little horn ramps plans up, breaks strong covenant.
        1. He stops sacrifices, sets up talking image.
        2. Declares himself God.
        3. Blasphemous mouth against God and His dwelling.
        4. Given 42 months authority over tribes/peoples/nations.
    B. Anti-Christ/false prophet supports and reinforces little horn.
        1. Forces worship of little horn, kills those who don't.
        2. Deceiver like his father, uses fire signs from heaven.
        3. Has people make an image of beast, gives it breath.
        4. Tramp stamp to all on right hand or forehead with 666.
            a. Probably identification with beast's injuries.
            b. No buying or selling without mark.
            c. Mark probably like a business license.
    C. First bowl poured out on earth, painful sores.
    D. Second bowl into the sea, becomes blood, all creatures die.
    E. Third bowl into rivers and springs, they become blood.
    F. Fourth bowl on the sun, people scorched with fierce heat.
        1. True, man caused, global warming.
    G. Fifth bowl dumped on beast's throne, darkness felt.
    H. Sixth bowl dries Euphrates, prepares for kings of the east.
    I. Unclean demon/frog spirits from gang of three enlist armies.
        1. Armies gather at Armageddon.
    J. Seventh bowl: "It is done!"
        1. Lightening, rumblings, peals of thunder.
        2. Earthquake like no other, matching sixth seal of Scroll.
            a. Jerusalem split into three parts.
            b. Cities fall.
            c. All mountains flattened.
            d. All islands disappear.
            e. "Fall on us" Hosea 10:8, Luke 23:30, Rev. 6:16.
        3. Hail stones of 100 pounds level what's left Rev. 16:21.
        4. Great city Babylon toast; destroyed by beast Rev. 17:16.

        a. Religion and city of merchants gone.
        b. Made desolate and naked.
        c. Flesh devoured and burned with fire.
        d. Done in a single day, a single hour.
        e. Death, mourning and famine.
        f. Weeping merchants, no one buys cargo.
  K. Rejoicing in heaven.
  L. Marriage supper of the Lamb - Armageddon.
    1. First resurrection/rapture, Rev. 19:6-9
        a. Righteous/martyrs only.
    2. White horse rider Yeshua with armies of heaven.
        a. Angels, more than 12,000, Matthew 26:53.
    3. Yeshua sets foot on the Mount of Olives.
        a. Mount splits in two making a valley.
        b. Israel/believers flee down valley.
        c. 144,000 probably seen at this time.
    4. Angel standing in sun calls carrion birds to feast.
    5. Beast & false prophet thrown alive into lake of fire.
    6. Armies summarily slaughtered, birds get fat.
    7. Deceiver locked in jail, thousand-year sentence.
VII. The Kingdom of God on earth established.
  A. Yeshua takes the throne of David.
  B. Other thrones set up.
  C. Law goes forth from Jerusalem Isa. 2:3.
  D. Temple of Ezekiel 40-47 built.
  E. Healing river flows through new valley Ezekiel 47.
  F. Trees grow for healing of nations Ezekiel 47.
  G. Dead Sea no longer dead.
  H. Swords to plowshares, spears to pruning hooks Isa. 2:4.
  I. Wolf and lamb graze together, children play with cobras.
  J. Nations go up to Jerusalem for Tabernacles Zech. 14:6.
VIII. End of thousand years, rebellion again led by deceiver.
  A. Fire from heaven destroys the last army.
  B. Great white throne, books are opened.
    1. Resurrected unrighteous dead judged by works written in books.

      2. Cowardly, faithless, detestable, murderers, sexually immoral, sorcerers, idolaters, liars in lake of fire.
   B. Death and Hades thrown into lake of fire.
IX. New heaven and new earth.
   A. Former things pass away.
      1. No sea.
      2. No tears, death, pain or mourning
   B. New Jerusalem from heaven, about 1,400 miles square.
      1. Temple is God and the Lamb.
      2. No need of sun or moon, light comes from God's glory.
      3. River of life flows down the street lined with trees.
      4. Outside/lake of fire are dogs, sorcerers, sexually immoral, murderers, idolaters, lovers of falsehood.
      5. Of His Kingdom there is no end, Isa. 9:7, Luke 1:33.

Image: Yeshua Takes the Throne of David

Yeshua Takes David's Throne—Kingdom of Heaven on Earth

Let not the foreigner who has joined himself to the LORD say, "The LORD will surely separate me from his people," and let not the eunuch say, "Behold, I am a dry tree." For thus says the LORD: "To the eunuchs who keep my Sabbaths, who choose the things that please me and hold fast my covenant, I will give in my house and within my walls a monument and a name better than sons and daughters; I will give them an everlasting name that shall not be cut off. And the foreigners who join themselves to the LORD, to minister to him, to love the name of the LORD, and to be his servants, everyone who keeps the Sabbath and does not profane it, and holds fast my covenant—these I will bring to my holy mountain, and make them joyful in my house of prayer; their burnt offerings and their sacrifices will be accepted on my altar, for my house shall be called a house of prayer for all peoples."

Yeshua haMashiach ascends to the throne of David. Other thrones set up, probably for the 24 elders.

Isaiah 57:15-16 ESV. For thus says the One who is high and lifted up, who inhabits eternity, whose name is Holy: "I dwell in the high and holy place, and also with him who is of a contrite and lowly spirit, to revive the spirit of the lowly, and to revive the heart of the contrite. For I will not contend forever, nor will I always be angry; for the spirit would grow faint before me, and the breath of life that I made."

Temple of Ezekiel 40-47 built. Healing waters flow through new valley made by Yeshua splitting the Mount of Olives in two. Trees grow on banks for the healing of the nations. Dead Sea revives.

End of 1,000 year jail term for the deceiver. Starts another rebellion which is squashed by fire from heaven.

Law goes forth from Jerusalem.

Swords made into plowshares and spears into pruning hooks.

Nations go up to Jerusalem for Tabernacles.

Great White Throne, books are opened. Resurrected unrighteous dead judged by works. Cowardly, faithless, detestable, murders, sexually immoral, idolaters, and liars sent to lake of fire. Death and Hades sent also.

Wolf and lamb graze together. Children play with cobras.

| New heaven, new earth, new Jerusalem. |

Former things pass away. No tears, death, pain or mourning. No sea.

New Jerusalem comes down from heaven. About 1,400 miles square. Temple is God and the Lamb. No need of sun or moon, light comes from God's glory. River of Life flows down the street lined with trees.

Of His kingdom there is no end. Isaiah 9:7.

Outside are dogs, sorcerers, sexually immoral, murderers, idolaters, lovers of falsehood.

462

Kingdoms and Spiritual Forces

Earthly kingdoms come and they go. But they rarely come or go peacefully. The fights between earthly kingdoms for dominance are vicious and destructive, but don't hold a candle to the fights behind the scenes of the spiritual powers. Earthly or visible kingdoms are led and influenced by spiritual powers that can't be seen as easily as humans see each other. The deceiver has been using fallen angels (now called demons) to wage war against God since the beginning, and earthly kingdoms are just a reflection of this spiritual war.

In the beginning, God created various angelic beings that had powers, sort of like the super heroes of modern movies. Before sin was found in the deceiver, and before the fall, angels were all good and holy. After sin entered the world, war was declared and some of those angels followed the deceiver. For instance, there's the destroyer (Exodus 12:23), a fallen angel called Death, and one called Hades (Revelation 20:14).

Some of the angels who remained with God, such as Michael and Gabriel, were assigned to counter these agents of the deceiver's kingdom by keeping them from going hog wild whenever they wanted. The deceiver apparently had the most power, and was a cherub (Ezekiel 28:14) or guardian of God's holiness (Isaiah 14 and Ezekiel 28). Some of the fallen angels used their powers to control what we call "nature," such as the angels in charge of the four winds (Revelation 7:1). But much of the spiritual warfare concerns itself with angels controlling human kingdoms, especially with the leaders.

It's important to remember that the deceiver has been at war with God almost from the moment he was created. He keeps trying to use human kingdoms to upset God's plans and natural order, building his own kingdom to unseat God and take His place.

Remember too that most, if not all, modern inventions such as TV and automobiles come from these demonic, anti-God powers. Not that the inventions themselves are demonic, and God's people can use them for great benefit, but they were specifically designed to further the kingdom of the deceiver first and foremost. The "fallen kingdom" needs these tools because the agents are not all-knowing or all-powerful. Plus, their other tools, the humans who follow the deceiver, are likewise weak and need assistance to control others in the kingdom.

An important concept to note is that these inventions will develop only as far as the deceiver needs the power they give for challenging God with his own kingdom. This means that all the future stories of technology solving the world's problems are just stories, and will never see fruit (thank God). We're not going to fly faster-than-light starships to colonize other planets with our sinful seed. Nor is knowledge (without God), however beneficial, ever going to be our salvation.

As Paul says, we don't wrestle against flesh and blood (although it's a factor in daily living) but against "the rulers, against the authorities, against the cosmic powers over this present darkness, against the spiritual forces of evil in the heavenly places" (Ephesians 6:12). Prophecy contains a promise that these powers will not win. God's kingdom will triumph, and those not with God will be consigned to a place suitable to their natures and choices.

What Do We Do?

Everyone wants to know what happens in the future so we can prepare. However, when it comes right down to it we can't really know the details of what and when. To know, or to think we know definitely, is sort of like a security blanket. A lot of people will fight tooth and nail to keep their blankies. They won't listen to any Scripture that seems to take away the security. The question is, can we prepare adequately, in terms of a place to live or supplies to buy, for any possibility? The answer to that is, sadly, no.

Should we flee into the nearest wilderness when we see the Abomination of Desolation standing in the holy place? Perhaps. Although Yeshua does limit that action to those in Judea (Matthew 24:16). But if the people of the prince who is to come want to find someone, they certainly have the technology to do it. Satellites, night vision goggles, helicopters fitted with thermal imaging, drones and so on are just the tip of proverbial iceberg of tools that are available for tracking.

Can God hide His people anyway? Sure. In that case, we would have to be able to hear His voice or decide which way He is directing. Our hearing is improved when we read His Word and do what He says in normal daily living. If we can't do that, how in the world would we be able to tell what He is directing when it isn't spelled out in a handbook somewhere? If we don't listen when things are relatively quiet, how will we hear when worldwide calamities are falling all around?

Should we stay where we are? Depends on the situation. The judgments God will be handing out could be either mostly in the Middle East or worldwide. If the judgments are worldwide, fleeing wouldn't be much of an option unless God has a place for us. If the judgments are mostly in and around the Middle East, then staying put might be the best possible or wisest choice if you are not living there.

How about gathering in camps, perhaps in Israel? The problem with this option is that camps are an easier target (unless you assume God will miraculously hide the camp) and Israel at the present time only accepts Jewish immigrants. If Israel was to open up immigration to, say, all believers or even all people, we might consider that. We can get ready by, for instance, making sure our passports are up to date.

Except Israel is going to be the focus of the little horn's attentions, and might not be so safe. God won't let Israel get wiped out, but that doesn't mean there won't be collateral damage. Israel as a whole is not really following God now, so there's some doubt that He would protect them anyway. They may be in for more chastisement because they are still mostly secular. Plus they are still doing stupid, worldly things, like requiring every citizen to get jabbed with a deadly experimental non-vaccine against that mythical flu virus released by China.

The desire to run and hide is understandable. It may be what is in store for us. None of us want to be rounded up and executed wholesale as Hitler did with the Jews in World War 2. Most of us would rather die on our feet facing the enemy than live on our knees in a concentration camp facing horrible tortures like cattle. We may not have a choice though in some instances.

Revelation 13:10 ESV. If anyone is to be taken captive, to captivity he goes; if anyone is to be slain with the sword, with the sword must he be slain. Here is a call for the endurance and faith of the saints.

It's worth emphasizing again that God determines our fates, and if we are to die, let it be while we are standing firm in the faith and steadfast in the testimony of Yeshua haMashiach. Remember that the point of all of this is glory for a loving, holy, just and righteous God who knows the count of every hair on our heads and knows even when a sparrow falls to the ground dead. He is in control at all times, even when we don't think so. Our bodies may perish, but He will take care of our souls for eternity.

The possibility of martyrdom is one of the reasons for "counting the cost," as Yeshua said. Most of the disciples were martyred. Many in Israel were blamed for events that weren't their fault, but were killed anyway. Believers the world over even now are being martyred at alarming rates. Following God and His Son, persevering through threats and actual death, is not a walk in the park. They killed Yeshua and they certainly won't stop at killing believers whenever they can.

Luke 14:33 ESV. So therefore, any one of you who does not renounce all that he has cannot be my disciple.

One other admonition from Yeshua worth mentioning (and overlooked by The Church) is recorded for us in Luke.

Luke 22:35–38 ESV. And he said to them, "When I sent you out with no moneybag or knapsack or sandals, did you lack anything?" They said, "Nothing." He said to them, "But now let the one who has a moneybag take it, and likewise a knapsack. And let the one who has no sword sell his cloak and buy one. For I tell you that this Scripture must be fulfilled in me: 'And he was numbered with the transgressors.' For what is written about me has its fulfillment." And they said, "Look, Lord, here are two swords." And he said to them, "It is enough."

When Yeshua sent out the disciples to announce that the kingdom was at hand, they didn't take a sword. Afterward, Yeshua tells them it is time to sell something if you have to in order to buy a sword. Yeshua is most definitely not a pacifist. He just knows when it is time to fight and when it is not time. Apparently, now it is time to fight. Not to go hunting evildoers. That would be an offensive strategy. Yeshua is recommending a defensive strategy. We are commanded to defend others or ourselves as needed.

On the other hand, Yeshua also told us that if we are in Jerusalem and see it surrounded by enemies to flee.

Luke 21:20–24 ESV. "But when you see Jerusalem surrounded by armies, then know that its desolation has come near. Then let those who are in Judea flee to the mountains, and let those who are inside the city depart, and let not those who are out in the country enter it, for these are days of vengeance, to fulfill all that is written. Alas for women who are pregnant and for those who are nursing infants in those days! For there will be great distress upon the earth and wrath against this people. They will fall by the edge of the sword and be led captive among all nations, and Jerusalem will be trampled underfoot by the Gentiles, until the times of the Gentiles are fulfilled.

Some people think this just applies to the destruction of Jerusalem in 135 A.D., but the language of "great distress" suggests otherwise. It is an example of the cycle of prophecies, where things seem to happen again and again. Believers can stay "dressed for action" by dedicating themselves to adhering to God's instructions in every way possible. We are to persevere, remain faithful, endure and conquer by keeping the commandments of God and holding to the testimony of Yeshua.

The message of this book will not be popular. It won't earn a lot of money from advertising or speaking engagements. The truth of the Word is presented here to help others prepare by fortifying them with that Truth. Hopefully the deceptive visions have been dispelled and true believers will use this book to grow in spiritual maturity. Fatalism or pessimism is not an option. The hope is that your feet are more firmly on the Word and your trust in God is strengthened. It's up to each believer to count the cost and decide for himself or herself how much he or she is willing to pay to follow Yeshua. Trust in our Father and His Son Yeshua haMashiach and lean not on your own understanding. In all your ways acknowledge Him and He will direct your paths.

Choose God

Daniel 12:3 NASB95. "Those who have insight will shine brightly like the brightness of the expanse of heaven, and those who lead the many to righteousness, like the stars forever and ever.

Daniel 12:8-10 NASB95. As for me, I heard but could not understand; so I said, "My lord, what *will be* the outcome of these *events?*" [9]He said, "Go *your way,* Daniel, for *these* words are concealed and sealed up until the end time. ¹⁰"Many will be purged, purified and refined, but the wicked will act wickedly; and none of the wicked will understand, but those who have insight will understand.

Daniel is told that the words he was given are concealed and sealed up until the end time. But there are those who will lead many to righteousness as they are purged, purified, and refined. This is a reference to the fact that believers are subject not only to the normal trials and tribulations of life, but also to direct hatred from the world. This hatred is to the point of murder for holding to the commandments of God and the testimony of Yeshua. We are not immune to suffering, whatever the cause. In fact, just as our Messiah was perfected through suffering (Hebrews 2:10), we will be also. We can, however, have comfort and a peace that passes understanding because we have the hope of our God and Messiah Yeshua.

1 Peter 5:8–10 ESV. Be sober-minded; be watchful. Your adversary the devil prowls around like a roaring lion, seeking someone to devour. Resist him, firm in your faith, knowing that the same kinds of suffering are being experienced by your brotherhood throughout the world. And after you have suffered a little while, the God of all grace, who has called you to his eternal glory in Christ, will himself restore, confirm, strengthen, and establish you.

We get protection from His Word. For instance, if we follow His commands on avoiding sex outside of marriage, we won't have to hassle with disease and pregnancy complications the way others will who ignore them. If we are hungering and thirsting after His righteousness and His kingdom, which means to hear and obey every single word as best as we are able, then we are protected from many of the evils that come from disobedience.

In the coming time of trouble which the world has not seen before, the target for the anger of the deceiver will be the visible representatives of the God who is causing the tribulation. The choice, as always, will be the God of life or continued separation from Him and resulting destruction. Isaiah records God encouraging us to choose the things that please Him.

Isaiah 56:1–8 ESV. Thus says the LORD: "Keep justice, and do righteousness, for soon my salvation will come, and my righteousness be revealed. Blessed is the man who does this, and the son of man who holds it fast, who keeps the Sabbath, not profaning it, and keeps his hand from doing any evil." Let not the foreigner who has joined himself to the LORD say, "The LORD will surely separate me from his people"; and let not the eunuch say, "Behold, I am a dry tree." For thus says the LORD: "To the eunuchs who keep my Sabbaths, who choose the things that please me and hold fast my covenant, I will give in my house and within my walls a monument and a name better than sons and daughters; I will give them an everlasting name that shall not be cut off. "And the foreigners who join themselves to the LORD, to minister to him, to love the name of the LORD, and to be his servants, everyone who keeps the Sabbath and does not profane it, and holds fast my covenant— these I will bring to my holy mountain, and make them joyful in my house of prayer; their burnt offerings and their sacrifices will be accepted on my altar; for my house shall be called a house of prayer for all peoples." The Lord GOD, who gathers the outcasts of Israel, declares, "I will gather yet others to him besides those already gathered."

Choosing God means to choose the behavior that pleases Him rather than pleasing ourselves. People who choose what He does not delight in are choosing the sword.

Isaiah 65:12 ESV. I will destine you to the sword, and all of you shall bow down to the slaughter, because, when I called, you did not answer; when I spoke, you did not listen, but you did what was evil in my eyes and chose what I did not delight in."

Harsh treatment is coming for those who have treated others harshly and rejected the Author of love and life, and it will be of their own choosing. A person can go through the motions, trying to appear as if they've chosen Him, but ignoring parts of his Word means they are choosing their own ways and rejecting His. Offerings of frankincense and sacrifices that look like they are for Him but are done in "their own ways" are like abominations.

Isaiah 66:3–4 ESV. "He who slaughters an ox is like one who kills a man; he who sacrifices a lamb, like one who breaks a dog's neck; he who presents a grain offering, like one who offers pig's blood; he who makes a memorial offering of frankincense, like one who blesses an idol. These have chosen their own ways, and their soul delights in their abominations; I also will choose harsh treatment for them and bring their fears upon them, because when I called, no one answered, when I spoke, they did not listen; but they did what was evil in my eyes and chose that in which I did not delight."

When He calls, we must answer. When He speaks, we must listen, which means actually doing what God says when He says it. When we follow all of His Words, even the hated (by the Church and the world) Law, we choose what delights God and is a pleasing aroma to Him.

The harsh treatment of believers by unbelievers will not continue. Believers don't have to be much concerned with tribulation, or even The Tribulation. God gives us hope that He is watching out for those who choose Him, those who are contrite of spirit. We can take solace in the fact that He will not leave us bereft of help and support in times of tribulation. He is dwelling in us and will dwell with us soon, to revive our spirits.

Isaiah 57:15–16 ESV. For thus says the One who is high and lifted up, who inhabits eternity, whose name is Holy: "I dwell in the high and holy place, and also with him who is of a contrite and lowly spirit, to revive the spirit of the lowly, and to revive the heart of the contrite. For I will not contend forever, nor will I always be angry; for the spirit would grow faint before me, and the breath of life that I made.

Revelation 22:12–13 ESV. "Behold, I am coming soon, bringing my recompense with me, to repay each one for what he has done. I am the Alpha and the Omega, the first and the last, the beginning and the end."

Matthew 28:19–20 ESV. Go therefore and make disciples of all nations, baptizing them in the name of the Father and of the Son and of the Holy Spirit, teaching them to observe all that I have commanded you. And behold, I am with you always, to the end of the age."

Topical/Scripture Index

1

1 Chronicles 1:1-6 · 178
1 Chronicles 12:8 · 288
1 Chronicles 17:1-15 · 111
1 Chronicles 25:1-3 · 32
1 Corinthians 11:31–32 · 56
1 Corinthians 12:28-29 · 119
1 Corinthians 13:8 · 45
1 Corinthians 14:3 · 106
1 Corinthians 14:42-49 · 414
1 Corinthians 15:22-26 · 384
1 Corinthians 15:24–28 · 433
1 Corinthians 15:26 · 428
1 Corinthians 15:50-52 · 376
1 Corinthians 15:50-58 · 296
1 Corinthians 15:51 · 299
1 Corinthians 2:14 · 40, 71
1 Corinthians 9:5 · 335
1 John 1:6–10 · 429
1 John 2:20 · 25, 223
1 John 2:22 · 317
1 John 2:27 · 223
1 John 2:3–6 · 40
1 John 4:2 · 13
1 Kings 14:15 · 355
1 Kings 17 · 209
1 Kings 18 · 178, 209
1 Kings 19:11 · 204
1 Kings 19:18 · 261
1 Kings 8 · 178
1 Kings 9:15 · 370
1 Peter 4:17 · 3
1 Peter 4:17–18 · 56
1 Peter 5:8 · 126, 303
1 Peter 5:8–10 · 469
1 Samuel 10 · 31
1 Samuel 14 · 390
1 Samuel 14:41 · 390
1 Samuel 2 · 309
1 Thessalonians 1:10 · 381
1 Thessalonians 4:13-18 · 376
1 Thessalonians 4:15–18 · 380, 440
1 Thessalonians 5:1–3 · 259
1 Thessalonians 5:3 · 447
1 Thessalonians 5:9–10 · 397
1 Thessalonians 5:9-11 · 381
1 Timothy 6:10 · 113
144,000 · 79, 101, 119, 236, 254, 257, 258, 261, 262, 264, 291, 335, 396, 448, 455, 460

2

2 Chronicles 35:22 · 345
2 Chronicles 36:16 · 297
2 Chronicles 4:10 · 417
2 Corinthians 1:21–22 · 223
2 Corinthians 11:12–15 · 115
2 John 7 · 317
2 Kings 13:23 · 118
2 Kings 2:11 · 295
2 Kings 23:29 · 371
2 Kings 7 · 61
2 Peter 3:3–4 · 57
2 Peter 3:8–13 · 126, 443
2 Peter 3:9 · 337
2 Peter 3:9–10 · 275
2 Peter 3-7 · 92
2 Samuel 7:12-16 · 111
2 Samuel 7:12–16 · 111
2 Samuel 7:19 · 47
2 Thessalonians 2:11-12 · 313
2 Thessalonians 2:1-12 · 304, 386
2 Thessalonians 2:1–4 · 401
2 Thessalonians 2:3 · 307, 315
2 Thessalonians 2:3-4 · 305, 387

2 Thessalonians 2:3–4 · 228
2 Thessalonians 2:8 · 387
2 Thessalonians 2:8–10 · 372
2 Timothy 2:14 · 99

6

666 · 101, 329, 459

7

70th week of Daniel · 224, 251

A

abomination of desolation · 50, 51, 211, 314, 315, 316, 447
abortion · 91, 122, 132, 244, 251
Acts 16:6 · 214
Acts 17:11 · 272
Acts 17:30 · 30
Acts 2 · 379
Acts 2:17-21 · 413
Acts 2:19–20 · 255
Acts 20:29-30 · 72
Acts 20:29–30 · 14
Acts 20:29–30 · 318
Acts 24:14-15 · 383
Acts 6:7 · 31
Acts 7 · 393
Acts 7:38 · 12
Acts 7:38-39 · 13
Acts 7:43 · 205
Age of Enlightenment · 88, 89, 92
altar · 178, 179, 180, 211, 229, 253, 254, 258, 265, 273, 276, 286, 315, 331, 351, 388, 393, 414, 421, 448, 470
Amos 1:1 · 204
Amos 3:6-8 · 35
Amos 5:10 · 33

Amos 5:26 · 205
Amos 5:6–7 · 279
Amos 7:7-8 · 111
Amos 8:11 · 246
Amos 8:4–6 · 198
animal sacrifices · 186, 187
antichrist · 51, 130, 301, 317, 319
Antifa · 82
Antiochus · 211, 212, 306, 307, 308, 310, 315, 388
apostasia · 401
Arabia · 74
Ararat · 281, 282
ark of his covenant · 229, 298
Ark of the Covenant · 158, 177, 184, 186, 276, 409
Armageddon · 52, 97, 130, 139, 152, 178, 209, 229, 243, 252, 257, 264, 265, 266, 281, 320, 340, 344, 346, 348, 350, 354, 366, 368, 370, 371, 374, 386, 400, 406, 408, 410, 448, 459, 460
Ashtaroth · 88, 231, 359
Asia · 133, 214, 265
Assyria · 42, 67, 147, 196, 213, 270, 292, 340
Astarte · 88, 90
astrology · 16, 17, 38, 232
Astronomy · 232
Aztec · 124

B

Babel · 45, 144, 146, 147, 194, 213, 340, 359
Babylon · 42, 136, 146, 175, 192, 194, 199, 205, 332, 333, 340, 347, 356, 359, 362, 364, 366, 445, 450, 452, 455, 459
Babylonian · 175
Balaam · 15, 89, 111, 216, 239, 360, 395, 409
balance · 165, 220, 287, 429, 435
baptism · 368

Bible codes · 102
bitter · 26, 90, 144, 276, 278, 279, 280, 292, 293, 456
Black Lives Matter · 82
Body of Christ · 11, 12, 13, 15, 20, 53, 116, 117, 120, 150, 259, 343, 388, 391, 392, 412
Bride · 11, 60, 150, 200, 230, 245, 386, 388, 406, 434
Buddhism · 123
Byzantium · 96, 133, 214, 364, 455

C

calendars · 98, 100, 127
Canaanites · 138, 140, 145
capitalism · 197, 198
captivity · 61, 101, 120, 153, 167, 175, 188, 189, 217, 218, 220, 225, 255, 279, 389, 445, 466
Catholics · 10, 75, 88, 90, 137
Chaldea · 192, 196
Chaldean · 193, 194, 196, 287
charagma · 327, 328
China · 82
church · 11, 19, 59, 136, 141, 150, 163, 255, 326, 391
churchgoer · 2, 11, 88, 141, 159, 255, 271, 295, 312, 319, 395, 399
coliseums · 134, 365
commandments · 8, 26, 37, 40, 64, 107, 126, 137, 180, 230, 231, 252, 253, 325, 327, 341, 342, 343, 392, 425, 469
communism · 82, 197, 198, 199
communist · 82, 247, 334
communists · 82, 246, 439
conquer · 9, 65, 68, 136, 146, 153, 201, 218, 243, 254, 296, 338, 345, 367, 430, 455
Constantine · 137, 215, 365
Constantinople · 96, 133, 214, 215, 364, 455
covenant of grace · 58

covenant of redemption · 58

D

Daniel 10:13, 20 · 44
Daniel 10:13–14 · 285
Daniel 11 · 194, 211, 446
Daniel 11:29-12:13 · 453
Daniel 11:31 · 314
Daniel 11:38–39 · 122
Daniel 11:41 · 453
Daniel 12 · 211
Daniel 12:1 · 47
Daniel 12:11 · 73, 191, 206, 208, 314
Daniel 12:11-12 · 453
Daniel 12:12 · 191, 206
Daniel 12:1-3 · 382
Daniel 12:3 · 468
Daniel 12:7 · 206
Daniel 12:8-10 · 468
Daniel 12:9 · 208
Daniel 2 · 68, 69, 140, 445
Daniel 2:31–35 · 418
Daniel 2:35 · 74
Daniel 2:44–45 · 420
Daniel 2:47 · 298
Daniel 3 · 68, 133
Daniel 3:26–27 · 398
Daniel 4 · 192, 205
Daniel 5:27 · 287
Daniel 7 · 61, 82, 96, 161, 169, 192, 216, 235, 244, 289, 304, 307, 428, 445, 452
Daniel 7:2 · 258
Daniel 7:21 · 308
Daniel 7:25 · 193, 206, 308
Daniel 7:26 · 308
Daniel 7:6 · 210
Daniel 7:7 · 82
Daniel 7:8 · 307
Daniel 8 · 216, 244, 308, 445, 452
Daniel 8:10 · 205
Daniel 8:14 · 207
Daniel 8:17 · 445

476

Daniel 8:19 · 207
Daniel 8:23 · 309
Daniel 8:25 · 307
Daniel 8:26 · 47, 207
Daniel 8:9 · 208, 216, 308
Daniel 9 · 224, 445
Daniel 9:24 · 53, 208, 224, 237, 452
Daniel 9:26 · 226, 308
Daniel 9:26–27 · 227, 446
Daniel 9:27 · 206, 227, 314, 447
Daniel 9:27-24 · 51
Daniel 9:3–5 · 26
Daniel: 8:14 · 206
dark · 255, 256, 280, 281, 353
Day of Christ · 401
day of smoke and burning · 49, 105, 158, 191, 219, 267, 347, 378, 400
Day of the Lord · 49, 105, 143, 152, 159, 191, 206, 211, 212, 221, 224, 274, 281, 297, 301, 316, 342, 347, 378, 400, 449, 450, 453
Dead Sea · 408, 409, 410, 416, 417, 460
Death · 127, 246, 249, 273, 428, 460, 461, 463
deceiver · 27, 28, 38, 39, 41, 42, 43, 44, 45, 49, 52, 53, 59, 62, 67, 68, 69, 73, 86, 92, 97, 110, 112, 113, 114, 122, 129, 130, 131, 132, 141, 143, 145, 146, 147, 149, 151, 161, 162, 173, 174, 194, 195, 199, 200, 204, 206, 209, 211, 212, 214, 215, 216, 218, 220, 骗221, 222, 223, 226, 228, 231, 238, 242, 244, 246, 274, 275, 281, 297, 298, 301, 302, 303, 304, 307, 311, 316, 317, 319, 320, 321, 327, 338, 340, 348, 359, 363, 366, 368, 372, 374, 395, 400, 405, 408, 421, 426, 427, 442, 444, 448, 449, 450, 452, 456, 459, 460, 463, 464, 469
deep state · 59
Deuteronomy 1:4 · 359
Deuteronomy 11:18 · 325
Deuteronomy 12:26–27 · 179
Deuteronomy 13:1–4 · 36
Deuteronomy 14:3 · 73

Deuteronomy 17:18 · 238
Deuteronomy 17:6 · 294
Deuteronomy 18:9-14 · 38
Deuteronomy 19:15 · 294
Deuteronomy 25:15 · 333
Deuteronomy 29:18–19 · 278
Deuteronomy 30:1 · 295
Deuteronomy 30:19 · 294
Deuteronomy 31:28 · 294
Deuteronomy 32:4 · 85
Deuteronomy 32:8 · 138
Deuteronomy 4:25–31 · 190
Deuteronomy 4:26 · 294
Deuteronomy 4:6–8 · 442
Deuteronomy 6:4-8 · 324
Deuteronomy 7:20 · 283
Deuteronomy 9:10 · 136
Dome of the Rock · 286
dry bones · 87, 153, 188

E

Ecclesiastes 5:10 · 113
Edom · 74, 85, 86, 87, 245, 369, 407
Egypt · 47, 77, 104, 117, 133, 141, 142, 149, 152, 153, 154, 158, 166, 167, 174, 184, 185, 187, 210, 213, 218, 270, 276, 280, 292, 325, 328, 349, 351, 354, 407, 419, 446, 452
eisegesis · 80
ekklesia · 11, 12, 136
elders · 79, 119, 199, 236, 254, 257, 264, 265
elections · 134, 244
Elijah · 4, 52, 178, 209, 261, 295, 296
endure · 342
Ephesians 1:13 · 217
Ephesians 2:1–3 · 40
Ephesians 2:2 · 205
Ephesians 2:4–8 · 432
Ephesians 3:6 · 299
Ephesians 4 · 217
Ephesians 4:11 · 119
Ephesians 4:30 · 217

Ephesians 5:5–11 · 118
Ephesians 6:12 · 39, 44, 205, 464
Ephesians 6:17 · 367
Epimanes · 211
Epiphanes · 211, 306, 307, 310, 315, 388
erchomai · 387
eschatology · 57
Euphrates · 285
Exegesis · 80
Exodus 10:21–23 · 354
Exodus 11:6 · 190
Exodus 12:23 · 205, 270
Exodus 13:14 · 104
Exodus 13:7–10 · 328
Exodus 13:9 · 325
Exodus 2:24 · 118
Exodus 20:24–25 · 179
Exodus 23:28 · 283
Exodus 28 · 223
Exodus 3:2 · 85
Exodus 7:1 · 306
Exodus 7:21 · 351
Exodus 7:24 · 351
Exodus 9:8–9 · 349
Ezekiel 10 · 175
Ezekiel 10-11 · 183
Ezekiel 13:4–5 · 33
Ezekiel 16 · 67
Ezekiel 16:29 · 196
Ezekiel 17:4 · 196
Ezekiel 20:11-12 · 325
Ezekiel 20:33–38 · 187
Ezekiel 20:35-38 · 418
Ezekiel 21:27 · 239
Ezekiel 22 · 333
Ezekiel 22:12 · 333
Ezekiel 27 · 195
Ezekiel 27:13 · 139
Ezekiel 27:33 · 350
Ezekiel 28 · 42, 195, 362, 463
   13 · 45
Ezekiel 28:11-19 · 42, 195
Ezekiel 28:14 · 463
Ezekiel 29 · 407

Ezekiel 3:1-3 · 293
Ezekiel 3:3 · 292
Ezekiel 31 · 407
Ezekiel 32 · 407
Ezekiel 32:26 · 139
Ezekiel 32:38 · 139
Ezekiel 32:39 · 139
Ezekiel 32:7 · 255
Ezekiel 32:7–8 · 280
Ezekiel 33:11 · 221
Ezekiel 33:31–33 · 7
Ezekiel 36:25–27 · 117
Ezekiel 36:8–11 · 418
Ezekiel 37 · 87, 188, 262
Ezekiel 37:12-14 · 382
Ezekiel 37:9 · 259
Ezekiel 38 · 407
Ezekiel 38:1–6 · 370
Ezekiel 38:19 · 407
Ezekiel 38:19–20 · 203, 256
Ezekiel 38:19-23 · 371
Ezekiel 38:7 · 407
Ezekiel 39 · 407
Ezekiel 39:11–16 · 410
Ezekiel 39:17 · 406
Ezekiel 39:3 · 81
Ezekiel 40:2 · 181
Ezekiel 40-47 · 182, 187, 229, 415, 419
Ezekiel 47 · 416
Ezekiel 47:12 · 415
Ezekiel 5:12 · 219
Ezekiel 5:5–8 · 55
Ezekiel 7:26 · 2
Ezekiel 8 · 315
Ezekiel 9 · 325
Ezekiel 9:1-2 · **258**
Ezekiel 9:1–6 · 258
Ezekiel 9:4 · 258
Ezekiel 9:4-6 · 322, 323
Ezra 3:1-3 · 179

F

faith · 3, 10, 13, 19, 22, 32, 38, 39, 60, 65, 70, 71, 75, 78, 99, 111, 113, 118, 121, 135, 136, 138, 141, 150, 159, 164, 217, 220, 255, 261, 265, 298, 299, 341, 343, 380, 383, 398, 399, 401, 404, 418, 466
faithful · 9, 85, 106, 163, 165, 181, 192, 219, 252, 254, 406, 431
falling away · 401, 402
false prophet · 32, 36, 38, 52, 67, 84, 114, 212, 244, 253, 291, 301, 306, 314, 318, 319, 320, 327, 329, 330, 336, 354, 395, 400, 426, 427, 450, 455, 459, 460
false prophets · 37, 51
feast of Tabernacles · 158
Feasts · 105
feasts of God · 423
Fertile Crescent · 143, 212, 213, 214, 289, 412
flip · 26
flood · 17, 18, 94, 142, 173, 174, 185, 190, 227, 295, 332, 359, 389, 403, 422, 423, 424, 446
Folly · 88
fracking · 244
fruit of the Spirit · 9, 118, 151
future · 3, 9, 16, 17, 22, 32, 36, 38, 46, 47, 50, 51, 62, 67, 77, 86, 96, 99, 102, 108, 125, 139, 140, 157, 158, 159, 161, 178, 187, 189, 216, 224, 232, 265, 286, 302, 303, 315, 360, 365, 366, 423, 432, 439, 444, 447, 464

G

Gaia · 88
Galatians 1:23 · 29
Galatians 3:7 · 119
Galatians 5:22–23 · 118
Galileo · 89
Genesis 1:14–15 · 232, 301
Genesis 10 · 138, 139, 140, 142, 144, 445, 449
Genesis 10:25 · 142
Genesis 11 · 142, 194
Genesis 11:1 · 142
Genesis 11:1-9 · 194
Genesis 12:1–3 · 110
Genesis 13 · 110
Genesis 15 · 110
Genesis 15:18 · 355
Genesis 17 · 110
Genesis 18:17-19 · 34
Genesis 2:14 · 355
Genesis 2:7 · 431
Genesis 20 · 35
Genesis 22 · 110
Genesis 24 · 110
Genesis 25:14 · 74
Genesis 26 · 110
Genesis 28 · 110
Genesis 28:18 · 222
Genesis 3:1 · 304
Genesis 3:15 · 21, 35, 109, 359
Genesis 3:24 · 205
Genesis 3:7 · 103
Genesis 35:14 · 222
Genesis 37 · 230
Genesis 37:1-11 · 77
Genesis 37:9 · 205
Genesis 37:9-10 · 399
Genesis 4:15 · 328
Genesis 40 · 77
Genesis 41:32 · 77, 101, 330, 343
Genesis 41:57 · 141, 142
Genesis 46:3 · 118
Genesis 49:10 · 239
Genesis 49:16–17 · 260
Genesis 6:1 · 425
Genesis 6:18 · 110
Genesis 9:11 · 190
Genesis 9:25-27 · 110
Genesis 9:4 · 351
Genesis 9:9 · 110

globalist · 28, 59, 84
Goddess of Reason · 87, 88, 89, 90, 91, 92, 122, 140, 231, 284, 340, 359
Goddess of wisdom · 91
Gog · 139, 370, 407, 410, 426, 451
grace · 21, 22, 60, 118, 121, 165, 242, 412, 417
Gradualism · 58, 59
Great Tribulation · 52, 105, 212, 216, 450, 471
Greece · 133, 147, 192, 193, 213, 215, 285, 289, 311, 340, 445, 455
Greek · 11, 98, 133, 136, 147, 192, 194, 210, 211, 250, 283, 308, 309, 317, 328, 359, 368, 376, 387, 388, 395, 401, 446, 452
gross · 336

H

Hades · 246, 249, 273, 428, 461, 463
Haditha · 285
Hal Lindsey · 81
hard heart · 7
har-megiddone · 344
harpazo · 376
heart · 2, 4, 5, 6, 7, 8, 20, 36, 37, 55, 56, 61, 77, 80, 100, 107, 117, 118, 119, 137, 155, 168, 181, 184, 186, 190, 245, 250, 261, 278, 291, 295, 324, 333, 350, 367, 369, 385, 440, 444, 451, 471
Hebrews 1:10–12 · 201
Hebrews 1:1-2 · 34
Hebrews 1:1–4 · 291
Hebrews 13:5 · 113
Hebrews 2:10 · 469
Hebrews 4:12 · 367
Hebrews 4:12–13 · 291
Hebrews 4:2 · 13, 110, 111
Hebrews 5:12-13 · 7
Hebrews 9:27 · 60, 295
heretics · 89
his day · 5, 24

holidays · 149, 157, 159, 161, 162, 193, 269, 377, 419, 423
Hosea 10:8 · 204, 455, 459
Hosea 12:10 · 76
Hosea 12:7 · 333
Hosea 14:9 · 16
Hosea 6:5 · 291

I

idolatry · 37, 89, 90, 114, 122, 123, 153, 168, 180, 204, 216, 278, 279, 334, 340, 360, 407
Idolatry · 31, 37, 121, 122, 123, 360
idols · 3, 89, 90, 107, 117, 123, 154, 205, 273, 284, 359, 374
Iesou · 98
Immanuel · 110, 292, 415, 420, 429, 430, 437
iniquity · 3, 53, 111, 117, 135, 155, 164, 165, 208, 224, 237, 333, 398, 446, 447
Inquisitions · 89
Instructions · 9
intercede · 35
interpretation · 23, 58, 60, 65, 70, 71, 80, 87, 92, 94, 95, 295, 388, 404, 420
Isaiah 1:10 · 74
Isaiah 10:14 · 447
Isaiah 10:20-23 · 447
Isaiah 11:1 · 111
Isaiah 11:6 · 425
Isaiah 11:6–9 · 421
Isaiah 13:10 · 256
Isaiah 13:13 · 203
Isaiah 13:6 · 256
Isaiah 13:9 · 191
Isaiah 14 · 42, 44, 463
Isaiah 14:12 · 42, 205
Isaiah 14:12-20 · 195
Isaiah 2 · 447
Isaiah 2:17–19 · 123
Isaiah 2:2–3 · 420

Isaiah 2:3 · 417
Isaiah 2:4 · 120, 190, 422
Isaiah 21:11 · 74
Isaiah 23 · 67
Isaiah 24:19–20 · 202
Isaiah 24:5–6 · 54, 299
Isaiah 26:19-21 · 398
Isaiah 27:12–13 · 270
Isaiah 29:13 · 11
Isaiah 29:18 · 39
Isaiah 29:5–6 · 292
Isaiah 29:5–7 · 347
Isaiah 30:26 · 434
Isaiah 30:29–33 · 451
Isaiah 34:1–2 · 86, 143
Isaiah 34:4 · 353
Isaiah 34:5–7 · 86
Isaiah 34:8–9 · 86
Isaiah 4 · 447
Isaiah 4:2–6 · 412
Isaiah 4:3–4 · 347
Isaiah 40:12–15 · 287
Isaiah 40:3-4 · 182
Isaiah 40:3-5 · 203
Isaiah 41:18 · 422
Isaiah 42:9 · 57
Isaiah 43:2 · 398
Isaiah 45:1 · 223
Isaiah 48:17–19 · 107
Isaiah 48:3 · 212
Isaiah 48:3–5 · 121
Isaiah 48:6–8 · 107
Isaiah 5:24 · 289
Isaiah 55:8–9 · 226
Isaiah 56:1–8 · 470
Isaiah 56:6-8 · 189
Isaiah 56:6–8 · 414
Isaiah 57:15–16 · 471
Isaiah 57:17 · 333
Isaiah 57:4–6 · 54
Isaiah 59:1–4 · 135
Isaiah 60:19–20 · 436
Isaiah 60:5 · 350
Isaiah 61:10 · 200
Isaiah 61:10–11 · 421
Isaiah 62:2 · 414
Isaiah 63:1–6 · 245, 369
Isaiah 65:12 · 470
Isaiah 65:19–20 · 423
Isaiah 65:19–23 · 120
Isaiah 65:23 · 425
Isaiah 65:25 · 422
Isaiah 66:3–4 · 471
Isaiah 7:14 · 111
Isaiah 8:11–13 · 130
Isaiah 8:5–8 · 292
Isaiah 9:11 · 447
Isaiah 9:6-7 · 447
Isaiah 9:6–7 · 421
Ishtar · 88, 231
Islam · 123
Istanbul · 96, 133, 215, 281, 364

J

James 2:17–19 · 343
James 3:3–6 · 290
James 4:13–15 · 331
James 5:17 · 209
Jeremiah 12:4-9 · 407
Jeremiah 13:27 · 67
Jeremiah 15:2 · 218
Jeremiah 15:3 · 407
Jeremiah 17:13 · 133
Jeremiah 2:2 · 231
Jeremiah 21:4 · 81
Jeremiah 23:16–17 · 2, 37
Jeremiah 23:18–20 · 107
Jeremiah 23:20 · 80
Jeremiah 23:6 · 99
Jeremiah 25:11 · 224, 225
Jeremiah 25:11-12, 29:10 · 61
Jeremiah 25:15, 28-29 · 56
Jeremiah 25:27–29 · 268
Jeremiah 25:4–7 · 123
Jeremiah 3:15–17 · 184
Jeremiah 31:31-34 · 295
Jeremiah 31:31–34 · 117
Jeremiah 33:14-17 · 111

Jeremiah 43:11 · 218
Jeremiah 46:7–8 · 292
Jeremiah 48:44 · 218
Jeremiah 49:36 · 259
Jeremiah 5:14 · 290
Jeremiah 50:29 · 363
Jeremiah 51:27 · 282
Jeremiah 51:60–64 · 339, 363
Jeremiah 6:10 · 39
Jeremiah 6:11 · 390
Jeremiah 6:16–19 · 275
Jeremiah 6:17 · 270
Jeremiah 7:21–24 · 186
Jeremiah 7:33 · 407
Jeremiah 7:8–15 · 181
Jeremiah 9:10 · 407
Jeremiah 9:13–15 · 279
Jesus · 403
Jezebel · 15, 89, 178, 192, 215, 263, 338, 360, 363, 395
Jezreel · 344, 371, 373, 400
Job 1:7 · 206, 304
Job 2:2 · 206
Job 2:4 · 304
Job 32:17–18 · 69
Job 33:15–18 · 76
Job 33:5–7 · 104
Job 38:7 · 205
Joel 2:10–11 · 284
Joel 2:22–27 · 422
Joel 2:28–30 · 413
Joel 2:31 · 255
Joel 2:3–5 · 282
Joel 2:4–5 · 287
Joel 3 · 417
Joel 3:13–14 · 343
Joel 3:14–15 · 374
Joel 3:16 · 401
Joel 3:18 · 409
John · 387
John 10:11–16 · 313
John 10:35 · 15
John 11:1 · 286
John 11:51 · 31
John 12:3 · 223

John 12:31 · 303
John 14:1–3 · 436
John 14:15–17 · 180
John 14:30 · 368
John 21:20–23 · 95
John 3:10–13 · 160
John 4:21–24 · 180
John 5:28-29 · 383
John 6 · 106, 167
John 6:52-58 · 6
John 6:53-58 · 31
John 6:63 · 7
John 7:17–18 · 32
John 8:43 · 70
Joseph · 77, 78, 101, 141, 225, 230, 260, 279, 330, 399
Joshua 24:12 · 283
Joshua 24:2 · 355
Jude 3 · 29
Judges 1:27 · 370
Judges 7 · 269
Judges 9 · 223

K

Karaite Judaism · 98
katabaino · 387
Kidron Valley · 97
kingdom of heaven · 4, 5, 28, 103, 118, 298, 375

L

labor pains · 191
lake of fire · 411
Lamentations 2:14 · 3
Lamentations 3:31–33 · 402
latter days · 191
Law · 9, 13, 20, 25, 32, 37, 38, 40, 56, 58, 59, 64, 79, 91, 110, 117, 119, 153, 161, 165, 185, 191, 193, 202, 211, 230, 238, 253, 260, 279, 307,

313, 318, 328, 333, 335, 342, 360, 383, 395, 411, 417, 420, 424, 460, 471
lawlessness · 17, 53, 228, 299, 305, 307, 318, 384, 386, 387, 402, 447, *See* iniquity
leaven · 103, 104, 138, 167, 328
Levite · 5
Leviticus 17:12 · 352
Leviticus 17:7 · 122
Leviticus 17:8–9 · 179
Leviticus 18:22, 20:13 · 73
Leviticus 19:35 · 333
Leviticus 23 · 377
Leviticus 23:2 · 193
Leviticus 25:10 · 378
Leviticus 25:9 · 377
Leviticus 26 · 118, 267, 347
Leviticus 26:14–20 · 267
Leviticus 26:42 · 118
Leviticus 3:17 · 351
Leviticus 7:26-27 · 351
light · 26, 43, 51, 104, 115, 118, 130, 160, 186, 201, 232, 236, 253, 255, 256, 261, 280, 281, 291, 301, 353, 354, 357, 373, 385, 426, 432, 434, 436, 437, 438, 439, 461, 464
little horn · 42, 43, 51, 52, 67, 69, 74, 83, 101, 114, 124, 131, 141, 147, 174, 178, 192, 193, 194, 204, 207, 208, 209, 211, 212, 216, 218, 219, 223, 225, 226, 227, 229, 243, 244, 246, 253, 262, 264, 265, 289, 290, 291, 296, 306, 307, 308, 309, 310, 311, 312, 314, 315, 316, 326, 327, 328, 329, 335, 336, 338, 340, 351, 353, 361, 362, 365, 366, 371, 372, 386, 400, 417, 445, 446, 447, 449, 450, 451, 452, 455, 456, 459, 466
locusts · 205, 272, 273, 281, 282, 283, 284, 349, 456
Luke 10:18–19 · 303
Luke 11:17 · 301
Luke 11:23 · 130
Luke 11:29–30 · 73
Luke 12:35–38 · 202
Luke 14 · 407
Luke 14:33 · 467
Luke 16:10 · 342
Luke 17 · 389
Luke 17:26–30 · 332
Luke 17:6 · 30
Luke 18:7–8 · 135
Luke 19:44 · 6, 64, 225
Luke 21 · 236, 385, 389
Luke 21:20–24 · 467
Luke 21:25–28 · 380
Luke 21:6 · 64, 225
Luke 22:19 · 167
Luke 22:30 · 257
Luke 22:35–38 · 467
Luke 23:30 · 455, 459
Luke 3:22 · 223
Luke 3:4–6 · 5
Luke 4:25–26 · 209
Luke 4:42–43 · 109
Luke 6:46 · 13
Luke 8:10 · 298
Luke 8:9–10 · 298

M

Maccabees · 211
Magog · 139, 370, 371, 407, 426, 451
Malachi 1:2–3 · 26
Malachi 3:1–4 · 124
Malachi 3:1-5 · 66
Malachi 3:1–5 · 66
Malachi 3:16-18 · 399
Malachi 3:16–18 · 202
Malachi 4:1–6 · 1
Mark 13 · 314
Mark 13:2 · 64, 225
Mark 13:27 · 259
Mark 3:24-25 · 301
Mark 4:11 · 298
Mark 4:26–29 · 128
Mark 6:13 · 222
Mark 9:9 · 387

mark of the beast · 9, 116, 161, 261, 262, 272, 312, 318, 321, 324, 325, 326, 327, 335, 338, 345, 349, 411, 412, 450
Martin Luther · 89
martyrs · 75, 88, 90, 236, 252, 254, 264, 265, 391, 393, 460
Mary · 88, 223, 391
Matthew 1:13 · 225
Matthew 10:28 · 221
Matthew 10:34 · 366
Matthew 12:25 · 43, 301
Matthew 12:25-26 · 68
Matthew 13:11 · 298
Matthew 13:24–30 · 426
Matthew 13:24-43 · 345
Matthew 13:33 · 103
Matthew 13:40-42 · 384
Matthew 13:42 · 430
Matthew 15:7–9 · 137
Matthew 16:6, 11, 12 · 103
Matthew 19:28 · 257
Matthew 2:1-2 · 302
Matthew 21:12 · 66
Matthew 21:12–13 · 331
Matthew 21:13 · 181
Matthew 22:30 · 120, 425
Matthew 23:1–4 · 5
Matthew 24 · 49, 50, 51, 103, 170, 225, 236, 273, 314, 385, 389, 447, 455
Matthew 24:10–12 · 318
Matthew 24:14 · 337
Matthew 24:15 · 50, 315
Matthew 24:15–18 · 314
Matthew 24:16 · 465
Matthew 24:2 · 64
Matthew 24:21-22 · 49
Matthew 24:21–22 · 51
Matthew 24:21–22 · 191
Matthew 24:21–22 · 226
Matthew 24:22 · 209, 242
Matthew 24:23–24 · 222
Matthew 24:24 · 36, 143, 223, 309
Matthew 24:26-27 · 385
Matthew 24:29 · 256, 353

Matthew 24:29-31 · 385
Matthew 24:3 · 50
Matthew 24:31 · 259, 270
Matthew 24:3–5 · 317
Matthew 24:36 · 226
Matthew 24:36-37 · 128
Matthew 24:37-39 · 402
Matthew 24:45–46 · 5
Matthew 24:4–8 · 240
Matthew 25 · 63, 202
Matthew 25:11 · 13
Matthew 25:13 · 85, 442
Matthew 25:34 · 116
Matthew 28:18 · 242
Matthew 28:19–20 · 85, 472
Matthew 3:16 · 223
Matthew 4 · 132
Matthew 4:17 · 4
Matthew 4:8–9 · 132
Matthew 6:17 · 222
Matthew 6:24 · 113
Matthew 7:15–16 · 14
Matthew 7:21 · 13
Matthew 8:12 · 430
meadow of acacias · 409
Media · 147, 192, 213
Media/Persia · 192
Medo-Persian Empire · 192
Megiddo · 52, 96, 344, 370, 371
Meshech · 139, 370
meta tauta · 395
Micah 4:11–12 · 343
Micah 4:11–13 · 369
Micah 4:2 · 417
Micah 4:3 · 120, 422
Middle East · 212, 277, 284, 465
mother earth · 88
Mother Nature · 88
Mount of Olives · 50, 155, 177, 181, 182, 183, 229, 317, 356, 372, 373, 406, 408, 409, 410, 417, 448, 451, 460
multitude · 236, 257, 264

N

Nahum 1:11 · 67
Nahum 1:15 · 67
Nahum 1:8 · 67
Nahum 3:16 · 196
narcissism · 17
Nebuchadnezzar · 126
Nehemiah 9:13–14 · 9
Nehemiah 9:29 · 272
New Covenant · 119
newspaper exegesis · 80
Nicolaitan · 14, 55, 137
Nicolaitans · 15, 16, 32, 137, 193, 215, 313, 360, 391, 395, 402
Noah · 110, 128, 139, 185, 186, 332, 402, 403, 445
Numbers 10 · 269
Numbers 11:25-26 · 31
Numbers 21 · 46
Numbers 24:17 · 205, 240
Numbers 25 · 409

O

Obadiah 10–11 · 151
Obadiah 15 · 152

P

Palestinians · 145
parousia · 387
Pergamum · 192, 205, 214, 215, 281, 304, 455
persevere · 9, 64, 106, 155, 166, 201, 219, 254, 342, 346, 440
Persia · 44, 139, 147, 193, 213, 215, 285, 305, 340, 370, 407, 445, 455
pharmakeia · 250
Philippians 2:12 · 202
Philippians 3:19 · 122
Philippians 3:6 · 260
Philippians 3:8-11 · 383
philosophies of men · 15, 17, 21, 25, 38, 58, 71, 104, 150, 255, 341, 395, 433, 444
place of acacias · 409
Plain of Jezreel · 373
poisoning the well · 359
poisonous · 278, 279
priest · 5, 19, 200, 235, 308, 421
Promise · 109, 110, 111, 112, 118, 119, 418
prophecy · 1, 2, 3, 6, 7, 8, 9, 10, 16, 18, 21, 22, 23, 26, 27, 31, 32, 36, 39, 46, 47, 48, 49, 57, 60, 61, 62, 64, 65, 66, 68, 69, 70, 71, 72, 76, 77, 80, 82, 83, 84, 85, 92, 94, 95, 99, 101, 102, 105, 106, 107, 108, 109, 111, 112, 125, 127, 128, 139, 140, 143, 144, 153, 156, 157, 158, 159, 160, 166, 189, 200, 211, 217, 222, 225, 252, 259, 262, 267, 287, 300, 303, 330, 397, 410, 413, 417, 446
prophet · 4, 9, 32, 35, 36, 58, 62, 63, 66, 95, 187, 188, 223, 300, 306, 314, 365, 445
Prophet · 31
prophetess · 34
Protestants · 10, 12, 137, 359
Protoevangelium · 110
Proverbs 1 · 85
Proverbs 1:20–31 · 91
Proverbs 2:7 · 85
Proverbs 20:10 · 333
Proverbs 5:3–6 · 90
Proverbs 9:10 · 89
Psalm 102:25–27 · 201
Psalm 104:1–2 · 201
Psalm 104:15 · 248
Psalm 109:18–19 · 200
Psalm 110:1-7 · 235
Psalm 119:103 · 293
Psalm 130:1-4 · 324
Psalm 18:13 · 276
Psalm 2:7–9 · 424
Psalm 22 · 76

Psalm 23 · 367
Psalm 27:4-5 · 398
Psalm 27:5 · 177
Psalm 37:3–4 · 113
Psalm 50:14-15 · 399
Psalm 73:6 · 200
Psalm 79:2–3 · 406
Ptolemaic · 211
Ptolemy · 210

Q

qahal · 136

R

radioactive · 411
rapture · 1, 55, 84, 136, 189, 217, 218, 219, 255, 264, 305, 375, 376, 377, 378, 379, 380, 381, 382, 386, 387, 388, 389, 390, 392, 394, 396, 397, 400, 401, 402, 404, 442, 451, 460
religion · 88, 90, 114, 115, 119, 123, 124, 134, 138, 145, 149, 174, 194, 196, 359
religious · 5, 76, 140, 175, 186, 194, 195, 196, 216, 319, 326, 340, 358, 359, 455
Repent · 3, 4, 5, 363, 374
repentance · 4, 5, 6, 17, 54, 127, 129, 169, 182, 192, 204, 271, 272, 275, 284, 324, 326, 336, 337, 347, 349, 351, 354, 374, 442, 443, 444, 456
resurrection · 46, 60, 66, 73, 75, 112, 120, 167, 168, 169, 170, 172, 187, 189, 203, 219, 254, 263, 264, 265, 295, 335, 375, 376, 377, 379, 382, 383, 384, 385, 386, 388, 389, 394, 400, 401, 402, 404, 415, 418, 423, 425, 430, 439, 440, 442, 451, 460
Revelation 1:1 · 77
Revelation 1:10 · 270
Revelation 1:16 · 205, 289, 366
Revelation 1:2 · 392
Revelation 1:3 · 63
Revelation 1:7 · 140, 412
Revelation 1:9 · 49, 251, 254, 265, 392
Revelation 10:10–11 · 144
Revelation 10:11 · 144
Revelation 10:1–4 · 443
Revelation 10:5–7 · 292
Revelation 10:7 · 274
Revelation 11:1-14 · 52
Revelation 11:13 · 203
Revelation 11:15 · 237, 298, 405
Revelation 11:15-18 · 254
Revelation 11:18 · 54
Revelation 11:19 · 203, 298
Revelation 11:3 · 206
Revelation 11:3–4 · 294
Revelation 11:6 · 210
Revelation 11:8 · 74
Revelation 11:9 · 144
Revelation 12 · 78, 124, 126, 230, 232, 304, 450
Revelation 12:1 · 205, 301
Revelation 12:11 · 338
Revelation 12:12 · 299, 304
Revelation 12:1-2 · 391
Revelation 12:14 · 206
Revelation 12:15 · 300
Revelation 12:1-5 · 302
Revelation 12:17 · 64, 117, 230, 231, 252, 392
Revelation 12:4 · 205
Revelation 12:5 · 400
Revelation 12:6 · 206, 300, 399
Revelation 12:7-13 · 303
Revelation 12:8 · 304
Revelation 12:9 · 141, 143
Revelation 13 · 65, 73, 79, 116, 146, 193, 215, 217, 290, 296, 309, 310, 315, 320, 345, 448
Revelation 1-3 · 75
Revelation 13:10 · 65, 254, 342, 466
Revelation 13:11 · 73
Revelation 13:11-18 · 199, 320

Revelation 13:16–17 · 330
Revelation 13:17 · 326
Revelation 13:5 · 296
Revelation 13:5–8 · 430
Revelation 13:7 · 144, 218, 308
Revelation 13:8 · 182
Revelation 13:9–10 · 255
Revelation 14 · 270, 448
Revelation 14:1 · 262
Revelation 14:11 · 326
Revelation 14:12 · 64, 65, 254
Revelation 14:12-13 · 342
Revelation 14:12–13 · 341
Revelation 14:13 · 262
Revelation 14:1-4 · 254
Revelation 14:14-16 · 270
Revelation 14:14-20 · 343
Revelation 14:15 · 129
Revelation 14:1-5 · 335
Revelation 14:16 · 344, 345
Revelation 14:20 · 373, 408
Revelation 14:4-5 · 259
Revelation 14:5 · 260, 291
Revelation 14:6 · 144
Revelation 14:6-13 · 336
Revelation 14:6–7 · 337
Revelation 14:8–11 · 339
Revelation 14:9 · 321, 326
Revelation 14:9–11 · 341
Revelation 15:1 · 102
Revelation 15:2 · 338, 345
Revelation 15:2-4 · 345
Revelation 15:5 · 177
Revelation 16 · 358
Revelation 16:1 · 349
Revelation 16:10–11 · 353
Revelation 16:11 · 349
Revelation 16:12-16 · 320
Revelation 16:12–16 · 354
Revelation 16:13 · 291
Revelation 16:13–14 · 400
Revelation 16:15 · 254, 346
Revelation 16:17–21 · 256, 356
Revelation 16:18 · 203, 204, 236
Revelation 16:2 · 326, 349
Revelation 16:20 · 182, 203, 204
Revelation 16:3 · 349
Revelation 16:4–7 · 351
Revelation 16:8 · 352
Revelation 16:8-11 · 338
Revelation 17 · 48, 67, 75, 76, 87, 90, 114, 144, 146, 230, 299, 358, 360
Revelation 17:12 · 362
Revelation 17:15 · 144
Revelation 17:16–17 · 361
Revelation 17:8 · 13, 430
Revelation 17-18 · 79
Revelation 18 · 116, 134, 199, 230
Revelation 18:1 · 396
Revelation 18:10 · 347, 364
Revelation 18:11 · 332
Revelation 18:11-13 · 48
Revelation 18:11–13 · 196
Revelation 18:15–18 · 114, 332
Revelation 18:17 · 364
Revelation 18:19 · 364
Revelation 18:21 · 339, 364
Revelation 18:23 · 250
Revelation 18:24 · 365
Revelation 18:4-5 · 363
Revelation 18:8 · 347, 364
Revelation 19 · 116, 134, 244, 358, 407
Revelation 19:1 · 396
Revelation 19:10 · 252, 392
Revelation 19:11-16 · 366
Revelation 19:1-3 · 119
Revelation 19:14 · 386, 448
Revelation 19:1–4 · 263
Revelation 19:15 · 289, 367, 402, 424
Revelation 19:16–18 · 406
Revelation 19:20 · 326
Revelation 19:21 · 289
Revelation 19:7 · 230
Revelation 19:7–8 · 200
Revelation 19:7–9 · 406
Revelation 19:8 · 230, 386
Revelation 2 · 214, 338, 360
Revelation 2:10 · 252
Revelation 2:13 · 206, 214, 304
Revelation 2:16 · 63, **289**

Revelation 2:17 · 414
Revelation 2:19 · 252
Revelation 2:2 · 252
Revelation 2:21-22 · 338
Revelation 2:22 · 263
Revelation 2:3 · 252
Revelation 2:9 · 13
Revelation 20 · 304
Revelation 20:11–15 · 428
Revelation 20:4 · 252, 326, 338, 392
Revelation 20:4-6 · 254, 375
Revelation 20:4–6 · 439
Revelation 20:7–10 · 426
Revelation 20:8 · 139
Revelation 21:12 · 257
Revelation 21:14 · 257
Revelation 21:18 · 434
Revelation 21:1-8 · 254
Revelation 21:2 · 231
Revelation 21:21 · 257
Revelation 21:22 · 438
Revelation 21:23-27 · 436
Revelation 21:7 · 338
Revelation 21:8 · 439
Revelation 21:9–11 · 434
Revelation 22:1–2 · 415
Revelation 22:12–13 · 472
Revelation 22:14 · 85
Revelation 22:1-4 · 254
Revelation 22:16 · 205
Revelation 22:18–19 · 84
Revelation 2-3 · 15, 219
Revelation 3 · 214, 338, 360
Revelation 3:10 · 252
Revelation 3:12 · 414
Revelation 3:16 · 289
Revelation 3:20 · 313
Revelation 4 · 235, 257
Revelation 4:1 · 270
Revelation 4:1,2 · 169
Revelation 4:4 · 119
Revelation 5 · 235
Revelation 5:9 · 144
Revelation 5:9–10 · 235
Revelation 6 · 447

Revelation 6:12 · 203
Revelation 6:12–14 · 201, 255
Revelation 6:13 · 205
Revelation 6:14 · 203, 236
Revelation 6:15–17 · 357
Revelation 6:16 · 455
Revelation 6:5 · 296
Revelation 6:9 · 252
Revelation 6:9-11 · 393
Revelation 6-18 · 391
Revelation 7:1 · 257, 396
Revelation 7:10 · 263
Revelation 7:1-3 · 262
Revelation 7:13-14 · 394
Revelation 7:14 · 263, 264, 393
Revelation 7:8 · 296
Revelation 7:9 · 144, 396
Revelation 7:9-17 · 119, 254, 263
Revelation 8:12 · 280
Revelation 8:13 · 270
Revelation 8:5 · 203
Revelation 8:7 · 275
Revelation 8:8 · 296
Revelation 8:8–9 · 277
Revelation 8-10 · 448
Revelation 9 · 205, 314, 321
Revelation 9:1-11 · 281
Revelation 9:13 · 285
Revelation 9:14 · 259
Revelation 9:17 · 193
Revelation 9:17-19 · 290
Revelation 9:20 · 284
Revelation 9:20-21 · 338
Revelation 9:20–21 · 273
Revelation 9:20–21 · 374
Roman · 12, 46, 51, 64, 100, 133, 134, 135, 137, 147, 192, 194, 207, 208, 215, 226, 227, 228, 286, 306, 307, 310, 315, 317, 365, 366, 387, 445, 452
Romans · 41, 51, 64, 112, 115, 116, 119, 121, 122, 134, 149, 153, 173, 188, 192, 196, 206, 207, 208, 225, 226, 227, 315, 431
Romans 1:1–4 · 112

Romans 1:18–23 · 29
Romans 10:8–10 · 261
Romans 11:25 · 298, 412
Romans 11:4 · 261
Romans 12:3 · 28
Romans 16:18 · 122
Romans 16:25–27 · 31, 299
Romans 5:1–5 · 121
Romans 9:6 · 418
Romans 9:6–8 · 119
rotting flesh · 411
Russia · 82

S

sacrifices · 88, 122, 164, 165, 179, 183, 187, 207, 211, 222, 229, 276, 309, 366, 414, 415, 419, 459, 470, 471
Satan · 330
Satanism · 123
Satan's throne · 205, 455
science · 88, 90, 91, 93, 94, 108, 130, 312, 321, 432
Scripture · 1, 5, 16, 25, 49, 50, 60, 80, 81, 102, 105, 133, 156, 169, 176, 187, 189, 194, 208, 253, 262, 265, 291, 295, 296, 307, 312, 322, 329, 350, 356, 359, 368, 370, 377, 382, 388, 397, 400, 403, 416, 433, 439, 465
Scriptures · 3, 84, 112, 188, 239, 268, 321, 383, 397, 400, 422
seed · 7, 39, 70, 76, 110, 111, 128, 391, 464
Seleucid · 210, 211, 216, 309, 452
seven congregations · 191
sexual immorality · 73, 75, 88, 114, 138, 195, 231, 273, 278, 279, 284, 312, 313, 339, 340, 358, 359, 360, 374, 395, 409
Shalom · 420
Shittim · 409
singularity · 321
slavery · 77, 91, 92, 104, 197, 198, 334

soft heart · 7
strong covenant · 207, 227, 314, 366, 446, 447, 448, 449, 455, 459
supernatural · 120, 171, 248, 280, 281, 353
survivors · 119, 284, 411, 412, 414, 422, 425
sword · 192, 219, 220, 243, 245, 246, 249, 289, 291, 319, 357, 366, 367, 425
Syria · 139, 145, 194, 207, 210, 211, 215, 216, 259, 309, 355, 446, 449, 452

T

tabernacle · 111, 149, 176, 177, 178, 180, 183, 222, 223, 229, 260, 269, 398, 409, 415
Taoism · 123
temple · 52, 64, 66, 124, 125, 129, 175, 176, 177, 178, 180, 181, 182, 183, 184, 185, 186, 187, 226, 228, 229, 256, 286, 287, 298, 305, 323, 331, 343, 349, 356, 377, 386, 387, 388, 393, 398, 401, 409, 415, 416, 419, 434, 438, 447, 449, 450, 452
Temple · 41, 50, 51, 52, 64, 111, 149, 174, 176, 177, 178, 179, 182, 207, 208, 211, 222, 223, 225, 227, 228, 229, 248, 260, 286, 287, 314, 315, 316, 336, 393, 402, 416, 438, 446, 453, 455, 456, 460, 461
ten horns · 147
Tetragrammaton · 98
that day · 24, 39, 105, 123, 128, 173, 191, 203, 226, 228, 256, 270, 328, 331, 372, 373, 401, 408, 409, 410, 412, 416, 417, 421, 432
the adulteress · 88
the beast · 147, 318
The Beast · 82
The Caliphate · 361

The Church · 1, 2, 6, 9, 10, 13, 14, 15, 37, 40, 56, 58, 59, 60, 71, 75, 76, 82, 84, 88, 89, 90, 94, 100, 104, 107, 115, 119, 133, 135, 136, 150, 151, 161, 162, 193, 214, 215, 217, 253, 259, 295, 299, 308, 312, 313, 317, 318, 319, 342, 360, 362, 366, 377, 388, 391, 392, 394, 395, 396, 402, 404, 455, 471
The Day · 4, 48, 158, 190, 191, 377, 378, 459
the day of wrath · 191
the forbidden woman · 88
The Fourth Turning · 50
The Late Great Planet Earth · 81
the Sea · 417
the time of Jacob's trouble · 191
The Tribulation · 52, 56, 191, 378, 444, 471
the valley of my mountains · 408
throne · 4, 5, 17, 28, 45, 91, 109, 111, 114, 119, 155, 175, 184, 206, 214, 215, 225, 229, 235, 237, 244, 256, 257, 263, 281, 296, 304, 314, 348, 353, 354, 356, 358, 404, 415, 417, 419, 420, 421, 428, 429, 430, 441, 447, 452, 459, 460
Tower of Babel · 15, 100, 132, 138, 140, 141, 142, 146, 149, 150, 185, 194, 435
Trajan · 365
Tubal · 139, 370
Turkey · 133, 139, 148, 185, 194, 205, 207, 210, 211, 213, 214, 215, 216, 281, 285, 309, 355, 446, 449, 452, 455

U

United States · 45, 59, 75, 82, 132, 133, 134, 135, 152, 198, 199, 231, 247, 248, 250, 251, 310, 311, 335, 435, 442
USSR · 82

V

vaccines · 243, 244, 250, 334
Valley (or plain) of Jezreel · 344
Valley of Decision · 97, 344, 345, 373, 374, 386, 406, 407, 410, 451
Valley of Jehoshaphat · 97, 344, 373, 400, 410, 450
Valley of Jezreel · 97, 344, 410
Valley of Shittim · 409
Valley of Vision · 373
visitation · 6
voodoo · 360

W

watch · 9, 50, 63, 84, 128, 202, 325, 367
Whole Bible Christianity · 6
Wicca · 123
Wiccans · 124
witchcraft · 123
wormwood · 90, 273, 278, 279

Y

Y2K · 83
Yeshua · 98, 109, 112, 118, 156, 158, 166, 170, 172, 173, 188, 218, 239, 293, 305, 313, 325, 338, 343, 415, 425, 427, 431, 433, 452, 466

Z

Zechariah 1 and 6 · 241
Zechariah 10 · 240
Zechariah 11:16–17 · 310
Zechariah 11:17 · 67, 211
Zechariah 12:10 · 412, 417
Zechariah 12:10-11 · 371

Zechariah 12:11 · 345, 371
Zechariah 13:1 · 416
Zechariah 14:12 · 411
Zechariah 14:12–13 · 373
Zechariah 14:1-5 · 451
Zechariah 14:1–6 · 372
Zechariah 14:16–19 · 419
Zechariah 14:20 · 421
Zechariah 14:20–21 · 331
Zechariah 14:3–5 · 408
Zechariah 14:4 · 448
Zechariah 14:5 · 408
Zechariah 14:6–7 · 432
Zechariah 14:8 · 416
Zechariah 14:9 · 417
Zechariah 2:6–9 · 188
Zechariah 3:8-9 · 111
Zechariah 4:11–14 · 294
Zechariah 9:10 · 76
Zephaniah 1:11 · 196
Zephaniah 2:3 · 397
Zephaniah 3:9 · 100
Zerubbabel · 224, 225